COLONIAL COMMON AND CIVIL LAW

LEGAL REGIMES IN WORLD HISTORY

COLONIAL COMMON AND CIVIL LAW

LEGAL REGIMES IN WORLD HISTORY

Ehlimana Memisevic
Anamarija Musa

Kruger Brentt
Publishers

2025

Kruger Brentt Publishers UK. LTD.
Company Number 9728962

Regd. Office: 68 St Margarets Road, Edgware, Middlesex HA8 9UU

ISBN: 978-1-78715-323-3

For information on all our publications visit our website at http://krugerbrentt.com/

PREFACE

"Colonial Common and Civil Law: Legal Regimes in World History" offers a comprehensive exploration of the legal systems that emerged during the era of colonialism, shedding light on their origins, development, and enduring legacies in contemporary legal regimes around the world. This book serves as a valuable resource for scholars, students, and practitioners in the fields of law, history, and colonial studies, providing a nuanced understanding of the complex interactions between colonialism, law, and society.

The colonial period witnessed the imposition of European legal systems on indigenous societies across Africa, Asia, the Americas, and Oceania, leading to profound transformations in legal norms, institutions, and practices. These legal regimes, which drew upon both common law and civil law traditions, reflected the power dynamics and cultural encounters inherent in the process of colonization, shaping the legal landscapes of diverse societies for generations to come.

As editors of this volume, we have endeavored to compile a diverse array of perspectives, methodologies, and case studies from leading scholars and researchers in the field of colonial legal history. Through a blend of historical analysis, comparative studies, and interdisciplinary insights, this book examines the complexities of colonial legal regimes, including their impact on indigenous legal systems, the role of law in colonial governance, and the legacy of colonialism in post-colonial legal systems.

Our overarching goal in presenting this book is to foster a deeper understanding of the historical roots and contemporary implications of colonial legal regimes, while also promoting dialogue, reflection, and critical engagement with issues of law, power, and justice in colonial and post-colonial contexts. By illuminating the intersections of law, colonialism, and society, we aim to contribute to broader conversations about the legacies of colonialism and the quest for justice and reconciliation in the modern world.

We extend our sincere gratitude to all the contributors who have generously shared their expertise, experiences, and insights in the field of colonial legal history. It is our hope that this book will serve as a catalyst for further research, teaching, and advocacy in the pursuit of a more just and equitable legal order, both globally and locally.

Ehlimana Memisevic
Anamarija Musa

CONTENTS

PREFACE .... **V**

1. **INTRODUCTION: SITUATING, RESEARCHING, AND WRITING COMPARATIVE LEGAL HISTORY** **1**

The Subject Matter of Comparative Legal History 3

What Sort of Legal History? 4

Making Comparisons 4

Researching and Writing Comparative Legal History 6

Exploring Legal Transplants 8

Investigating Broader Geographical Areas 10

Case Law, Precedent, and Relationships between Legal Systems 11

Exploring past Comparativists and the Challenges of Writing Comparative Legal History 13

2. **'IN ALIQUIBUS LOCIS EST CONSUETUDO': IN THE MID-THIRTEENTH CENTURY, FRENCH LAWYERS WERE INVOLVED IN THE LOMBARD CUSTOMS OF FIEFS** **25**

From the era of feudal law in the medieval state to the reemergence of the Libri feudorum is a significant development. 26

The Libri feudorum's Influence and Impact 28

Recontextualizing the Lombard Custom 30

Feudal Law as a Legal Precedent? The Provençal Practise and Jean Blanc 31

Jean de Blanot and the Dominance of Indigenous Traditions 34

Aurelianus' perspective on the Feudal Contract and Customary Law 37

The Influence of Feudal Law on the Formation of the ius commune 38

Footnote 39

3. **THE PHRASE "REGIAM MAIESTATEM" CONVEYS A SPECIFIC MESSAGE (AND WHAT DOES IT MEAN)?** **47**

The Subsequent Development of Regiam maiestatem 48

The Evolution of Regiam maiestatem in the Context of Survival 52

An Analysis of the Most Ancient Remaining Version and the Compiler's Contributions 53

Glanvill's Selection as Textual Authority 57
In Regiam maiestatem, maiestas 59
Parallel Legal Discourses: Maiestas and Communitas 63
Concise Summary 66
4. JAMES VI AND I, REX ET IUDEX: ONE KING AS JUDGE IN TWO KINGDOMS 87
James VI and I rendered judgments in various cases. 89
James and the King in the Role of Judges 93
When should the monarch make a decision? 96
James therefore explained that he came to judge the assize of error 99
A Comparative Conclusion 105
A constitutional amendment 106
5. THE COMPARATIVE LEGAL BACKGROUND OF THE FIRST ENGLISH TRANSLATION OF JUSTINIAN'S INSTITUTES, AS EXAMINED BY GEORGE HARRIS..........123
Introduction: An Overview 123
George Harris 124
Translation of the Institutes: The Editions 125
Translation of the Institutes: Content 127
Assessments of Harris's Translation 133
Concise Summary 134
6. LEGAL SCIENCE AND COMPARATIVE LEGAL HISTORY IN BLACKSTONE'S COMMENTARIES: AN EXAMINATION OF THE ESSENCE OF CUSTOM 143
Why? Because 149
7. THE EXAMINATION OF ENGLISH COMMON LAW FROM THE PERSPECTIVE OF THE GÖTTINGISCHE GELEHRTE ANZEIGEN (EIGHTEENTH CENTURY): A CRITICAL ANALYSIS 163
Introduction: An Overview 163
Gelehrte Zeitschriften 164
The Göttingische Gelehrte Anzeigen 165
English Law in the Anzeigen 165
German Learned Journals and English Law 174
8. EXAMINING THE ORIGINS OF CONTINUOUS EASEMENTS IN ENGLISH LAW FROM A FRENCH PERSPECTIVE 187
Introduction: An Overview 188
French Rule's Reception in England 189

The Origins and Current Success of the Rule in France 192
Disregarding the Current Discourse in France: An Exclusion from English Perspective 193
Examining the Origins of the English (Mis)Interpretation Analysis 195
Lessons for Comparative Law and Legal History: Three Key Takeaways 198
Concise summary 200

9. CASE LAW IN GERMANY: THE SIGNIFICANCE OF SEUFFERT'S ARCHIV ..211

Introduction: An Overview 211
The Importance of Providing Justifications for Judicial Rulings 212
Collections of Decisions 213
Seuffert's Innovative Collection 213
Precedents according to Nineteenth-Century German Doctrine 215
The One and Only Decision 216
Issue and Method 217
A Court File Becomes an Entry in Seuffert's Archiv 217
Headline and Guiding Principles 219
First Question of Law 219
Second Question of Law 220
Three Opinions 220
Statement of the Judge 221
Application of the Legal Rule to the Case 222
Concise Summary 222

10. THE HISTORICAL SIGNIFICANCE OF LEONE LEVI (1821–1888) IN THE FIELD OF COMPARATIVE COMMERCIAL LAW 229

Introduction: An Overview 229
Commercial Law of the World 231
From the comparative legislation to the process of codification 238
Concise Summary 241

11. THE CROWN'S RADICAL TITLE AND ABORIGINAL TITLE: NORTH AMERICA IN 1763, NEW SOUTH WALES IN 1788, AND NEW ZEALAND IN 1840...253

12. CONCEALED FRUSTRATIONS, PRIVATE ADVOCACY, AND THE BREAK WITH ENGLISH LAW IN THE MID-CENTURY: AN ANALYSIS OF THE HIGH COURT OF AUSTRALIA 279

A Unified Common Law: At What Cost? 281
The Privy Council's Unwitting Role in Parker 285

Failed Advocacy 288
Denouement 291
13. THE COMPREHENSIVE SLAVE LAWS OF THE BRITISH WEST INDIES CAN BE TRACED BACK TO THE ORIGINS OF ENGLISH SOCIETAL LAWS..297
Introduction: An Overview 297
The Barbados Slave Code introduced in 1661 298
English Property Law: Slaves as Chattels 299
Villeinage's Significance 301
Law pertaining to police conduct, vagrancy, and martial law 305
Concise Summary 308
INDEX 315

INTRODUCTION: SITUATING, RESEARCHING, AND WRITING COMPARATIVE LEGAL HISTORY

This volume is a selection of essays taken from the excellent range of papers presented at the British Legal History Conference hosted by the Institute for Legal and Constitutional Research at the University of St Andrews, 10–13 July 2019. The theme of the conference gives this book its title: 'comparative legal history'. The topic came easily to the organisers because of their association with the St Andrews-based European Research Council Advanced grant project 'Civil law, common law, customary law: consonance, divergence and transformation in Western Europe from the late eleventh to the thirteenth centuries'. But the chosen topic was also connected to the fact that this was, we think, the first British Legal History Conference held at a university without a Law faculty. Bearing in mind the question of how far institutional setting determines approach, our hope was that an element of fruitful comparison would stimulate people to think further about the range of approaches to legal history. With its explicit agenda of breaking down barriers, comparative legal history provided a particularly suitable focus for this investigation. After situating the subject matter of comparative legal history, and then discussing the levels of comparison that may be most fertile, this introduction moves on to considering the practical tasks of researching and writing such history, using the essays included in the volume to suggest ways ahead. The introduction groups the essays under certain headings: 'Exploring legal transplants'; 'Investigating broader geographical areas'; 'Case law, precedent and relationships between legal systems'; and 'Exploring past comparativists and the challenges of writing comparative legal history'. Yet the essays could be kaleidoscopically rearranged under many headings. We hope that the book, like a successful conference, includes many stimulating conversations.

F. W. Maitland wrote that 'history involves comparison ... an isolated system cannot explain itself, still less explain its history'. [1] Comparative approaches are vital for answering broad questions and understanding specific issues. Investigating both difference and similarity, they can seek patterns, construct narratives and test theories of causation. Sometimes they are explicit, sometimes implicit. Comparison, conscious or unconscious, is inevitably present in producing and testing analyses, in asking 'what if this were not the case?', 'what if we change certain conditions?' Such has been described as the 'quasi-Popperian' role of comparison: 'comparison is the closest that historians can get to testing, attempting to falsify, their own explanations'. [2] At the same time, comparison may also produce fresh hypotheses, for example, asking 'is this pattern of change replicated elsewhere?' or 'are differences more assumed than real?', hypotheses that may be more resilient after themselves being tested through further comparison.

Comparison has long featured in investigation of legal development, be it between the Germanic and the Roman in the great founding works of German legal historical scholarship, or between Common law and Civil law in classic works on English legal history. Studies of comparative legal history have grown in the twentieth- and the twenty-first centuries, [3] along with some studies of the history of comparative legal history. [4] The work has been conducted predominantly by scholars situated – by disciplinary formation or institutional affiliation – within Law rather than History. This is evident, for example, when examining the list of contributors to volumes such as the 2019 collection *Comparative Legal History*, which describes itself as 'an emblematic product of the *European Society for Comparative Legal History*'. [5] This predominance is true both of studies of specific legal topics and of writings on approaches. [6] In the latter, it is manifest in the focus upon the relationship of comparative legal history to law and comparative law, with little or no mention of a relationship to history and comparative history. [7]

The present volume is deliberately subtitled 'Essays *in* comparative legal history'; the essays tackle aspects of law, including practice, doctrine, and academe, rather than being theoretical or methodological papers *on* comparative legal history. Likewise, this introduction concentrates on possibilities and problems of practice, rather than on the philosophical, unless one counts pragmatism and pluralism as philosophies. Such is not to put a perspective from History in place of a perspective from Law. Nor is it simply advocacy of pluralism from two authors who are hybrids in their own disciplinary formation and/or attachment. A similarly pragmatic desire resonates from at least some lawyers' methodological studies:

Comparative legal historians should find a middle road between elaborating a potentially overly sophisticated comparative methodology and simply getting on with research without a conscious or at least obvious one. ... [The] final element of comparative methodology that the comparative legal historian can take from comparative law is ... a lesson in when to stop, in this case when to stop discussing it and actually use it. [8]

THE SUBJECT MATTER OF COMPARATIVE LEGAL HISTORY

A preliminary question must be 'what is the subject matter of legal history?' The simple answer of course is 'Law' – or 'law' or possibly 'the law'. [9] However, as comparative legal scholars are particularly aware, considerable difficulty remains in defining this subject matter. [10] Modern definitions or characterisations of law are contested. The effect of different definitions upon the writing of legal history is readily apparent. [11] So too is the effect of characterisations of law that rest less on definition of what a law or the Law is than on the perceived functioning of law, be they, for example, Marxist or Ehrlich's 'living law'. These produce a different approach to the relationship between law and context. [12] The notion of the 'relative autonomy' of law provides a partial solution, but only if 'relative' is a notion acutely interrogated rather than what Maitland might describe as 'a useful word [that] will cover a multitude of ignorances'. [13] Such pondering and investigation in turn may produce the type of metaphorical language that sometimes also appears in writings on comparative legal history, E. P. Thompson's 'imbrication' being one such metaphor. [14]

The comparative and historical aspects increase the difficulties still further. What is legal history about, if both law and concepts of law are not constant but shaped by context? [15] Can modern jurisprudential tests as to what is law, or what are rules of law, be employed to indicate the limits of law in past societies? Such tests impose socio-culturally determined ideas, ironically sometimes applied to convict others of anachronism in depiction of past 'law'. Verbal contortions arising from, and perhaps required for sustaining, a highly specific definition of law go back in English jurisprudence at least to the nineteenth century with John Austin's use of the phrase 'laws improperly so called'. [16]

So, would it be better for the legal historian, especially when also a comparativist, to work with a broader definition, or at least a broad core categorisation, to answer 'what is law?', 'what is the object of study?' The aim must be to avoid easily criticised supposed universals or precise but unhelpful hyper-nominalism. This may involve thinking about practice and abstraction therefrom, about the field of study being a particular area of practice and knowledge in which certain people have expertise. [17] Take the following suggestion by Brian Simpson:

The predominant conception today is that the common law consists of a system of rules; in terms of this legal propositions (if correct) state what is contained in these rules. I wish to consider the utility of this conception, and to contrast it with an alternative idea – the idea that the common law is best understood as a system of customary law, that is, as a body of traditional ideas received within a caste of experts.[18]

Focus on knowledge linked to practice resonates with ideas of legal cultures or 'law in minds' as the proper subject for comparative study. [19] It may provide, if not a definitive solution to the problem of the field of comparative study, at least a way forward, and it requires the necessary examination of the definitions, categorisations and vocabulary used by those studied, and dialogue between such terminologies and our own.

WHAT SORT OF LEGAL HISTORY?

The next, related, issue is what sort of legal history comparative legal historians are doing, an issue that methodological writings only occasionally raise. [20] The issue is pressing because of the extensive divisions between varieties of legal history, partly although not solely disciplinary. [21] Is the concentration to be the internal history of law, described by David Ibbetson as follows: 'A legal system does have its own separate history ... and even though it is inevitably embedded in the extra-legal world ... legal change takes place within this system and can only be understood in terms of it'? [22] Or is it to be the external history: 'External legal history is the history of law as embedded in its context, typically its social or economic context.' [23] Or should the two be integrated, not least because some views of law render the division more difficult? Is integration particularly necessary regarding causation, periodisation and construction of a narrative? [24] Likewise, is the focus– in Roscoe Pound's useful if contested phrase – 'Law in books' or 'Law in action'? And is there a point where the social history of law – as epitomised, for example, in *Albion's Fatal Tree* – ceases to be a form of legal history? [25]

To argue that any particular method is the sole correct one may require a degree of circularity: that an internal history of law is the only proper one because that is what the history of law is, or that a social history of law is the only proper one because law can only be considered in social context. Instead, a single, holistic approach, incorporating elements of all others, might be considered the correct method. However, it may be necessary in practical terms – and indeed desirable in theoretical terms, as well as best fitting personal aptitude – that individuals pursue different approaches, whilst ensuring those approaches are explicit and in dialogue: what may be called legal historical pluralism.

MAKING COMPARISONS

Beyond these issues, there are further clear difficulties in conducting comparative studies. Familiar from many discussions are difficulties such as the comparative use of concepts such as 'ownership' or 'crime'. [26] A solution – be it functionalist or other – again must avoid treating such concepts as unchanging, uncontextualised universals, whilst not lapsing into uninformative, irreducible nominalism where all that is apparent is difference. In contrast, theoretical writings are sometimes surprisingly vague as to what comparative legal history is seeking to explain. Two related aspects that have received attention are legal transplants and entanglements.[27] Whilst such analyses sometimes are comparative, and can indeed benefit greatly from a comparative aspect,[28] sometimes they are not, and perhaps need not be; rather, they are intent on creatively disrupting supposedly separate units. However, topics such as transplants do emphasise that comparative legal history must help to explain not just the particular legal systems compared but also the nature, processes and causes of legal change.[29] Such is yet another reason for the difficulty of comparative legal history. To the difficulties of comparative law, it adds a third dimension of comparison: time.

Bearing in mind the above, what are the possible units of comparison for the legal historian?[30] Generally, comparison has been between 'legal systems' – archetypically between Civil law and Common law – or between geographical areas, especially between political units.[31] Comparison could also be between types of law – unwritten and written, custom and academic – or across time as well as place and system, as in comparisons between procedures in English Common law and Roman law.[32]

A further issue is level of comparison and consequent generalisation. The 'comparative method' was crucial to the developing social sciences in Victorian England, including comparative law and legal history, personified by Sir Henry Maine. Supported by ideas of evolution, writers were confident in generalisations not just about specific or common patterns but about necessary and universal ones. Deprived of this belief in broad evolutionary patterns for human social and cultural development, and subjected to detailed empirical criticism, such theories have gone out of academic fashion. Only occasionally are writers prepared to speculate on whether legal systems have a 'natural history' or to attribute to them anthropomorphic characteristics.[33]

Still, there is an opposite – probably reactive – danger, of insufficiently broad comparison. This may lapse into lists of similar or dissimilar rules or procedures. Rather than comparing individual rules or attempting to uncover universal patterns, therefore, the task is to find an intermediate level of comparison, to seek contrasting or shared patterns of legal norms, processes and change.[34] Very useful lists for comparison have been offered, for example: '1. Fact patterns. 2. Institutions. 3. Reasoning. 4. Principles and concepts. 5. Substantive legal rules. 6. Procedure. 7. Outcomes.'[35] Objects of comparison may range from the broad to the very particular, from structures of legal thought, through legal learning and education, [36] clusters of rules and practices, to individual rules or the related functions of different rules in the compared systems, and on to the very specific, for example the judicial activities of one individual in different courts. [37] Multiple perspectives can contribute: be it in litigation or transaction, starting from the participant point of view – 'actor-based' analysis – may reveal similarities and differences between types of law hidden to comparative analysis starting from legal rules or procedure.

Such explorations can also be formulated in specific research questions, again of differing scope. For example, such questions may form part of a wider analysis of the generation, development, and functioning of legal norms. Are clashes between unwritten customs resolved in different ways from clashes between written rules? Is there a difference in the strictness of application of procedural and of substantive norms? How far are norms brought into play by litigants, how far by those presiding over courts? In what ways do legal norms and processes fit diverse circumstances into set forms, and how are problems arising from such constrictions then remedied? [38] Such analysis will return to questions such as that of the relationship of procedure and substantive norms, and to Maine's oft-quoted but rarely tested suggestion that 'substantive law has at first the look of being gradually secreted in the interstices of procedure'. [39]

Similarities uncovered by comparison may thus be in patterns of law or legal development, rather than identical rules. The focus may be on what notions structure legal thought. There may be similarities or differences in assumptions, in underlying principles or pervasive ideas, in what S. F. C. Milsom described as 'elementary legal ideas' so fundamental that they are rarely stated yet must be uncovered to allow any possibility of further understanding. [40] Investigation at this level may also allow exploration, not just of what existed, what changed, or when and why, but also of how law worked and developed, for example through replicable and adaptable units. Such intermediate level comparisons of groupings of ideas, assumptions and practices may analyse what Duncan Kennedy termed a 'subsystem' in legal consciousness, 'a small set of conceptual building blocks, along with a small set of typical arguments as to how the concepts should be applied, to produce results that seem to the jurists involved to have a high level of coherence with and across legal fields'. [41] Such analysis may in turn reveal the coexistence of competing subsystems or models, the interaction of which may be central to legal development. [42]

RESEARCHING AND WRITING COMPARATIVE LEGAL HISTORY

The above discussion has been punctuated with statements of difficulties and with numerous questions. And, one fears, the problems are not yet exhausted. A further reason for the absence in particular of book-length comparative studies is the sheer amount of research required. Maitland encapsulated the difficulty in his requirement that 'The first step towards an answer must be a careful statement of each system by itself. We must know in isolation the things that are to be compared before we compare them.' [43] All too easy are flawed shortcuts, particular in researching comparators beyond the author's particular speciality. Such shortcuts are manifest in assumptions of uniformity within the systems compared – including such casual contrasts as 'Anglo-American Common Law' and 'Continental European Civil Law' [44] – or in comparing a full picture of law on one side with a picture solely of 'Law in books' on the other. The challenge of the balance between the possible and the ideal, present in most research, is especially prominent here. The sheer bulk of material multiplies particularly if the approach emphasises the external or the social history of law, [45] but also if it involves a widely defined notion of 'legal culture'. [46] Moreover, volume of research looms still more threateningly if it is felt methodologically desirable to have more than two comparators in order to avoid coincidental patterns achieving mistaken significance. Collaboration provides an answer, but the danger remains of a plethora of fragmented studies, awaiting the immensely challenging process of synthesis: more data does not automatically provide more explanation. [47]

The hope will be that comparison provides better explanation. Take analysis of causation of legal change, with an external perspective: if similar legal developments occur in markedly different socio-economic settings, apparent links between legal and socio-economic change must be rejected in favour of other or more complex explanations. Comparison may often have a destructive rather than constructive effect. This may be particularly true of causal explanation within external approaches to legal history, but is not limited to such: [48]

> comparative law and legal history working together can prevent three methodological assumptions: that a common rule across jurisdictions results from common needs, that a common or similar rule has been adopted solely on its merits in the marketplace of ideas, and that a rule which has flourished in more than one place can be explained by the circumstances of only one time and place. [49]

These are indeed general problems in analysis of historical causation and in construction of narrative. [50] However, rather than the scholarly reaction being one of defeat, we may welcome the opportunities for removing misinterpretation, for accepting the role of contingency, [51] and for redoubling efforts to construct and test explanation.

The essays presented in this volume illustrate some of the ways in which comparative legal history may be approached, and how such studies can test all-too-easily accepted narratives or provide fresh perspectives on familiar legal and historical developments. The approaches that have been taken vary, all in their different ways examining and illuminating the causes and nature of legal change. Several essays directly explore legal 'transplants'. Others consider the uniformity of legal development across broad geographical areas. Further authors examine a related issue, the role of case law and precedent in legal development, an examination which not only challenges an oft-assumed bright line between Common and Civil law systems, but also encourages examination of the relationship between jurisdictions sharing a Common law heritage. A final strand of essays concerns the work of past comparativists, which can reveal much about how fundamental units of comparison such as 'legal systems' have been understood historically. These essays also allow us to compare our own experience of comparative study with the endeavours of those attempting such work in the past.

EXPLORING LEGAL TRANSPLANTS

A comparison of the essays concerning legal transplants reveals a variety of forms that such transplants can take, and how they may or may not work. Alice Taylor discusses the transplant of a text from one legal system to another; that is, the appearance of much of the content of the twelfth-century English legal treatise known as *Glanvill* in the fourteenth-century Scottish treatise *Regiam maiestatem*. This is a cross-border transplant for which the probable passage of time between the production of the *Glanvill* text and its introduction into another system adds not only complexity but also explanatory potential. The similarities between *Glanvill* and *Regiam maiestatem* have long been recognised, but Taylor offers a new explanation of why *Glanvill* was used so extensively. *Regiam maiestatem*, she argues, may be seen as an 'intercontextual translation', whereby the authority of *Glanvill* was used as a vehicle for conveying an argument for the *maiestas* of Scottish kings during the reign of Robert I. Traditional narratives have emphasised the importance during this period of ideas about the 'community of the realm'; the idea of royal *maiestas*, Taylor argues, represents an important alternative strain of political thought, which offers a new interpretation of the intellectual underpinnings of Robert I's kingship. Taylor's essay thus illustrates how the study of legal transplants can disrupt familiar narratives. It also shows how such transplants may create only the illusion of legal change or convergence, and therefore be of little obvious consequence to the internal history of law, yet nevertheless be extremely politically significant and also have a long-term effect on legal culture.

Taylor's essay focuses more on the broad political principle that could be promoted through *Regiam maiestatem* and less on the individual rules contained in the text. In contrast, Ciara Kennefick's essay addresses the transplant of an aspect of a particular rule from one system to another. This is the concept of 'continuous' in relation to the rule that an easement which is 'continuous and apparent' may be created in certain circumstances by implication, rather than by express grant, when land held by one owner is subsequently divided. Following the point made by Simpson in an earlier article, Kennefick shows how this rule concerning servitudes can be traced to an idea in the French Civil Code. [52] It crossed the sea and entered English law when it was included in Charles Gale's *Treatise on Easements*, published in 1839, and from that moment it caused difficulties of interpretation. Kennefick adds another perspective to Simpson's argument by analysing this development from a comparative perspective. She shows that this was a transplant of a legal rule that was also problematic in the donor jurisdiction, an insight which adds a fresh perspective to the struggles of the English courts to interpret it. Kennefick's study thus provides three lessons for legal history, one general, two specific: (i) we must not always assume that a rule being transplanted was a good fit even for the donor system; (ii) the influence of the French Civil Code on the Common law has been underestimated; and (iii) English legal treatises were an important influence (for better or worse) on the development of certain areas of English law. By studying transplants from an explicitly comparative perspective, Kennefick's essay also illustrates how change may not occur because of deep-rooted and widely shared structures of legal thought. Instead, it emphasises, as mentioned above, the potential role of contingency in legal development.

The complexities that may be caused by the transplantation of legal doctrine are also evident in Justine Collins's essay, which discusses the way in which pre-colonial English law crossed the ocean and served as a basis for the slave laws of the British West Indies. This essay focuses on three broad areas: (i) the idea of slaves as chattels; (ii) the overlapping idea that slavery was analogous in many respects to villeinage; and (iii) the influence on West Indian slavery legislation of attitudes and laws concerning the control and subjugation of the lower orders in England. A related concern is the way in which colonial administrators seized upon ideas concerning the use of martial law and applied them to the governance of their territories. The legal transplants discussed by Collins operated in a system quite different from that of England, and, as Collins explains, their introduction involved a degree of improvisation. As such, attempts to connect the law of chattels and villeinage to slavery created a plethora of issues that were never fully reconciled. [53] This was especially clear when the transplanted ideas that had been adopted and adapted in the British West Indies returned to their donor system in cases requiring adjudication by the English Common law courts. Through her discussion of this last point, Collins's essay also reveals how these cases, which stimulated debate about the precise nature of a transplanted rule or concept (such as villeinage), are very useful sources for legal historians seeking to understand attitudes towards the rule or concept in question.

The discussion of transplants in this volume is not limited to the transplantation of texts or of disembodied legal ideas. Ian Williams discusses the transplant of a *person*, James VI Scotland, who progressed ceremonially from Edinburgh to London in the days following the death of Elizabeth I of England in 1603 and acceded to the English throne that same year. As Williams notes, 'While law as idea is important, law can only be applied (at least for now) by people. As people move, the law in practice can change.' [54] Although considerable attention has been devoted to James's attempts to influence the work of his judges, Williams's essay addresses the less-studied area of the king's own judicial activity in both England and Scotland. As the author explains, it was not unusual for a king to act as a judge in Scotland during this period. This was not the case in England, although Williams notes that such a practice was 'not unthinkable'. Williams investigates whether James applied his ideas about how and when a king should sit in judgment consistently, not just within each country, but also between realms. Such a consideration introduces another unit of comparison to the study: the potential differences between theory and practice. Williams shows that James certainly did seem to act according to some discernible principles applied uniformly in his activities throughout England and Scotland. However, Williams also adds a chronological dimension to his comparative matrix. James's views on certain subjects changed over time, but Williams argues that he nevertheless continued to apply them consistently irrespective of realm: 'The comparative exercise here lets us reach a conclusion which would surely have delighted James himself: in his ideas and practice of royal judgment we have an example of genuinely British legal history.' [55]

INVESTIGATING BROADER GEOGRAPHICAL AREAS

Discussion of legal transplants is not confined to the above essays, [56] although they are the ones that deal most directly with such issues. It is clear that transplants can lead to the implementation of the same legal rules in different places, and another significant theme of the essays in this volume concerns similarities of legal development over a broad geographical area. Attilio Stella's essay examines narratives of legal change and the development of 'feudal law' in Western Europe during the late twelfth and early thirteenth centuries. He focuses on the activities of five lawyers, two from Italy (Obertus de Orto and Iacobus de Ardizone) and three from France (Jean Blanc, Jean de Blanot and Iacobus de Aurelianis), and compares the way in which they related local practice and custom to 'learned' doctrine and written law, particularly that contained in the *Libri feudorum*, a highly influential composite work concerning north Italian custom, produced in various stages between *c.* 1150 and *c.* 1250. His conclusion disrupts the simplistic narrative that in this period there was a wholesale replacement of the 'warm natural custom', which reflected the spirit of the people, by the uniform 'cold artificial law' of professional lawyers. Instead, unwritten local legal traditions often survived and shaped Western European experiences of law during this formative period of the *ius commune*.

David Williams likewise considers legal doctrine. He examines the development of the doctrine of radical title – the underlying title of the Crown to Commonwealth land – and the response of courts to the question of whether this title would be burdened by the pre-existing interests of the indigenous population. Three main jurisdictions are considered – Canada, Australia and New Zealand – and reference is made to some Privy Council decisions concerning smaller territories. As Williams notes, 'A reasonably coherent account of legal history on this topic might seem possible, and even plausible, if one focused on the development of the Common law in just one of the three legal systems.'[57] However, comparison of the case law relating to all these jurisdictions reveals that the development of the Common law in this area has been unsystematic and often directed by policy decisions and pragmatism rather than clear legal principles.

A central, sometimes implicit, concern of Williams's essay is the value that courts have been willing to attach to indigenous peoples' own understanding of their relationship to their land, a relationship not necessarily expressed in legal concepts or even perhaps a form of 'law', familiar to a Common law lawyer. Here then, like Stella, Williams provides another insight into how a developing legal system may (or may not) integrate pre-existing normative structures into its overarching system of rules. This perhaps surprising connection between the two essays illustrates well the creative possibilities of using issues such as 'integration' as a tool for comparison.

CASE LAW, PRECEDENT, AND RELATIONSHIPS BETWEEN LEGAL SYSTEMS

Williams's and Stella's essays both raise questions about the use of past cases, and how they may be employed either to integrate local circumstances into the interpretation and development of norms, or to ensure the consistent development of legal principles. Case law is most strongly associated with Common law systems, where the doctrine of precedent provides the foundations and framework for much legal development. In contrast, it is often regarded – at least in the Common law world – as less important to Civil law systems. Without deeper comparison, however, this casual contrast between Common law and Civil law jurisdictions may obscure similarities or distort differences.

As a direct response to such a casual comparison, Clara Günzl's essay examines the so-called 'case-law revolution' which took place in Germany between 1800 and 1945. Despite clear doctrinal rules that prior decisions were not formally binding on courts, during this period case law began to play a more important role in the decision making of the German judiciary. In particular, the collection of decisions printed from 1847 to 1944 in 'Seuffert's *Archiv*' did much to increase awareness of previous judicial decisions and the reasoning applied in past cases. Günzl first introduces us to the debates that took place surrounding the use of case law in the period. She shows that jurists recognised the value of taking into account past decisions, but also feared the consequence that an incorrect decision would prevent courts from reaching 'the only true and right solution' in subsequent cases. This discussion naturally invites comparison of how different traditions of legal learning may view essential questions such as the existence of a single right answer to every legal problem, and how legal certainty corresponds to more abstract notions of justice. Günzl then uses a case study to show us how the knowledge of past decisions might, nevertheless, influence the outcome of a case in practice, and how this outcome could, in turn, become part of the collection of case law which circulated nationwide and influenced other decisions. In this sense, these judgments in past cases, *Präjudizien*, 'resemble most closely those of persuasive precedents in Common law countries today'. [58]

While Günzl's essay encourages comparison between Common and Civil law systems, Josev's essay concerns the relationship between two jurisdictions within the Common law world. Her essay examines the period leading to Australian High Court Chief Justice Sir Owen Dixon's statement in *Parker* v. *The Queen* (1963) that Australian courts should no longer consider themselves bound by English precedent. As the author explains, this came after a period in which the Australian judiciary are usually perceived as having displayed almost complete deference towards the English courts, and the decision has sometimes been regarded 'as the most sensational judicial *volte-face* in Australian legal history'. [59] However, Josev goes beyond this traditional account and reveals differing and evolving attitudes towards the relationship between English and Australian law in this period. Despite the desire of many Australian judges to maintain the unity of the Common law, Josev argues, considerable tensions existed in the years preceding *Parker*. These arose from differing individual attitudes between judges, as with Dixon's disapproval of Lord Denning's judicial activism in England, from wider dissatisfaction in Australia with some of the directions that English law was taking, and from serious concerns among some of the Australian judiciary about the activities of the Privy Council. Against this backdrop, Josev argues that it is difficult to celebrate the *Parker* judgment as a bold declaration of judicial independence. Rather, it should be seen as the consequence of a 'relatively gloomy period in English–Australian legal history'. [60] Meanwhile the contribution of elements such as the cooling of Dixon's admiration for Denning re-emphasises the need to consider the contingent as well as the more structural in explaining significant legal change.

EXPLORING PAST COMPARATIVISTS AND THE CHALLENGES OF WRITING COMPARATIVE LEGAL HISTORY

A fertile alternative approach to comparative legal history is to examine the work of past comparativists. This can help us better appreciate historical understandings of the nature of various legal systems, their relationships to each other, and the bounds and functions of law within these systems. The preoccupations of the past can also aid us in reflecting upon units that may be used in our own comparisons, be they between 'written' and 'unwritten' law, or between 'Civil' and 'Common' law, or between substantive rules and principles.

Several essays in this volume are dedicated to the history of comparative law. Carsten Fischer discusses the way in which the English Common law appeared in the pages of the *Göttingische gelehrte Anzeigen*, a German scholarly journal first published in 1739. A small but significant proportion of its pages were devoted to reviews of books of, or concerning, English law. Fischer concentrates on two reviews in particular, both of works published by Göttingen law professors: Christian Hartmann Samuel Gatzert's *De iure communi Angliae*, published and reviewed in 1765; and Justus Claproth's partial translation of Blackstone's *Analysis of the Laws of England*, published in 1767 and reviewed in 1769. Both the content of the works reviewed in the *Anzeigen* and the reviews themselves reveal how English law was regarded and understood in Germany during this period. Fischer points out, for example, that an interest in the applicability of Roman law to English law may be found in the works of both Gatzert and Claproth. In general, however, there does not seem to have been any criteria for the selection of works reviewed in the *Anzeigen*. Nor is there anything more than a modest understanding of English law on display, and furthermore, as we shall see, problems of language affected the nature and quality of the comparisons made between English and German law. [61]

Andrew Cecchinato also examines an eighteenth-century attempt to compare English law with that of the Continent. In this instance, however, the individual engaged in the comparison was very familiar indeed with the Common law. Cecchinato's essay explores Sir William Blackstone's attempt to situate English law within the broader legal experience of Western Europe, and thus within a shared human endeavour to give positive expression to the eternal law of God's will. Cecchinato first draws attention to Blackstone's interpretation and grounding of the *ius commune* maxim *rex... in regno suo est imperator* within the English legal system, through which he was able to justify the preeminence of the Common law as a body of 'particular law'. Cecchinato then turns to Blackstone's attempts to reconcile the fact that, while judicial decisions could be taken as strong *evidence* of long-standing custom, it did not necessarily follow that this evidence provided *authority* for the custom. How, therefore, could it be claimed that court decisions had acquired such authority? Again, Blackstone turned to civilian legal sources, comparing the manner in which the English courts dealt with custom to the way in which the emperor had the authority to 'interpret' law with normative force, as exemplified in the *lex Si imperialis maiestas*. In turn, this gave force to Blackstone's view that judges were the 'oracles of the law', a metaphor which itself has roots in classical jurisprudence. Blackstone did not, however, uncritically adopt all aspects of European legal thought. His views on the importance of custom within the English legal system led him to view with disapproval how unwritten law, 'approved by the judgment of the people', had diminished in importance by the later years of imperial Rome.

While Blackstone was firmly rooted in the English Common law tradition, the subject of another of the essays, George Harris, had a background in Civil and ecclesiastical laws. Harris was an eighteenth-century civilian who was a member of the College of Advocates and who also engaged in judicial work. Łukasz Korporowicz examines his production of the first English translation of Justinian's *Institutes*, published in the mid-eighteenth century. In particular, Korporowicz draws attention to how the translation itself is accompanied by numerous notes, 'arguably the most significant element of the translation'.[62] Korporowicz goes on to show that these notes contain references to classical sources, legal and non-legal, different traditions of Civil law authors, and, notably, an array of Common law treatises and works of writers on English law. Harris was not formally trained in the Common law, so the inclusion of this latter material is particularly striking.

Monti's essay concerns the comparative work of Leone Levi, an Italian-born merchant who moved to England at the age of fifteen and later became a jurist, statistician and economist. Levi spent much of his life involved in commerce, and Monti shows how this eventually led to the production of his *Commercial Law of the World*. The first edition of this work, published in two volumes in 1850 and 1852, took a rather different form to the revised version, *International Commercial Law*, which appeared in 1863. Monti points out that the full title of the earlier edition named no less than fifty-nine 'countries' as the subject of comparison. The later work named only twenty-five, although the words 'and others', added to this list, also suggest that more might have been included. Together with this change, the geographical focus of the study changed somewhat. Furthermore, the first edition set out in tabular form the laws of various countries, polities and regions which were to be compared. The plan was abandoned in the later work, and a comparison was made in discursive form.

A comparison of these essays is instructive. For one, they reveal different motives for the past employment of the comparative method. Cecchinato shows how Blackstone used comparison for justificatory purposes; he sought to explain and legitimise aspects of English law. Korporowicz, on the other hand, shows that Harris intended his translation to make the *Institutes* more widely accessible in England, and that the copious notes that accompanied the translation were intended to arouse curiosity about English law. Levi's comparative works on mercantile law were likewise intended to educate, but Monti makes it clear that they were also intended to aid merchants in their dealings overseas, and to act as a step towards an international commercial code.

These essays, furthermore, provide a historical perspective on the practical challenges faced by those who have attempted and still attempt to employ a comparative method, as raised earlier in this introduction. In doing so, they encourage reflection about the process of comparative work. The issues that can arise concerning language and terminology are clear. Ideally comparatists would be highly skilled linguists, but Fischer's, Korporowicz's, and Monti's essays also highlight the importance of accurate translations for the study of comparative law. However, the accurate translation of unfamiliar and highly technical legal material is no easy task, especially when the subject matter seems so alien to the reader. These linguistic challenges are made clear in Fischer's essay, which suggests that the eighteenth-century German jurists did not enjoy their first contact with what Maitland would describe as the Common law's 'whole scheme of actions with repulsive names'. [63] Gatzert, in particular, complained (perhaps not unreasonably) about the 'adventurous and un-English' nature of the English legal language. [64] Fischer also notes how attempts made in the *Anzeigen* to explain the English system through analogies and descriptive terms familiar to German jurists would, in fact, have seriously misled the German reader. Here, then, is a very clear example of comparison being made through a familiar frame of reference which has the effect of distorting one's understanding of the subject matter.

Also clear is the problem of the sheer bulk of research. Blackstone had the luxury of being able to select the principles he wished to use for the purpose of his argument. In contrast, as Monti shows, Levi presented himself with the enormous task of producing a comprehensive comparison of the mercantile law of as many as fifty-nine countries. The later reduction of this number highlights the sheer work required if such an approach is to be successful, where 'a careful statement of each system by itself' is indeed the necessary starting point. [65] The amount of labour required for comparative work is also evident from the reviews contained in the *Anzeigen*. For example, Fischer notes that in Gatzert's review (of his own work) the author questions whether he will continue down 'this arduous path'. [66] Harris's work, as described by Korporowicz, represents an intermediate approach, sitting between those taken by Blackstone and Levi. Here, a detailed commentary is provided on selected parts of a specific text. In his essay, Korporowicz clearly illustrates the astonishing depth and breadth of these comments. Still, Harris's aim was to pique his reader's interest and stimulate comparative thought; comprehensive study of several bodies of law requires still greater labours.

Perhaps just as importantly, comparative legal history may provide salutary lessons for modern comparative endeavours. It may seem obvious to note that the method employed must fit the aim of the project. However, Monti's essay shows that this may not be achieved as easily as one might hope, and that problems can arise because of assumptions that one makes about one's audience and, perhaps, oneself. She argues that the tabular comparative format of Levi's first edition of his *Commercial Law* might have been readily accessible to Continental lawyers, but to British lawyers, 'the presentation might not have been self-explanatory, and would most likely have appeared complicated and somewhat cumbersome'. [67] In contrast, the more discursive revised edition was 'better suited to the needs and expectations of an English-speaking readership'. [68] Significantly, Monti argues, 'Levi was now a British citizen who was attuned to the needs of the Empire and its colonies; he was no longer an "outsider".' [69]

Study of Levi has taken us back to James VI and I and consideration of the significance of the transplant of an individual, demonstrating how this introduction's arrangement of essays into groups is just one of many possible patterns, each capable of fertile outcomes. The valuable quasi-Popperian falsifying role is but one important function of comparative approaches to legal history. Their falsifying role, for example in breaking down assumptions of uniformity within systems, coexists with producing illuminating questions and improved hypotheses. They can generate a more precise understanding of particular rules or concepts, as understood by contemporaries. They can refine our understanding of historical attitudes to law and the legal systems or doctrines that are being compared. Moreover, the pluralism of approach advocated above can produce stimulating conversation between different levels of study, from the specific to the deeper structures of Milsom's 'elementary legal ideas' or Kennedy's 'subsystems' of legal consciousness, and with a particular focus on processes of legal change. [70] Such investigation and such conversation can provide fresh perspectives that do not necessarily require the abandonment of a previous narrative, but instead suggest improvements to accommodate different evidence and different ideas. And perhaps just as importantly, comparative legal history may provide salutary lessons for modern comparative endeavours.

Footnote

1. F. W. Maitland, 'Why the History of English Law is Not Written', in The Collected Papers of Frederic William Maitland, ed. H. A. L. Fisher, 3 vols. (Cambridge, 1911), vol. I, 480–97, at 488–9.
2. The work presented in this introduction has been supported by the European Research Council, through the Advanced grant n. 740611, 'Civil law, common law, customary law: consonance, divergence and transformation in Western

Europe from the late eleventh to the thirteenth centuries' (see http://clicme.wp.st-andrews.ac.uk/). We would like to thank Matt Dawson, our co-editors and the other members of the ERC project for their comments on drafts of this introduction. John Hudson would also like to thank Susan Reynolds for her comments and for decades of exhortation always to compare.

3. C. Wickham, Problems in Doing Comparative History (The Reuter Lecture, 2004; Southampton, 2005), 3.

4. Possible starting points include W. W. Buckland and A. D. McNair, Roman Law and Common Law: A Comparison in Outline, 2nd edn (Cambridge, 1952); A. Watson, Legal Transplants (Edinburgh, 1974); R. Sacco, La comparaison juridique au service de la connaissance du droit (Paris, 1991); R. Zimmermann, 'Savigny's Legacy: Legal History, Comparative Law, and the Emergence of a European Legal Science', Law Quarterly Review, 112 (1996), 576–605; A. A. Levasseur and M. Reimann, 'Comparative Law and Legal History in the United States', American Journal of Comparative Law, Supp. *1*, 46 (1998), 1–15; M. Graziadei, 'Comparative Law, Legal History, and the Holistic Approach to Legal Cultures', Zeitschrift für Europäisches Privatrecht, 7 (1999), 531–43; D. Heirbaut, 'Comparative Law and Zimmermann's New Ius Commune: A Life-Line or a Death Sentence for Legal History? Some Reflections on the Use of Legal History for Comparative Law and Vice Versa', Fundamina, 11 (2005), 136–52; D. J. Ibbetson, 'Comparative Legal History: A Methodology', in A. Musson and C. Stebbings (eds.), Making Legal History: Approaches and Methodologies (Cambridge, 2012), 131–45; M. Reimann and R. Zimmermann (eds.), The Oxford Handbook of Comparative Law (Oxford, 2006); K. Å. Modéer, 'Abandoning the Nationalist Framework: Comparative Legal History', in H. Pihlajamäki, M. D. Dubber and M. Godfrey (eds.), The Oxford Handbook of European Legal History (Oxford, 2018), 100–13; O. Moréteau, A. Masferrer and K. Å. Modéer (eds.), Comparative Legal History (Cheltenham, 2019). Also relevant are works more particularly on comparative law, but with a strong legal historical dimension: e.g. W. Ewald, 'Comparative Jurisprudence (I): What was it Like to Try a Rat?', University of Pennsylvania Law Review, 143 (1995), 1889–2149; H. P. Glenn, Legal Traditions of the World, 2nd edn (Oxford, 2004).

5. E.g. A. Giuliani, 'What is Comparative Legal History? Legal Historiography and the Revolt against Formalism, 1930–60', in Moréteau et al. (eds.), *Comparative Legal History*, 30–77.

6. Moréteau et al. (eds.), *Comparative Legal History*, vii–xiii for list of contributors, xiv for quotation.

7. There are exceptions, with writings by historians such as D. L. D'Avray, 'Weber and Comparative Legal History', in A. Lewis and M. Lobban (eds.), *Law* and History: Current Legal Issues, Volume 6 (Oxford, 2004), 189–99; S. M. G. Reynolds, 'Early Medieval Law in India and Europe: A Plea for Comparisons', The Medieval History Journal, 16 (2013), 1–20.

8. E.g. Graziadei, 'Comparative Law', 532; D. Michalsen, 'Methodological Perspectives in Comparative Legal History: An Analytical Approach', in Moréteau et al. (eds.), *Comparative Legal History*, 96–109, at 97, 100, 108–9; Modéer, 'Abandoning the Nationalist Framework'; J. Gordley, 'Comparative Law and Legal History', in Reimann and Zimmermann (eds.), *Oxford Handbook of Comparative Law*, 754–71, at 754; A. Masferrer, K. Å. Modéer, and O. Moréteau, 'The Emergence of Comparative Legal History', in Moréteau et al. (eds.), *Comparative Legal History*, 1–28, at 7. M. Dyson, 'Comparative Legal History: Methodology for Morphology', in Moréteau et al. (eds.), *Comparative Legal History*, 110–38, at 119, includes history in a list of 'cognate disciplines', along with economics, sociology and philosophy. Absent from citations are works such as Wickham's *Problems in Doing Comparative History*, familiar in the footnotes of historians. Note also, e.g. the focus of Levasseur and Reimann, 'Comparative Law', esp. 1, 13, 15, on scholarship in Law schools with only a passing reference to History departments; also D. Ibbetson, 'What Is Legal History a History of?', in Lewis and Lobban (eds.), *Law and History*, 33–40, at 34. There are exceptions amongst those writing on comparative legal history; e.g. Heirbaut, 'Comparative Law', 147; M. Lobban, 'The Varieties of Legal History', Clio@Thémis, 5 (2012), 1–29, at 19, 21–2.

9. Dyson, 'Comparative Legal History', 112, 118; see also 112–13, 119, 120 ('Comparative legal history must avoid the "surfeit of methodology and self-inspection" that comparative law has borne'), 124, 137. Note also, e.g. Ibbetson, 'Comparative Legal History', esp. at 134. For pluralism, note the pertinent comments of D. Kennedy, The Rise and Fall of Classical Legal Thought (Washington, D.C., 2006), xiv: 'The point was to add structuralist and critical techniques to the repertoire available for understanding law as a phenomenon too large and messy and complex to be fully grasped within any one theoretical frame.'

10. Such matters of terminology differ between languages. Also very stimulating is J. Gardner, 'Legal Positivism: 5½ Myths', American Journal of Jurisprudence, 46 (2001), 199–227.

11. A point also made e.g. by Michalsen, 'Methodological Perspectives', 98, and Ibbetson, 'What Is Legal History?', 34. Differing conceptions of history will likewise affect our understanding of and approach to the subject.

12. See e.g. R. Gordon, 'Critical Legal Histories', in his Taming the Past: Essays on Law in History and History in Law (Cambridge, 2017), 220–81, at 229–30.
13. E. Ehrlich, Fundamental Principles of the Sociology of Law, trans. W. L. Moll (Cambridge, MA, 1936), on which see, e.g. S. P. Donlan, 'Comparative? Legal? History? Crossing Boundaries', in Moréteau et al. (eds.), *Comparative Legal History*, 78–95, at 85–6. For 'relative autonomy', see, e.g. E. P. Thompson, Whigs and Hunters (London, 1975), 258–69; Kennedy, *Rise and* Fall, x, 2; Gordon, 'Critical Legal Histories', 224, 248–53, 266.
14. F. W. Maitland, 'The Law of Real Property', in *Collected Papers*, ed. Fisher, I. 162–201, at 175–6 (the word about which he is talking here is feudalism).
15. Thompson, *Whigs and Hunters*, 261. Other metaphors include, for example, the 'stickiness' of legal rules, and also 'transplant', on which see below, 13–16.
16. Here comparative legal history may feed back into theories about law; note, e.g. M. Lobban, 'Legal Theory and Legal History: Prospects for Dialogue', in M. Del Mar and M. Lobban (eds.), Law in Theory and History (Oxford, 2016), 3–21. For relevant discussion of other issues that may be described as ones of 'legal theory', note J. Whitman, 'The World Historical Significance of European Legal History: An Interim Report', in Pihlajamäki et al. (eds.), *Oxford Handbook of European Legal History*, 3–21.
17. See e.g. J. Austin, The Province of Jurisprudence Determined, ed. W. E. Rumble (Cambridge, 1995), 18, 106 (the opening of Lectures I and V).
18. Note P. Bourdieu, 'The Force of Law: Toward a Sociology of the Legal Field', Hastings Law Journal, 38 (1987), 805–53. More specifically legal historical comments appear in D. Freda, 'Legal Education in England and Continental Europe between the Middle Ages and the Early Modern Period', in Moréteau et al. (eds.), *Comparative Legal History*, 242–66.
19. A. W. B. Simpson, 'The Common Law and Legal Theory', in his Legal Theory and Legal History: Essays on the Common Law (London, 1987), 359–82, at 361–2. See also, e.g. J. H. Baker, The Law's Two Bodies: Some Evidential Problems in English Legal History (Oxford, 2001). Simpson sees this as true of the period in England from the late medieval development of the Inns of Court up to the mid-nineteenth century, when expansion of the legal profession, numerically, geographically and socially, ended the dominance of this caste. Yet elements of his point remain true today, at least within particular areas of the legal profession; note the interviews in the University of St Andrews project 'The Law's Two Bodies': http://ilcr.wp.st-andrews.ac.uk/institute-projects/the-laws-two-bodies/.

20. See Dyson, 'Comparative Legal History', 117–18, for a helpful summary and references; also e.g. Modéer, 'Abandoning the Nationalist Framework', 109. Note also Kennedy, *Rise and Fall*, 27, defining his notion of 'legal consciousness' as 'the particular form of consciousness that characterizes the legal profession as a social group, at a particular moment. The main peculiarity of this consciousness is that it contains a vast number of legal rules, arguments, and theories, a great deal of information about the institutional workings of the legal process, and the constellation of ideals and goals current in the profession at a given moment.'
21. E.g. Michalsen, 'Methodological Perspectives', 96, 98. Cognate issues arise with studies of comparative law as well as legal history.
22. E.g. Lobban, 'Varieties of Legal History'; Ibbetson, 'What Is Legal History?'.
23. Ibbetson, 'Comparative Legal History', 132.
24. Ibbetson, 'What Is Legal History?', 34.
25. Note e.g. Dyson, 'Comparative Legal History', esp. 128–31, 138; Donlan, 'Comparative? Legal? History?', 83; Kennedy, *Rise and Fall*, xxvii. A further highly pertinent critique is provided by P. Legrand, e.g. in his 'On the Unbearable Localness of the Law: Academic Fallacies and Unseasonable Observations', European Review of Private Law, 1 (2002), 61–76, esp. 63–4, 66. On the significance of the specific context for court decisions that will assume a major, differently contextualised place in the internal history of law, see A. W. B. Simpson, Leading Cases in the Common Law (Oxford, 1995); external context, specific or general, may be particularly important to decisions in the type of difficult case that may drive Common law development, and to the later utilisation of those decisions.
26. D. Hay (ed.), Albion's Fatal Tree: Crime and Society in Eighteenth-Century England (London, 1975). Ibbetson, 'What Is Legal History?', 33, distinguishes 'legal history' and 'history of law'. The discussion here does not exhaust possible types of legal history; see also, e.g. below, 10–11, on structures of legal thought. Another type is 'presentist' legal history, on which see e.g. D. V. Williams, 'Historians' Context and Lawyers' Presentism: Debating Historiography or Agreeing to Differ', New Zealand Journal of History, 48 (2014), 136–60; see also Whitman, 'World Historical Significance'; Heirbaut, 'Comparative Law', 143–8; Lobban, 'Varieties of Legal History', 24–5; Zimmermann, 'Savigny's Legacy', esp. 598–601. For a critique of certain forms of presentism, helpfully formulated in terms of the 'instrumental impulse', see Legrand, 'Unbearable Localness'.
27. On problems of terminology, see, e.g. J. Vandelinden, 'Here, There and Everywhere ... or Nowhere? Some Comparative and Historical Afterthoughts

about Custom as a Source of Law', in Moréteau et al. (eds.), Comparative Legal History, 140–66. Developing interest in comparative legal history is linked to, but not identical with, developing interest in global perspectives, with its broadening of geographical perspectives, emphasis on interconnectedness, and questioning of assumed concepts and values; see esp. T. Duve, 'European Legal History – Concepts, Methods, Challenges', in T. Duve (ed.), Entanglements in Legal History: Conceptual Approaches (Frankfurt am Main, 2014), 29–66, esp. 30–1, 55, 56; also T. Duve, 'Global Legal History: Setting Europe in Perspective', in Pihlajamäki et al. (eds.), *Oxford Handbook of European Legal History*, 115–38. Note further G. Frankenberg, Comparative Law as Critique (Cheltenham, 2016).

28. See esp. Watson, *Legal Transplants*; Duve (ed.), *Entanglements in Legal History*. The word 'transplant' for the introduction of English laws to Scotland was already used three centuries earlier bySirMathew Hale in his The History of the Common Law of England (London, 1713), 200.
29. See below, 13–16; see also, e.g. W. Swain, 'The Common Law and the *Code Civil*: The Curious Case of the Law of Contract', in Moréteau et al. (eds.), *Comparative Legal History*, 379–99.
30. See below, 12–13, on causation.
31. Note also, e.g. Michalsen, 'Methodological Perspectives', 106–7.
32. For problems with 'legal systems' as a basis for comparison, see, e.g. Gordley, 'Comparative Law and Legal History', 761–4, Dyson, 'Comparative Legal History', 114–16.
33. Note, e.g. S. F. C. Milsom, The Natural History of the Common Law (New York, 2003).
34. E.g. Milsom, *Natural History*; Buckland and McNair, *Roman Law and Common Law*, xxi. Note also E. Conte, Diritto comune (Bologna, 2009). On broad generalisation, see also Duve, 'European Legal History', 45. For caution as to the extent of decline in influence of evolutionary assumptions and models, see e.g. Gordon, 'Critical Legal Histories', 225–7, 231–4. For an invigorating reassertion of the importance of the broad generalisation and comparison, see Whitman, 'World Historical Significance'. For pertinent comments on non-legal historians using anthropomorphic and other metaphors, see E. A. R. Brown, 'The Tyranny of a Construct: Feudalism and Historians of Medieval Europe', American Historical Review, 79 (1974), 1063–88, at 1075–6.
35. Wickham, *Problems in Doing Comparative History*, 11–15, reaches a similar conclusion.
36. Dyson, 'Comparative Legal History', 120.

37. E.g. Freda, 'Legal Education'.

38. See J. G. H. Hudson, The Oxford History of the Laws of England, Volume 2: 871–1216 (Oxford, 2012), 533, for the possible wider consequences of this point.

39. Note Y. Thomas, 'Présentation', Annales HSS, 50 (2002), 1425–8, at 1425–6.

40. H. S. Maine, Dissertations on Early Law and Custom (London, 1883), 389.

41. S. F. C. Milsom, The Legal Framework of English Feudalism (Cambridge, 1976), esp. 37; Milsom, *Natural History*.

42. Kennedy, *Rise and Fall*, xiv, and also, e.g. viii, ix–xi, xiii, xxxiv, 3, 5, 6, 7, 16–17, 21, 26, 27, 43, 192–3, 205, 208–9, 250–1, 256–7.

43. Ibbetson, 'What Is Legal History?', 36–9; Hudson, *Oxford History*, 375. Exploration of a different but sometimes related kind of competition may start with R. Cover, 'Nomos and Narrative', Harvard Law Review, 97 (1983), 4–68. Note also Ibbetson, 'Comparative Legal History', 136: 'A further facet of the level of legal doctrine ... is the degree to which it allows a substantial measure of indeterminacy.'

44. F. Pollock and F. W. Maitland, The History of English Law before the Time of Edward I, 2nd edn, reissued with a new introduction by S. F. C. Milsom, 2 vols. (Cambridge, 1968), vol. I, cvi.

45. See e.g. D. Osler, 'The Myth of European Legal History', Rechtshistorische Journal, 16 (1997), 393–410. To the medieval English legal historian, familiar with the resounding baronial expression of preference for 'English laws' over Canon law on the issue of whether subsequent marriage of parents legitimised children born before marriage, it comes as a salutary awakening to find the Orléans jurist Jacques de Revigny mentioning a similar local preference for 'our laws' (iura nostra) on this issue; K. Bezemer, What Jacques Saw: Thirteenth-Century France through the Eyes of Jacques de Revigny, Professor of Law at Orleans (Frankfurt am Main, 1997), 5, 11; cf. e.g. J. G. H. Hudson, The Formation of the English Common Law: Law and Society in England from King Alfred to Magna Carta, 2nd edn (London, 2018), 206.

46. Note Maitland's response to a request that he write a chapter on the early modern reception of Roman law in Germany: 'I have seen just enough to know that the subject, if it is to be made interesting, is beset by enormous difficulties. For instance the writer would be expected to say whether Roman law really harmed the peasantry, and that is a matter about which I dare not give any opinion. No one ought to have any opinion about it who does not know the economic position of the German peasants before and after the Reception, and even such a one would be in great danger of arguing from *post* to *propter* if he

did not know France and England also'; *The Letters of Frederic William Maitland*, ed. P. N. R. Zutshi (Selden Society, Supplementary Series, xi, London, 1995), no. 174.

47. The advantages of using clearly comparable bodies of source material are clear in, e.g. P. R. Hyams, 'The Common Law and the French Connection', Anglo-Norman Studies, 4 (1982), 77–92, 196–202. Note also Wickham, *Problems in Doing Comparative History*, 5; Donlan, 'Comparative? Legal? History?', 84.
48. Note also Gordon, 'Critical Legal Histories', 237.
49. See e.g. Gordley, 'Comparative Law and Legal History', 763–6, 770; Gordon, 'Critical Legal Histories', 237–43; Ibbetson, 'Comparative Legal History', 143–5. Note further M. Lobban, 'The Politics of English Law in the Nineteenth Century', in P. Brand and J. Getzler (eds.), Judges and Judging in the History of the Common Law and Civil Law (Cambridge, 2012), 102–37.
50. Dyson, 'Comparative Legal History', 110.
51. Note, e.g. Gordon, 'Critical Legal Histories', 243, 248, 270–2; Ibbetson, 'Comparative Legal History', 141–2; and, in particular for construction of analytical narrative, Dyson, 'Comparative Legal History', 128, 130–1, 136, 138.
52. Dyson, 'Comparative Legal History', 110: 'the comparative link will help historians to appreciate the role of chance in legal development'. Also Ibbetson, 'Comparative Legal History', 139–40 (including use of the word 'capricious').
53. A. W. B. Simpson, 'The Rule in Wheeldon v. Burrows and the Code Civile', Law Quarterly Review, 83 (1967), 240–7, at 240.
54. This is not to suggest that laws introduced with considerable thought for their place in their respective legal framework cannot also lack consistency and coherence.
55. Below, 87.
56. Below, 117.
57. For example, Cecchinato's essay on Blackstone's use of Civil law principles to address issues arising from the largely customary nature of English law may lead us to ask whether we can see this as a transplant of legal ideas. See below, 140–160.
58. Below, 261.
59. Below, 223.
60. See below, 289.
61. See below, 304.

62. See below, 22.
63. See below, 130.
64. Maitland, 'Why the History of English Law is Not Written', 486.
65. Below, 176.
66. Above, 11.
67. Below, 174.
68. Below, 247.
69. Below, 248.
70. Below, 249.
71. See above, 10–11.

01 'IN ALIQUIBUS LOCIS EST CONSUETUDO': IN THE MID-THIRTEENTH CENTURY, FRENCH LAWYERS WERE INVOLVED IN THE LOMBARD CUSTOMS OF FIEFS

The issue of customary authority has been a longstanding concern for legal historians, and its evolution during the twelfth and thirteenth centuries has held a prominent position in this debate.[1] This period was indeed a highly constructive one, being at the intersection of a series of processes which would lead to a wealthier, more populated and better-organised society and thus lay the foundations of modern Europe. The emergence of the *ius commune* and its relations with local legal traditions consequently lie at the core of various paradigms concerning the history of Continental law and European legal systems. Studies on the legal and institutional processes of this period have shed much light upon the revival of Roman law, the new ways of conceiving of law and the legal profession, as well as the progressive bureaucratisation of power relationships and an ever more widespread commitment of law to writing.[2] In this essay, I consider one of the most powerful among the narratives that have informed historical interpretations of this age of change. It became widespread in modern scholarship thanks to the influence of the nineteenth-century German constitutionalists, who envisaged this period as a transition from an age dominated by customary law to an age governed by the new law of the 'learned'.[3] Following old anti-Romanist sentiments – the first examples date to sixteenth-century France – this view found one of its most prominent supporters in Fritz Kern. In an influential article on law and constitution in the Middle Ages (1919), then translated into English in his book Kingship and Law (1939), the German scholar deemed custom to be the only true law of medieval people.[4] Resting on habit (Sitte) and popular belief (Volksglaube), custom was 'warm-blooded, vague, confused, and impractical, technically clumsy, but creative, sublime, and suited to human needs'. At the opposite end, Roman law was considered a cold artificial construct, alien to medieval societies, made up of 'unintelligible laws [that] seem to be made arbitrarily by men, or even to be taken over from the heathen Romans, and resurrected at Bologna in lecture-rooms and folio volumes'. [5]

The conflict between 'cold new law' and 'warm old custom' can be attributed to the 'Italophobia' that emerged among early modern French intellectuals. However, this sentiment was later transformed into a Romanticized notion of custom's alignment with the national spirit. [6] It would be redundant to repeat here the various criticisms brought against this ideological stance. [7] It is important to acknowledge, however, that the compelling story of a distinct movement from custom-based societies to systems founded on positive, codified law has demonstrated remarkable durability, permeating contemporary historical readings of the transformation that occurred throughout the twelfth and thirteenth centuries. In order to gain an understanding of how historians persist in presuming the model, it is necessary to examine the substantial body of legal anthropological research carried out in the pre-transition era, as well as the prominence of meticulously legal studies undertaken in the post-transition period. [8]

FROM THE ERA OF FEUDAL LAW IN THE MEDIEVAL STATE TO THE REEMERGENCE OF THE LIBRI FEUDORUM IS A SIGNIFICANT DEVELOPMENT.

The study of feudal law emerging in the twelfth and thirteenth centuries represents a privileged vantage point to reappraise this transition since it lies at the core of old and recent debates on the relationship between law and custom. Our point of departure will be the paradigm of feudalism developed by François-Louis Ganshof, one of the most resilient legal interpretations of feudal relationships. In his most famous book, *Qu'est-ce-que la féodalité?* (1944), Ganshof relied on the foundational idea that feudal law was the law of the medieval state par excellence. An earlier formulation of this idea was proposed by the German historian Heinrich Mitteis, who, in his book *Lehnsrecht und Staatsgewalt* (Feudal Law and State Power, 1933), framed within a coherent constitutional theory the shared conviction that feudalism had first emerged in the Merovingian and Carolingian eras. In Mitteis's and Ganshof's view, feudal law was a very apt example of law emerging from raw practice, in a way that in many aspects matched the constitutionalist idea of custom. Feudal law, indeed, was thought to stem naturally from the power relationships that kept the nobility together in the heartland of the Carolingian empire. Here, feudal relationships were nothing more than private agreements between lords and their followers. The Carolingians, however, created a constitutional precedent by using them as vital tools for the creation of imperial authority. The progressive formalisation of the rules governing the exchange of fiefs and protection in return for fidelity and military aid, sealed through precise rituals, would develop only later, from the tenth to the thirteenth centuries, the age of classic feudalism. Concerned as they were with suggesting a coherent model potentially applicable to all of medieval Europe, Mitteis first and Ganshof afterwards proposed that the feudal law developing from the Carolingian era was the only possible means by which any medieval form of territorial power could guarantee constitutional order and become a state. [9]

The main criticisms brought against this model concern the conviction that feudal law was a spontaneous phenomenon inherent to medieval values – i.e. that it was the law of a profoundly feudal society. [10] The main fault of Mitteis and Ganshof was to have neglected in their shaping of the feudal categories the role of a book, the *Libri feudorum*, that had been compiled in twelfth- and thirteenth-century Italy. [11] To be sure, the book had been studied almost uninterruptedly for centuries, but most modern scholars had (to some extent rightly) deemed it to be nothing more than the local custom of northern Italy, and hence evidence for the Lombard fief alone. [12] Nonetheless, the extraordinary afterlife of the *Libri* deserved a more thorough analysis. In its first version, the book was a compound of early twelfth-century source material on fiefs, written and collected by Lombard practitioners to help other Lombard practitioners. Seven short tracts were first put together about 1150, but other texts were continuously added for about a century. [13] By 1207, an incomplete apparatus of *glossae* was compiled, and, by about 1250, Accursius, the most famous law professor in Bologna, concluded this work. The completion of the apparatus allowed the inclusion, apparently by Accursius himself, of the *Libri* in the new editions of the *Corpus iuris civilis* produced in Bologna. The *Libri* thus became the tenth book of the *Authenticum* – the collection of Justinian's *Novels* until then subdivided into nine books. [14] This insertion, of course, would grant to the book an exceptional and enduring success. The *Libri* became *the* reference book to drive doctrinal debate on fiefs in a way that makes it very difficult to doubt its long-term influence in shaping late medieval and modern notions of feudal law and feudalism. This may also make it 'incomprehensible', as Dirk Heirbaut suggests, that views such as Mitteis's and Ganshof's could survive well into the 1990s. [15]

Susan Reynolds, the most radical opponent of the Ganshofian model, holds that the *Libri feudorum* was probably principally responsible for the construction of a 'feudal vocabulary' through four centuries of scholarly debate on feudal law and feudalism. [16] Her views have gained considerable authority among medievalists, but have been criticised by historians of medieval law mainly on the grounds that, at least from the twelfth century onwards, more or less formalised norms regulating feudal practices and institutions existed independently of any scholarly interpretation of the *Libri*. [17] I argue that holding that the new law – or the *new fief* – was entirely a product of the professionalisation of law or, more precisely, of the combined action of rulers and their bureaucrats may be seen as bearing the same original sin as the old German constitutional theory of custom vis-à-vis law. It rests on the assumption of a gap between custom accessible by any common man and the merely artificial new law. The relevant question here goes beyond whether the *Libri feudorum* related to the socio-political developments of twelfth-century Lombardy – and thus whether the book contained customary law or not. The principal problem, which I am going to tackle, is understanding how some of the 'learned' agents of this process, the alleged makers of the artifice, conceived of the practices and customs of fiefs they described in their treatises, and arguably taught to their students, in relation to the *Libri feudorum.* Tackling this issue compels us to consider, on the one hand, the possible normative value of the *Libri* and, on the other, the mechanisms of its absorption in the system of Civil law, that is, the extent to which the making of the *ius commune feudorum* related to issues emerging from practice. In what follows I try to answer these questions by briefly considering the impact of the *Libri* in the thirteenth century and its relations with the customary reality of Italy according to two early authors on feudal law: Obertus de Orto and Iacobus de Ardizone. I move then to a broader analysis of the first treatises on fiefs produced by lawyers from beyond the Alps, to reassess the authoritative and normative value of the Libri outside Italy.

THE LIBRI FEUDORUM'S INFLUENCE AND IMPACT

The existence and existence of the Libri provide evidence for the hypothesis that the text spread widely starting from the mid-thirteenth century. During the latter part of the twelfth century, the source material gathered in Lombardy underwent scientific examination by the Civilians. It is quite probable that Pillius de Medicina was the first individual to utilize this material as an instructional resource, commencing in Modena in 1182. This can be deduced from the observation that he created a glossae apparatus for the Libri and a Summa feudorum, which regrettably remains destroyed and is only known through a significant revision, presumably conducted by Accursius.. [18] Thus, the *Libri* is the first and maybe the only example of a medieval custumal to be accepted as an authoritative source – a teaching book, and hence a citable text – in open contravention of the demand by the Bolognese scholars to cite only the *Corpus iuris civilis.* However, it was only decades later that experts in law continued the tradition initiated by Pillius. The mysterious Symon Vicentinus (d. before 1263) left some *glossae*, and he is also known for a *Liber domini Symonis*, likely to be a lost recompilation of the *Libri feudorum.* He may have used it as a textbook when he taught in Padua, perhaps in 1222–8, but this hypothesis is purely speculative. [19] Iacobus de Ardizone and Odofredus produced *glossae* and recompilations of the *Libri* and also two famous *Summae feudorum* based on the book, probably both written in the 1230s. About 1250, or slightly earlier, the *Margarita feudorum* by Dullius Gambarini, active in Naples, would attest to the need to normalise the practical application of the book. [20] On the canonistic side, *glossae* and commentaries on fiefs flourished after the title *De feudis* (X. 3.20) was inserted in the *Compilatio tertia* (1210), but canonists relied almost exclusively on Gratian's *Decretum*, collections of decretals, and imperial decrees. Only with the *Summa decretalium* by Hostiensis, concluded about 1253, did the *Libri* appear as an established source in the Canon law literature, even though the commentary on X. 3.20 contained in this treatise was mostly an adaptation of Accursius's reworking of Pillius's short treatise. [21] In sum, the so-called *ius commune feudorum* did not emerge until the second half of the thirteenth century. This success was due principally to the fact that the Justinianic sources did not contain any reference to 'fiefs' and 'vassals' and the glossators felt at some point compelled to find an authoritative source relating to these matters. This limitation of the *Corpus iuris civilis* was a prevalent complaint among the authors on feudal law, and it also served as a justification for the utilisation of the *Libri*. [22]

Nonetheless, there are at least three good reasons to believe that such general acceptance of the *Libri* was neither easy nor immediate. In the first place, the book was not part of the ordinary curricula of the law schools but was taught only in extraordinary lectures; consequently, its teaching was not as widespread as one might think. [23] In the second place, direct citations of the *Libri* in charters and court proceedings were quite rare, and such evidence emerges only in the late thirteenth century. [24] Finally, until then, the ranks of commentators on the *Libri* – no more than fifteen authors – were tiny if compared with the vast legions of commentators on the *Corpus iuris civilis*. [25] Therefore, there is enough evidence to argue that although most Italian lawyers accepted the *Libri* as both an authoritative source to drive scholarly debate on fiefs and a normative text, most non-Italian lawyers struggled to accept its authority and normativity.

This criticism, indeed, would lie at the core of the sixteenth-century Gallican polemics following the controversy concerning the origins of fiefs, in which Charles Dumoulin played the leading role. The debate was sparked by the fifteenth-century philologists, engendering a series of different interpretations of the historical roots of the fief. It was Dumoulin who put an end to it by imposing the idea that the origins of the fief had been in early medieval Gaul. This was an attempt to undermine any interpretation of the *Libri feudorum* as a text possessing binding force or even scientific value for French lawyers. Indeed, Dumoulin was a strenuous advocate of the absolute power of the French Crown, and most of his intellectual efforts aimed at stressing the independence of French law from any foreign influence. He refused to accept the binding force of the *Corpus iuris civilis*, although he could not afford to reject its value in terms of legal science. [26] The *Libri*, on the other hand, became a much easier target for such a polemical impetus. The book, he thought, should not be considered part of the *Corpus* as it was the mere creation of private persons, who had no authority to establish any universal custom or law. It was nothing more than the local custom of Lombardy. [27]

The long-standing success of Dumoulin's theories, along with his depiction of them as a break with the whole medieval tradition of the Glossators and Commentators, has obscured the fact that their germs were already growing in the Middle Ages. For instance, in the mid-fourteenth century, the Auvergnat lawyer Pierre Jame d'Aurillac, then teaching at Montpellier, accepted the text as a citable source but firmly opposed its binding force. He asserted that the written customs of the book of fiefs, from top to bottom, ought not to be held at all as far as it concerns us in the entire kingdom of France. They do not bind us in any way and deservedly so, because they have no authority over us and because they are local. Indeed, if a controversy arises over a fief and there is a custom on that matter that is legally prescribed where the controversy takes place, that [custom] ought to be observed. [28]

Several decades before him, the great Orleanais master Jacques de Revigny (d. 1296) had already taken a very similar stance: even if he considered feudal law to be written law, he scarcely mentioned it, even in his *quaestiones* on fiefs, and, in his *Lectura authentici*, he did not consider it as the tenth book of the collection, in contradiction to the Bolognese school. [29] As we will see, similar disagreements emerged at the very outset of the Civilians' discussion on fiefs.

RECONTEXTUALIZING THE LOMBARD CUSTOM

One of the most common objections to the authority of the *Libri* was its localised nature. Grants of fiefs in exchange for allegiance, political support or service emerged in several regions of Europe, but regional variations could be substantial, so that a fixed set of rules could hardly be applicable universally. [30] The *Libri*, of course, reflected the substantive and procedural rules of twelfth-century Lombardy and not the customary law developing in other regions or times. One of its authors, Obertus de Orto, declared that the 'custom of the realm', i.e. the kingdom of Italy, varied according to the 'diverse practices (*mores*) of different courts and regions'. For this reason, he could describe nothing more than the 'usage (*usus*) of fiefs that is held in our lands', i.e. the Milanese territory, wherein he was one of the highest political and judicial authorities. [31]

It took the encounter of the Civilians with the *Libri* to change the nature of the book radically. By the early thirteenth century, many of the customary norms it contained were obsolete even in Milan, where only some sections of the book would be inserted in the 1216 'book of the customs of Milan' after thorough selection and updates. [32] As a source for the study – or the creation – of feudal law it served an entirely different purpose, that is, to offer a shared, no matter how inconsistent, set of notions and problems which the Glossators could use to control doctrinal debate about issues that continued to emerge from practice. [33] This is evident in Ardizone, who in his *Summa feudorum* quite plainly followed Obertus in acknowledging the highest authority of custom. Obertus, overturning the meaning of a famous rescript by Constantine on the supremacy of law over custom (C. 8.52[53].2) had suggested that 'in the judgment concerning fiefs, it is common to say what is contrary to our laws: the authority of the Roman laws is not negligible, but they do not extend their force so far as to override usage and practice (LF 2.1)'. This provocative statement worked as a justificatory opening for Obertus's treatment of the Milanese custom of fiefs by contrast with a broader custom of the realm, which remains in the background of Obertus's tracts without ever being revealed in full. Eighty-odd years later, in the first chapters of his *Summa*, Ardizone developed this argument by suggesting that unwritten custom was of the highest authority, regardless of its crystallisation in a legal text. In what appears to be a vigorous defence of the helpfulness of the *Libri*, he went on to say that 'it was necessary and useful to write about the controversies [over fiefs], not because they would not be valid otherwise, since they would obtain the force of the laws even if they remained in [unwritten] custom. ... On the contrary, they are written down to be better committed to memory.' [34]

Ardizone's treatise is an excellent example of cross-fertilisation among the various bodies of law. Sources of Roman law, Canon law, Lombard law, and even the Statute Book of Verona are used all together to analyse what the author considered the custom of fiefs only partly reflected in the *Libri*. [35] In order to expand his arguments, especially when the *Libri* or other sources were silent on a matter or perceived of as insufficiently detailed, he did not hesitate to bring in the local custom of Verona, his hometown, where he worked as a judge and public officer and, most likely, taught law. [36] This attitude reflects the bestowal of the highest authority upon unwritten custom on the matter of fiefs: the *Libri feudorum*, in this sense, is a contingent reflection – one of the many possible ones – of a broader, changing body of unwritten law which needed constant update and expansion.

FEUDAL LAW AS A LEGAL PRECEDENT? THE PROVENÇAL PRACTISE AND JEAN BLANC

Like with Russian dolls, Obertus's statement on the authority of custom is embedded in Ardizone's, and both are reported almost literally – one might even suggest copied – in the *Epitome feudorum* by Iohannes Blancus (Jean Blanc) from Marseille. Blanc was a Provençal law expert who, in the 1230s, like many of his colleagues, studied in Italy, more precisely at the *studium* of Modena, where Pillius's teachings were still very influential. There he learned Roman law and familiarised himself with the *Libri*; in about 1250, perhaps slightly later, he was the first to write a treatise on the book outside of Italy. Because of its apparently unambiguous acceptance of the authority of the *Libri* and its heavy reliance on Ardizone's *Summa feudorum*, the *Epitome* has been said to appear like an Italian treatise in all respects. [37] In this work, Blanc tended to pass over in silence the fact that he was taking more than inspiration from his sources, which in some cases he copied word for word. Nonetheless, his copying entailed selection. Alterations and addition of material reveal that his agreement was only partial. It was not just passive transcription but an active process of appropriation and recontextualisation. When he discussed the authority of custom and the *Libri feudorum*, he reported, without citing the source, Ardizone's treatment of the opening of Obertus's tract. In this case, the argument is nearly identical: feudal customs were written down because some disputes over fiefs were solved by Roman law, others by Lombard law, the custom of the realm, or unwritten feudal custom. [38] It is custom that approves these unwritten rules and procedures, which do not need to be crystallised into a text to gain authority. The only practical reason for their commitment to writing is their usefulness for lawyers who need to judge similar disputes; in other words, precedents possess, to some extent, legal authority in feudal matters regardless of their oral or written nature.

This attitude towards practice is well reflected in Blanc's *Epitome*, which, to my knowledge, is the feudal law treatise that mentions the highest number of real cases, the second one being, not surprisingly, Ardizone's *Summa*. In the text, Blanc's modus operandi appears in full clarity: in several *quaestiones*, he begins by displaying an argument derived from one of the *Libri*, Ardizone's treatise or one of his teachers, but often conceals his source. He then develops it by abstracting a principle and sometimes considering its application to real cases that he witnessed or judged, from which he eventually reaches an original conclusion. These cases are not just informative examples but are used, to some extent, to shape new arguments. Blanc reports disputes involving the Templars, the Cistercians, Provençal bishops, barons, and noblemen, which attest to his fieldwork in Provence in a period spanning from 1237 to the 1250s. [39] For instance, the most famous one, the *bishop of Apt* v. *Bertrand de Simiane* (1247), is used to develop the old question 'whether jurisdiction adheres with castles'. Following a *quaestio* by Pillius, Blanc proved that the enfeoffment of the *donjon* of a castle entailed the concession of the rest of the fortification and, by extension, the jurisdiction over the inhabitants of the surrounding territory. [40] Another case, opposing the Templars against the canons of Pignans, served to develop this argument further, by upholding the thesis that even after the destruction of a castle the jurisdiction over its former district would remain united. [41]

One of the most insightful examples, however, is the *quaestio* concerning whether ecclesiastics can hold fiefs. Blanc began his building of the argument from a passage of Ardizone's *Summa*, which he reported almost verbatim before expanding it in light of a novel case. The Veronese lawyer held that any churchperson could receive fiefs in a personal capacity since LF 2.40.3 implied that royal fiefs granted to a church ought to revert temporarily to the king should its rector – i.e. the bishop or the abbot – commit a wrong. According to Ardizone, the fact that other sources pointed in another direction – i.e. a fief-holder who becomes a cleric ought to lose the fief – would not constitute an impediment, and so he resolved the matter without further analysis. [42] Blanc, for his part, had several reservations. He copied Ardizone's short treatment – again, with no mention of the source – and added that ecclesiastics could theoretically receive a fief as long as the grantor was aware of their clerical status. [43] However, he saw 'no reason why a cleric should receive a fief from a layperson' because in that case he would be subject to the secular jurisdiction of the grantor and not the ecclesiastical jurisdiction of his primate, as established by four decretals (X. 2.2.12, 5.39.45, 3.50.3, 3.50.6). [44] The principal point of friction concerned the prohibition on Cistercians holding any secular power, which was expressed in the rule of the order and later confirmed by Alexander III in the decretal *Recolentes* (X. 3.35.3). [45] Blanc decided to mention here a case he saw in Provence, of which there is, unfortunately, no other extant evidence. [46] He remains silent on many details, but lets us know that, at some point, one party had exhibited a letter by which Innocent III confirmed to the Cistercians of Thoronet the enfeoffment of a castle by the count of Provence. Blanc's doubts concerned the validity of this confirmation. He suggested that this open breach of the Cistercian rule might still be considered lawful as long as it was demonstrated that it benefited the monks without damaging anyone else (C. 1.19.7, Decr. C. 25 q. 2 c. 15). Nonetheless, for this to happen the confirmation should have made clear that it was meant to break a law, i.e. the decretal *Recolentes*. Since it did not mention the decretal, and since not even the pope could relieve monks from their own rule (X. 3.35.6), he continued:

> it seems to me that this confirmation damages rather than benefits the plaintiffs, for it goes against the rule of their Order and may cause the waiver or forfeiture of the privileges of the Cistercian Order. If the Cistercians accepted such things, which are against the statutes of their Order, they would be judged by the law that is common to everyone and not by the [special law] of the Cistercians, as said in the decretal *Recolentes*. [47]

On this basis, Blanc ends up declaring this confirmation not only void and useless but most likely false, since it was not credible that the papal curia would overlook such a significant matter.

These instances show very clearly how Blanc did not use actual cases to highlight how existing custom or law ought to be applied in court practice. Rather, he saw in them the generative force of practice. Blanc took novel cases as precedents that could serve to expand the horizons of feudal law, encouraging the creation of new principles. Of course, Blanc was using the interpretative tools provided by the rising *ius commune*, which entailed a high degree of abstraction and often induced him to conceal his sources or pass over in silence essential details of the cases he took as precedents. But he intended to move seamlessly in the wake of Obertus and Ardizone. The example of Blanc ultimately suggests that the mechanisms of the 'Romanisation' of the fief entailed a process of abstraction that obscures the connections of the 'new' law with practice more to us than to thirteenth-century lawyers.

JEAN DE BLANOT AND THE DOMINANCE OF INDIGENOUS TRADITIONS

Blanc had considered the *Libri* not only as an authoritative source for doctrinal uses but also as a text reflecting custom that needed constant expansion and updates in light of novel cases. Jean de Blanot took a very different stance. Blanot was born in Mâcon (Burgundy) before 1230 to a tax collector of Cluny Abbey. He completed his studies *in utroque iure* at Bologna, attending the lectures of Odofredus, and he taught in the same university in the 1250s. Later back in Burgundy, he served Duke Hugh IV (d. 1272) and, in exchange for his service, received the castellany of Uxelles as a fief in 1263. [48] Blanot published his most famous treatise, a commentary upon the title *De actionibus* of Justinian's *Institutes*, at the time of his Bolognese teaching. There is no reason to doubt that he wrote it in Italy, but it is nevertheless clear that he had the Burgundian context in mind and, most likely, a Burgundian audience. Emanuele Conte has noted how the aim of this treatise was 'to cast the social and customary reality of his age in the abstract categories offered by Roman law' and 'to teach practitioners in his homeland how to fit the real relationships prevailing in that region of Europe to the procedural patterns described by Roman institutions'. [49]

A point of particular interest is that Blanot decided to discuss homage and the nature of the feudal bond within a broader treatment of the *actio praeiudicialis in rem*. In Roman law this *actio* allowed owners to retrieve the service of their freed slaves (*liberti*). Blanot implied that the act of homage creating the feudal bond was somehow analogous to the act of manumission of a slave – i.e. it generated similar duties connected to the personal status created by the act. [50] To be sure, these notions were not entirely new. The analogy between vassals and *liberti* had already been suggested by Iohannes Bassianus (d. 1197) and Ardizone. [51] By 1233, Roffredus Beneventanus had discussed the opportunity for lords to use the *actio praeiudicialis* in the same terms as Blanot did. [52] However, the chapters on homage, overlordship, and *lèse-majesté* that the Burgundian lawyer decided to insert in his treatise on legal actions would enjoy an independent and very successful afterlife, being a valuable source for Guillaume Durand's famous *Speculum iudiciale* and Pere Albert's *Customs of Catalonia Between Lords and Vassals.* [53]

The key aspect to emphasize is that Blanot choose to utilize renowned historical events as examples pertaining to his homeland, in contrast to Blanc's Epitome, which relied on specific court cases attended by the author. Blanot drew inspiration from the conflict between the French Crown and the count of Toulouse (1209–29) when examining the concept of lèse-majesté. This concept was founded on a quaestio, which had already been formulated by Blanot's mentor, Odofredus, in comparable language. [54] Other arguments on overlordship are built on the examples of the 1203 war between Burgundy and Lorraine (ch. XIV) and the paradoxical situation in which the king of France found himself when he inherited the county of Mâcon in 1239, being at once overlord and vassal of the bishop of Mâcon (ch. XV). [55] Blanot's reliance on historical situations and informative examples has been deemed to be an obstacle to our understanding of how practice or local custom shaped his theoretical building. [56] However, I believe that a closer look into the text proves the contrary.

One must first note that the history of Blanot's chapters on homage is quite problematic. One fourteenth-century code, in MS Parma, Biblioteca Palatina 1227, transmits them as an independent short treatise on fiefs and homage – a *Tractatus super feudis et homagiis*. In 1906, Jean Acher was misled by the unknown compiler of this only witness and edited this *Tractatus* as a self-standing work. Acher had noticed some issues concerning the reliability of this compiler, but he did not realise the extent of his manipulations on the texts contained in the code. Several tracts are misattributed, and nearly all contain deceptive interpolations. [57] Blanot's text, in particular, though rightly attributed to the Burgundian author, was not only misleadingly reported as a self-standing tract, with no connection to the broader treatise *De actionibus* of which it was an extract; it was also interpolated with several additions and citations from the *Libri feudorum* that were in fact not present in the original text of Blanot's *De actionibus.* [58] Therefore, the reliance of Blanot on the *Libri* is much less significant than historians have thought in the past. This is very important, since the treatise *De actionibus* was most likely written in Italy in the mid-thirteenth century, i.e. when the Bolognese scholars were well acquainted with the *Libri* and the *glossae* apparatus was near completion, if not already completed. Notwithstanding this, Blanot developed his arguments on feudal homage – i.e. homage which entails the grant of a fief (*homagium ratione feudi*) – without considering the scholarly interpretations of the book that were available at the time.

The insertions by our unknown interpolator correspond mostly with arguments that Blanot built considering the customs held 'in some places' ('in aliquibus locis'), 'parts' (*partes*), 'regions' (*regiones*) or even the entirety of France ('per vulgare

Francie'). This positioning suggests that our unknown interpolator was interested in highlighting the divergences between the local customs of France and the *Libri*. The contrast between the two, however, was implicitly subsumed in nearly all of Blanot's treatment of homage and fiefs. This contrast emerges very clearly in the argument concerning the heritability of the feudal bond, in which Blanot asked whether succession into fiefs was like other kinds of succession. His answer was negative, because neither women nor monks nor the maimed could succeed into fiefs, and this was 'according to the custom approved by Lord Frederick I, as it is contained in the constitution concerning the usages of fiefs' – this is as far as Blanot went in mentioning the *Libri*, without citing any specific chapter of the book. [59] However, he went on to say that in some regions the custom was ('in aliquibus locis est consuetudo') that women, agnates, cognates, and even non-relatives may succeed in the absence of closer relatives. [60] In another passage, he questioned the principle of egalitarian inheritance in fiefs that underpinned most of the *Libri*, this time not even mentioning the book, by expounding a 'statement of custom' ('declaratio consuetudinis'):

> in many places, it is observed by custom that if someone is my man and holds all his property in fief from me, his firstborn takes an oath of fidelity to me and is bound to serve me against my enemies, for ... it is rightful to choose one [heir], and custom chooses the firstborn ... The same way custom burdens the firstborn on the one hand, so on the other one it benefits him because his younger brothers are bound to do homage and take an oath of fidelity to him ... and this is the custom in the regions beyond the Alps. [61]

Custom – and in no way the *Libri* – governs succession in fiefs. The authority of local custom was then restated in the description of the nature of the feudal contract. The point of departure was the acknowledgement that if not even death could free a man from the obligations of homage – since his heirs would inherit them – the waiver of the fief would in no way suffice to exempt the vassal from such obligations. Blanot first discarded the opinion held by 'some people' ('ut voluerunt quidam dicere') according to which the feudal contract was 'innominate', i.e. a contract which does not conform to a standard set by law and which parties create ad hoc based on specific needs. More specifically, Blanot challenged the idea that the feudal contract was of the kind 'do ut facias', a service contract by which someone gives something in exchange for a performance. He found a more fitting analogy with other 'nominate' contracts founded in Roman law, such as emphyteusis, according to which withdrawal was not allowed after the closing (D. 12.4.16, C. 4.10.5, C. 4.66.1) – a good analogy with the impossibility of a vassal withdrawing from feudal obligations. However, since the feudal contract did not rest on written law, Blanot went on to suggest that even though it was derived from custom ('inductus de consuetudine'), it was nonetheless 'nominate': it conformed to a standard. This standard was provided by the binding force of custom, which, as Blanot asserted throughout the tract, was an unwritten tradition substantially diverging from the content of the *Libri*. [62]

AURELIANUS' PERSPECTIVE ON THE FEUDAL CONTRACT AND CUSTOMARY LAW

The notions on which Blanot rested his arguments on custom are strikingly similar to the ones utilised by another French lawyer active in the mid-thirteenth century: Iacobus de Aurelianis, or Aurelianus (Jacques d'Orleans). He was the author of some *glossae* and *additiones* to the *Libri feudorum* and possibly the compiler of an alternative version of the *Libri*, known as the *Liber domini Iacobi de Aurelianis*. In a recent essay, I suggested that Aurelianus was the author of the mysterious *Summa feudorum* transmitted by MS Parma 1227, the authorship of which has been the object of several speculations. [63] This *Summa* is an unfinished work, the definitive version of which is unfortunately lost. Like Blanc's *Epitome*, it is a commentary upon the *Libri feudorum*, written in the wake of the Italian tradition. While it has been seen as a practice-oriented treatise, there is scarcely a mention of specific cases and usages. [64] Nonetheless, even if Aurelianus moved more comfortably than Blanot within the maze of Canon law sources and his pattern of reasoning denoted much stronger influences of the liberal arts, this *Summa* presents several points of convergence with the work of the Burgundian lawyer.

In particular, the two authors seem to share the same ideas about primogeniture and the nature of the feudal contract. [65] Concerning the former, we have seen that in his 'statement of custom' Blanot suggested that the *consuetudo* of the regions beyond the Alps ('partes ultramontanas') was to choose the firstborn ('consuetudo eligit primogenitum'). Aurelianus suggested that by the custom of 'our regions' ('in partibus nostris'), the lord chooses the firstborn urged by the necessity of custom ('dominus primogenitum eligit necessitate consuetudinis suadente'). [66] The idea is the same and is expounded through a strikingly similar vocabulary. What is more, precisely like Blanot, Aurelianus thought of the feudal contract as a nominate contract founded in custom ('contractus nominatus consuetudine inventus'). In his *Summa*, however, the argument is much more sophisticated than in Blanot's tract. Aurelianus developed it very carefully, weighing all the elements, in a skilful application of logic to legal reasoning. [67] He first reported two different opinions: some authors say that the feudal contract is a service contract ('do ut facias') which is 'innominate' and thus with no foundation in Civil law; some others, including Roffredus, hold that it is a *donatio sub modo*, a donation given on determined conditions, hence a nominate contract, the substance and form of which was provided by Roman law. From the synthesis of these two elements, Aurelianus suggests the emergence of a third one:

I say that it is a contract in itself which has something of the aforementioned service contract and something of the *donatio sub modo*. Hence a *tertium quid* is obtained which possesses its own nature, conception, and definition ... I say that if we consider its form, this is a nominate contract founded in custom, but if we consider its matter, it took its origin from the *ius gentium* (see the argument as in D. 43.26.1 and 43.26.14). [68]

Resorting to the notions of matter and form (*materia* and *forma*), he asserts that the substantial existence of the feudal contract could derive its form only from customary law. He cites the *Libri feudorum* (LF 2.32), where it is said that the 'solemnity of custom', i.e. right customary procedure, is needed to consider a feudal grant to be valid. On this specific point, Aurelianus did not use the book to provide a statement of custom but as a source to prove the vital function of custom in shaping the feudal contract. This is even clearer from the following step of the argument, in which Aurelianus compared this contract with verbal agreements, such as *stipulatio* and *acceptilatio*, and with serfdom. By their substance, they all originally belonged to the *ius gentium*, i.e. the composite body of unwritten laws and principles which, according to Roman law, were innate and common to all peoples (D. 1.1.1.5, 1.1.5). These analogies led the argument to its finale: since 'the form gives existence to the substance' ('forma dat esse rei'), a maxim possibly borrowed from Peter of Spain's treatise on logic, Aurelianus concluded 'daringly that it must be held that the feudal contract is a nominate contract founded in custom, for it takes its existence (*esse suum*) from custom'. [69] The bottom line is that the verbal agreements between lords and vassals would be no 'contract' were it not for the crystallisation granted by custom. Interestingly, the *Libri* entered this argument as an authoritative source to prove that certain formalised practices and rituals were needed for the feudal contract to subsist. However, the *ius consuetudinarium* that provided these agreements with a *nomen* was not the text of the *Libri feudorum*, which, as the author admitted, 'is most disorganised and averts me, and perhaps many others, from the way of truth'. [70] The form, and hence the existence of the feudal contract, could only be provided by unwritten custom.

THE INFLUENCE OF FEUDAL LAW ON THE FORMATION OF THE IUS COMMUNE

This initial contribution to the study of the geographical dimensions of feudal law, its interrelations with local custom and its long-standing yet unsettled dialectics with the *Libri feudorum* has been suggestive from several points of view. In the first place, the three examples we have observed attest to very different approaches to the relationship between custom and the *Libri*. Blanc and Aurelianus took it as a reference book but did not share the same view on its nature and function. Blanc seems to have pursued a project of expansion of the boundaries set by the *Libri*, accepting both its normative potential and its authority as a source for legal arguments. Aurelianus, on his part, did not spare criticism of the *Libri*, but he nonetheless decided to dedicate a treatise to it. Although he did not question its utility as a text to drive doctrinal debate on fiefs, he shared Blanot's mistrusting attitude towards its normative value and its applicability to non-Italian contexts. Coming to Blanot, further analysis is needed to clarify his actual reliance on the *Libri*. Nonetheless, he certainly believed that the book was not an appropriate tool for describing homage and the feudal bond to a Burgundian or French audience. This sentiment, we know, was shared by generations of later French scholars, even those who cited and commented upon the *Libri*. The roots of the sixteenth-century debate on the authority and normativity of the book in the French contexts thus originated at the very first encounter of French scholars with it.

In the second place, the reliance of the norms regulating fiefs and homage on local usages compelled lawyers to take a clear stance on the matter of custom. The survival of unwritten legal traditions and the fact that 'learned' lawyers were ready to receive them and combine them within more or less structured theories of 'authority' and 'normativity' would suggest some continuity, if not circularity, between the two spheres of social practice and legal doctrine. Such circularity narrows significantly the alleged gap dividing 'warm natural custom' from 'cold artificial law', a gap that, as we have seen, underpins several historical paradigms of legal and institutional change in twelfth- and thirteenth-century Western Europe. In particular, this circularity questions the very idea that 'learned law' should be seen just as a product of the professionalisation, or bureaucratisation, of the legal profession, and casts doubts on the foundations on which models of the twelfth- and thirteenth-century 'transition' rely.

Ultimately, by pointing at the geographical dimensions of these doctrinal debates and their relationship with local and unwritten customs, our examples provide a vantage point to observe some underestimated processes at work in the making of the *ius commune*. Legal historians have often tended to stress uniformity and unity in explaining its emergence. [71] Feudal law and its absorption within the system of the *ius commune* offer a slightly different perspective, telling us a story in which local legal traditions not only survived but remained a constitutive element of the Western European experiences of law.

FOOTNOTE

1. V. Scialoja, 'Sulla const. 3 Cod. Quae sit longa consuetudo e la sua conciliazione col fr. 32, § 1, Dig. De legibus: difesa di un'antica opinione', Archivio giuridico, 24 (1880), 420–30; E. Cortese, La norma giuridica. Spunti teorici nel diritto

comune classico, 2 vols. (Milan, repr. 1995), vol. II, 101–67; A. Gouron, 'Coutume contre Loi chez les premiers glossateurs', in A. Gouron and A. Rigaudiére (eds.), Renaissance du pouvoir législatif et génese de l'Etat (Montpellier, 1988), 117–30; E. Conte, 'Roman Law vs Custom in a Changing Society: Italy in the Twelfth and Thirteenth Centuries', in P. Andersen and M. Münster-Swendsen (eds.), Custom: The Development and Use of a Legal Concept in the Middle Ages (Copenhagen, 2009), 33–50.

2. H. J. Berman, Law and Revolution: The Formation of the Western Legal Tradition (Cambridge, 1983), 120–64; M. Bellomo, The Common Legal Past of Europe, 1000–1800 (Washington, DC, 1995); S. Reynolds, 'The Emergence of Professional Law in the Long Twelfth Century', Law and History Review, 21(2) (2003), 347–66.
3. Conte, 'Roman Law'; E. Conte, 'Consuetudine, Coutume, Gewohnheit and Ius Commune: An Introduction', Rechtsgeschichte, 24 (2016), 234–43; L. Gilissen, La coutume (Turnhout, 1982), 24–32.
4. F. Kern, 'Recht und Verfassung im Mittelalter', Historische Zeitschrift, 120 (1919), 1–79, translated into English as F. Kern, Kingship and Law in the Middle Ages: A Classic Study of Early Constitutional Law, trans. S. B. Chrimes (Oxford, 1939).
5. Kern, *Kingship*, 179–80.
6. D. R. Kelley, 'De Origine Feudorum: The Beginnings of an Historical Problem', Speculum, 39(2) (1964), 207–28, at 207–8.
7. Andersen and Münster-Swendsen (eds.), *Custom*; M. Ryan, 'Feudal Obligations and Rights of Resistance', in N. Fryde, P. Monnet, and O. G. Oexle (eds.), Die Gegenwart des Feudalismus (Göttingen, 2002), 51–78.
8. W. Davies and P. Fouracre (eds.), The Settlement of Disputes in Early Medieval Europe (Cambridge, 1992); C. Wickham, Courts and Conflict in Twelfth-Century Tuscany (New York, 2003); F. Cheyette, 'Suum cuique tribuere', French Historical Studies, 6(3) (1976), 287–99. Criticisms of this methodological divide come from: S. Teuscher, Lords' Rights and Peasant Stories: Writing and the Formation of Tradition in the Later Middle Ages (Philadelphia, PA, 2012); B. Lemesle, Conflits et justice au Moyen Âge. Normes, loi et résolution des conflits en Anjou au XIe et XIIe siècles (Paris, 2008).
9. H. Mitteis, Lehnsrecht und Staatsgewalt. Untersuchungen zur mittelalterlichen Verfassungsgeschichte (Weimar, 1933); F.-L. Ganshof, Qu'est-ce-que la féodalité? (Brussels, 1944).
10. See the outline in D. Heirbaut, 'Feudal Law', in H. Pihlajamäki, M. D. Dubber and

M. Godfrey (eds.), The Oxford Handbook of European Legal History (Oxford, 2018), 528–48.

11. LF 1 and LF 2 refer respectively to book 1 and book 2 of the *Libri feudorum*, edited in K. Lehmann, Das Langobardische Lehnrecht (Handschriften, Textentwicklung, ältester Text u. Vulgattext): Nebst den Capitula Extraordinaria (Göttingen, 1896). All translations of this text are mine.
12. The title of the 1896 edition, 'The Feudal Law of the Lombards' reveals this conviction: Lehmann, *Das Langobardische Lehnrecht*. The same idea is expounded by the influential Italian author P. Brancoli Busdraghi, La formazione storica del feudo Lombardo come diritto reale (Spoleto, 1999).
13. P. Weimar, 'Die Handschriften des Liber Feudorum und seiner Glossen', Rivista Internazionale di Diritto Comune, 1 (1990), 31–98.
14. A. Rota, 'L'apparato di Pillio alle Consuetudines feudorum e il ms. 1004 dell'Archivio di Stato di Roma', Studi e memorie per la storia dell'Università di Bologna, 14 (1938), 61–103; Weimar, 'Handschriften'.
15. Heirbaut, 'Feudal Law'; K. Pennington, 'Feudal Oath of Fidelity and Homage', in K. Pennington and M. Harris Eichbauer (eds.), Law as Profession and Practice in Medieval Europe: Essays in Honor of James A. Brundage (Farnham, 2011), 93–115; M. Ryan, 'Ius commune feudorum in the Thirteenth Century', in A. Romano (ed.), "... colendo iustitiam et iura condendo ..." Federico II legislatore del Regno di Sicilia nell'Europa del Duecento (Rome, 1997), 51–65.
16. S. Reynolds, Fiefs and Vassals: The Medieval Evidence Reinterpreted (Oxford, 1994), 1–74.
17. Pennington, 'Feudal Oath'; Heirbaut, 'Feudal Law'.
18. E. Cortese, 'Pillio da Medicina', in I. Birocchi, E. Cortese, A. Mattone, and M. N. Miletti (eds.), Dizionario biografico dei giuristi italiani (XII–XX secolo), 2 vols. (Bologna, 2013) (henceforth, DBGI), vol. II, 1587–90; E. Conte, 'Modena 1182: The Origins of a New Paradigm of Ownership. The Interface Between Historical Contingency and the Scholarly Invention of Legal Categories', GLOSSAE. European Journal of Legal History, 15 (2018), 4–18.
19. E. J. H. Schrage, 'Symon Vicentinus, un docteur très excellent du XIIIe'siècle', Tijdschrift voor Rechtsgeschiedenis, 55 (1987), 297–320.
20. A. Stella, 'The Liber Ardizonis: Reshaping the Libri feudorum in the Thirteenth Century', Studi Medievali, 58 (2017), 175–227; M. Montorzi, Processi istituzionali: episodi di formalizzazione giuridica ed evenienze d'aggregazione istituzionale attorno ed oltre il feudo: saggi e documenti (Padua, 2005), 135–259.
21. K. Pennington, 'Enrico da Susa, cardinale Ostiense', in DBGI, vol. I, 795–8;

M. Ryan, 'The Libri feudorum and the Roman Law', unpublished PhD thesis, University of Cambridge (1994), 134–220.

22. Ryan, 'Ius commune feudorum'.
23. M. Huneke, Iurisprudentia romano-saxonica. Die Glosse zum Sachsenspiegel Lehnrecht und die Anfänge deutscher Rechtswissenschaft (Harassowitz, 2014), 298–9.
24. See the *consilia* by Dino del Mugello: Ryan, 'Ius commune feudorum', 56–65; A. Stella, 'Bringing the Feudal Law Back Home: Social Practice and the Law of Fiefs in Italy and Provence (1100–1250)', *Journal of Medieval History*, 46 (2020), 396–418.
25. G. Giordanengo, 'La littérature juridique féodale', in J.-F. Nieus (ed.), Le vassal, le fief et l'écrit (Louvain-la-Neuve, 2007), 11–34, at 11–12.
26. D. R. Kelley, Foundations of Modern Scholarship: Language, Law, and History in the French Renaissance (New York and London, 1970), 151–82.
27. C. Dumoulin, Opera Omnia (Paris, 1612), cols. 12–13; Kelley, 'De Origine'. The terms of this debate were very far from the concerns of the thirteenth-century jurists. Dumoulin and the French legal antiquarians were rejecting the authenticity of the *Libri*, as well as its authority and validity, in order to claim the authority, in the kingdom of France, of French customary law.
28. My translation from Petrus Jacobi de Aureliaco, Aurea practica libellorum (Cologne, 1575), fo. 273b.
29. L. Waelkens, La théorie de la coutume chez Jacques de Révigny (Leiden, 1984), 176–8.
30. Heirbaut, 'Feudal Law'.
31. LF 2.1. On Obertus: L. Loschiavo, 'Oberto dall'Orto', in DBGI, vol. II, 1448–9.
32. Liber consuetudinum Mediolani anni 1216. Nuova edizione interamente rifatta, ed. E. Besta (Milan, 1949), 119–32; H. Keller, 'Die Kodifizierung des mailänder Gewohnheitsrechts von 1216 in ihrem gesellschaftlich-institutionellen Kontext', in Milano e il suo territorio in età comunale (Spoleto, 1999), 145–72.
33. Ryan, 'Ius commune feudorum', 51–56.
34. My translation from Iacobus de Ardizone, Summa Feudorum (Asti, 1518), fo. 3r.
35. Stella, 'Bringing the Feudal Law'.
36. G. M. Varanini and A. Stella, 'Scenari Veronesi per la Summa feudorum di Iacopo di Ardizzone da Broilo', in P. Maffei and G. M. Varanini (eds.), Honos alit

artes. Studi per il settantesimo compleanno di Mario Ascheri. La formazione del diritto comune (Florence, 2014), 266–80.

37. G. Giordanengo, 'Blanc, Jean', in J.-L. Halpérin, J. Krynen, and P. Arabeyre (eds.), Dictionnaire historique des juristes français, XIIe–XXe siècle (Paris, 2015) (henceforth, DHJF), 114; G. Giordanengo, 'Jean Blanc, feudiste de Marseille XIIIe siècle', Annales de la Faculté de droit de l'Université de Bordeaux, 2 (1978), 71–93.

38. J. Blanc, Epitome feudorum (Cologne, 1565), fos. 17–18.

39. Giordanengo, 'Jean Blanc', 72–79.

40. Stella, 'Bringing'.

41. Blanc, *Epitome*, fos. 542–50.

42. Ardizone, *Summa*, fo. 8ra.

43. The habit of concealing sources in legal writings was not uncommon among the Glossators, but the matter, to my knowledge, has not been treated in full. I consider some examples in Stella, 'Bringing'. See also E. Conte, 'Framing the Feudal Bond: A Chapter in the History of the Ius Commune in Medieval Europe', Tijdschrift voor Rechtsgeschiedenis, 80 (2012), 481–95, at 490–1.

44. Blanc, *Epitome*, fo. 98.

45. The decretal implied that some Cistercian monks had forgotten the pristine nature and rule of their institution in coming to possess towns, mills, and churches, to receive oaths of fidelity and homage, and to hold judicial and fiscal authority.

46. Blanc, *Epitome*, fos. 100–3.

47. Ibid., fo. 103.

48. P. Arabeyre, 'Blanot, Jean de', in DHJF, 115–17. Although he was bailiff of Charles d'Anjou in 1275–7, his career developed almost exclusively in Burgundy, at the service of Hugh IV and, after him, his son Robert II.

49. Conte, 'Framing', 486.

50. Ibid., 487.

51. Ardizone, *Summa*, fo. 9ra: 'Habita similitudine de liberto cui possunt imponi operae tam certae quam incertae ... Nam dominus Io‹hannes Baxianus› ait quod ea quae in legibus leguntur de libertis etiam a vasallis ex regni consuetudine sunt servanda, et hoc in summa Quibus modis quis possit ab ecclesia repellere in nomine Domini Iesu Christi'.

52. Roffredus Beneventanus, Tractatus iudiciarii ordinis (Cologne 1591), fos.

166ra–170rb.

53. Conte, 'Framing', 490–1.

54. J. Acher, 'Notes sur le droit savant au moyen age', Revue historique de droit français et étranger, 30 (1906), 138–78, at 160–1 (Ch. XIII); Odofredus Denari, Summa feudorum (Alcalá de Henares, 1584), fo. 112r.

55. Acher, 'Notes', 161–4; J. Richard, 'Les exemples bourguignons dans le traité des hommage et des fiefs de Jean de Blanot', Mémoires de la Société pour l'Histoire du Droit et des Institutions des anciens pays bourguignons, comtois et romands, 18 (1956), 107–12.

56. Richard, 'Les exemples'; remarks shared by Giordanengo, 'Jean Blanc', 76 n. 29; Reynolds, *Fiefs and Vassals*, 281–3.

57. Acher, 'Notes'. See some remarks and bibliography in A. Stella, 'The Summa Feudorum of MS Parma 1227: A Work by Iacobus Aurelianus?', Reti Medievali Rivista, 20(2) (2019), 271–327, at 273–5.

58. There is no critical edition of *De actionibus*. I have derived these conclusions from E. Conte, Servi medievali. Dinamiche del diritto comune (Rome, 1996), 230–4, and from two manuscripts: Sion, Archives et Bibliothèque Cantonales (ABC), S. 102; Paris, Bibliothèque Nationale de France, Lat. 4106.

59. Sion, ABC, 102, fo. 20rb: 'non, quia nec mulier, nec monachus, nec mancus succedit in feudum, secundum consuetudinem approbatam per dominum Fredericum seniorem, ut in const(itutione) de usibus feudorum continetur.' The unknown interpolator at this point cites eight chapters of the *Libri*: LF 1.8.2, 1.4, 2.11, 2.17, 2.50, 2.21, 2.26.6, 2.30.

60. Sion, ABC, 102, fo. 20rb.

61. Acher, 'Notes', 156–7.

62. Ibid., 149 and 171. On later interpretations of this definition, see A. Massironi, Nell'officina dell'interprete. La qualificazione del contratto nel diritto comune (secoli XIV–XVI) (Milan, 2012), 312 n. 44.

63. Stella, 'The Summa Feudorum', 272–85, with an updated edition of the *Summa* at 287–327.

64. E. Cortese, 'Scienza di giudici, scienza di professori tra XII e XIII secolo', in E. Cortese, Scritti, ed. I. Birocchi, 2 vols. (Spoleto, 1999), vol. I, 93–148, at 143–4.

65. It seems possible that Aurelianus knew Blanot's work – one might even wonder if he attended Blanot's lectures in Bologna. The attendance of French students at Blanot's Bolognese lectures would explain Blanot's choice to clarify legal arguments in light of customs and examples from Burgundy and France. One

of the main problems, nonetheless, is that Aurelianus was keen on mentioning very explicitly the authors on whom he relied, but he did not cite Blanot at all.

66. Stella, 'The Summa Feudorum', 290, at lines 107–13.
67. Ibid., 297–8, at lines 375–424.
68. Ibid., 298, at lines 398–401.
69. Petrus Hispanus, Summule logicales, ed. L. M. de Rijk (Leiden, 1972), 68; Stella, 'The Summa Feudorum', 299, at lines 420–424.
70. Stella, 'The Summa Feudorum', 278.
71. Bellomo, *The Common Legal Past*; P. Grossi, A History of European Law (Chichester, 2010), 24–38.

02 THE PHRASE "REGIAM MAIESTATEM" CONVEYS A SPECIFIC MESSAGE (AND WHAT DOES IT MEAN)?

In 1609, Sir John Skene, a Scottish lawyer and Lord Advocate, released two editions of Scotland's ancient laws. One edition included the contents in Latin, while the other edition was published in Scots. [1] Both were entitled *Regiam maiestatem and the Auld Lawes and Constitutions of Scotland.* Skene's book was the first to print *any* Scottish legal material which pre-dated the 1424 parliament of James I, king of Scots, and contained 'ancient law' from the early eleventh century to the early fifteenth. [2] In 1609, Sir John Skene, a Scottish lawyer and Lord Advocate, released two editions of Scotland's ancient laws. One edition included the contents in Latin, while the other edition was published in Scots. [3] He wrote:

While after only a short time looking into these early and ancient laws, I fell into an Augean stable which not even the labours of Hercules could ever cleanse or purge. Many books were thrown before me, some of ancient authority – now feasts for moths and worms. In these books, there is much that the passage of time has made unknown to us ... all of which is easier to admire than to interpret. In these books, there is unwise and careless writing, much of which is corrupt, contrary, abbreviated and confusingly rendered, which falsifies the meaning and renders it as nothing.

These despairing words have been quoted many times, so much so that the manuscript corpus of early Scottish law has become almost a totemic lacuna in the history of early Scots law. [4] Yet, although these books as a whole are not, perhaps, as unyielding and forbidding as Skene has had us imagining, their contents still need a great deal of illumination. Chief among their contents is Skene's headline piece, *Regiam maiestatem*, a work which survives in multiple manuscript copies in various forms from the late fourteenth to the early seventeenth century. It was probably *Regiam* which caused the most difficulty for Skene, and it would continue to do so for generations of lawyers and legal scholars down to the present day. For, although Skene's edition of *Regiam maiestatem* became the one most widely circulated and, indeed, was the 'standard' text used by lawyers and scholars well into the twentieth century, it did not illuminate what *Regiam* was, and how it had come into being, as much as one might have hoped. [5] This was, in part, because Skene had what might loosely be called a flexible attitude towards the authority of his texts, making clear emendations, deletions of entire chapters and chunks of text, and often preferring the readings of the latest manuscripts instead of the earliest ones. Almost three hundred years *after* Skene's edition had been published, George Neilson (1858–1923), the Scottish historian and antiquary, wrote in 1891 that 'thick Cimmerian darkness girds the *Regiam* round: its date, its object, its history, lie in primeval doubt. The cobwebs have closed over it once more'. [6] Nearly 130 years after Neilson's plaint, this essay offers a reconsideration, not only of how *Regiam* survives but also of its original state and, crucially, its intended purpose. In so doing, it will be argued that not only would *Regiam*'s content have mattered very much indeed, but, moreover, the example of *Regiam* adds something to how we understand late thirteenth- and early fourteenth-century political and legal thought in Western Europe.

THE SUBSEQUENT DEVELOPMENT OF REGIAM MAIESTATEM

That *Regiam* should be subject to so much doubt is, at first glance, odd. From the beginning of the second quarter of the fifteenth century onwards, *Regiam* was first understood as the kingdom's 'auld law', and was later used as an authoritative source of law. The tractate is first mentioned in 1426, under James I, with the well-known provision that six wise and discreet men should examine the two books of law of Scotland – *Regiam* and *Quoniam attachiamenta* – to discover what they had to say about exceptions. [7] Parliamentary attempts were made to reform and codify the kingdom's ancient law in 1469 and 1473; [8] *Regiam*'s chapters were cited (correctly) in parliamentary legislation of 1471 and 1475; [9] another was reformed in parliament in 1481–2. [10] Hector MacQueen has shown that *Regiam* is also cited chapter and verse in notarial instruments (sometimes correctly) and in lawyers' notes to pleading. [11] In short, the fifteenth-century status of the lawbook known as *Regiam maiestatem* is not in doubt: it was the ancient law of the kingdom of the Scots, had received parliamentary sanction and was the subject of law reform. [12]

Regiam continued to be influential well into the early modern and modern periods. Over the sixteenth century, the authority of *Regiam* was discussed in the context of wider conversations about which kind of legal authority should take precedence in the judicial decisions of the Court of Session: Roman or Scottish Common. [13] The discussion was to change emphasis in the seventeenth century: by

1604, it had been discovered that *Regiam* was not an 'original' compilation (in the modern sense) of Scots law but, instead, derived mostly from the twelfth-century English tractate on jurisdiction, law and procedure known as *Glanvill*, itself written between 1187 and 1189. [14]

The implications of the suddenly discovered link between the English *Glanvill* and the Scottish *Regiam* were explosive. Hector MacQueen has emphasised that the issue was not simply the immediate one of how far *Regiam* was derived from *Glanvill*, but the potential consequence of that question: how far medieval Scots law was 'simply a version of the English common law'. [15] This was no small question: in the context of the Union of Crowns (1603), a union of law between England and Scotland was a real possibility; if Scots law was derived from English law, could it, indeed should it, be subsumed by it? Quite understandably, many thought *Regiam* was not part of Scots law. But, although the political implications of *Regiam*'s origins had grown gradually less significant by the end of the eighteenth century – particularly after the 1707 parliamentary union between England and Scotland and the quashing of the 1745/6 Jacobite rising against the Hanoverian dynasty – nothing like consensus as to where, when, how and why *Regiam* had been composed emerged. [16] Theories ranged from *Regiam* being compiled on the orders of Edward I of England to its belonging to the last few years of Alexander II's reign in 1240s, and the sheer range of opinion makes Neilson's complaint of 'Cimmerian darkness' surrounding *Regiam* understandable, particularly as the debate was no longer raging quite so fiercely by the end of the nineteenth century. [17]

It is thus worth recapping what is, currently, known – or thought to be known – about the composition of *Regiam maiestatem*. It is known that it is the earliest surviving jurisprudential tractate to have survived from Scotland. It must have been compiled before 1424/5, because its earliest surviving manuscript was in existence by that point as it was sold on 20 January 1424 (it is unclear whether the year started on Lady Day or not). [18] The manuscript in question – known as 'the Bute manuscript' – may have been produced as early as the very late 1380s or 1390s, as, in its current form, the codex is composite, with the first two gatherings being added on to what palaeographically looks like a volume of the late fourteenth century, and, indeed, the latest date in it (1389) seems to be near-contemporary, with Robert Stewart (II) being described as 'reigning' (he died in 1390). [19] But if the later fourteenth century is the terminus ante quem of *Regiam maiestatem*, what is its terminus post quem? Internally, *Regiam* states that it was compiled on the command of King David I (1124–53). [20] Yet, despite the attribution, it cannot have been compiled during David I's reign because much of it is derived or taken verbatim from *Glanvill* (1187×9). [21] In addition, there is a substantial section at the end of its books 1 and 2, taken from the Canon law *Summa super titulis decretalium*, compiled by Goffredus Tranensis – or Goffredo di Trani – between 1241 and 1244. [22]

Any twelfth-century origin for *Regiam* should therefore be discounted, and indeed, although there were attempts in the mid-twentieth century to date the tractate to the mid-thirteenth century, research undertaken since the 1960s has located the treatise in the early fourteenth century, during the reign of Robert I (1306–29). [23] In particular, A. A. M. Duncan reexamined a passage in book 1 of *Regiam* which was also found, near-verbatim, in a chapter of a well-circulated piece of legislation enacted by Robert I in his parliament held at Scone on 3–5 December 1318. [24] Duncan concluded that, *pace* Lord Cooper, this passage could not be an interpolation but was instead so fundamentally integrated into and expanded in *Regiam* that *Regiam* had to have been compiled after the issue of the legislation in December 1318, not before. [25] Yet the post-1318 date is, in fact, debatable, as new material has recently been discovered and edited which has questioned whether the passage in *Regiam* was directly derived from the 1318 legislation and whether *Regiam* was, in fact, developing provisions first laid down in that legislation. [26] Instead of *Regiam* directly developing the 1318 legislation, it is more probable that *Regiam* and the 1318 legislation share a common source or, even, that the 1318 legislation was derived from the work which came to be known as *Regiam maiestatem*, rather than the other way around. [27]

It will be outlined below that *Regiam*'s content and emphasis echo other changes to royal charter diplomatic occurring in the 1310s, thus creating a wider context for its compilation in the 1310s. As a result, the cumulative effect of the new evidence destabilising the post-1318 date is, happily, to locate the text more precisely in the reign of Robert I (1306–29). Indeed, in 1984, Alan Harding drew attention to how well *Regiam* broadly fitted Robert's reign, seeing in it (although without any probative evidence) a desire to concoct ancient law which was probably located in Robert I's own political insecurity. [28] Despite his later mythologised role as national hero 'The Bruce', Robert's reign was extremely tumultuous, controversial and thus necessarily full of new ideas about Scottish kingship and government. [29] It began in a period when Scotland had been conquered by the English king, Edward I, in 1304–5. Robert was inaugurated king of Scotland in late March 1306, not as an obvious successor to the previous king John Balliol, but in an attempt to resurrect the very idea of an autonomous kingship of the Scots. This move was an even more audacious one since it was done less than two months after he had murdered his main political rival, John Comyn, in a church in Dumfries in February 1306. The early years of his reign were marked by warfare, exile and severe internal political divisions, and, although a famous military victory at Bannockburn in 1314 granted him some time and space to stabilise his rule, his government was extremely uncompromising and could be experienced as ambitious, radical and divisive. Chief among Robert's innovative ideas was the formation of a joint-Bruce-kingship in Scotland and Ireland through his brother Edward Bruce's invasion of

Ireland and Edward's proclamation as king of Ireland in 1314. In 1314, Robert's government effectively made cross-border landholding illegal, enacting in a parliament held that year that anyone who refused to swear fealty to him for their lands against all others would be disinherited and treated as his enemy. The unrest around him continued to bubble until his kingship was finally recognised in 1328 (the year before he died). Until that point, he was repeatedly excommunicated; his kingship was not recognised by either the English kings or popes Clement V or John XXII; and, indeed, he had a rival for the Scottish kingship in the figure of Edward Balliol, son of the earlier king of Scots John (1292–1314, deposed 1296 but still recognised), with whom members of the Scottish nobility aimed to replace Robert in an assassination attempt now known as the Soules Conspiracy of 1320. Contextualising these undoubtedly tumultuous political circumstances, the power of Harding's piece lay in its emphasis on law's capacity to offer a salve to ease and cover much more profound political divisions. By attributing *Regiam* to David I, Robert's own kingship was confirming the work of *the* great law-giving and, crucially, undisputed king of Scots. [30] Harding thus stressed that it was *Regiam*'s symbolic value which mattered far more than its procedural and legal content.

This was an important position because it at least directly confronted one of the, perhaps-surprising, problems which has long bedevilled *Regiam*: its content does not make very much sense, despite its later medieval parliamentary sanction. [31] As stated above, much of it is derived from *Glanvill*. In fact, from about a third of the way through, the text is essentially *Glanvill* verbatim, minus its writ formulae, until the last book, when *Regiam* becomes a miscellany of Scottish legal chapters, mostly witnessed in other sources. [32] *Regiam*'s reliance on *Glanvill* has caused historians many headaches because *Regiam* imports long sections on rules, jurisdictions and procedures, some of which were never part of Scots law or its judicial system. For example, *Regiam* contains *Glanvill*'s passage on the assize *utrum*, which determined whether land was alms or lay fee, despite *utrum* never having been adopted as Scots legal procedure. [33] *Regiam* preserves a reference to the King's Bench – never a Scottish institution. [34] *Regiam* also contains long sections taken entirely verbatim from *Glanvill* on the writs of novel disseisin, mort d'ancestor and right, and it is unclear how far these were intended to mirror the procedure of their Scottish equivalents (dissasine, mortancestor, and right). [35] Susan Marshall has shown how misleading *Regiam*'s testimony banning inheritance by children born before their parents' marriage was as a statement of Scots law. *Regiam* had adopted *Glanvill*'s view (which said pre-nuptial children could not inherit) despite Canon law later stipulating the opposite. *Regiam*'s testimony has been the basis for subsequent historical work which has argued that pre-nuptial children could not inherit in fourteenth-century Scotland, even though, as Marshall points out, there is no evidence save *Regiam* that they could not and, indeed, more evidence to show that the Canon law doctrine of legitimation *per subsequens matrimonium* did apply. [36] The authority of *Regiam* as an authority on fourteenth-century Scots law is therefore ambiguous because of the seemingly automatic dependence on *Glanvill* in its middle section. Indeed, the change in quality of work by the compiler of *Regiam* has led historians to argue that its compiler either lost interest in the task about a third of the way through (after the first thirteen chapters in book 2), and thereafter completed his job at a shoddy standard, *or* that a skilled compiler was 'interrupted' at his task and replaced by someone else who did not have the skill or knowledge to continue the work at the level of his predecessor. [37]

There are thus many reasons why historians have been wary about tackling the content of *Regiam*. Combined with a complicated and changing manuscript tradition, and three editions which do not in any way represent this tradition effectively, *Regiam*'s position within Scottish legal and medieval history remains ambivalent and its content viewed as a minefield abandoned after generations of Anglo-Scottish political and legal conflict. [38] This essay reconsiders the original form, intended content and purpose of *Regiam* based not on any published edition of the work, but on the evidence offered by its two earliest surviving manuscripts which, unless other manuscripts are rediscovered, contain the only two witnesses to its earliest surviving form.

THE EVOLUTION OF REGIAM MAIESTATEM IN THE CONTEXT OF SURVIVAL

Regiam survives in over thirty manuscripts as either a Latin or a Scots text. [39] The earliest manuscript dates from the later fourteenth century (*c.* 1389); manuscripts were still being produced in the last third of the sixteenth. [40] The Scots translations represent, on the whole, a later tradition that is first derived from and then responds to changes in the Latin text. [41] The earliest Scots manuscripts containing *Regiam* date from the third quarter of the fifteenth century at the earliest. [42] Not all Scots manuscripts are the same, suggesting that there was not a single 'official' translation made, but rather continually evolving ones which were responding to changes made to the Latin text over the fifteenth century. [43]

Two points have to be made about the manuscript corpus as a whole. First, all the known surviving books containing texts of *Regiam* are consciously archaicising in their form and content. That is, they all contain texts of *veteres leges* – of old law. Even the earliest manuscript to survive, the so-called Bute manuscript, is a book containing works of law mostly attributed to a king, David I, who ruled almost three hundred years before the production of that particular codex. [44] But the Bute manuscript also contains works attributed to kings Mael Coluim mac Cinaeda (1005–34), William the Lion (1165–1214) and Alexander II (1214–49). [45] By the end of the fifteenth century, the self-consciously archaic nature of these books was proclaimed in a contents' list which appears to have been understood as the 'official' order in which the works should appear. [46] Thus, throughout its later medieval life, *Regiam* was not only understood by external sources as ancient law, but also survives wholly within a manuscript tradition which explicitly identifies it as such. There is thus no firm evidence to suggest that, even when *Regiam* was originally circulated, it did so as anything other than as part of a broadly based tradition of 'auld law'. [47]

Second, despite the consistently archaic presentation of these books, the texts within them do change. As the fifteenth century progressed, the books become more ordered, and more likely to contain the same corpus of texts. More works were added, and all works within them, including *Regiam*, become longer; but not all these 'additions' were of new work, as certain texts which first appear as autonomous legal 'works' become incorporated into other, large tractates, *within the same book*, with the result that some texts appear two or three times, leading to several desperate declarations from scribes. [48] The increasing tendency to standardise the order of these 'books of law' seems to have been a response to central directives of the parliaments of James II and III which were concerned at certain points with the precise content of ancient law and aimed to create an authoritative 'book of law'. [49]

Consequently, it is not possible to examine these later fifteenth-century manuscript-texts of *Regiam* and treat them as though they represent *Regiam* as it was first compiled and, possibly, circulated. *Regiam* as it appears in these later manuscripts is connected with its contemporary context, first within a burgeoning interest in old law in the first half of the fifteenth century – particularly within the institutional Church, religious houses and the burghs, and also among *magistri* – then in centralised efforts to control the circulation of that ancient law and what authority certain texts had. [50] This is a particularly important point to grasp for *Regiam*, given that even the best of the four editions currently available (that by Thomas Thomson, published in 1844) is based predominantly on a mid-fifteenth-century manuscript of *Regiam* whose text of *Regiam* contains material resulting from an extension and revision which had already occurred. [51] Thus, in order to understand what *Regiam* originally intended to say, we have to look at its text only as preserved in its earliest surviving version, which is in only two manuscript witnesses, one from the last quarter of the fourteenth century, the other from the early fifteenth. One is the Bute manuscript (NLS, MS 21246); the other is known by its modern repository and shelfmark, BL Additional MS 18111. [52]

AN ANALYSIS OF THE MOST ANCIENT REMAINING VERSION AND THE COMPILER'S CONTRIBUTIONS

Full manuscript descriptions of both these manuscripts can be found elsewhere. [53] It suffices to say here that the Bute manuscript's text of *Regiam* is dated palaeographically to the last quarter of the fourteenth century, and the manuscript itself probably does not long post-date 1389; the Additional manuscript's text dates to the first quarter of the fifteenth century, and that manuscript may well have been produced at or commissioned by Dunfermline Abbey. [54] Despite the Additional manuscript being the later, it has been postulated by A. A. M. Duncan that it preserves a slightly earlier text, and, indeed, further work has only strengthened this conclusion. [55] The work by John Reuben Davies on the two manuscripts preserving the earliest-known version of *Regiam maiestatem* is demonstrating that both manuscripts preserve predominantly the same text, divided into four books. This quadripartite structure was, most probably, the work of the original compiler. [56] On occasion, there are notes or citations in the main text in *Regiam* which are expanded in notes and commentary in the margin in the Bute manuscript, but not the Additional manuscript. [57] Equally, there are some occasions when Bute highlights in the margin a *Questio/Solucio* structure to the text where it is not explicitly made in the main text, and it also makes marginal cross-references where none appear in the Additional manuscript. [58] Bute also contains two extra chapters on the end which are not present in the Additional manuscript's text, and, of the two, only the Additional manuscript includes a clear *explicit*, stating that the work (called here the *Constitutiones regie regni Scocie*) has ended, saving the *Constitutiones burgorum*, suggesting that *Regiam* was conceived as *part* of the kingdom's constitutions, rather than constituting their entirety. [59] The Additional manuscript also has a more fluid structure, with some chapters containing multiple rubricated sub-sections, many of which have hardened into separate chapters in the Bute manuscript. As a result, Duncan's position is borne out by further work on the texts: although preserving in general the same version of the text, the Additional manuscript should be preferred over the Bute manuscript as representing the earliest-known text of *Regiam*, even if, on occasion, the Bute manuscript preserves better readings.

What, then, is the status of the text contained in both manuscripts? Do they confirm the consensus of current scholarship, that *Regiam* is divided into a polished first third and an unfinished and unpolished second two-thirds? What follows summarises extensive research into what can be discerned about the original compiler's editorial techniques, to be set out fully in the introduction to the forthcoming edition of *Regiam*. Two points here are most relevant. First, these two manuscripts show that *Regiam* was originally conceived as a single work: it calls itself a 'book' and contains internal cross-references. [60] Second, it has been possible to identify five editorial techniques that appear throughout the book, to greater and lesser degrees. [61] All concern the compiler's treatment of his sources, whether *Glanvill*, Goffredo's *Summa* or the Scottish legal material. The techniques range from simple interventions in the compiler's source material (removing almost all the writ formulae from *Glanvill*, for example), to slightly altering technical words or phrases to make them better fit the Scottish situation, to wholesale rewrites of passages within *Glanvill.* [62] These editorial interventions, particularly the smallest ones, appear consistently throughout *Regiam*: this suggests that *Regiam* does not contain, as is currently thought, a 'finished' section and an 'unfinished' section, nor does it constitute the work of two compilers, one diligent, the other lackadaisical; instead, it is unfinished all the way through, albeit to greater and lesser degrees. *Regiam* is most finished in the prologue and in book 1, as has long been acknowledged, but there are also relatively finished passages in book 2 and also, most interestingly, at the start of book 4, normally castigated as just a mishmash of Scottish legal chapters. In addition, there are passages in book 1 whose text has been subjected to minimal editorial intervention, and, conversely, even the long-ignored book 3 displays a degree of editorial intervention which is wholly consistent with the basic techniques identified in more heavily edited sections. [63] Thus the earliest manuscripts of *Regiam* reveal it to be originally unfinished all the way through: there was no replacement of one compiler by another. The interesting question is how and why this clearly unfinished work was then recopied and circulated *as though* it was a finished authority. This point will be returned to briefly at the end of this article.

But what is the significance of this conclusion? Two points about both his editorial work and his knowledge of the law are key to appreciating what the original compiler of *Regiam* was trying to do with his work. First, what he would have done with the figure of David I, the king to whom *Regiam* is attributed, had he finished his work, and second, why and how he relied so heavily on *Glanvill.* It is well known that he attributed the tractate to an unknown compiler working on the command of King David, who, as shown above, had a long-standing reputation as a law-maker and law-giver. Indeed, when Edward I set out the plans for governing his newly conquered kingdom in 1305, he equated the entire law of Scotland with the figure of King David, relegating all David's successors to having simply provided additions and emendations. [64] Yet the position of David throughout *Regiam* is rather ambiguous because, perhaps surprisingly for a work which attributes its existence to his command, David rarely appears. This would not be so problematic had David *only* appeared in *Regiam* in the prologue: the laws of Hywel Dda, for example, do not refer explicitly to Hywel himself as a legislator; some manuscripts of *Glanvill* attribute the work to Henry II without Henry appearing in a similar role. [65] Yet, other than in the prologue, David appears in *Regiam* as a named legal actor twice, and there are further references to an unnamed 'lord king' enacting (*statuit*) various provisions. [66] This choice, therefore, marks a departure in *Regiam* from its main source, *Glanvill.*

In the context of a work containing over 32,000 words, these few references to David do not stand out; yet it is possible that David's role as law-giver might have been more prominent had the compiler finished his work. As John Reuben Davies has pointed out, the two earliest surviving manuscripts of *Regiam* not only contain references to Roman and Canon law, but also to their major commentaries and glosses. [67] These cross-references are quite accurate, although not always perfectly preserved in the two manuscripts. Whoever made them was demonstrably learned in the most up-to-date thought on Canon and Civil law in the early fourteenth century: most of the references are to the *Digest*, the *Institutes* and the Canon law collections the *Liber extra* (1234), the *Liber sextus* (compiled on the command of Boniface VIII in 1298) and the ordinary gloss of the *Liber extra* by Bernardus Parmensis (d.1266). [68] No later manuscript contains these references in this form: they are edited out or expanded in the margins, or readmitted to the main text and discussed further. [69] What is particularly interesting is that *all* these references to Roman and Canon law in any manuscript of *Regiam*, early or late, have been removed from all print editions. This was, perhaps, not a particularly surprising action for post-Reformation editors to have taken. Yet, as a result, these editions of *Regiam* have confined the Roman and Canon law material in *Regiam* to the unattributed material from Goffredus's *Summa*. [70] Examining this extra material across the manuscript tradition of *Regiam* is not the subject of this article; what is pertinent here is that not only were these citations probably part of the original work of the compiler himself but that, as will be shown below, they might also have been more elegantly incorporated into *Regiam*'s text, had the compiler finished his work.

There are two places in the main text of *Regiam* where David I's name is explicitly invoked. The first is in book 1, where a lengthy text on warranty, originating, probably, after 1184 in the reign of William the Lion, has been edited slightly and ascribed wholly to the actions of David I. [71] The second is slightly more complex and more revealing of how the compiler might have treated the direct citations of Roman and Canon law texts had he finished. It also occurs in book 1, in a relatively heavily edited section on essoins (lawful excuses for non-appearance in court), based on *Glanvill*. [72] The passage starts with *Glanvill*, taking the problem outlined there of when plaintiffs or pursuers come into a vill, initiate their plea, but suddenly essoin themselves owing to illness. [73] The passage in *Regiam* is, however, concerned with a different problem to the one in *Glanvill*: *Regiam* was not, as *Glanvill* was, outlining what should happen if this occurred (essentially a procedural matter), it was questioning the legality of this happening in the first place. [74] It asks: 'should such an essoin ever by law be received?' *Regiam* then states that the problem was solved by a statute enacted by King David, which answered, yes, they were to be received, if such essoins were lawful in the first place. [75] The reason David gave was as follows: 'since law is made for the common profit (*communis utilitas*) of both parties – both the pursuer and the tenant – it would indeed be a wickedness if the remedy of benefit was taken away, because the actor and the *reus* ought not to be judged unequally or for the detriment of one over the other'. [76] This last sentence, beginning *quia actor*, is first found as part of what became the ordinary gloss to the *Liber sextus*, a collection of papal decretals compiled by Pope Boniface VIII in 1298; the ordinary gloss was compiled by Giovanni d'Andrea in 1306. [77] Thus, if the ordinary gloss to the *Liber sextus* was being used here, it was not only incorporated into the compiler's prose, its authority was also transposed from its canonical context and placed into the mouth of King David. What this might conceivably suggest is that the original compiler had intended to write these citations of Roman and Canon law into the prose of his text and, on occasion, even transform their authority into statutory pronouncements – one might even say, legislation – of King David I. [78] Had the compiler of *Regiam* finished his work, the figure of David I might have appeared much more frequently as a *Gesetzgeber* than he currently does in any known version of *Regiam*. [79]

GLANVILL'S SELECTION AS TEXTUAL AUTHORITY

In this context, why was *Glanvill* chosen as the textual authority through which these aims could be communicated? Although there are long passages taken from Goffredo di Trani's *Summa*, the structure of *Regiam* follows *Glanvill*: its prologue is based on *Glanvill*; it starts, like *Glanvill*, with a description of jurisdictions and pleas; and then, like *Glanvill*, it takes the reader through the process of making a plea – from summons and essoins, to the pleading of the case itself, to visnet and judgment, and so on. In this way, the underpinning structure, the literary model and, thus, the authority of *Regiam* is taken from *Glanvill*, not from any other legal work. This is important, as the compiler's choice of *Glanvill* seems even more deliberate given his expertise in *four* kinds of law: Canon, Civil, English Common and Scottish Common. Why *Glanvill* was used is often the question which is first asked about *Regiam* before its content is ever analysed. The underlying issue, of course, is: surely Scottish law was not so similar to late twelfth-century English procedures on writ that *Glanvill* was the most appropriate choice of text?

The very formulation of this question reveals the basic assumption behind any treatment of *Regiam*: it is approached as a ‘legal transplant’, a borrowing from one legal system and implanting it into another, thus stimulating legal development in the recipient system. [80] While *Regiam* eventually had this effect, it is suggested here that the compiler of *Regiam* wanted to takeover and transform the *authority* of *Glanvill*, not its legal content per se. Although in the least finished sections, *Glanvill*'s prose is reproduced almost verbatim in *Regiam* (leading, as was noted above, to the inclusion of procedures and judicial fora which were never part of the Scottish legal system), the same is *not* true in what look like the most finished sections, mainly in books 1, the start of book 2 and book 4. Here, we can see that *Glanvill*'s prose often provided the skeletal structure of each chapter – its first sentence, or first few sentences, its last sentence, its area of concern – but, to follow through with the image, not the muscle, ligaments, tendons or organs. [81] As a result, it is helpful to see *Regiam* not as transplant but as translation, thus serving the same appropriative functions which Rita Copeland has identified for medieval interlingual translations of literary works from Latin into the vernacular.

On this subject, Copeland has written of medieval translation that 'translation reinvents its source and appropriates it'. [82] She expands:

The aim of translation is to reinvent the source, so that ... attention is focused on the active production of a new text ... translation seeks to erase the cultural gap from which it emerges by contesting and displacing the source and substituting itself: it forges no synthetic links with its source. [83]

To translate is therefore to appropriate and, potentially, to displace and to challenge. To forge 'no synthetic link' with its source raises the possibility that *Regiam*'s reliance on *Glanvill* might not be an obviously imitative act; it might instead have served a more disruptive function. How, then, might *Regiam* be functioning as a translation of *Glanvill*? As a Latin text, *Regiam* is not an interlingual translation. Rather, it should viewed as an intercontextual translation, that is, the 'making legible' of one text in another social, political or legal context. [84] Instead of 'matching form and substance [of the original] in a different language', as Copeland has written about interlingual translation, an inter-contextual translation matches the 'form and substance' of the source in a different *context*, here, a legal context. [85] This explains the compiler's ultimate approach to *Glanvill*: to replace much of its precise procedure but retain the verbatim shell of the work as a whole. A 'new text', to use Copeland's phrase, would have been produced, but one which retained the outward form of its source. [86] This method of working suggests that the aim of *Regiam* was not to transplant rule and procedure; it was to translate – and thus appropriate – *Glanvill*'s authority in a different context. It reinvented *Glanvill* while still constituting it.

But what authority did *Glanvill* have to offer? This question has baffled historians, who have thought that, by the early fourteenth century, *Glanvill* is the last work one would use: there were many other more up-to-date legal tractates written within the English judicial system, not only *Bracton*, but also *Hengham Magna*, which survives in multiple manuscript copies by the early fourteenth century. [87] However, this ignores the manuscript evidence of *Glanvill* and, of course, its very antiquity. *Glanvill was* old and it was outdated, but it was still known. Of the forty-one surviving manuscripts of *Glanvill* which survive from (perhaps) the late twelfth century to the first quarter of the fourteenth, over half (twenty-one) were put together in the last quarter of the thirteenth and beginning of the fourteenth. *Glanvill* was still popular. [88] Most of these manuscripts were in England, but we can surmise that *Glanvill* was circulating in Scotland too from as early as 1230, if not before, and influenced other legal compilations dating from the late thirteenth and early fourteenth centuries. [89] By 'translating' *Glanvill*, the compiler of *Regiam* was appropriating its status as a crucially old but still-foundational text of the English Common law to reinvent its authority to serve the law and legal procedure of the Scottish kingdom.

This reinvention was simple but would have been extremely effective, particularly had the compiler finished his work. It could also have unsettled *Glanvill*'s reputation. By invoking David I, the compiler of *Regiam* was not only invoking the authority of the king whose law was, by a conquering government, held to be equivalent in 1305 to the law of the entire kingdom, but a king of more ancient authority than the king whose name was associated with *Glanvill*, Henry II. [90] *Regiam*, if taken at face value, was the earlier work; *Glanvill* derived from it, not the other way around. It may have been in the compiler's mind for someone to look at *Glanvill* and look at *Regiam* and ask which text was the legal authority? Which one was the foundational text of both legal systems? The fact that these were the very questions asked when the link between *Glanvill* and *Regiam* was rediscovered in the early seventeenth century might have amused the original compiler as much as irritated him that it took so long for anyone to ask the question that the compilation of *Regiam* may well have been originally designed to prompt. The choice of *Glanvill* as the structuring source for *Regiam* was probably far more strictly political than legal. In the context of early fourteenth-century Anglo-Scottish relations, the audacious aim of using *Glanvill* – as opposed to any other legal text – was to displace that text's authority and relocate it in a Scottish context as a Davidian invention, a statement of the Scottish king's legislative power and his position as the inventor of law. This proposition receives further evidential support from an analysis of the surviving content of *Regiam*, as witnessed by its two earliest manuscripts.

IN REGIAM MAIESTATEM, MAIESTAS

Can any theoretical ideas about authority be identified in *Regiam*? Concerns about its content as well as the absence of an authoritative edition have prevented this question from being asked of *Regiam*, and, in consequence, it is best to start from the beginning, which, in the case of *Regiam*, is its opening prologue. As is well known, both *Regiam* and *Glanvill* use the opening lines of Justinian's *Institutes* for the opening of their prologue. In the *Institutes*, this is: 'imperial majesty must not only be decorated with arms but also be armed with laws'. [91] In *Glanvill*, however, the text opens with the words *regia potestas* – royal power – and continues with the more verbose injunction that 'royal power must not only be decorated with arms against the rebels and peoples who rise up against it and the kingdom but it is also fitting that it is decorated with laws to rule its subjects and peoples peacefully'. [92] The compiler of *Regiam*, however, changed *Glanvill*'s *regia potestas* half-back to the reading of the *Institutes*. Its opening words are, of course, *regiam maiestatem*, royal majesty. The injunction then follows *Glanvill*, sometimes returning tellingly to the prose of the *Institutes*: royal majesty must not only be 'decorated with arms against the rebels who rise up against it and the kingdom but it is also fitting to be armed with laws for subject and peaceful peoples'. [93]

Despite *Regiam*'s unfinished state, it is clear that the compiler intended for the *maiestas* of the Scottish king to be advanced throughout the work. It was not only in the prologue that the compiler substituted *Glanvill*'s words to emphasise royal *maiestas*. For example, in *Glanvill*, no one accused of homicide could be released on bail save 'ex regie dispensationis beneficio'; this stipulation is repeated in *Regiam* but the exception is 'nisi ex regie maiestatis beneficio' – 'save with the benefit of royal majesty'. [94] The king in *Regiam* was thus a king who exercised *maiestas*.

Maiestas is an odd word. Although transposed into English as 'majesty', its direct translation is 'greaterness'. Its legal origins lie in Roman law, in the first-century BC *Lex Julia* on *maiestas*, where it was defined as any action which acted against the Roman people or their security. [95] Recorded in the *Digest*, Ulpian's opinion was that the crime of offended or harmed *maiestas* was the crime closest to sacrilege, *sacrilegium*, because it so endangered authority and public order. By the early fourteenth century, *maiestas* was a key concept in political and juristic thought, and it was invoked to represent the authority of a ruler who had no temporal superior. It is sometimes asserted (if not interrogated) that, for most of the twelfth century, if anyone thought much about the issue at all, the emperor was the only secular ruler who exercised *maiestas* (then in Staufer hands). [96] This is, however, questionable, particularly if one looks *outside* juristic sources and towards visual, diplomatic and literary ones. Yet, as the thirteenth century progressed, the possession of *maiestas* became increasingly discussed, contested and politicised. Whom it could be applied to and with what justification needed to be made more explicit. [97] Did all kings have *maiestas* or was it only the Roman emperor? What constituted an offense against that *maiestas*, once demonstrated? [98] Could treason only be committed against a ruler who held *maiestas*? [99]

Most of these discussions focused on the relationship between the kings of Sicily, the pope and the emperor because of their peculiar political relationships, or between the emperor and the king of France. In the 1280s, the preface and gloss to Frederick II's *Liber Augustalis* by Marinus de Caramanico focused on the very right of kings – and particularly the kings of Sicily, the role in which Frederick had legislated – to make law. [100] Since Francesco Calasso published an edition of the preface, Marinus's arguments have been given much attention, so it is unnecessary to repeat them here. [101] His basic point, however, was that there was no difference between the authority of a king and the authority of an emperor: even a king who was a vassal of the pope had the authority to make law as superior lord over the *singula* of his kingdom. For Marinus, kings, as much as emperors, deserved the name prince, exercised *maiestas* and thus could punish the crime of *lesa maiestas* for offences against their own *maiestas.* [102]

Maiestas was used alongside a few other highly contestable and politically volatile legal terms, in particular *princeps* and *superior.* [103] Some jurists (particularly in France) argued that a ruler who exercised *maiestas* was a prince who ruled without any superior (although, as Kenneth Pennington has shown, even this was debated, even within France). [104] Others disagreed, like Marinus, and thought that some kings could be princes and exercise *maiestas* even though they had superior and direct lords according to feudal law. In a lovely parallel to the opening words of *Regiam*, Marinus even argued against those who made the rather facile point that it could only be the emperor who exercised *maiestas* because the opening words of the *Institutes* were 'imperial majesty' and not 'royal majesty'. [105]

These words – *maiestas*, *superior*, *princeps* – were thus part of a live juristic discussion that was erupting in the later thirteenth and early fourteenth centuries, even though this discussion is often written about as though it was only occurring in Italy, France and the Empire. [106] Yet the compiler of *Regiam* situated his work within this much broader conversation. This is obvious from its first few chapters. We already know that the king in *Regiam* exercised 'royal *maiestas*'. In the prologue we learn that the 'king' in *Regiam* governs, his 'rule committed to him by God', and 'has no *superior* save the Creator of heaven and earth himself, who governs all things, and the most holy mother, the Roman Church'. [107] In the prologue again, the compiler of *Regiam* emphasised the sceptre of the king as the rod of equity which crushed the ungovernable and overmighty and provided justice for the meek and humble – the sceptre being one of the six items of regalia which Marinus had argued signified the *maiestas* of a sacred ruler. [108] Moreover, the compiler made even more effort to present its king *as a princeps*, a prince. In a section based on Goffredus's *Summa*, the compiler substituted Goffredus's *praetor* for *princeps uel balliuus suus.* [109] The overall view of the compiler of *Regiam* on the status of the Scottish kingship is clear: the king was a prince, exercised *maiestas* and had no superior save God and the Church.

But would the participation of *Regiam* in this juristic discussion have been legible or understandable at all within an Anglo-Scottish political context? The letters exchanged between Alexander III and Edward I offer a rich avenue of enquiry for how the authority of the king of Scots was perceived by the English chancery and vice-versa, and how far the two perceptions matched up to one another. [110] The potential of letters to be a mine for political thinking is often dismissed by both political historians and legal historians: by the former because letters often explicitly say that the *real* message they were conveying would be delivered orally, and by the latter because the ideas expressed within them are often referred to in passing rather than developed. Only when dossiers of letters were explicitly composed as part of legal struggles are letters given real attention. [111] Yet letter writing was an 'art': manuals of dictamen survive which tried to educate individuals in the *ars dictaminis* to avoid causing offence to the other party and increasing the chances of a good outcome on behalf of the sender. [112] The most important part of a letter to get right was the order of a letter's address, its *salutatio*, because that was the place where relative status was asserted. If an individual was writing to a person of higher status, the recipient's name and title was put first; if the sender was of higher status, then his or her *intitulatio* was placed first. [113] If there was any doubt, then it was safer to put the recipient first: better to be humble than to immediately offend someone you were hoping to persuade by making an ill-advised claim of higher status.

The letters exchanged between Alexander III and Edward I leave no doubt as to relative status. Edward's always put Alexander second, addressing him from first position in the letter, and calling him his *dilectus frater* and his *fidelis*, the language of family *and* service (*dilectus et fidelis* was the standard address to royal officials). By contrast, Alexander III's *capella regis* did not assert the king's status in his replies: they always addressed Edward as Alexander's *frater* (the two were related by marriage) but, crucially, as his *serenissmus princeps*, his most serene prince, or *magnificus princeps*, magnificent prince. [114] *Princeps* was not a title used in any of Edward's surviving letters to Alexander. This does not mean they were devoid of affection: Edward addressed Alexander as his *karissimus frater*, his dearest brother, in his letter of condolence sent on hearing of the death of Alexander III's eldest son, Alexander, in 1284 (all three of Alexander's children – as well as his own mother – had died within three years of each other). [115] Yet Edward's letters were still soaked through with a language expressing juristic hierarchy. Indeed, it was not uncommon for Alexander's letters in their *conclusio* to refer to Edward's *maiestas*, and reassure him (often because the two kings were in conflict) that he and his men would do nothing that would harm Edward's *maiestas* or, once, his *regia maiestas*. [116] *Serenissimus princeps* was also the formal title adopted by Edward during the Great Cause of 1291–2. [117] While contemporary political and legal thought thus provided the immediate contemporary context for the implications of a theory of Scottish royal *maiestas* to be understood, the correspondence between Edward I and Alexander III provided more local contextual power: these were concepts and ranks which the king of Scots had long been excluded from in his immediate dealings with the English king, and which *Regiam* was explicitly claiming. [118]

Regiam was intended to be a treatise setting out the Scottish king's *maiestas*, thus situating itself within the major political discussions of the day and resonating deeply with, but challenging, a longer-held hierarchy between the English and

Scottish rulers. The aim was obviously to present the Scottish kingship as one without any superior, thus creating a legal argument for jurisdictional autonomy. It is probable that one of the intended audiences was the pope, then John XXII: Robert was a king without papal recognition and *Regiam* did, after all, stress in the prologue that the king had no superior 'save God and the sacrosanct mother, the Roman Church', an emphasis which Sir John Skene, writing in the generations after the Scottish Reformation, removed from his edition. In the summer of 1320, John XXII would be the recipient of the Declaration of Arbroath, an appeal by the Scottish *communitas regni* which used (partly) history to try to persuade the pope of the legitimacy and antiquity of the Scottish kingship and, more particularly, the right of Robert Bruce to hold it. Expecting the pope to issue a written confirmation of kingship was not unusual: in September 1319, John XXII was to use apostolic authority to 'promote' (literally) Duke Władysław as king of Poland, granting him a royal diadem. [119] But that *Regiam* was written with one eye on the papal curia did not mean it was originally intended only for an exterior purpose. Even in its unfinished form, *Regiam*'s aim of emphasising Scottish royal *maiestas* not only affected its presentation of the Scottish legal system but also highlights that there was an additional political discourse circulating in Scotland to the 'community of the realm' traditionally focused upon by historians. [120]

PARALLEL LEGAL DISCOURSES: MAIESTAS AND COMMUNITAS

How did *Regiam*'s aims affect its content? First, *Regiam* contains the first formal reference to treason – lese-majesty – in Scotland. While the *crimen lese maiestatis* was referred to in the 1266 Treaty of Perth between Alexander III and Magnus VI of Norway, we have no explicit reference to *treason* legislation or law within Scotland before its appearance in *Regiam*, where it is listed at the beginning as the first plea belonging only to the Crown: the 'crime of lese-majesty' or 'of harmed or offended *maiestas*', that is, for the death of or *sedicio* against the king, kingdom or army. [121] Indeed, the opening sentence of *Regiam* highlights an underlying concern for internal order upheld by legitimate royal authority: whereas *Glanvill* follows the *Institutes* by saying that royal power must be decorated with arms against the 'rebels and peoples' (*rebelles et gentes*) who rise up against it, *Regiam* says that 'royal majesty must be decorated with arms to act against *rebels*', consciously avoiding the diluting effect of the *gentes*. [122]

The stress on royal *maiestas* was not confined to *Regiam*. In the 1310s, the clerks of Robert I's 'chapel', or chancery, were developing the position that the Scottish king exercised *maiestas*, offending which constituted a crime risking life, limb or disinheritance, and made reference to the king's *maiestas* in his charters for the first time. Formulae mentioning the crime of offending the king's *maiestas* started to appear in royal charters from 1310 onwards. [123] Some royal charters even set out a conception of princely authority mirroring that which is found in *Regiam*. An intriguing letter – which now only survives as an inspection of James I made in 1424, but which was originally drawn up in 1315 and confirms the possessions of Kinloss Abbey – unusually calls all Scottish kings *princes*: in this document, Robert was following in the footsteps of those 'most serene princes' (*serenissimi principes*), his predecessors, the kings of Scotland. [124] The charter then ends with the injunction that Kinloss Abbey should hold all their lands peacefully, on pain of the king's full forfeiture and 'offence of our royal majesty'. This is particularly interesting as it suggests an extremely wide and flexible definition of treason which included harming the property of a monastery under the king-prince's protection. 'Lese-majesty' is also included in another legal compilation compiled in Robert's reign, known as the Assizes of David I (not to be confused with *Regiam*). [125]

Indeed, that Robert and his government were actually following through on their own idea of *maiestas* is shown not only in the parliament held at Scone in early December 1318 but also by the way they treated the so-called Soules Conspiracy in 1320, a plot to assassinate Robert himself. [126] The parliament held at Scone not only issued a series of rather influential legislation, but also recognised Robert's nephew Robert Stewart as his heir (his brother and heir, Edward, had been killed earlier in the year, after having been proclaimed king of Ireland). In addition, Thomas Randolph was named guardian of the kingdom if Robert Stewart succeeded as a minor (in the event he succeeded over half a century later). Crucially, anyone who went against these provisions would be treated as 'a traitor to the kingdom and guilty of the crime of *lesa maiestas* in perpetuity' – a reference to *maiestas* otherwise absent in the 1318 legislation itself. [127]

The so-called 'Soules Conspiracy' of 1320 showed that Robert and his government would be true to their legislative word. Although later chroniclers have the rather odd story that the coup was to raise to the kingship the relatively minor political actor, William de Soules, it has been convincingly argued that this conspiracy aimed at replacing Robert with Edward Balliol. [128] Edward was the son of the king of Scots, John Balliol (1292–6), who had substantial English backing and who indeed would be consecrated as a rival king of Scots to Robert's young son, David, following Robert's death and as externally sponsored civil war broke out again. [129] The charge against these conspirators was *lesa maiestas*, according to *Gesta annalia* II and Walter Bower. [130] Horrific executions are an accepted part of the political narrative of this period: a decade and a half earlier the body parts of William Wallace had been displayed in four towns (three Scottish, one English) following his conviction for treason and sacrilege, while Robert I's younger brother, Niall, had been hanged, drawn and quartered at Berwick in 1306, to name but two high-profile mutilations. [131] Yet it is still worth pointing out that not only was the fate of the conspirators in the Soules Conspiracy unprecedented in a Scottish judicial forum (one unfortunate even sentenced to being hanged, drawn and quartered despite already being dead, and two others to be pulled apart by horses), so too was the very idea of a formal treason trial. [132] The formal legal category of treason, of lese-majesty, against the Scottish king should perhaps be seen as a picking up of the pace of Robert's reign, with *Regiam* being an early manifestation of its more prominent conceptualisation.

A further way in which *Regiam*'s aim of stressing royal *maiestas* is developed is in its presentation of jurisdiction and courts. *Regiam* depicts jurisdiction, substantive law and procedure as being clearly hierarchical, bounded, co-dependent and, more importantly, completely royal. *Regiam* only describes procedure in royal courts, those of the justiciar and the sheriff. We see this hierarchical element clearly in *Regiam*'s presentation of the procedure to be followed in a case of rape, which is to be found in book 4: the victim has to show injuries first to the leading men of the vill, then to the sheriff, then to the justiciar. [133] In addition, *Regiam* also minimises non-royal secular jurisdiction. This is important because Scottish royal justice explicitly incorporated non-royal temporal jurisdiction to a much greater extent than its English counterpart, with certain individuals and institutions able to hear pleas of the Crown. [134] Not only does *Regiam* explicitly deny this jurisdictional *fact*, its compiler also describes such courts as *curie private* – private courts – to be contrasted with the *res publica* over which the law of the king ran. [135]

What this suggests, therefore, is that the emphasis on the *maiestas* of thc Scottish king may have quite significantly affected the presentation of Scottish law and its legal system within *Regiam* itself, had the compiler finished his work. The emphasis on royal *maiestas* could well have resulted in a presentation of the relationship between the king and the law in which the king was the sole source of law and the conduit by which other sources of law – particularly Roman and Canon – were upheld within his kingdom. All this suggests a rather different idea of kingship than is normally emphasised in scholarship of this period, where the political dominant idea examined has been that of the community of the realm. [136] This is a powerful narrative: after the death of Alexander III, the elite of the kingdom bound together as the *communitas regni* to guard it, first until its minor heiress came of age and, then, against English aggression. The new and controversial king, Robert, had then to align himself with this notion, for, in addition to being a member of the aristocracy himself, the *communitas regni* was the basis of his own legitimate authority. [137] In this way, the *communitas regni* became a historical witness to the idea of a Scottish political nation. [138] But *Regiam* allows us to identify an alternative and not-necessarily-conflicting strain of thought around royal *maiestas*: a conception of singular legal authority residing in the king alone which could have been just as influential as *communitas* in our understanding of political thought during this period, had *Regiam* been finished and circulated. Indeed, the compiler of *Regiam* himself seems to have shied away from developing the idea that legal authority resided in the *communitas* as opposed to the *maiestas* of the prince, for he removed the sections of *Glanvill*'s prologue which mentioned counsel and consent from its counterpart in *Regiam*. [139] The word *communitas* appears only once in *Regiam*, in one of its least-edited sections. [140]

CONCISE SUMMARY

Despite the presence of moths and worms in Skene's 'ancient books', it is worthwhile to attempt to comprehend the true meaning of Regiam maiestatem and its implications. The oldest surviving copies of Regiam are incomplete and likely originated as an unfinished piece. It is necessary to inquire about the methods, reasons, and timing of the transformation of this incomplete work, perhaps through the creation of an accurate replica, and its subsequent dissemination as if it had been completed. It has been contended in other sources that Regiam experienced a revival during the second reign of David II. During this period, David II enacted a comprehensive and diverse set of laws in the 1360s, which appears to have resulted in the revision of the kingdom's 'auld law'. This revision is evident in the composition of works such as Leges Malcolmi Mackenneth, Ordo justiciarie, and potentially the legal compilations attributed to William the Lion (1165–1214) and Alexander II (1214–49). [141] Regardless of immediate origin, however, *Regiam* had obtained the status of an authoritative source of law by 1426 and, in the fifteenth century, was circulated and revised as the kingdom's 'auld law', thus ushering in centuries of confusion about why a lawbook which did not make much sense as a guide to the early Scottish Common law could have achieved such authoritative status.

Yet, moving aside centuries of textual accretion, we can still see the original conception of *Regiam* as a work of political legal theory by a well-ordered, knowledgeable and intellectually creative mind of the early fourteenth century. Much like the reason why *Regiam* was circulated in its unfinished state, the identity of the compiler of *Regiam* will never be known definitively. Whoever he was, he was closely connected with promoting the legitimacy of Robert's kingship, knew Canon, Civil and Common law, was informed of the latest commentaries, and was probably acquainted with the major controversies over legal authority and jurisdictional boundaries which were coursing through France, the Empire and Sicily in this very period. Given that context, it is tempting to see the compiler as the university-educated Robert Wishart, bishop of Glasgow (1273–1316), auditor and defender of the Bruce claim in the Great Cause, stalwart supporter of Robert's incipient and controversial kingship in 1306, and captive of the English from 1308 to 1315, when he was released, blind (although this is according to John Barbour in his vernacular epic, *The Brus*, produced in the 1370s) but still politically active, and returned to Scotland. [142] The possibility that Robert was the compiler of *Regiam* is suggested by his university education, the presence of Roman law terminology in some charters closely associated with his episcopate and the fact that he spent some of his captivity at the papal curia (and seemingly witnessed at least the early stages of the conflict between Robert of Naples and Henry VII play out, a conflict which in part raised the question of each ruler's *maiestas*). [143] Wishart's death on 26 November 1316 might also provide an explanation of why *Regiam* was left unfinished: if Robert were the compiler, he might have been mid-way through his work when he died.

Robert Wishart's authorship will never be proven and remains only a likelihood or a possibility. What can be said is that the aim of *Regiam*'s compiler was to show, through a variety of techniques – hidden intertextual citation, intercontextual translation and explicit statement – and a variety of legal authorities that the king in his kingdom had no superior other than God and the Church, and certainly not, by implication, the king of England. This intention behind *Regiam* reveals not only that a polity on the 'periphery' of Europe was as engaged in debates about authority as any jurist in Paris or Naples, but also highlights how far our understanding of political thinking during the thirteenth and fourteenth centuries is still framed by the big political crises and intellectual centres of the 'core' areas of Europe. *Regiam* instead reveals how widely embedded this legal language was, both geographically and, also through letters and more ephemeral sources, in political communication.

Finally, *Regiam* reveals an alternative conceptualisation of the Scottish king's political authority which centred around his *regia maiestas*, and only a long-standing but perhaps uncritical focus on the idea of 'the community of the realm of Scotland' has prevented the identification of this strain of thought in Robert's kingship, as much as the fact that *Regiam* was unfinished. Indeed, that *Regiam* may have intended to create a new – or at least different – legal underpinning for Scottish kingship is suggested not only by its innovative content but also by its presentation of royal jurisdiction as the only legitimate temporal forum. But *Regiam* was *not* finished, the aims and ambitions of its compiler were abandoned and what survives of it retains only the foundations of its original design, buried beneath a mass of *Glanvill* unadapted to its intended field of application. In 1681, Viscount Stair wrote in his *Institutions of the Law of Scotland* that *Regiam*, because of its heavy dependence on *Glanvill*, was 'no part' of Scots law. [144] Stair may have been taken aback by the revelation that a historian, writing almost three centuries and fifty years later, now considers the possibility that the original author of Regiam, had they witnessed what is presently acknowledged as Regiam maiestatem, they could have potentially concurred with the Viscount's condemnatory assessment.

Footnote

1. J. Skene, ed., Regiam majestatem Scotiæ veteres leges et constitutiones ... opera et studio Joannis Skenaei (Edinburgh, 1609); J. Skene, ed., Regiam majestatem. The Auld Lawes and Constitutions of Scotland ... Be Sir John Skene of Curriehill, Clerk of our Soveraigne Lordis Register, Counsell and Rollis (Edinburgh, 1609).
2. *The Actis and Constitutiounis of the Realme of Scotland ... Anno. Do. 1566* (Edinburgh, 1566). A facsimile is available in K. Luig, ed., The Acts and Constitutions of the Realm of Scotland, Edinburgh 1566: 'Black Acts': Faksimiledruck mit einer Einleitung von Klaus Luig (Mittelalterliche Gesetzbücher Europäischer Länder in Faksimiledrucken; Glashütten (Taunus), 1971).
3. Skene, ed., *Regiam majestatem*, note 'candido lectori'. The Scots version was rather less dramatic about the labour involved, but more dramatic about the role that Latin had played in supporting the dominance of the pope and his bishops; Skene, ed., *Regiam majestatem* (Scots), vi, ix.
4. See, for discussion, A. Taylor, The Shape of the State in Medieval Scotland, 1124–1290 (Oxford, 2016), 457–9; for a reassessment, see The Laws of Medieval Scotland: Legal Compilations from the Thirteenth and Fourteenth Centuries, ed. A. Taylor (Stair Society, 66; Edinburgh, 2019).
5. See the brief discussion by Lord Cooper in Regiam Majestatem and Quoniam Attachiamenta Based on the Text of Sir John Skene, ed. T. M. [Lord] Cooper (Stair Society, 11; Edinburgh, 1947), 3–8, 16–18. This was despite Thomas Thomson preparing an edition based primarily but not exclusively on the Cromertie manuscript (Edinburgh, National Library of Scotland (NLS), Advocates MS 25.5.10), which was published under the editorship of Cosmo Innes in 1844: *Acts of the Parliaments of Scotland, Volume 1: 1124–1423*, ed. C. N. Innes and T. Thomson (Edinburgh, 1844), 597–641 (all page references are to the red foliation; henceforth, citations of the various volumes of *Acts of the Parliaments of Scotland* will be referred to as *APS*). During the first half of the 1940s, Lord Cooper was preparing another edition of *Regiam* for the Stair Society (he had drafted the introduction by early 1944), which was published in 1947. Cooper decided to use Skene's edition as the basis for his own, despite the known issues with Skene's editorial techniques. Cooper not only believed that 'the practice of "Skene-baiting" has been carried much too far' but also thought that, given that his edition would be used by 'lawyers and students of legal history', Skene's was anyway the most valuable because to edit a text based on the earliest manuscripts would be redundant as 'it would not be the text of the Regiam Majestatem of professional tradition familiar to Scottish lawyers for 350 years' (Cooper, ed., *Regiam Majestatem*, 18). The major difference between Skene's and Cooper's editions was Cooper's inclusion as a supplement of chapters from

book 4 excluded by Skene but present in Thomson's and in some form in all the manuscripts of *Regiam maiestatem* (Cooper, ed., *Regiam Majestatem*, 18–20, with the Supplement at 280–304).

6. G. Neilson, 'The Study of Early Law', Juridical Review, 3 (1891), 12–20, at 17; also G. Neilson, Trial by Combat (Glasgow, 1890), 103. For an earlier comment on this passage, see A. Harding, 'Regiam Majestatem amongst Medieval Law-Books', Juridical Review, new ser., 19 (1984), 97–111, at 98.
7. It has long been thought that the object of consulting *Regiam* and *Quoniam* in 1426 was to reform them. This is due to the words 'and mend the lawis that nedis mendment' after the injunction to consult both books in the edition of the 1426 statutes printed by Thomson in *APS, Volume 2: 1424–1557*, ed. T. Thomson (Edinburgh, 1814), Acta Parliamentorum Jacobi I, 10 (black foliation). However, Andrew Simpson and Adelyn Wilson have noted that these words are not, in fact, in the earliest manuscripts of this legislation nor those which seem to preserve copies distributed to the localities. Instead, they are in the 'semi-official' copies which may well preserve edits inserted after a legal reform made in 1450: see A. R. C. Simpson and A. L. N. Wilson, Scottish Legal History, Volume 1: 1000–1700 (Edinburgh, 2017), 59–60. As a result, Simpson and Wilson argue that the remit of the original clause in the 1426 legislation was to consult *Regiam* and *Quoniam* to discover which exceptions could be admitted and which not, as the courts were facing delays.
8. *RPS*, 1469/34; *RPS*, 1473/7/17. *RPS* here and henceforth refers to the online resource *The Records of the Parliaments of Scotland to 1707*, eds. K. M. Brown et al. (St Andrews, 2007–20), available at https://rps.ac.uk (accessed 28 February 2020).
9. *RPS*, 1471/5/9; *RPS*, 1475/34.
10. *RPS*, 1481/4/13; *RPS* 1482/3/22 See the broader commentary and analysis in H. L. MacQueen, Common Law and Feudal Society in Medieval Scotland, 2nd edn (Edinburgh, 2016), 91–4.
11. MacQueen, *Common Law*, 94–8.
12. Ibid., 91–8; H. L. MacQueen, '*Regiam Majestatem*, Scots Law, and National Identity', Scottish Historical Review, 74 (1995), 1–25.
13. For a starting point, see A. R. C. Simpson, 'Legislation and Authority in Early-Modern Scotland', in M. Godfrey (ed.), Law and Authority in British Legal History, 1200–1900 (Cambridge, 2016), 85–119.
14. *Tractatus de legibus et consuetudinibus regni Anglie qui Glanvilla vocatur: The Treatise on the Laws and Customs of the Realm of England Commonly Called Glanvill*, ed. G. D.

G. Hall, with a guide to further reading by M. T. Clanchy (Oxford, repr. 2002); H. L. MacQueen, 'Glanvill Resarcinate: Sir John Skene and Regiam Majestatem', in A. A. MacDonald, M. Lynch and I. B. Cowan (eds.), The Renaissance in Scotland: Studies in Literature, Religion, History and Culture Offered to John Durkan (Leiden, 1994), 385–403.

15. MacQueen, '*Regiam Majestatem*', 16; MacQueen, 'Glanvill Resarcinate', 385–7.
16. MacQueen, '*Regiam Majestatem*', 19–23, disputing and developing C. Kidd, Subverting Scotland's Past: Scottish Whig Historians and the Creation of an Anglo-British Identity, 1689–c. 1830 (Cambridge, 1993), 148–50.
17. MacQueen, '*Regiam Majestatem*', 23–4. In his reissue of Skene's edition of *Regiam* for the Stair Society in 1947, Lord Cooper argued that *Regiam* was 'compiled in the later years of Alexander II and was intended to describe the law as it then prevailed': Cooper, ed., *Regiam Majestatem*, 45.
18. This is the Bute manuscript, now NLS, MS 21246 (henceforth, **C**), fos. 27r–62r. The note of sale is on what looks like the original outer leaf of the original manuscript on fo. 178v.
19. Taylor, ed., *Laws of Medieval Scotland*, 49–54; **C**, fo. 119v.
20. *Regiam*, prologue: 'set ad iuuandam memoriam ad modum necessariam quandam particulam ad mandatum domini regis Dauid cum sano consilio tocius regni sui'. All references to *Regiam* are to the forthcoming edition being prepared by John Reuben Davies, with editorial and historical commentary from me. This edition will be based on the earliest-known text of *Regiam* as it survives in London, British Library (BL), Additional MS 18111 (elsewhere denoted as **F**) and the Bute manuscript (NLS, MS 21246, known as **C**). This will be published by the Stair Society and is part of the research being conducted on the AHRC-funded project 'The Community of the Realm in Scotland, 1249–1424: History, Law and Charters in a Recreated Kingdom' (AH/P013759/1).
21. What kind of *Glanvill*-text lies behind *Regiam* is rather difficult to ascertain, although this will be developed in the forthcoming Stair edition of *Regiam* (ed. Davies with Taylor). One key diagnostic is the inclusion in the earliest manuscripts of *Regiam* of the cross-references contained in some beta-manuscripts of *Glanvill* to the recognitions on the assize *utrum* (referred to but not inserted in the main edited text of *Glanvill*, XIII, 31). No currently available edition of *Regiam* includes these references, so their inclusion has not been remarked upon. They are present in the earliest beta-manuscripts of *Glanvill*, such as BL, Additional MS 24066 (*Glanvill* manuscript *B*), which dates from the early thirteenth century. Sarah Tullis suggested that, based on 'more systematic study', *Regiam* might have been derived from a manuscript like *E* (BL, Additional

MS 35179) or 'one that is now lost': S. Tullis, '*Glanvill* after *Glanvill*', unpublished DPhil thesis, University of Oxford (2007), 165. BL, Additional MS 35179, fo. 71r, does have these cross-references.

22. P. Stein, 'The Source of the Romano-Canonical Part of Regiam Maiestatem', Scottish Historical Review, 48 (1969), 107–23. There is no modern critical edition of Goffredo's *Summa*, so all references are to Goffredus Tranensis, Summa super titulis Decretalium (Lyon, 1519; repr. 1968). Aberdeen Cathedral's library is known to have had two copies: *Scottish Libraries*, ed. J. Higgitt, with J. Durkan (London, 2005), 17 (S1). I am grateful to Richard Sharpe for his help with Goffredo.
23. Cooper, ed., *Regiam Majestatem*, 43–45.
24. A. A. M. Duncan, 'Regiam Majestatem: A Reconsideration', Juridical Review, new ser., 6 (1961), 199–217.
25. Ibid., 210–16.
26. The passage in question is the 'brieve of right in the burgh', which is a short procedural tract for how to plead and propone exceptions to a brieve of right in the burgh court in the form of a brieve of right of Alexander III: Ayr Miscellany, c. 2, in Taylor, ed., *Laws of Medieval Scotland*, 448–53.
27. Taylor, ed., *Laws of Medieval Scotland*, 274–80.
28. Harding, '*Regiam Majestatem*'.
29. The two major biographies of Robert Bruce take a rather different view of his post-1314 kingship, with Michael Penman preferring to stress the insecurity of Robert's position, particularly in the years 1318–20 following the death of his brother, while Geoffrey Barrow stresses unity and the perseverance of the Bruce government to the challenges of 1319–20: M. Penman, Robert the Bruce: King of the Scots (New Haven, 2014), 177–234; G. W. S. Barrow, Robert Bruce and the Community of the Realm of Scotland, 4th edn (Edinburgh, 2005), 393–404. A new interpretation of Robert and his reign is being developed as part of the research on the AHRC-funded project, 'The Community of the Realm in Scotland, 1249–1424: History, Law and Charters in a Recreated Kingdom' (https://cotr.ac.uk), which this paragraph represents in simplified form.
30. The position of David I as *the* lawmaking king had a long history within and outwith Scotland. In his posthumous *Life of David*, written shortly after the king's death in May 1153, Aelred of Rievaulx had extolled David's delivery of justice and his protection of the poor and vulnerable (Oxford, Bodleian Library, MS Digby 19, fos. 7v–8v, 10r–v). When David's grandson, Mael Coluim, succeeded him in 1153, David's relationship to law was retained and indeed promoted by

the king's *capella*. The most famous example is the illuminated majuscule 'M' in a royal charter to Kelso Abbey, printed in *Regesta Regum Scotorum Volume 1: The Acts of Malcolm IV, 1153–1165*, ed. G. W. S. Barrow (Edinburgh, 1960), no. 131. The laws of Mael Coluim's brother and successor, William, were sometimes even portrayed as mere *confirmations* of David's law, despite the institutional structures to which these laws referred not existing in David's reign (for an example, see *Regesta Regum Scotorum Volume 2: The Acts of William I, 1165–1214*, ed. G. W. S. Barrow with W. W. Scott (Edinburgh, 1971), no. 281, discussed in Taylor, *Shape of the State*, 63–4, 180–6. When, in 1305, following his successful – but temporary – conquest of Scotland, Edward I had an ordinance drawn up to lay down how the conquered kingdom would be governed under the new regime, he asked the good men of the land to gather together and literally 'recherche' the laws which King David had made, as well as any amendments and additions made by any of his (unnamed) predecessors. The laws of Scotland were, in some senses, understood by outsiders to be a corpus made by David. For the 1305 ordinance, see *Anglo-Scottish Relations 1174–1328: Some Selected Documents*, ed. and trans. E. L. G. Stones (Oxford, repr. 1970), no. 33 (240–59, at 250–1).

31. Harding, '*Regiam Majestatem*', 108–10.

32. As we shall see, book 4 actually begins with edited material from *Glanvill*, XIV ('de criminalibus'), before moving on to legal chapters first attested in *Leges Scocie* (*Regiam*, cc. 142–8), then to those later attested in *Statuta Regis Alexandri* (*Regiam*, c. 149), and then material first attested in the Ayr Miscellany (*Regiam*, cc. 150–68), in one case extending what was originally in the Ayr Miscellany (*Regiam*, c. 158*). Further chapters attested in the Ayr Miscellany can be found at cc. 170–9, 181–5. The only chapters not attested in the Ayr Miscellany are *Regiam*, cc. 168–9, 172, 180, 186; however, since the Ayr Miscellany survives only in an incomplete form, it is possible that these chapters too might have been included in it. *Regiam* finishes with four chapters first attested as *Leges Scocie*, c. 21. For the relationship between *Regiam* and the Ayr Miscellany, see Taylor, ed., *Laws of Medieval Scotland*, 265–8, 274–80.

33. *Regiam*, cc. 124–5, 130; *Glanvill*, XIII, cc. 2, 23–5.

34. *Regiam*, c. 120.

35. Ibid., cc. 125–33; *Glanvill*, XIII. Some information here is attested in other pieces of Scots law (for example, that there be no essoins for novel dissasine and mortancestor), but other detail is not (for example, socage).

36. S. Marshall, Illegitimacy in Medieval Scotland (Woodbridge, forthcoming, 2020), ch. 2. I am grateful to Dr Marshall for sharing her chapter with me before its publication.

37. The change in the use of *Glanvill* around thirteen chapters into book 2 was first noted by Lord Cooper and then developed by A. A. M. Duncan (in the edition based on the two earliest manuscripts, 'book II, c. 13' is *Regiam*, c. 47): Cooper, ed., *Regiam Majestatem*, 22; Duncan, 'Regiam Majestatem', 205. For a different view of the compiler's editorial methods, see below, 62–67.

38. There are currently four editions of *Regiam* in print, but, as two derived directly from Skene's edition, only the two remaining differ substantively from one another. Those two are that of Skene, published in 1609, and that by Thomas Thomson for the Record Commission, published under the overall editorship of Cosmo Innes in 1844 as an Appendix to *APS*, volume 1. Lord Cooper based his edition on Skene's text, as did David Hoüard (1725–1802), a French advocate and member of *parlement*, who published Skene's text together with a French commentary in 1776 (*Traités sur les coutumes anglo-normandes*, ed. D. Hoüard, 4 vols. (Rouen, 1776), vol. II, 36–267).

39. This list is roughly coterminous with the manuscripts of *Quoniam attachiamenta*, provided in *Quoniam Attachiamenta*, ed. T. D. Fergus (Stair Society, 44; Edinburgh, 1996), 5–6. The list also includes NLS, Acc. MS 11218/5 and St Andrews University Library, MS 39000.

40. See, for example, BL, Additional MS 48032 and BL, Additional MS 48033.

41. Later fifteenth-century Scots manuscripts preserve the earlier version (of *c.* 190 chapters, divided into four books; see, for example, NLS, Advocates MS 25.4.15) when it was far more common for Latin *Regiam* texts to contain either a three-book *Regiam* (which had already been revised) *or* a four-book *Regiam* derived from this *three*-book *Regiam*, *or*, even, a four-book *Regiam* which had been wholly revised and extended. For a brief survey of these differences, see Taylor, ed., *Laws of Medieval Scotland*, 376–7.

42. NLS, Advocates MS 25.4.15.

43. Indeed, the Scots texts are generally more fluid than the Latin ones, and require further study. For example, the Marchmont *Regiam* is a three-book text, but only because it does not include the 'fourth' book, supposedly devoted to crime (St Andrews University Library, MS 39000). One manuscript, written in 1470, contains a four-book *Regiam*, but only around 177–80 chapters, missing out ones found in the Latin tradition (e.g. the chapter on *cró*, at the end of the fourth book): NLS, Advocates MS 25.5.7.

44. NLS, MS 21246. The first two items in the original codex are *Regiam maiestatem* and an 'Assise Regis Dauid', a witness to the alpha-version of *Capitula Assisarum et Statutorum Domini Dauid Regis Scotie*. The first sixty-seven folios, therefore, of the Bute manuscript are taken up entirely with items attributed to David I; see

Taylor, ed., *Laws of Medieval Scotland*, 53–5. There is, however, good evidence that the codex had a practical use, or at least was intended to inform practice.

45. Taylor, ed., *Laws of Medieval Scotland*, 55–60.
46. Commented on in Taylor, ed., *Laws of Medieval Scotland*, 129, 387–8.
47. Although there is not space to develop the implications of this point here, the fact that *Regiam* – as it survives – exists only within a self-conscious tradition of 'auld law' raises questions about its immediate circulation. Was *Regiam* publicly circulated immediately after its compilation (even in its unfinished state)? The paucity of fourteenth-century legal manuscripts means that this question is impossible to answer in its own right.
48. Taylor, ed., *Laws of Medieval Scotland*, 366–90.
49. Ibid., 387–90.
50. Ibid., 61–218, 363–90.
51. This is the Cromertie manuscript (NLS, Advocates MS 25.5.10).
52. BL, Additional MS 18111, fos. 1r–76r. This manuscript had not been studied until its existence was rediscovered by A. A. M. Duncan in, presumably, the late 1950s/early 1960s, who used it as the basis of his reassessment of *Regiam*. Since then, T. D. Fergus has used it as one of two early witnesses of *Quoniam* (the other being the Bute manuscript): Fergus, ed., *Quoniam*, 19–23.
53. Taylor, ed., *Laws of Medieval Scotland*, 49–60, 72–78.
54. Ibid., 50–51, 73; R. J. Lyall, 'Books and Book-Owners in Fifteenth-Century Scotland', in J. Griffiths and D. Pearsall (eds.), Book Production and Publishing in Britain, 1375–1475 (Cambridge, 1989), 239–56, at 244.
55. Duncan, '*Regiam Majestatem*', 202–4; *Regiam*, ed. Davies with Taylor (forthcoming).
56. Both manuscripts number *Regiam*'s chapters in continuous sequence, not restarting as new books begin. Although both state that they have *c.* 190 chapters, the Bute MS text is actually numbered in six score hundreds, making a total of 213 chapters. Both manuscripts have a contents list prefacing the text, although a folio is missing from the Additional manuscript so we cannot see how it would originally have been introduced. The Bute MS contents list makes a clear division between chapters 44 and 45, indicating the start of the second book with the words 'in secundo libro' (fo. 22v). The same division is indicated between chapters '100' (*recte* 120) and '101' (*recte* 121) with the words 'in tercia parte' (fo. 23r). By contrast, there is no division indicated in the contents list between books 3 and 4, which should have occurred between chapters '131' (*recte* 151) and '132' (*recte* 152), at fo. 23v. Subsequently two later hands added this division. When it comes to the main text in the Bute MS, there are clear

divisions between parts 1 and 2 (fo. 34r, with the sections called *partes*); parts 2 and 3 (fo. 46v); and parts 3 and 4 (although here the 'fourth' part is mistakenly called *tercia pars*). The Additional manuscript has, in its contents list, a division between parts 1 and 2 between chapters 33 and 34 (BL, Additional MS 18111, fo. 1r); between 2 and 3 between chapters 107 and 108 (fo. 3r); and between 3 and 4 (cc. 133–4: fo. 3v). These are also reflected in the text (divisions noted at fos. 19r, 46r and 62v at the correct chapters). The Additional manuscript divisions are less intrusive than the Bute ones (there is a tendency in the Bute manuscript to suggest that the first rubric of each book is the 'title' of the book, something which later manuscripts absolutely do represent): the Additional manuscript divisions are called only *partes*, with no titles. Thus, although the Bute manuscript contains some ambiguity about the divisions in *Regiam*, the Additional manuscript, which preserves an earlier structure, does not, suggesting, at most, that *Regiam* was originally intended to be divided into four books and, at least, that its earliest-known version was divided into four books. For the note that later manuscripts sometimes preserve a three-book text, see MacQueen, *Common Law*, 93, and, for a brief explanation, see Taylor, ed., *Laws of Medieval Scotland*, 375–7. John Reuben Davies and I will comment on the 'three-book'-*Regiam* in our introduction to the forthcoming edition of *Regiam*.

57. See the margins in NLS, MS 21246, fos. 30r, 34r, 35v, 43r, 45r, and so on.

58. See, for example, the *Questio/Solucio* imposed onto regulations about warrantors in theft accusations in the Bute manuscript (*Regiam*, c. 23, in the Bute manuscript, fo. 31v). The text says that if a far-away warrantor refused to answer or if the accused man could not produce him, then the king's sergeands would go to the lord of the warrantor and make him come. The situation is, in the margin, described as a *questio*, and the procedure (what the king's sergeands would then do) is described as a *solucio*: NLS, MS 21246, fo. 31v.

59. The additional chapters in Bute are c. '192' (*recte* c. 212) 'de illis qui sunt conuicti de periurio' and c. '193' (*recte* c. 213), 'nullus seriandus potest esse prolocutor nec attornatus'; NLS, MS 21246, fo. 62r. The *explicit* in the Additional manuscript is found after its chapter 190 ('de effusione sanguinis') and reads: 'expliciunt constituciones Regie [*sic*; possibly a scribal error for *Regis*] Regni Scocie preter constituciones burgorum edite per Dauid Regem Scocie'.

60. *Regiam*, cc. 2, 9, 19 (following and summarising *Glanvill*, III, 4 (40), although *Glanvill* does not contain the cross-reference), c. 21; see also c. 45.

61. These will be developed in the forthcoming Stair edition of *Regiam* (ed. Davies with Taylor). For now, they will just be listed. (1) The simplest phase of editing was the removal of almost all writ formulae from *Glanvill* and any mention of them. (2) Passages where *Glanvill*'s content has, broadly, been maintained, but

slightly abridged and/or summarised. The most obvious example is actually present throughout *Regiam*: the compiler never included *Glanvill*'s rather tedious description of what happened on each of the three days of essoining but instead just jumped straight to the fourth day, when all lawful essoins have been used, and stipulates what should happen then (for example, *Regiam*, c. 47). (3) Small editorial changes, without any real substantive change to the procedure or rule. For example, the English royal *iusticie* – justices – in *Glanvill* are consistently rendered as *iusticiarii* in *Regiam* to denote the regional justiciar. (4) Small editorial changes to a source which nonetheless result in substantive change. For example, the compiler changed Goffredo's statement that arbiters must be over the age of twenty-five to over the age of twenty-one, the age of majority in Scotland. In a passage on essoins based on *Glanvill*, the compiler of *Regiam* added the words 'de Forth' to the words 'de ultra mare', thereby effectively changing the location of the sea in question from the English Channel to the Firth of Forth. (5) The most substantial changes, elaborated below, in which the material from the source – normally *Glanvill*, as it is the Glanvillian sections in book 1 which have been the most heavily edited – provides the bare bones of the structure of a particular chapter and section, but the material has either been completely written for Scotland or 'Scottish' material has been inserted.

62. All save seven of the writ-formulae in *Glanvill* are absent in *Regiam*. Five occur in *Regiam*, c. 47, in book 2, under the title 'de donacionibus inter uirum et uxorem et de dote', which Duncan described as 'Glanville *totally unrevised*, and includes even the Glanvillian writs' (Duncan, '*Regiam Majestatem*', 205). These writs are: the writ of right for dower land (*Glanvill*, VI, 5); the writ for transferring a case from the county to the king's *curia* (*Glanvill*, VI, 7); the writ for summoning the heir to warrant the dower (*Glanvill*, VI, 9); the writ for making a summons for dower when the woman does not have the land (*Glanvill*, VI, 15); and the writ for measuring dower if it is claimed the widow has more than her reasonable share (*Glanvill*, VI, 18), only here there has been a haplographic error between the two *sine dilacione* so the injunction to the sheriff to measure the dower land is not preserved in *Regiam*, both in the earliest manuscripts and in later ones (*Regiam*, c. 47; and, further, the 'Cromertie' manuscript, NLS, Advocates MS 25.5.10, fo. 48v; the Monynet manuscript, NLS, Advocates MS 25.5.6, fo. 17v). However, it is not the case, first, that this is the only place where the writ formulae have not been retained nor, second, that this chapter is *Glanvill* 'totally unrevised'. Two more writ formulae appear, both later in book 2 (*Regiam*, c. 54, on withholding chattels of a testate dead man (*Glanvill*, VII, 7); *Regiam*, c. 81, on the illegitimacy of children born before their parents' marriage (*Glanvill*, VII, 14)). This lengthy chapter 47 of *Regiam* is indeed revised, albeit lightly.

63. *Regiam*, cc. 19–27 (based on *Glanvill*, III, 4–8); *Regiam*, c. 127 contains some rather interesting abridgements of *Glanvill*, XIII, 13–15; *Regiam*, c. 133 says that the pursuer in a case of dissasine will be compensated up to the value of ten marks from the chattels and fruits of the land; cf. *Glanvill*, XIII, 38.

64. *Anglo-Scottish Relations*, ed. and trans. Stones, no. 33, 240–59, at 250–1: 'et des gentz qui y seront assemblez soient rehercez les leis que le roy David fist, et ausint les amendementz et les addicions qui unt esté puis faites par les roys'.

65. *Glanvill*, incipit, 1. Like *Glanvill*, some scribes of manuscripts of the *Laws of Hywel Dda* refer explicitly to Hywel making this law, but not as a legislator; the prologue to the *Ior.* recension makes it clear that Hywel called wise men and clerics to him to examine the old law, and to make new law where appropriate, and on occasion, later changes to the law are referred to: *The Law of Hywel Dda: Law Texts from Medieval Wales Translated and Edited*, ed. and trans. D. Jenkins (Llandysul, 1986), xxiii–xiv.

66. *Regiam*, cc. 6, 14. Both references are in book 1. For the references to *dominus rex statuit* (or variant), see *Regiam*, cc. 6, 15, 21 (again, in book 1) and 171, 187 (in book 4).

67. These references are discussed in J. R. Davies, 'References to Roman and Canon Law in Regiam Maiestatem', *The Community of the Realm in Scotland, 1249–1424: History, Law and Charters in a Recreated Kingdom*, www.cotr.ac.uk/blog/regiam1. All these references – and how they develop in later manuscripts – will be discussed in detail in the forthcoming Stair edition of *Regiam* (ed. Davies with Taylor).

68. References to the *Digest* can be found in *Regiam*, cc. 11, 39, 40, 114; references to the *Institutes* at *Regiam*, cc. 9, 32, 109, 114, 150; and to the *Liber extra*, at cc. 39, 42, 47–8, 119, 127–8. For the *Liber sextus*, see *Regiam*, cc. 28, 127; for the Gloss of Bernardus Parmensis, see *Regiam*, c. 158. Some of these are also found in one of *Regiam*'s sources, Goffredus, but by no means all, and not all of Goffredus's internal references are to be found in *Regiam*: see J. R. Davies, 'The Reception and Identification of Roman and Canon Law in *Regiam Maiestatem*', forthcoming.

69. The presence of Roman and Canon law material in later manuscripts of *Regiam* will be developed in more detail in the introduction of the forthcoming Stair edition of *Regiam* (ed. Davies with Taylor). Lord Cooper was aware of this material in the early manuscripts but thought it a work of a later scribe and judged Skene correct to have removed all references. Needless to say, neither Skene's nor Thomson's editions acknowledged the full extent of Roman and Canon law throughout the manuscript tradition of *Regiam*; Cooper, ed., *Regiam Majestatem*, 16–17, 27–32.

70. Stein, 'Source of the Romano-Canonical Part', 107.

71. This is the law long known by the name *Clurmathan* or *Claremathan*, a word which had become attached to the law by the time it had been incorporated into the compilation *Statuta Regis Alexandri*, attributed to Alexander II and probably drawn up in the late 1350s or 1360s (*Statuta Regis Alexandri*, c. 12; Taylor, ed., *Laws of Medieval Scotland*, 231–3, 341–2, 590–5). However, it first appears as the first chapter of *Leges Scocie*, a compilation dated to 1210X72, but whose chapters mostly date from the reign of William the Lion (ibid., 231–3).

72. *Regiam*, c. 6, 'de essoniis', with seven rubricated sections, based on *Glanvill*, I, 12, 18, 25, 27–9, 33. There is a lawful essoin in *Regiam* which is not in *Glanvill* that is about going to a fair (*Regiam*, c. 6.5).

73. *Glanvill*, I, 28.

74. *Regiam*, c. 6.5. The chapter is widening the remit of *Glanvill* as well, as it includes an essoin for 'any other reason' than illness for which the defendant has found a pledge.

75. *Regiam* then returns to *Glanvill*, and states that the tenant would have at least a further fifteen days until he must appear in court again: *Glanvill*, I, 28.

76. *Regiam*, c. 6.5.

77. Johannes Andreae *ad* VI.2.13.3, *Liber sextus Decretalium d. Bonifacii papae VIII*, in UCLA Digital Library Program, *Corpus Juris Canonici (1582)*, available at http://digital.library.ucla.edu/canonlaw (accessed 28 February 2020).

78. Not all internal citations answer questions posed in the text, although some do. For example, in book 3, *Regiam* includes and abridges *Glanvill*'s chapter on loans for use (*comodata*; *Glanvill*, X, 13).

79. This is despite the figure of David being invoked more in later manuscripts than he is in the earliest ones. See the transformation of the phrase 'ergo contra eorum personas dominus rex distinguit in hunc modum' (*Regiam*, c. 6.3) into 'ergo circa [sic] eorum personas dominus Rex Dauid precepit distinguere in hunc modum'; NLS, Advocates MS, 25.4.13 (**D**), fo. 16v.

80. A. Watson, Legal Transplants: An Approach to Comparative Law (Edinburgh, 1974); see, for an analytical response, J. W. Cairns, 'Watson, Walton, and the History of Legal Transplants', Georgia Journal of International and Comparative Law, 41 (2013), 637–96; for a critique, see P. Legrand, 'The Impossibility of "Legal Transplants"', Maastricht Journal of European and Comparative Law, 4 (1997), 111–24, and, in this context, MacQueen, *Common Law*, 264–5.

81. Most obviously in book 1, the section on pleading; *Regiam*, c. 8; cf. *Glanvill*, II, 3, 13, 17–18. For example, the beginning of book 4 starts with *Glanvill* with a

few changes, and then slowly its content gets replaced, with *Glanvill*'s dismissal of robbery being rewritten, as is the whole procedure on rape; *Regiam*, cc. 139–40; cf. *Glanvill*, XIV, 5–6. *Regiam* also has a chapter on theft (first attested as *Leges Scocie*, c. 4 and Ayr Miscellany, c. 9) where *Glanvill* states that it is not appropriate to mention theft, which belongs in the county court, not the king's court (*Glanvill*, XIV, 8).

82. R. Copeland, Rhetoric, Hermeneutics and Translation in the Middle Ages: Academic Traditions and Vernacular Texts (Cambridge, 1995), 35.
83. Ibid., 30.
84. 'Intercontextual' translations have received little attention as a practice, although translation as a 'method' of conceptual history has been discussed since the 1970s, albeit within an interlingual context. See, for example, K. Palonen, Politics and Conceptual Histories: Rhetorical and Temporal Perspectives (London, 2016), 145–60.
85. Copeland, *Rhetoric, Hermeneutics and Translation*, 30. The phrase intercontextual translation is not used in Copeland; her points about interlingual translation are being used here to illuminate the compilation methods in *Regiam*.
86. This is particularly important given the clear attribution to David I in the early manuscripts of *Regiam*, while *Glanvill* was not always known as *Glanvill*, even by the early fourteenth century. It was known by a variety of titles in the surviving manuscripts: 'Regia Potestas' (MSS *O* and *W*); 'Leges Henrici Secundi' (MSS *Co*, *G*, *Or*); 'Liber Curialis' (*Ab*). All *sigla* are those used in the modern editions of *Glanvill* (see *Glanvill*, ed. Hall, ix; Tullis, '*Glanvill* after *Glanvill*', 5–7). Others call it *Suma que uocatur Glaunuile*, or similar (*J*, *P* and also *Co*).
87. P. Brand, 'Hengham Magna: A Thirteenth Century English Common Law Treatise and its Composition', Irish Jurist, new ser., 11 (1976), 147–69; T. J. McSweeney, 'Creating a Literature for the King's Courts in the Later Thirteenth Century: Hengham Magna, Fet Asaver, and Bracton', The Journal of Legal History, 37 (2016), 41–71.
88. Tullis, '*Glanvill* after *Glanvill*', ch. 1 and appendix 1.
89. It is clear that a copy of *Glanvill* had influenced the drafters of Scottish statutes as it influenced the style and content of the statute introducing novel dissasine in Scotland, enacted in October 1230. This survives as *Statuta Regis Alexandri*, c. 7, in Taylor, ed., *Laws of Medieval Scotland*, 586–7; discussed in MacQueen, *Common Law*, 136–7; Taylor, *Shape of the State*, 285–93. *Glanvill* was also used in *Capitula assisarum et statutorum domini Dauid regis Scocie* (henceforth *CD*), cc. 32 and 36, and influenced a passage in the Ayr Miscellany, cc. 1, 34 (Taylor, ed., *Laws of Medieval Scotland*, 446–7, 480–1, 518–19, 522–3).

90. Sarah Tullis has shown that the *incipit* which refers to Henry II is preserved in twenty-seven of the surviving manuscripts of *Glanvill*. MSS *G* and *Or* (originally the same volume) contain a miniature of Henry II with an archbishop and four knights (Tullis, '*Glanvill* after *Glanvill*', 19). The French translation (mid-thirteenth century) calls him 'del secund roy Henry de Engleterre'; Tullis, '*Glanvill* after *Glanvill*', 40 and n. 130.

91. *Institutes*, prologue: 'Imperatoriam maiestatem non solum armis decoratam sed etiam legibus oportet esse armatam ut utrumque tempus et bellorum et pacis recte possit gubernari et princeps Romanus victor existat non solum in hostibus proeliis sed etiam per legitimos tramites calumniantium iniquitates expellens et fiat tam iuris religiosissimus quam victis hostibus triumphator.'

92. *Glanvill*, prologue: 'Regiam potestatem non solum armis contra rebelles et gentes sibi regnoque insurgentes oportet esse decoratam sed et legibus ad subditos et populos pacificos regendos decet esse ornatam.'

93. *Regiam*, prologue: 'Regiam maiestatem non solum armis contra rebelles sibi regnoque insurgentes oportet esse decoratam set eciam legibus ad subditos et populos pacificos oportet esse armatam.'

94. *Glanvill*, XIV, 3; *Regiam*, c. 137.

95. *Digests* 48.4.1: 'proximum sacrilegio crimen est'. The literature is vast. See W. Ullmann, 'The Development of the Medieval Idea of Sovereignty', *English Historical Review*, 64 (1949), 1–33; K. Pennington, The Prince and the Law, 1200–1600: Sovereignty and Rights in the Western Legal Tradition (Berkeley, CA and Los Angeles, CA, 1993), 90–106; A. Bryen, 'Labeo's iniuria: Violence and Politics in the Age of Augustus', Chiron: Mitteilungen der Kommission für alte Geschichte und Epigraphik des deutschen Archäologischen Instituts, 48 (2018), 17–52, at 26–32, 42–3.

96. A rather famous bull of Paschal II addressed to Emperor Henry V in 1111 referred to the *divina maiestas* flowing through priests and the *regalis maiestas* which should prevent dissension and conflict over episcopal elections; Constitutiones et Acta Publica Imperatorum et Regum inde ab A.DCCCXI usque ad A.MCXCVII, ed. L. Weiland (Monumenta Germaniae Historica; Hanover, 1893), no. 96.

97. See the summary in K. Pennington, 'Law, Legislative Authority and Theories of Government, 1150–1300', in J. H. Burns (ed.), The Cambridge History of Medieval Political Thought, c. 350–c. 1450 (Cambridge, 1988), 424–53.

98. Thus, in 1313, in *Pastoralis Cura*, Pope Clement V explained that Henry VII had engaged in an offence of his *maiestas* by creating *confederationes* and *conspirationes*; *Clem.* II.11, accessed from *Clementis papae V. Constitutiones*, in

UCLA Digital Library Program, *Corpus Juris Canonici (1582)*, available at http://digital.library.ucla.edu/canonlaw (accessed: 28 February 2020).

99. Pennington, *Prince and the Law*, 95–7; S. H. Cuttler, The Law of Treason and Treason Trials in Later Medieval France (Cambridge, 2003), 8–15.

100. See F. Calasso, I glossatori et la teoria della sovranità: studio di diritto comune publico, 3rd edn (Milan, 1957), 177–205.

101. See, among many, Pennington, *Prince and the Law*, 102–5; M. Ryan, 'Political Thought', in D. Johnston (ed.), The Cambridge Companion to Roman Law (Cambridge, 2015), 423–51, at 438–9; Daniel Lee, Popular Sovereignty in Early Modern Constitutional Thought (Oxford, 2016), 60–1.

102. The question of what constituted the royal *dignitas* in Scotland was raised explicitly in the Great Cause in 1292; see, more broadly, the still important discussion in B. C. Keeney, 'The Medieval Idea of the State: The Great Cause, 1291–2', The University of Toronto Law Journal, 8 (1949), 48–71.

103. Calasso, *I glossatori*, 106–23; cf. Pennington, *Prince and the Law*, 97–98, 102–5. In the twelfth century, the word *princeps* could be used in a narrower sense by single authorities. The *Kanzlei* of the German king-emperors, for example, used it not only to denote the king-emperor, but also high-ranking nobles and *ministeriales*: see H. Koller, 'Die Bedeutung des Titels "princeps" in der Reichskanzlei unter den Saliern und Staufern', Mitteilungen des Instituts für österreichische Geschichtsforschung, 68 (1960), 63–80.

104. Pennington, *Prince and the Law*, 95–103.

105. Marinus, 'Prooemium', in Calasso, *I glossatori*, 199–200.

106. J. P. Canning, 'Law, Sovereignty and Corporation Theory, 1300–1450', in Burns, ed., *Cambridge History of Medieval Political Thought*, 454–76, at 464–9; G. Jostkleigrewe, '"Rex imperator in regno suo" – An Ideology of Frenchness? Late Medieval France, its Political Elite, and Juridical Discourse', in A. Pleszczyński, J. Sobiesiak, M. Tomaszek and P. Tyszka (eds.), Imagined Communities: Constructing Collective Identities in Medieval Europe (Leiden, 2018), 46–84.

107. Regiam, prologue.

108. Ibid., prologue: 'ut effrenatorum et indomitorum detera fortitudinis elidendo superbiam et humilium ac mansuetorum uirga equitatis que sceptrum dicitur moderando iusticiam'. The link between the sceptre and the 'staff of equity' was made explicitly by the compiler of *Regiam*; it is not present in *Glanvill*, prologue. For the reference in Marinus, see Marinus, 'Prooemium', in Calasso, *I glossatori*, 185. Marinus wrote of the sceptre: 'Licet ista duo ultima, scilicet sceptrum et malum, possint etiam in alia representatione accipi, videlicet quod rex in una

manu portat iustitiam et in alia gratiam sive misericordiam ... Vigor quidem iustitie representatus per sceptrum idest virgam, ut XLV. dist., c. Disciplina' (Marinus, 'Prooemium', in Calasso, *I glossatori*, 186).

109. Regiam, II, c. 39; noted also in Stein, 'Source of Romano-Canonical Part', 110.

110. What follows has learnt much from the approach and insights of Anaïs Waag in her doctoral thesis, 'Forms and Formalities in Thirteenth-Century Queenship: A Comparative Approach', unpublished PhD thesis, King's College London (2020); see, more generally, B. Grévin, 'Les mystères rhétoriques de l'état médiéval. L'écriture du pouvoir en Europe occidentale (XIIIe–XVe siècle)', Annales, 63 (2008), 271–300.

111. B. Grévin, Rhétorique du pouvoir médiéval: les lettres de Pierre de la Vigne et la formation du langage politique européen (XIIIe–XVe siècle) (Rome, 2008).

112. M. Carmago, Ars Dictaminis, Ars Dictandi (Turnhout, 1991); M. Carmago, 'What's the Brief? The Ars Dictaminis and Reading/Writing Between the Lines', Disputatio, 1 (1996), 1–18; and, most recently, F. Hartmann and B. Grévin, Ars Dictaminis: Handbuch der mittelalterlichen Briefstillehre (Stuttgart, 2019).

113. Waag, 'Forms and Formalities', chs. 1, 3.

114. London, The National Archives (henceforth, TNA), C47/22/9/15 (abbreviated copy of exchange between Edward I and Alexander III in 1277 over the border). Alexander III's letter is abbreviated, not containing the protocol or the eschatocol.

115. N. Reid, Alexander III, First Among Equals (Edinburgh, 2019), 246–68. The address reads: 'karissimo fratri suo Alexandro eadem gratia Regi Scot fideli suo salutem et sincere dilectionis semper augmentum'.

116. 'Nor is it our intention, nor will it be, by God's grace, in the future, to do anything which might or should offend (*ledere*) the extent (*culmen*) of your majesty'; TNA, SC1/20/150; body transcribed in TNA, C47/22/9/15; printed *Regesta Regum Scotorum Volume 4, Part 1: The Acts of Alexander III (1249–86)*, eds. C. J. Neville and G. G. Simpson (Edinburgh, 2013) (henceforth *RRS*, IV.1), no. 106.

117. Edward I and the Throne of Scotland, 1290–1296: An Edition of Sources for the Great Cause, eds. E. L. G. Stones and G. G. Simpson, 2 vols. (Oxford, 1978), vol. II, *passim*.

118. The only reference I have found to the Scottish king's *regia maiestas* is in a letter of the deans of Carrick and Cunningham, and the 'master of the schools at Ayr' to Alexander II in the early 1230s (before 25 April 1235) which refer to his *regia maiestas*; *Registrum Monasterii de Passelet: Cartas, Privilegias, Conventiones*, ed. C. N. Innes (Edinburgh, 1832), 169–70, commented on in Taylor, *Shape of the State*, 338. Clement III wrote to Henry II in January 1188, asking him to command

King William the Lion to accept the election of John the Scot as bishop of St Andrews, stating that John was prepared to be 'obedient and faithful to the royal majesty'; the bull was copied into Roger of Howden's *Gesta*, for which see *Gesta Regis Henrici Secundi Benedicti Abbatis*, ed. W. Stubbs, 2 vols. (London, 1866–7), vol. II, 57.

119. *Vetera Monumenta Poloniae et Lithuaniae Gentiumque Finitimarum Historiam illustrantia, vol. I: 1217–1409*, ed. A. Theiner (Rome, 1860), no. CCXXVI, 146–8, at 147.

120. It is of interest that, in his still-thought-provoking *Principles of Politics and Government* (intended for a popular audience), published in 1961, Walter Ullmann distinguished two 'types' of kingship which prevailed in the central/ late Middle Ages: 'feudal kingship', as typologised in the example of England, and 'theocratic kingship', typologised through the example of France. Ullmann presented these two types as, essentially, incompatible; the example of Scotland provides an interesting example of competing discourses within the same polity (at 211: 'the constitutional development depended, in short, on whether the theocratic or the feudal functions of kingship predominated').

121. *RRS*, IV.1, no. 61; *Regiam*, cc. 1, 134, 141. The only pre-1310 reference seems to be the news reported to the English king on 20 August 1299 and surviving in an enrolled chancery copy, which referred to William Wallace leaving Scotland 'without the leave or approval of the guardians' (translation in Barrow, *Robert Bruce*, 140–1, referring to TNA, C47/22/8 (the words are in fact 'qe treson ov maeste fu purparle'). The Scottish King's Household mentions treason, but this might well date to the 1310s as well. See David Carpenter, '"The Scottish King's Household" and English Ideas of Constitutional Reform', *The Breaking of Britain: Cross Border Society and Scottish Independence, 1216–1314*, Feature of the Month, October 2011, available at www.breakingofbritain.ac.uk/blogs/feature-of-the-month/october-2011-the-scottish-kings-household/index.html. Even Robert I's 1314 legislation refers to *inimici regis et regni* rather than referring to the crime of offending the king's *maiestas* (*RPS*, 1314/1, editing Edinburgh, National Records of Scotland, SP13/6).

122. *Regiam*, prologue; *Glanvill*, prologue, transcribed above, notes 92–93.

123. *Regesta Regum Scotorum Volume 5: The Acts of Robert I, 1306–29*, ed. A. A. M. Duncan (Edinburgh, 1988) (henceforth *RRS*, V), no. 13: 'quia Johannes de Polloc contra fidem et fidelitatem nostram extitit et existit inimicis nostris adherendo et in lesione nostre regie magestatis totis viribus notorie machinando'; ibid., no. 140, remits the royal rancour against Henry, bishop of Aberdeen, and regrants him the temporalities of his episcopacy 'sub pena nostre plenarie forisfacture et offensionis nostre regis magestatis'. This was probably issued at the

parliament held at Scone 3–5 December 1318, which issued an important piece of legislation that in part dealt with questions of political loyalty and unity, yet *in that legislation* did not invoke the concept of *maiestas* (*RPS*, 1318; also *RRS*, V, no. 139), even though they mentioned royal majesty in the 1318 entail. See also *RRS*, V, nos. 416, 559; see *Scottish Formularies*, ed. A. A. M. Duncan (Stair Society, 58; Edinburgh, 2011), E55 (78) B37 (135).

124. *RRS*, V, no. 66 (NRS, Great Seal Register C2/2, no. 9, inspection by James I, 12 October 1424, also copied in a notarial instrument in 1413 in Kinloss's archive). For the dating, see *RRS*, V, 351.

125. *CD*, c. 32, in Taylor, ed., *Laws of Medieval Scotland*, 518–19.

126. See the most recent treatment in Penman, *Robert the Bruce*, 219–27.

127. *RPS*, 1318/30

128. Penman, *Robert the Bruce*, 221–7.

129. A. Beam, The Balliol Dynasty, 1210–1364 (Edinburgh, 2008), 223–34; M. Hammond, 'Scotland's Forgotten King', *The Community of the Realm in Scotland, 1249–1424: History, Law and Charters in a Recreated Kingdom*, available at https://cotr.ac.uk/blog/scotlands-forgotten-king/.

130. *Gesta annalia* II, in Joannis de Fordun Chronica Gentis Scotorum, ed. W. F. Skene (Edinburgh, 1871), 348–9; *Scotichronicon by Walter Bower*, gen. ed. D. E. R. Watt, 9 vols. (Aberdeen and Edinburgh, 1989–98), vol. VII, 2–3.

131. Barrow, *Robert Bruce*, 177–9, 209–10.

132. *Gesta annalia* II, in *Fordun*, ed. Skene, 348–9; Penman, *Robert the Bruce*, 221–6. This is not to say that horrific killings had not been part of the political landscape in Scotland, but the framing of them as formal punishments for treason was new.

133. *Regiam*, cc. 1–3 and, for rape, 140; cf. *Glanvill*, XIV, 6.

134. See, in general, Taylor, *Shape of the State*, 157–64, 334–43, 445–55.

135. *Regiam*, c. 18. This also affects how we understand the conceptualisation of major jurisdictions as regalities; see A. Grant, 'Franchises North of the Border: Baronies and Regalities in Medieval Scotland', in Liberties and Identities in Medieval Britain and Ireland, ed. M. Prestwich (Woodbridge, 2008), 155–99.

136. Most powerfully in Barrow, *Robert Bruce*, although in a more ambiguous way than is often stressed.

137. Barrow, *Robert Bruce*; see also M. Penman, '"The King Wishes and Commands?" Reassessing Political Assembly in Scotland, c. 1286–1329', in M. Damen, J. Haemers and A. Mann (eds.), Political Representation: Communities, Ideas and Institutions in Europe, c. 1200–c. 1690 (Leiden, 2018), 123–41.

138. Traditionally, this is thought to have manifested most clearly in the Declaration of Arbroath of 1320 (NRS, SP13/7), described as 'the most eloquent statement of regnal solidarity to come out of the middle ages'; S. Reynolds, Kingdoms and Communities in Western Europe, 900–1300 (Oxford, 1987), ch. 8 (250–331, at 274–6 for the Declaration).

139. *Regiam*, prologue; cf. *Glanvill*, prologue. *Regiam* does, however, miss out *Glanvill*'s injunctions that the king be guided by the laws and customs which are reasonable and long-standing, by those in his kingdom most learned in law, and *Glanvill*'s reference to what pleases the prince has the force of law (*Digests* 1.4.1; *Institutes*, 1.2.6). It is interesting that *Regiam* did not include the maxim *quod principi placuit legis habet uigorem*, but this might be because it was so embedded in a passage in *Glanvill* stressing the opposite (that princely authority was constrained by council). It may be that, had *Regiam* been completed, a stronger sense of the relationship between the Scottish prince to its law might have come through.

140. *Regiam*, c. 148. This was originally an oath sworn in 1197 to keep the peace. It first survives as *Leges Scocie*, c. 15, and was then incorporated and updated in *CD*, c. 27 (which may well post-date *Regiam*). The emphasis on *communitas regni* does not appear in this version of this chapter, although *CD* stresses its enactment 'de consensu magnatum'. The version in *Regiam* preserves (bar the reference to the community) more of the readings of the *Leges Scocie*-version than the *CD*-version. For the *Lege Scocie*, *CD*, and *Leges Willelmi* versions, see Taylor, ed., *Laws of Medieval Scotland*, 418–19, 512–15, 554–7.

141. For the laws of Malcolm Mackenneth and *Ordo justiciarie*, see A. A. M. Duncan, 'The "Laws of Malcolm MacKenneth"', in A. Grant and K. J. Stringer (eds.), Medieval Scotland: Crown, Lordship and Community – Essays Presented to G. W. S. Barrow (Edinburgh, 1993), 239–73; for the compilations attributed to William and Alexander, see Taylor, ed., *Laws of Medieval Scotland*, 351–6; see further A. Taylor, 'The Laws of the Realm in Fourteenth-Century Scotland', in S. Boardman (ed.), *The Community of the Realm in Scotland, 1249–1424: History, Law and Charters in a Recreated Kingdom* (forthcoming).

142. For Robert Wishart, see A. A. M. Duncan, 'Wishart, Robert (c. 1240–1316)', in Oxford Dictionary of National Biography (Oxford, 2004), available at www.oxforddnb.com/view/10.1093/ref:odnb/9780198614128.001.0001/odnb-9780198614128-e-29797?rskey=1Ig5WE&result=13; D. E. R. Watt, A Biographical Dictionary of Scottish Graduates to A.D. 1410 (Oxford, 1977), 585–90. Robert Wishart, who had also attended the Second Council of Lyon in 1274, was the first of Robert Bruce the Competitor's auditors in 1291 (Stones and Simpson (eds.), *Great Cause*, vol. II, 82). For some early documents drawn up for the

Abbey of Paisley, which are soaked in Roman law, but with the figure of the newly elected bishop looming large in the background, see *Registrum monasterii de Passelet*, ed. Innes, 180–3, 183–9, 192–5, 195–7 (note repeated pagination in this volume). Bishop Robert still witnessed two of Robert I's charters on 1 May 1315 after his release (*RRS*, V, nos. 64–5); for more of his activity, see Watt, *Graduates*, 590.

143. Watt, *Graduates*, 589–90 (where it is recorded that he was back in London by 24 March 1312 or 1313). Robert was present at the 1314 parliament at Cambuskenneth, where the 'enemies of the king and kingdom' were deprived of their lands; *RPS*, 1314/1.

144. Lord Stair, *Institutions of the Laws of Scotland*, ed. D. M. Walker, 2 vols. (Edinburgh and Glasgow, 1981), vol. I, book I, 16 (pp. 88–89).

03 JAMES VI AND I, REX ET IUDEX: ONE KING AS JUDGE IN TWO KINGDOMS

Four centuries ago, James I, the ruler of England, presided over a legal proceeding in the Star Chamber. This was the final instance in which a monarch of England or Scotland would publicly judge his subjects, marking the last time he would do so.[1] The son gained prominence for his practice of subjecting his subjects to pass judgment on him. James's endeavors to meddle in the proceedings of his judges have been a recurring feature of constitutional history and have been thoroughly examined.[2] However, James's own judicial endeavors have been disregarded. Interestingly, James VI and I served as both James VI of Scotland and James I of England, which aligns well with the theme of this volume. Despite his strong desire to become the ruler of the unified kingdom of Great Britain, his two realms remained distinctly separate.[3] James I of England was a monarch who was transplanted from another place, which allows for a comparison between two separate locations. Although comparative law primarily examines the transfer of legal principles, the migration of individuals can also hold considerable importance. Although the concept of law holds significance, its practical implementation is currently limited to individuals. The legislation can undergo changes in practice as individuals relocate. For anyone with a greater interest in political history, examining James's judicial actions in Scotland and England also contributes to a substantial debate around James in a broader sense. According to Jenny Wormald, should James VI and I be regarded as two monarchs, one representing Scotland and the other representing England, or as a single monarch?[4] An further form of comparison that can be conducted for James pertains to the juxtaposition of theory and practice. James was unabashed in expressing his ideas regarding kingship, as well as any other subject matter. By analyzing James's writings and speeches, we can gain insight into his perspectives on the king's function as a judge. Although James was not a frequent judge, he did exercise his judgment. By examining his judicial activity, we can draw comparisons between theory and practice, or alternatively, observe the interplay between theory and practice. This paper aims to present an argument that James regarded judging as a significant component of monarchy, both in a broader sense and specifically within the context of his own reign. In addition, James recognized that rendering judgment was a means via which he could not only assume the role of a king, but also effectively rule the nation - royal judgment was an integral component of royal governance. [5]

Before considering the cases in which James judged, an important concern is quite what is meant by James being a judge. This is trickier than we might think or want. First, in both Scotland and England, much was done in the name of the king, and technically was in fact done by the king. But it was not done by James. [6] This poses problems, especially when James appears to have been present when judicial activity took place, such as attending the Scottish Parliament and the Scottish Privy Council. [7] The approach taken here is to ignore such judicial activity unless sources show James's personal involvement as judge.

A second problem relates to identifying what is meant by judging. Several institutions in England and Scotland had a mixture of judicial and other functions. For example, in the prosecution of Nicholas Dalgleish in 1584, Dalgleish tried to argue that he should not be prosecuted before the Justiciary Court in Edinburgh because he had already been tried and convicted in the Privy Council the day before. For Dalgleish, these Privy Council proceedings were judicial. But the Council informed the court that the hearings were in fact *pro consilij*, rather than judicial. There would therefore be no principled objection to trying Dalgleish. [8] This is a particular issue in relation to James's 'Speach' in the Star Chamber in 1616, which will be considered below. [9]

Less formal situations are particularly challenging. James's conference with the English judges concerning the jurisdiction of the church courts could appear more like a discussion than James seeking to give judgment. [10] But the judges of England frequently held informal conferences in the Exchequer Chamber, and these conferences did determine the law and resolved individual cases. [11] Such informal discussions therefore look more like judicial activity in the context of the early-modern English legal system. It is this context which explains why Edward Coke could criticise James in these informal activities for seeking to be a judge. Furthermore, proceedings which appear to have begun judicially might be ended in a less formal way. For example, in one of David Black's appearances before the Scottish Privy Council, Black 'declynned the king's judicatorie', suggesting he perceived the case to be judicial. But the case ended with James and Black in 'privat and homelie' conference, to James's satisfaction. [12]

Similar problems of informality arise in relation to James's frequent involvement in resolving disputes. For example, James acted to bring feuds to an end in Scotland, but we should see this kind of activity as more like mediation or arbitration, rather than judging. [13] James also personally acted as an arbitrator in

England. [14] Contemporaries were aware of the distinction between arbitration and personal royal judgment, sometimes preferring the latter. For example, the earl of Exeter asked James to intervene 'as to a judge and a just judge, and not as an arbitrator'. [15]

A third exclusion relates to James's interventions in legal process. Aside from occasional direct intervention to obtain a desired outcome,[16] James often intervened in ongoing cases to expedite or delay proceedings. He is most well known for delaying cases in England, in the Case of Commendams and De Non Procedendo Rege Inconsulto.[17] But delays were also ordered in Scotland.[18] One case was even delayed so James could be present as a judge, although there is no record of him in fact sitting.[19] Records of English petitions to James contain several examples of orders for cases to be delayed [20] and others that it be expedited, for example by ordering a 'speadie Tryall'. [21] While these were doubtless important interventions in legal process by the king, there is no evidence of James determining the outcome of the cases, so these are not treated as part of James's judicial activities.

JAMES VI AND I RENDERED JUDGMENTS IN VARIOUS CASES.

The focus of this paper is on the best-evidenced examples of James's judicial activities, all of which are in some sense exceptional. However, another important consideration is the evidence of James's participation in the regular administration of justice, activity for which the evidence is more sparse.

James was involved in the regular administration of justice in Scotland. There are references to him attending criminal courts in 1589 [22] and 1590, [23] and to a court being delayed to enable James to attend in 1598, although there is no evidence that he did in fact subsequently sit. [24] What is less clear is whether James judged in these cases or merely attended, as he seemingly regularly did in the Court of Session. [25] In 1601, in a different court, it appears James was judging, at least to the extent of giving sentence. In that year, an English agent wrote to London saying that James VI 'is become a great "justicer" having executed a Douglas, a Maxwell, a Johnstone and 2 other gentlemen for stealing and coining'. [26]

James also attended the Scottish Privy Council, a body which undertook a wide range of judicial activities. He is recorded as having been present when cases were resolved, [27] as well as for interlocutory [28] and jurisdictional matters. [29] James's personal involvement in such cases cannot be shown. However, in *Basilicon Doron* James gave advice about sitting judicially in the Privy Council, suggesting that he did participate. [30] Scotland had a tradition of direct royal involvement in the administration of justice, especially criminal justice. All of James's sixteenth-century predecessors, and his regents, had done so, and this activity was seen as something a good king should do. [31]

The English situation was quite different. There is no evidence of James's direct judicial involvement in the regular dispensation of justice, but merely a handful of unusual cases. These better-evidenced examples of royal justice from Scotland and England are the focus of the rest of this paper.

The first group of cases concerned judicial activity in the Scottish Privy Council. The Privy Council had a wide jurisdiction, but James's personal involvement is clearly identified in cases about seditious or treasonous speech, in particular seditious sermons. [32] The first example is from December 1585, as James Gibson was brought before the Council. Gibson identified James VI as a judge in the case. [33] Gibson took the Council through his sermon step by step, with James personally commenting on the acceptability of Gibson's reasoning. Every step in the process of scriptural exegesis was accepted until the very last. Gibson concluded that a king 'mainteaning wicked acts against God, sould be rooted out'. James did not accept that a king could be deposed and highlighted this as Gibson's error. Gibson was imprisoned in Edinburgh Castle at his own expense.

As noted above, David Black also appeared in front of the Council. His first appearance, in August 1595, ended with an informal conference. [34] Black was back before the Council in November 1596, for preaching allegations that included lying by James VI, the Privy Council being atheists, insults to Elizabeth I of England and encouraging armed disobedience. [35] Black declined the Council's jurisdiction on the basis that the content of sermons was first a matter for the Kirk, being a question of doctrine. [36] That challenge was rejected by the king personally, as the case was 'altogidder civile and not spiritual'. [37] After subsequent discussion, the Privy Council as a whole, including James, found themselves competent judges in the case. [38] So far it is not clear that James personally acted as a judge. But once Black was found guilty by the Privy Council as a whole, the Council then ordered that Black's sentence be reserved to James's will alone. [39] No sentence is recorded in the Privy Council records, but James prohibited Black from returning to his post at St Andrews. [40]

On his return to Scotland in the summer of 1617, James VI again sat as a judge, not in the Privy Council, but in the Scottish High Commission at St Andrews, trying ministers who objected to the introduction of certain ceremonies into the Kirk. Two ministers were imprisoned and one exiled. These were not cases concerned with seditious ministers, as in the Privy Council. However, from James's perspective the case was still a political one, as the ministers disagreed with James's exercise of his royal power in relation to matters indifferent and refused to obey what were (to James) legitimate and lawful instructions. James's actions are recorded by David Calderwood, in this instance one of the accused (and convicted) with whom James disputed. [41] James's judicial action was also reported as news in London. [42]

Beyond the ecclesiastical context, James VI acted as a judge in one case in the North Berwick Witch Trials, a set of witchcraft cases in the early-1590s, printed reports of which informed *Macbeth.* [43] The particular case in which James became involved concerned the prosecution of Barbara Napier. She, like others in the trials, had been charged with seeking to cause the death of the king by witchcraft, raising storms while he was travelling by sea and melting his effigy in wax. This was alleged to have been at the suit of the earl of Bothwell, lending the cases a political dimension. Various other 'sorceries, witchcrafts, and consulting with witches' by Napier were also alleged. [44] Unlike other defendants in the various trials, Napier was convicted of consulting with witches, but acquitted of the most serious charges. As the English agent in Scotland noted '[t]his is not fallen out as was looked for'. [45]

What followed was unusual. In June 1591 the assize (jury) were prosecuted for error under a legal, but little-used, procedure. [46] James arrived in court to sit in judgment, at which point the defendants submitted to the King's will. James declared his will, which was described as being 'in Judgement'. James here acted as the sentencing authority in the case, deciding in fact to permit the assize members to leave without any further penalty. [47]

In England, James acted as a judge in the well-known attempt to resolve questions of jurisdiction between the common-law and church courts. [48] In 1608 and 1609 there were several conferences involving the common-law judges, ecclesiastical judges and bishops, all presided over by James, with the intention of resolving various outstanding issues. The conferences ultimately ended in acrimony with no resolution to the various controversies.

Although the accounts of the conferences vary considerably, James does seem to have thought that he was acting judicially. [49] According to one manuscript, James began by asserting his judicial authority, claiming that the King is 'the supreme judge' and 'may if he please, sit and judge in Westminster Hall in any Court there'. [50] Edward Coke, in his account, apparently engaged with and rejected the idea that the king could judge, corroborating the idea present in other accounts, that James asserted his judicial authority in the conferences. [51] After Coke's rejection of his judicial authority, James's remaining judicial activity all occurred in the Star Chamber, despite Coke's explicit denial of James's power to sit as a judge in that court. He began to sit in 1616, with his final case in 1619. [52] There were three occasions on which James appeared as a judge.

In the middle of the second decade of the seventeenth century, a conflict between the common-law courts and the Chancery (or perhaps between the chief justice of the King's Bench and the lord chancellor) became overt and awkward. The long-running issues and specific challenges have been discussed in considerable detail by historians. [53] What is usually passed over quickly is James's formal attempt to end the dispute in favour of the Chancery. James appeared in the Star Chamber for the first time in his reign, and delivered a lengthy speech which was subsequently printed in James's *Workes.* [54]

It is easy to see this speech as judicial activity by James, as he sought to do precisely what he had also tried to achieve in relation to the church courts: determine the jurisdictional relationship between two of his courts, in effect ruling on the law. However, James made clear in the 'Speach' that he was acting 'not judicially, but declaratorily', a point which he repeated on a later occasion in the Star Chamber. [55] Nonetheless, despite this statement, a considerable portion of James's 'Speach' is directed to the issue of kings judging. [56] James also referred to himself sitting in the 'seat of Judgement', [57] and observed to the regular judges that 'you are Judges *with mee* when you sit here' (emphasis added). [58] There is at the least an ambiguity here. James presented himself in the Star Chamber as a judge, even if in some sense he did not consider his activity to be truly judicial. For the purposes of this paper, the 'Speach' will therefore be treated as an example of James's judicial activity, although its judicial status is more ambiguous than the other cases discussed in the paper.

James next sat as a judge in February 1617, in the prosecution of *Christmas and Bellingham.* The defendants were two young men who had arranged a duel between themselves and attempted to leave the country to fight. They were stopped at Dover and prosecuted in the Star Chamber. The defendants had confessed, and so James's only role was to give sentence. James's speech, summarising short reports found in letters, is briefly reported in the *Calendar of State Papers.* [59] A much fuller version of James's speech exists, which appears to have been taken down (and probably circulated) by a witness to it, running to almost five-and-a-half-thousand words, but has been overlooked by historians. [60] That report of the speech correlates with the versions in the State Papers, but provides much more detail and enables a fuller consideration of James's own views.

The final case which James judged was in many respects the most difficult. Whereas in other cases James was resolving points of law or sentencing guilty defendants, in the collection of cases concerning Sir Thomas Lake, neither side was willing to admit anything. For the first time in England, James was involved in determining liability, as well as the consequences of it.

The case concerned important families, unhappy in their own particular, and particularly peculiar, way. On one side stood the Lake family, the head of which was Sir Thomas Lake, one of the king's secretaries and a privy councillor. On the other side was the earl of Exeter, his second wife, and his descendants by his first wife. Sir Thomas Lake's daughter had married the grandson of the earl of Exeter,

Lord Roos. The marriage was not happy, and the couple were soon living apart. As a consequence, Lady Roos wished to be given property for her maintenance, in particular the manor of Walthamstow. The earl of Exeter refused to relinquish his rights in the manor and the case escalated from there. To quote from Alastair Bellany's excellent summary, '[e]arly in the affair it was rumoured that [Lord] Roos had been coerced into surrendering property to the Lakes under threat of nullity proceedings that would expose his sexual impotence. Later, the Lakes alleged that the youthful countess of Exeter had had an incestuous relationship with her step-grandson', that very same Lord Roos. [61] We should doubtless ignore the seeming incompatibility of those two allegations. The case continued, with allegations that the countess of Exeter had plotted to have Lady Roos poisoned. Both sides sued the other. [62] Gossip about the case widened the range of allegations. By the time sentence was to be carried out, John Chamberlain wrote that the behaviour of Lady Roos 'by report was so filthy as is not to be named and that incest which they wold have imposed upon others returnes on theyre owne heads, betwixt her brother Sir Arthur'. [63]

The allegations were sufficiently complex that one commentator wrote that 'if all the examinations that belong to it should be read, I thincke all the Starchamber dayes of the Terme would be to fewe. The books on both sides contayne 19,000 sheets.' [64] Ultimately the case took five days in the Star Chamber, during which James sat 'in a chair of state elevated above the table about which his lords sat'. [65] The case clearly aroused great public interest, as might be expected for a case concerning 'so fowle scandalls of precontracts, adulterie, incest, murther, poison and such like peccadillos'. [66] A letter in late 1618 reported that the case was to be heard 'at the great banqueting house', presumably because the usual Star Chamber would have been too small to accommodate the expected audience. [67] Contemporary letters refer to the case frequently. [68] Ultimately the Lakes were found to have defamed members of the Exeter family. They were also found to have suborned false testimony, importantly by Lake's abuse of his official position.

JAMES AND THE KING IN THE ROLE OF JUDGES

James's idea of kingship, at least in the idealised form he presented in his writings, was principally described in biblical terms. [69] It hardly requires the wisdom of Solomon to find examples of biblical kings judging; indeed according to the Old Testament, the Israelites asked for a king expressly 'to judge us'. [70] From a biblical perspective, judging was at the core of kingship. References to biblical kings are frequent in James's political writings, especially references to Solomon and David. [71] Both appear in James's most abstract discussion of kingship, *The Trew Law of Free Monarchies*, referring to kings ministering judgment and deciding controversies between subjects. [72] In his *Basilicon Doron*, supposedly written as advice for Prince

Henry, James referred again to the king doing justice. Indeed, he explained that 'the most part of a Kings office, standeth in deciding that question of *Meum* and *Tuum*, among his subiects; so remember when ye sit in iudgement, that the Throne ye sit on is Gods'. [73] That reference to the throne echoes the paragraph in the *Trew Law* where James discussed the judicial role of a king.

The biblical idea of the king as judge was a constant in James's judicial activity. We have quite detailed records of James's speeches in the prosecution of the Napier assize and then James's various appearances in the Star Chamber. In all of them James legitimised his activity by scriptural references. In the prosecution of the Napier assize, James stated that 'God hath made me a King and judge to judge righteouse judgmente', and noted that he was doing what 'solomon teacheth'. [74] James began his 1616 'Speach' in the Star Chamber by referring to Psalm 72, 'Give the king thy judgments, O God', a psalm which continues, 'He shall judge thy people with righteousness', perhaps the influence for the language of 'righteouse judgmente' in the earlier Scottish case. [75] When sentencing *Christmas and Bellingham*, James approved a reference to Psalm 101 by the chancellor of the Exchequer, that 'Mercie and Judgment belonge to the kinge'. [76] Finally, in the Lake family litigation, 'The King made a speech in the Court of Star Chamber, comparing himself to Solomon, called to decide between two women.' [77] In that case, James also compared the defendants to Adam and Eve, implying that he was dispensing God's judgment. [78] Given the general cultural importance of the Bible in early-modern Britain, it is not surprising that these biblical ideas were mentioned by others too. In relation to the Lake litigation, the Marquess Hamilton was reported as saying 'that the King had need be another Salomon to judge between the harlots'. [79]

One other possible influence on James's views on judging might be the *République* of Jean Bodin, a copy of which was in James's library, probably from late 1577. [80] James's 1616 'Speach' in the Star Chamber did make use of a peculiarly Bodinian metaphor, like many other writers on the relationship between law and equity in England from around 1580 onwards. [81] Whether further influence can be identified is more difficult. Bodin discussed the possibility and desirability of kings judging in book four, chapters six and seven, of the *République*, acknowledging the possibility, but advising strongly against doing so, a conclusion which James rejected. [82] Nonetheless, as will be seen below, some of James's views about the king as judge seem to echo material found in Bodin. [83]

James's view that it was possible for a king to judge, and that it was part of the royal role, was not unique to him. Most obviously, James's use of biblical sources in relation to his judicial activities would have been both obvious and legitimate to his contemporaries. As Patrick Collinson notes, early-modern minds were 'saturated in scripture', [84] while Kevin Killeen has stressed that the biblical kings to whom

James referred 'constitute a major lexicon of early modern political thought'. [85] Related to scripture, sermons in both England and Scotland referred to the king as a judge. In a 1592 Scottish sermon, Robert Bruce complained 'that the king himself went not about in person to execute justice yeerelie, as Samuell did', drawing on a biblical example of a royal judge. [86] When James was involved in the decision to have the Catholic Boynton executed in 1601, 'Mr. Patrik Galloway commended and encouraged the King in his sermon for the justice done of Boynton, showing him how much it had won the people's hearts.' [87] In England, one of John Donne's sermons, preached at court in 1630, refers to the king as a judge. [88]

The idea of good kings as dispensing justice personally has been noted as a feature of sixteenth-century Scots kingship. [89] While the king as judge was less prominent in English thought, the idea was present. Both Archbishop Bancroft and Lord Chancellor Ellesmere apparently did consider James to have judicial power. [90] On his initial progress from Edinburgh to London, James ordered the immediate execution of a cutpurse in Newark. This was criticised by some contemporaries, but these criticisms were directed to the absence of trial, rather than the king's personal involvement. [91] William Hudson's mention of James's judicial role in the Star Chamber was not critical of James's activities. [92]

The ruler as judge is also visible in literary sources. The plot of *Measure for Measure* (a play performed at James's court in 1604) hinges on the judicial role of the ruler. [93] Philip Sidney's extremely popular prose work, *Arcadia*, features a duke who personally dispenses judgment from 'the throne of judgement seat'. [94] The 'protector' who temporarily takes the place of the duke similarly sits as a judge to 'see the past evils duly punished, and your weal hereafter established', suggesting that the personal dispensation of justice was there seen as part of ensuring the well-being of the state, similar to James's own views. [95]

Within the common-law tradition, Coke's remarks rejecting a judicial role for James have usually been taken as representative. [96] In fact the position was more complex. In the fifteenth century, John Fortescue wrote that 'none of the kings of England is seen to give judgement by his own lips', [97] while in 1557 William Staunford barred the king from judging in cases of treason or felony due to his partiality. [98] However, in 1505 Robert Brudenell was reported as calling the king the 'chief justice' of the realm. [99] This remark was used in James Morice's 1578 reading to justify a broader claim, that the king is 'the supreame Judg of the Realme, who only ought of his princely power and authoritie to preserve the Common peace, and Judge or cause to the Judged according to the Law all causes suites and Controversies whatsoever'. [100]

The king as judge was not unthinkable in early-modern England. However, there was no tradition of judicial activity by the king in England. James sought to provide a precedent for his appearance in the Star Chamber in 1616, observing that his predecessors, especially Henry VII, had done just that. [101] However, Henry VII's successors did not sit in the court, and James never became a regular participant there. Furthermore, personal royal justice was not so central to, or expected of, good kingship. In his funeral sermon for James, Bishop Williams highlighted 'the Actions of Iustice in this King'. [102] Nowhere in Williams's discussion of James's contributions to justice is there any mention of James himself acting as a judge. While Williams saw much to praise in relation to James and justice, James's own judicial activity was not so significant. [103]

WHEN SHOULD THE MONARCH MAKE A DECISION?

James's thought went beyond the simple idea that kings were judges, with a set of ideas about why kings should judge certain cases and not others. These ideas appear in his judicial remarks and so mostly have not featured in the usual corpus of James's works, leading to them being overlooked. [104]

While James stressed his power to judge, underpinned by scriptural authority, his judicial remarks also identify restrictions on doing so. In the prosecution of the Napier jury, James explained that '[u]pon crymes touching mens lyves – as adultery, murder, theft, rebellion – yf the prince should sit in person it might be a note of rigour. And therefore it is forbidden in the civil lawe.' [105] James here suggests, very unusually, that he could be controlled by law and barred from sitting as a judge in some cases. [106] Nevertheless, even if James believed that in 1591, he did not accept the position later. By 1601 he was apparently sitting in capital cases. [107]

In England, James never accepted any legal constraints on his power to judge. Nonetheless, in both his 1616 'Speach' and *Christmas and Bellingham*, James acknowledged that there were situations in which he ought not judge. In Scotland James referred to a normative limit on his judicial role. In England, his limits were more pragmatic.

The first of James's apparently self-imposed limitations was based on expertise. In his 1616 'Speach', James explained that he decided at the start of his reign that he would not act as a judge immediately; instead 'I resolued therefore with *Pythagoras* to keepe silence seuen yeeres, and learne my selfe the Lawes of the Kingdome.' [108] In 1616 James was willing to claim that he had sufficient expertise to judge, referring to himself as 'hauing passed a double apprentiship of twice seuen yeeres'. [109] This was probably a deliberate reaction, and provocation, to Edward Coke, just as the 'Speach' itself determined the relationship between the common-law courts and the Chancery in favour of the Chancery and against Coke's position.

In 1609 Coke had apparently told James that he could not judge as he lacked expertise; in 1616 James accepted the principle, although importantly as a self-imposed limitation, rather than one imposed upon him. However, James denied its practical application. [110] This discussion of expertise should also be related to James's remark, two weeks before the 'Speach', in the 1616 *Case of Commendams* (in which he did not judge), where James observed that 'although wee never studied the common lawe of Englaunde, yet are wee not ignoraunt of anie pointes which belonnge to a kinge to knowe'. [111] In 1616 James was clearly asserting an expertise to judge. James did not base this claim to expertise on detailed knowledge of English law, but rather his expertise as king, a view which would conform with the influence of Bodin on his 'Speach'. [112] Bodin viewed the relationship between law and equity as being a matter exclusively for the prince as 'that greatly concerned the rights of soveraigntie'. [113] The issue of expertise never reappeared in James's judicial activity. Once James had asserted himself over Coke by both demonstrating that in suitable cases the king could judge, and by dismissing Coke from office, perhaps there was no need to engage with the expertise issue.

Other limitations on James's judicial activity appear more frequently, both in the 'Speach' and *Christmas and Bellingham*. Their repetition suggests that these were more important for James. For example, one reason that James thought he ought not judge was partiality. For James this had two meanings. The first was that James was judging in a cause affecting his own interests, whether his 'Prerogative or profit'. [114] The second meaning was that James as judge might favour one party or another. [115] In *Christmas and Bellingham* James suggested that he ought not judge in a case concerning jurisdiction 'because in that I might bethought to carry some parcial inclinacion', showing that James's real concern was appearances, rather than normative objections to the king's partiality. [116] This concern with the appearance of partiality was also present in his speech in the prosecution of the Napier assize: 'And I would not that any of you should thinke that I prosecuted this in respect of myne owne particuler, for God is my judge I did it not.' [117]

This limitation on James's actions was pragmatic, based on the possible interpretation of James's judicial activity by others, rather than the substance of James's actions. James does not explain in his speeches why this appearance of partiality would be so problematic, but when he discusses the issue in the 1616 'Speach', there may be influence from Bodin. According to Bodin, when ending disputes, 'the prince above all things must beware that hee show not himselfe more affected unto the one part than to the other: which hath bene the cause of the ruine and overthrow of many princes and estates'. [118] Partiality here is not a substantive vice. But showing oneself to be partial is to be avoided, just like James's concern in his speeches.

James's final restriction on royal judgment was that the case was deserving of royal attention. As he observed in his 1616 'Speach', 'a meane cause was not worthy of mee'. [119] The same concern appears again in *Christmas and Bellingham.* James thought he should not sit in a case concerning 'to private a nature', nor would he sit in a case concerning 'people of so base Rancke'. [120] The same concern also appears in Bodin's advice on judging by a prince: a prince should only be involved in 'causes such as may seeme worthy the princes hearing and iudgement', [121] although Bodin does not explain what determines such worthiness.

James's restrictions did not clearly identify any particular cases in which he should judge. For several of these cases, James's intervention can be explained as politically expedient. David Black's prosecution occurred in the context of a 'wrestling match' between the king and Kirk. [122] Barbara Napier's prosecution was linked to alleged treason by the earl of Bothwell. Napier was alleged to have been part of a conspiracy which sought James's death and the death of his new wife. The witch trials were treason trials, concerned with the protection of the king's body. The link with the earl of Bothwell, who would have been a possible claimant to the throne on James's untimely childless death, only exacerbated this. [123] The acquittal of Napier challenged this narrative, so a conviction of the assize for acquitting in error helped to restore the credibility of the government's position. In England, while the individual defendants were of no particular significance, the prosecution of Christmas and Bellingham was part of a wider campaign against duelling. The case concerning Thomas Lake risked causing reputational damage to the Jacobean court, especially in the context of the Spanish Match. [124]

However, such political explanations are not sufficient. Other politically important cases did not lead to James sitting as a judge. As Julian Goodare has observed for Scotland, James not sitting as a judge 'did not limit him' because 'he appointed the judges' and the same held true for much of his reign in England. [125] James was able to resolve the Overbury scandal at his English court through an investigation and then prosecution by the regular judges. [126] In *Christmas and Bellingham*, James even highlighted that he had not sat in two other cases concerning duelling. [127] In his speeches, James identified a set of ideas which explain many of his interventions as a judge.

One recurring principle was that of performing the office of a king, linked to the scriptural examples of biblical kings who judged. In the Napier assize prosecution, James attributed the acquittal of Napier in that case to partiality on the part of the assize, which he identified as a particular problem in Scotland:

> all men set themselves more for freendes then for justice and obedience to the lawe ... And let a man commyt the most filthie crymes that can be, yet his freendes take his parte, and first keepe him from apprehencion, and after by feade or favour, by false assisse or some waie or other, they fynde moyne of his escape from punishmente. [128]

JAMES THEREFORE EXPLAINED THAT HE CAME TO JUDGE THE ASSIZE OF ERROR

Sithence the common assisses which are heere gyven doe not aswell *noxios condemnare* as *innocentes demittere*, condemne the guylty as cleare the innocent, which are alike abhominable before God, as Solomon teacheth ... I fynde men make no conscience to fynde the guylty, to the greate perverting of justice. Therefore was I mooved at this tyme to chardge this assisse of errour ... And this I doe of conscience of that office which God hath laid upon me. [129]

For James, ensuring that the justice system worked as it should, to do that which Solomon showed to be the will of God, was part of his office. Establishing and maintaining a functioning legal system was, to James, part of a king's role and had scriptural warrant.

The same idea, of ensuring that justice was done by ensuring actors within the justice system performed their roles appropriately, could explain more of James's judicial activity. James's interventions in relation to matters of jurisdiction could be viewed in the same way. The disputes between the common-law courts and both the church courts and the Chancery could be seen as preventing the legal system from functioning and justice being done.

The idea of performing a particular royal office is also visible in *Christmas and Bellingham*. James noted that the case 'concerne the peace of the kingdome, which is the proper office of a kinge'. [130] As in the prosecution of the Napier assize in Scotland, James stressed that the act of judging was part of performing his royal office, here in ensuring peace. Giving judgment was how James performed one of his duties. Related to this was how the problem of duelling needed to be addressed. As John Ford has noted, James accepted 'that it was the sovereign's prerogative "to supply the Law where the Law wants"'. [131] A writer on the Star Chamber in the reign of Charles I observed that the court existed to proceed 'against suche enormities and excesses as could not be sufficiently punished by the ordinary stroake of Comon lawe, And therefore it seemed requisite the Prince himselfe or they in neerest authority under him should there shew themselves'. [132]

In his speech in the case of *Christmas and Bellingham*, James noted this need to supply the law because the law was wanting. As he observed, 'no lawes have bene heretofore made against Duells, because till of late they were never practised'. [133] Like the Napier assize, or questions of jurisdiction, James's intervention in relation to duelling concerned a situation where the legal system was not working as it should. That failure was also highlighted by biblical norms, with James stressing that killing in general, and duels in particular, were prohibited in the Bible. [134] This securing of peace through royal justice as a royal duty is also visible in the

Trew Law. After James discusses the role of kings as judges, he observes that the obligation of a king, as noted by David, is to 'procure the peace of the people', alluding to Psalm 72. [135]

At first glance the litigation concerning Thomas Lake does not seem to fall into this model of performing royal duties. The dispute was between two important families, but the surviving reports of James's speech do not feature any explicit statement from James as to why he considered a defamation case worthy of his attention. There is no obvious royal duty affected by the throwing of insults between subjects, however prominent. However, the facts of the case and James's reported remarks suggest several reasons as to why the case was related to James's duties as monarch, and therefore worthy of his attention.

The first is that the alleged facts concerned members of James's court. As a matter of presentation, allegations of reprehensible behaviour at court in this case undermined James's prestige, just as they had in the Overbury scandal a few years earlier. [136] More importantly, however, James 'insisted that maintaining court morality was one of the duties of the good king'. [137] As James set out in the *Basilicon Doron*:

make your Court and companie to bee a patterne of godlinesse and all honest vertues, to all the rest of the people. Bee a daily watch-man ouer your seruants, that they obey your lawes precisely: For how can your lawes bee kept in the countrey, if they be broken at your eare? Punishing the breach thereof in a Courteour, more seuerely, then in the person of any other of your subiects: and aboue all, suffer none of them (by abusing their credite with you) to oppresse or wrong any of your subiects. [138]

The Lake case not only raised the spectre of reprehensible crimes such as incest, adultery and poisoning being committed at court, but also oppression by a privy councillor. Part of the allegations against Thomas Lake were that he had abused his office as privy councillor to have individuals arrested without cause, using the opportunity to suborn them into giving false testimony in the case. [139] The king's duty as a 'watch-man' over his secretary was therefore engaged, redressing oppression of subjects by his servants.

James saw his duty to be ensuring 'godlinesse and honest vertues', both of which were lacking in the Lake family. [140] James's intervention was probably triggered by two related underlying aspects of the case: gender and religion. The dispute between the earl of Exeter and Thomas Lake was referred to by one commentator as 'the famous womens cause'. [141] Although men were involved, it was presented as a case between women. For the Lake family, the matter was even more serious. In his speech, James 'spoke long and well, comparing Lake to Adam, Lady Lake to Eve, and Lady Roos to the serpent'. [142] The paterfamilias had been swayed to sin by his wife, who had herself been tempted by her daughter. This was not a well-ordered Jacobean family, and, as Jacobean thought would have predicted, this disorder in the family led to disorder in government. As one Jacobean household manual put it: 'It is impossible for a man to understand how to govern the common-wealth, that doth not know how to rule his own house, or order his own person; so that he that knoweth not to govern, deserveth not to reign.' [143] In the Lake family and household, the dominant figure was the daughter, a reversal of both gender and parental roles. Thomas Lake therefore demonstrated his unsuitability for government.

According to the earl of Exeter's allegations against Lake, which were accepted by the Star Chamber, Lake had not only arrested innocent subjects to pressure them into giving false testimony, he even allowed his wife to be involved in the questioning and pressuring of the prisoners. [144] One report of the case describes the finding 'that when he [Lake] had examined Williams on matter of state he gave him to his wife the other defendant to be examined again by her'. [145] James alluded to this aspect of the case as an important general lesson in his speech, as he 'bade all secretaries beware of trusting their wives with secrets of state'. [146]

Linked to this gendered aspect of the case lay a concern with religion. As Bellany notes, 'Rumours of religious deviance had swirled around the case from its beginnings in 1617. As the affair dragged on, these rumours focused increasingly on the Lakes.' [147] Contemporaries smelled popery, and in his speech James 'charged the Judges to beware of Papists, especially of women, who are the nourishers of Papistry'. [148] The inference is that a significant threat was posed if these women could then control the men in their family, especially a servant of the king. The litigation concerning Thomas Lake therefore did touch directly on issues that James considered his royal duty: the behaviour of his courtiers and servants, as well as godliness at court.

Cases in which James judged can therefore be linked to James's view of the duties of a king. However, the Lake litigation also reveals another recurring thread in James's judicial practice, which is the role of royal judgment as part of governing the country. Although James was judging in particular cases, he saw his judgments as having wider consequences, and this was an important aspect of his judicial activity. As the archbishop of Canterbury noted in relation to the Lake case, 'the matter is held so exemplary ... that the Kinge himselfe intendeth to bee present'. [149] James chose to be present on the basis of the exemplarity of the case, with the example serving to shape future behaviour.

James seems to have thought that his personal participation rendered the judicial process itself exemplary. That personal royal presence may have been necessary in some cases for the example to be effective and for the judicial process to be a useful tool of royal government. In the Napier assize, James explained that

'I see the pride of these witches and their freendes, which can not be prevented but by myne owne presence.' [150] In *Christmas and Bellingham*, James noted that a previous case had failed to serve as an effective example, perhaps thinking that his presence would make a difference in this respect. [151]

This idea of exemplarity is prominent in James's speech in the Napier assize prosecution: 'I mooved at this tyme to chardge this assisse of errour, that it may be an example in tyme commyng to make men to be more wary how they gyve false verdictes, not onely in this cause but in all other causes.' [152] In that case, James also took the opportunity to teach not just about false verdicts, but also about the substance of the offence for which Barbara Napier was acquitted: 'for them who thinke these witchcraftes to be but fantacyes, I remmyt them to be catechised and instructed in these most evident poyntes'. [153] This idea of using royal judgment as a means to educate James's subjects about important matters was also mentioned in his 1616 'Speach', where James acknowledged that he needed to learn the laws of England 'before I would take upon mee to teach them unto others'. [154] James judged the parties for their conduct in the past, as an example to the future. [155]

James gave his most complete statement as to the role of royal judgment in teaching the people in *Christmas and Bellingham*:

For what can belonge more properly to a kinge, then consideringe that all kingdomes, and states, are governed Cheifely by example, to make such an Example, As may hereafter curbe the insolent mindes of these Duellers; and by solempne decree provide that the Contrie may be reformed, and sheddinge of bloud hereafter stayed; For which I have such an accompt to make before God. [156]

Such an educative purpose explains why James made such a lengthy speech demonstrating the unlawfulness of duelling in scripture and in the law of nations. [157] Education through justice was a vital, albeit rarely deployed, tool of royal government, perhaps related to the educative role of judicial charges at assizes and quarter sessions in the English context. [158]

This was perhaps particularly important in the context of a case about duelling. *Christmas and Bellingham* occurred after serious royal attempts to curtail duelling in England, including two proclamations, a campaign of education in printed books written by royal servants and an earlier case setting an example. [159] An exemplary prosecution ending in personal royal judgment was another attempt to alter public behaviour when other means had failed. The same problem of failure may also have spurred James's intervention in Thomas Lake's case. That litigation occurred only after James had been instrumental in ensuring the murder prosecutions of courtiers in the Overbury scandal. [160] Despite this example, courtiers continued to misbehave, and many of the allegations in the Lake case were similar to those in the Overbury scandal. [161] James may have considered that the Overbury example had failed, and that direct personal intervention would have more effect than the normal process of the common law, just as he may have thought his personal presence would ensure a more effective example in *Christmas and Bellingham.*

This concern with examples and shaping behaviour in the future seems also to have been reflected in some of James's sentencing practices. In 1590, James Gyb was prosecuted for wearing and shooting of pistols within James's Palace of Holyrood. Gyb placed himself in the king's will. Departing from the typical practice, a full statement of the King's will and the reasons behind the decision as to sentence were delivered to the court, suggesting royal interest (perhaps by James personally) in the case. Gyb was sentenced to death, lest his behaviour 'offerit ane perellous preparative and example to the rest of our subiectis; ... gif it be nocht condignelie pwneist, to the example of utheris'. [162] James did subsequently show mercy, remitting the death penalty and simply banishing Gyb. However, the death sentence was publicly proclaimed, while the exercise of mercy was not, maintaining the exemplary effect of the punishment. [163] The same approach can be seen in *Christmas and Bellingham.* The two defendants were each fined £1,000 and imprisoned in the Tower of London at the king's pleasure. [164] However, a month later their fines and imprisonment were remitted. [165] The example had been made.

This idea of punishments as examples to the wider community to determine behaviour in the future was not peculiar to James personally. An Elizabethan statute referred to executions for felony as 'chieflye for Terrour and Example'. [166] The Jacobean Court of Exchequer noted in one judgment that had the defendants not died, 'some severe exemplar punishment such as might deterr others hereafter from committing the like' would have been imposed. [167] In 1622, the Star Chamber is reported as using one case as a 'precedent' because of 'the frequency of such offences', clearly hoping to deter such conduct in the future. [168] Jacobean proclamations also make reference to the Star Chamber having provided exemplary punishments in the past and doing so in the future, [169] while the sentences imposed by James in the Scottish High Commission in 1617 were described as being imposed 'in exemplum et terrorem'. [170]

Such an approach had not always been taken by James. In the prosecution of the Napier assize, James accepted them into his will and imposed no further punishment. James explained that he believed the jurors simply to have been ignorant, rather than corrupt. In such an instance, an educative speech, correcting the ignorance of the jurors, sufficed. The Napier approach was not typical, although it fits with some of James's thought as expressed in *Basilicon Doron*: 'mixe Justice with Mercie, punishing or sparing, as ye shall finde the crime to have bene wilfully or rashly committed'. [171] As the jurors had at best committed their wrong 'rashly', they could be spared.

James's remarks on the relationship between justice and mercy in *Basilicon Doron* are revealing, showing that by 1598 James stressed the importance of punishment as justice:

For if otherwise ye kyth your clemenice at the first, the offences would soone come to such heapes, and the contempt of you grow so great, that when ye would fall to punish, the number of them to be punished, would exceed the innocent; and yee would be troubled to resolve whom-at to begin: and against your nature would be compelled to wracke many, whom the chastisement of few in the beginning might have preserved. [172]

James warned that he had showed too much mercy early in his reign, and he 'found, the disorder of the countrie, and the losse of my thankes to be all my reward'. [173] James apparently experienced the same lesson during his initial progress from Edinburgh to London. Initial mercy was rapidly replaced by punishment. James ordered the execution of a cutpurse at Newark. According to Stow, the thief 'upon examination confessed, that he had from Barwicke to that place, played the Cut-purse in the Courte. The king hearing of this gallant, directed a warrant to the Recorder of New worke, to have him hanged, which was accordingly executed.' [174] James ordered punishment without trial, punishment which was carried out. According to Francis Ashley's later report of the matter at his reading in 1616, James had in fact twice pardoned this cutpurse. Execution was only ordered for the third offence. [175] After an initial attempt at mercy, James changed his practice to punishment of the thief.

In *Christmas and Bellingham*, James described the relationship between justice and mercy, and his approach to sentencing, again:

For as nothinge is more hurtfull then Cruell mercie soe nothinge is better then mercifull Justice, Cruell mercie is, where the pardon of one procured the faults of many, and mercifull Justice is, where the punishment of a fewe scarrs milions, for that is Gods ordinance in the seate of Justice upon earth, that the punishment of a few might adde feare to manie. [176]

By imposing a harsh sentence, James thought to make an example of a few particular offenders for the general good.

In England, the Star Chamber was an ideal venue for such exemplary activity. It was a court which people did visit. John Holles directly compared the court to a theatre (indeed, the Globe), advising his son that 'yow shall uppon this stage see what yow are to avoyd, what to follow, and by others errors, learn to play your owne part better, when your turn cums: or by others harms grow so wys, as yow may still conserve your self a spectator, and a philosopher'. [177] Another visitor, perhaps sharing similar views, paid about as much for seats in the Star Chamber as for those in the theatre. [178] Furthermore, those who attended the Star Chamber then circulated material about its activities to others. [179]

In these cases, James acting as a judge was therefore part of royal government, doing more than just determining the outcome of a particular dispute. He sought to shape wider behaviour in his realms. Such royal judgment was neither frequent nor regular, but James's judicial activities deserve to be considered in relation to James's ideas and practice of kingship.

A question which should then be addressed is really an impossible-to-answer counterfactual: why did James not judge in person more frequently? There are only a few examples of him sitting as a judge, all seen as noteworthy by commentators. If royal judgment was a tool of royal government, why not use that tool more often? Any answers to a counter-factual question will necessarily be speculative. In a few cases, James's personal appearance might have been politically counter-productive. This seems likely in relation to the prosecution of Thomas Howard in the Star Chamber. Thrush has argued that James's dismissal of Howard from the lord treasurership for corruption was seen as disproportionate, and that the Star Chamber prosecution was designed to show that James's actions were reasonable. In this, James was assisted by Edward Coke, whose speech in the Star Chamber presented examples of such dismissals. [180] For James to sit in such a case may have undermined its political purpose. Similarly, while James did attempt to assert his judicial role in the impeachment of Francis Bacon in 1621, he 'chose to sacrifice the constitutional point for the short-run objectives of his continental policy and the clearing of his honor'. [181] However, these political reasons probably fail to explain the general absence of royal judgment by James.

A more general explanation is simply pressure of business. Even if James wanted to sit, he may not have had the time to do so. The Lake litigation took five days, time which could have been devoted to other matters. [182] Some indication that James's time was too limited to judge regularly may be found in his speech in *Christmas and Bellingham*. During the speech, James apologised for its quality, explaining that his discussion had been affected by 'the Cold that I have gotten' and the 'small tyme that I have had to thinke of this (which was but since last night at tenne of the Clocke'. [183] James's time was limited, and he did not turn to preparing a deliberately exemplary speech on a significant issue of government policy until quite late the night before the case. Frequent judicial activity may simply have been unsustainable. [184]

A COMPARATIVE CONCLUSION

As a matter of comparative legal history, we have one clear distinction between James as judge in his two kingdoms, in James's participation in the regular dispensing of justice. A combination of institutional and cultural differences may have affected James's inclination to participate in judicial activity in England. However, in other respects the pattern looks quite similar. There is considerable congruity between James's activities in Scotland and England, as well as the views and ideas he expressed. In fact, the more pronounced difference, or comparison, is between James in the 1580s and early 1590s, on the one hand, and James from the later 1590s onwards, on the other. In 1595, James was happy to end his dispute with David Black in conference but was later directly involved in Black's prosecution and sentencing. In the Napier prosecution, James was happy to release the offending jurors with nothing more than a verbal punishment. But in *Basilicon Doron*, completed in 1598, James acknowledged that his view of mercy had changed due to his 'over-deare bought experience'. [185] That experience shaped James's ideas, ideas which he applied in fairly consistent ways in both Scotland and England. The comparative exercise here lets us reach a conclusion which would surely have delighted James himself: in his ideas and practice of royal judgment we have an example of genuinely British legal history.

A CONSTITUTIONAL AMENDMENT

James's judicial activity was unusual, particularly in the English context. However, there is no evidence that his subjects saw anything problematic in his judicial role. From the perspective of constitutional history, James was the end of an older tradition. But that end was not preordained. Why did James's successors did not continue his practice of publicly dispensed personal justice? In Scotland the answer is fairly simple. Public personal justice required personal presence, which was rare after 1603. [186] In England, this would not have been an issue, and the answers involve trying to explain an absence which no contemporaries seem to have regarded as notable. One explanation relates to the character of James's successors. James was not shy about engaging in debate and discussion with his subjects, just as he did in his English judicial activity. This was a feature of his Scottish practice, although less common in England. [187] His successors were heirs to the English tradition of a more distant monarch.

Royal judgment also required there to have been a perceived need for such activity. But most of the time English monarchs could achieve their objectives through the legal system without intervening personally, confident that their judges would reach the right decisions. [188] In England James only judged where the regular legal system failed to achieve his objectives, and such cases were unusual.

Culturally, there may have been a change in views about the acceptability of royal justice dispensed personally by the monarch. During the parliamentary debates concerning the abolition of the Star Chamber in 1641, the former chief justice of the King's Bench, Henry Montagu, asserted that the king had a personal judicial power. According to one newsletter writer, Montagu's remarks were 'high prerogative language' that was not acceptable to many. [189] Furthermore, once Coke's remarks about the king's inability to act as a judge were printed in the Interregnum, any attempt by a king to judge may have been likely to provoke criticism. [190] Such criticism might undermine the political benefits of personal intervention, rendering the monarch's judicial activity a misjudgement. Institutionally, after the abolition of the Star Chamber and judicial role of the council in 1640, it is less clear in which court a monarch could have sat. [191]

Ultimately, it might be argued that the most noteworthy element of James's judicial position was not his active engagement, but rather an occurrence of passivity. In the event that Parliament took the decision to impeach Francis Bacon, James had put out a proposition to the House of Commons, suggesting the establishment of a commission of members from both houses of parliament. This commission would be tasked with scrutinizing the evidence presented against Bacon. The commission would subsequently submit a report to James, who would act as the individual adjudicator of the case. Nevertheless, James failed to present the plan to the House of Lords, resulting in its dismissal due to James's prioritization of other things. [192] According to Zaller, with reflection, this choice can be regarded as the most significant one ever taken by King James. [193] The ruling yielded two notable ramifications. James's choice to abstain from assuming a judicial position during the reign of Charles I led to the occurrence of unwelcome parliamentary trials against royal servants, such as the attempted trial of the duke of Buckingham and the prosecution of the earl of Strafford. These trials had a significant impact on the relationship between Charles and Parliament. Furthermore, the lack of judicial action by James established a precedent of parliamentary judicature over individuals serving in the royal service, without any explicit authorization or control from the monarchy, except for the dissolution of Parliament. In his 1624 draft treatise on Parliament, Henry Elsyng incorporated a chapter dedicated to parliamentary judicature. It was evident that, in accordance with established legislative precedents, the authority to make judgments rested solely with the House of Lords, while the king's role was limited to granting assent to such judgments. [194] The lack of action on James's behalf created an opportunity for the legislative scrutiny and regulation of the conduct of royal servants, a provision that remains intended to be incorporated into the constitution of the kingdom that James sought to consolidate.

Footnote

1. Charles I was personally involved in the Privy Council's resolution of petitions concerning judicial proceedings about the Forest of Dean, but these proceedings appear to have been private; see *Newsletters from the Caroline Court, 1631–1638: Catholicism and the Politics of the Personal Rule*, ed. M. C. Questier (Cambridge, 2005), 232 n. 1094. Charles also observed the trial of the earl of Strafford in 1641, but did not preside; J. H. Timmis, Thine is the Kingdom: The Trial for

Treason of Thomas Wentworth, Earl of Strafford, First Minister to King Charles I, and Last Hope of the English Crown (University, AL, 1974), 65.

2. My thanks to Amy Blakeway and Adelyn Wilson for their assistance on Scottish material. Earlier versions of this paper were presented to the Cambridge Early-Modern British and Irish History Seminar, the Notre Dame Roundtable on History and Theory in Constitutional Development and the UCL Faculty of Laws Staff Seminar. My thanks to all participants for their comments and suggestions.
3. For Scotland, see T. M. Cooper, 'The King versus the Court of Session', in T. M. Cooper, Selected Papers 1922–1954 (Edinburgh, 1957), 116–23. For England, the various incidents are outlined in J. S. Hart, The Rule of Law, 1603–1660: Crowns, Courts and Judges (Harlow, 2003), 102–11.
4. For James and the union project, see B. Galloway, The Union of England and Scotland, 1603–08 (Edinburgh, 1986).
5. J. Wormald, 'James VI and I: Two Kings or One?', History, 68 (1983), 187–209.
6. On one level this should not be surprising. Law and litigation (and therefore judging) had a great significance in early-modern England. As Brooks observes, 'the great wave of litigation characteristic of the period brought a wide range of issues, stretching nearly from the cradle to the grave, into the courts'; C. W. Brooks, Law, Politics and Society in Early Modern England (Cambridge, 2008), 241. However, this practical importance of judging does not necessarily explain why James's personal activities as a judge in individual cases would be part of wider royal government.
7. As Goodare observes, James's 'personal initiative has to be argued specifically rather than merely by reference to the fact that it was done in his name'; J. Goodare, The Government of Scotland 1560–1625 (Oxford, 2004), 290.
8. By the reign of James VI, the Scottish Parliament's judicial competence was limited to treason cases; see M. Godfrey, 'Parliament and the Law', in K. M. Brown and A. R. MacDonald (eds.), Parliament in Context, 1235–1707 (Edinburgh, 2010), 157–68. On the judicial competence of the Scottish Privy Council, see P. G. B. McNeill, 'The Jurisdiction of the Scottish Privy Council, 1532–1708', unpublished PhD thesis, University of Glasgow (1960). This thesis does not consider the king's personal judicial role.
9. R. Pitcairn, Criminal Trials in Scotland from A.D. MCCCC.LXXXVIII to A.D. M.DC. XXIV, 2 vols. in 3 parts (Edinburgh, 1833), vol. I, part 2, 136–7.
10. See below, 94–5.
11. See below, 93–4.

12. On the informal Exchequer Chamber, see J. H. Baker, Introduction to English Legal History, 5th edn (Oxford, 2019), 150. There were two other bodies known as the Exchequer Chamber by 1600, both of them formal courts with statutory foundations; see ibid., 147–8.
13. D. Calderwood, The History of the Kirk of Scotland, ed. T. Thomason, 8 vols. (Edinburgh, 1842–9), vol. V, 376–81, quotes at 377 and 378.
14. On James's activity in relation to bloodfeud, see K. M. Brown, Bloodfeud in Scotland 1573–1625 (Edinburgh, 1986).
15. R. W. Hoyle, 'Fountains of Justice: James I, Charles I and Equity', in M. Lobban, J. Begiato and A. Green (eds.), Law, Lawyers and Litigants in Early Modern England: Essays in Memory of Christopher W. Brooks (Cambridge, 2019), 96–108.
16. The Letters of John Chamberlain, ed. N. E. McClure, 2 vols. (Philadelphia, PA, 1939), vol. II, 145.
17. For example, Cooper, 'The King versus the Court'. Hannay suspects that there were probably other incidents in Scotland too, but that they were less explicit or overt and so not recorded; R. K. Hannay, The College of Justice: Essays on the Institution and Development of the Court of Session (Edinburgh, 1933), 119.
18. See J. H. Baker, The Reinvention of Magna Carta 1216–1616 (Cambridge, 2017), 424–6; Hart, *The Rule of Law*, 104–7, and D. C. Smith, Sir Edward Coke and the Reformation of the Laws: Religion, Politics and Jurisprudence, 1578–1616 (Cambridge, 2014), 278–82.
19. E.g. Pitcairn, *Criminal Trials*, vol. I, part 2, 381 and 384.
20. Ibid., vol. II, part 1, 53–61.
21. E.g. London, British Library (henceforth, BL), MS Lansdowne 216, fo. 133v.
22. BL, MS Lansdowne 216, fo. 16v.
23. *Calendar of the State Papers relating to Scotland and Mary, Queen of Scots 1547–1603*, 13 vols. (Edinburgh, 1898–1969) (henceforth, CSPS), vol. X, 102, no. 123.
24. Ibid., vol. X, 370–1, no. 458.
25. *The Register of the Privy Council of Scotland*, ed. D. Masson, 14 vols. (Edinburgh, 1877–98) (henceforth, RPCS), vol. V, 449 and 452.
26. Hannay, *The College of Justice*, 119. References to James's attendance in the Session include Pitcairn, *Criminal Trials*, vol. I, part 2, 29–34; R. Pitcairn, Ancient Criminal Trials in Scotland, 3 vols. in 6 parts (Edinburgh, 1833), vol. II, part 2, 358–9; CSPS, vol. XI, 236, no. 178.
27. CSPS, vol. XIII, 834, no. 668. No further details have been found. My thanks to Stephanie Dropuljic for checking the Justiciary Court records.

28. E.g. RPCS, vol. V, 318–19, a contract dispute involving an English merchant.
29. E.g. ibid., vol. V, 6–8, warding parties in castles until a dispute could be put to an assize.
30. E.g. ibid., vol. V, 175–6, about jurisdiction involving a Scot resident in Denmark.
31. James VI and I, *Basilicon Doron*, in *King James VI and I: Political Writings*, ed. J. P. Sommerville (Cambridge, 1994), 1–61, at 45.
32. A. Blakeway, Regency in Sixteenth-Century Scotland (Woodbridge, 2015), 158–92. James's comment in the Napier assize prosecution that 'it hath not bene the custome that the Kings of this realme ... should sit in persone upon cryminall causes' (CSPS, vol. X, 523, no. 572) might suggest that such royal activity did not involve judging cases or may refer only to the cases heard centrally in Edinburgh. Godfrey notes that before 1532, kings also participated personally in the Session; M. Godfrey, 'Control and the Constitutional Accountability of the College of Justice in Scotland, 1532–1626', in I. Czeguhn, J. A. L. Nevot and A. S. Aranda (eds.), Control of Supreme Courts in Early Modern Europe (Berlin, 2018), 118–49, at 127–9.
33. Another example of James's judicial, but private, involvement in a seditious speech case is the sentencing of Thomas Ross in 1619. Ross, a Scot, had written a vehement anti-Scottish text and fixed it to the doors of a church in Oxford. James had Ross returned to Scotland, to be tried there. Ross sought to place himself in the king's will but was still tried by the assize and found guilty of offences, some of which carried a mandatory death penalty by statute. The Scottish Privy Council sought James's decision as to the punishment to be inflicted. Ross had his hand struck off and was then executed. Given the content of the Privy Council's communication with James, it seems likely that James determined that this was the appropriate punishment. For the facts and documents, see Pitcairn, *Ancient Criminal Trials*, vol. III, part 2, 445–54 and 582–90.
34. RPCS, vol. IV, 39. The *Register* includes only basic information. The detail of the process is found in Calderwood, *History of the Kirk*, vol. IV, 484–8.
35. See above, 88.
36. CSPS, vol. XII, 368–9, no. 301.
37. Ibid., vol. XII, 362–3, no. 292.
38. RPCS, vol. V, 326–7.
39. Ibid., vol. V, 336.
40. Ibid., vol. V, 341–2. For another example of James personally being given

sentencing power by the Privy Council, see ibid., vol. VI, 197–8.

41. J. K. Cameron, 'Black, David (c. 1546–1603)', in H. C. G. Matthew and B. Harrison (eds.), Oxford Dictionary of National Biography, from the Earliest Times to the Year 2000, 61 vols. (Oxford, 2004), vol. V, 895.

42. Calderwood, *History of the Kirk*, vol. VII, 261–8.

43. *Reports on the Manuscripts of the Most Honourable the Marquess of Downshire Formerly Preserved at Easthampstead Park, Berkshire, Vol. VI: Papers of William Trumbull the Elder September 1616–December 1618*, ed. G. D. Owen and S. P. Anderson (London, 1995), 246–7. For the proceedings and context, see A. R. MacDonald, The Jacobean Kirk, 1567–1625: Sovereignty, Polity and Liturgy (Aldershot, 1998), 158–9.

44. For the influence of reports of the North Berwick trials on the portrayal of witches in Macbeth, see E. H. Thompson, '*Macbeth,* King James and the Witches', *Studii de Limbi Şi Literaturi Moderne: Studii de Anglistică Şi Americanistică* (1994), 131–5, an unpaginated online version is available at http://faculty.umb.edu/gary_zabel/Courses/Phil%20281b/Philosophy%20of%20Magic/Arcana/Witchcraft%20and%20Grimoires/macbeth.htm.

45. CSPS, vol. X, 514–5, no. 561.

46. Ibid., vol. X, 515, no. 561. Two of those convicted subsequently confessed before their executions but said that they had slanderously accused Napier; L. Nomad and G. Roberts, Witchcraft in Early-Modern Scotland: James VI's Demonology and the North Berwick Witches (Liverpool, 2000), 46.

47. On the assize of error, see I. D. Willock, The Origins and Development of the Jury in Scotland (Edinburgh, 1966), 234–46; C. Jackson, '"Assize of Error" and the Independence of the Criminal Jury in Restoration Scotland', Scottish Archives, 10 (2004), 1–26.

48. CSPS, vol. X, 522–5, no. 572.

49. On the jurisdictional disputes, see especially Smith, *Sir Edward Coke*, 176–212.

50. R. G. Usher, 'James I and Sir Edward Coke', English Historical Review, 18 (1903), 664–75.

51. BL, MS Lansdowne 160, fo. 425.

52. *Prohibitions del Roy* (1609) 12 Co. Rep. 63–5.

53. According to Coke in the *Prohibitions del Roy* 'the king may sit in the Star-Chamber; but this was to consult with the justices ... and not *in judicio*'; 12 Co. Rep. 64. Coke sat as a member of the panel in the case concerning Sir Thomas Lake and the earl of Exeter, with James himself as a judge (see below, 96–7). For

Coke's participation, see McClure, ed., *Letters of John Chamberlain*, vol. II, 214.

54. J. P. Dawson, 'Coke and Ellesmere Disinterred: The Attack on the Chancery in 1616', 36 Illinois Law Review (1941–2), 127–52; J. H. Baker, 'The Common Lawyers and the Chancery: 1616', 4 Irish Jurist (1969), 368–92; L. A. Knafla, Law and Politics in Jacobean England (Cambridge, 1977), 155–81; I. Williams, 'Developing a Prerogative Theory for the Authority of the Chancery: The French Connection', in M. Godfrey (ed.), Law and Authority in British Legal History, 1200–1900 (Cambridge, 2016), 33–59, at 54–59.
55. James VI and I, *The Workes of the Most High and Mightie Prince, Iames by the Grace of God, King of Great Britaine, France and Ireland* (London, 1616), 549–69. Citations to James's 'Speach' are from James VI and I, 'A Speach in the Starre-Chamber, the XX. of June. Annoe 1616', in Sommerville, *Political Writings*, 204–28.
56. James, 'Speach', 207. For the repetition, see *Christmas and Bellingham*, in BL, MS Harley 1576, fo. 75v.
57. James, 'Speach', 204–7.
58. Ibid., 207 and 209.
59. Ibid., 219.
60. *Calendar of State Papers Domestic Series, James I*, ed. M. A. E. Green, 190 vols. (London, 1857–9) (henceforth, CSPD), vol. XC, 436, no. 65. The fuller text is in the manuscript, London, The National Archives, SP 14/90/65.
61. BL, MS Harley 1576, fos. 75v–80v.
62. A. Bellany, The Politics of Court Scandal in Early Modern England: News Culture and the Overbury Affair, 1603–1660 (Cambridge, 2002), 253.
63. The information and reply in the case of *Earl of Exeter* v. *Lake* can be found in *Calendar of the Manuscripts of the Most Honourable the Marquess of Salisbury preserved at Hatfield House (Hertfordshire), Part XXII (A.D. 1612–1668)*, ed. G. D. Owen (London, 1971), 61–76.
64. McClure, ed., *Letters of John Chamberlain*, vol. II, 217.
65. Owen and Anderson, eds., *Reports*, 596.
66. W. Hudson, A Treatise on the Court of Star Chamber, in Collectanea Juridica. Consisting of Tracts Relative to the Law and Constitution of England, ed. Francis Hargrave, 2 vols. (London, 1791), vol. I, 9. This probably does not include the twelve legal issues which the case apparently involved. Some of these were handled at a pre-hearing in December 1618; Owen and Anderson, eds., *Reports*, 596. Some of the legal issues are reported in *Lake* v. *Hatton* (1618/19) Hobart 252–3. A fuller report can be found in Washington, D.C., Folger Shakespeare

Library (henceforth, FSL), MS V.a.133, fos. 82–87v. According to this report, James expressly delegated the legal issues in the case to the chief justices (ibid., fo. 84v), so the five days of hearing were probably focused on the facts.

67. McClure, ed., *Letters of John Chamberlain*, vol. II, 145.

68. Owen and Anderson, eds., *Reports*, 574.

69. Ibid., 513, 530, 552, 574, 581, 596 and 624–6; McClure, ed., *Letters of John Chamberlain*, vol. II, 144, 145, 161, 213–14 and 215–17.

70. For a discussion of the importance of the Bible to early-modern English political thought, see K. Killeen, The Political Bible in Early Modern England (Cambridge, 2016).

71. 1 Samuel 8:5 and 20.

72. On the biblical image of James VI as Solomon, see J. Goodare and M. Lynch, 'James VI: Universal King?', in J. Goodare and M. Lynch (eds.), The Reign of James VI (East Linton, 2000), 20. On the importance of both Solomon and David to James I in England, see J. N. King, 'James I and King David: Jacobean Iconography and its Legacy', in Daniel Fischlin and Mark Fortier (eds.), Royal Subjects: Essays on the Writings of James VI and I (Detroit, MI, 2002), 421–53.

73. James VI and I, *The Trew Law of Free Monarchies*, in Sommerville, ed., *Political Writings*, 2–84, at 64. James also refers to subjects needing to acknowledge a king as 'a Iudge set by God ouer them, hauing power to iudge them' (ibid., 72).

74. James, *Basilicon Doron*, 22 and 24.

75. CSPS, vol. X, 523–4, no. 572.

76. James, 'Speach', 204. Citations of Psalms are from the King James Version.

77. BL, MS Harley 1576, fo. 76v.

78. CSPD, vol. CV, 11, no. 83.

79. Ibid., vol. CV, 14, no. 103. Although James does not draw this out, this would link to the idea of a king sitting on God's throne when dispensing judgment, as mentioned in *Basilicon Doron* (see above) and the beginning of Psalm 72, as mentioned in his 1616 'Speach' (see above).

80. McClure, ed., *Letters of John Chamberlain*, vol. II, 145.

81. G. F. Warner, 'The Library of James VI. 1573–1583', in Publications of the Scottish History Society, vol. XV (Edinburgh, 1893), x–lxxv, at xlii.

82. See Williams, 'Developing a Prerogative Theory', 42–8 and 54–9.

83. J. Bodin, The Six Bookes of a Commonweale, ed. and trans. K. Douglas McRae (Cambridge, MA, 1962), 500–44. Of course, James's copy was in the original

French. Pennington notes that Bodin's views on a prince's judicial powers were much more restrictive than the traditional *ius commune*, despite Bodin's reliance on *ius commune* writers earlier in his discussion of sovereignty; K. Pennington, The Prince and the Law, 1200–1600: Sovereignty and Rights in the Western Legal Tradition (Berkeley, CA and Los Angeles, CA, 1993), 280. However, Pennington does not observe that in the chapters discussing a prince's judicial role, Bodin is not discussing the law about the prince's powers but rather whether exercising judicial powers is prudent.

84. See below, 104–106.

85. P. Collinson, 'The Coherence of the Text: How it Hangeth Together: The Bible in Reformation England', in W. P. Stephens (ed.), The Bible, the Reformation and the Church (Sheffield, 1995), 84–108, at 103.

86. Killeen, *The Political Bible*, 3. For other examples of English monarchs being compared to David and Solomon, see S. Doran, 'Elizabeth I: An Old Testament King', in A. Hunt and A. Whitelock (eds.), Tudor Queenship: The Reigns of Mary and Elizabeth (New York, 2010), 95–110, at 98.

87. Calderwood, *History of the Kirk*, vol. V, 172.

88. CSPS, vol. XIII, 814, no. 654. Galloway's praise was directed at the execution of a Catholic, but James apparently stressed that the death penalty was the penalty imposed by law for stealing evidences of title, the offence for which Boynton had been convicted; ibid., vol. XIII, 809, no. 650 and 823, no. 660. It is not clear whether James was involved as a judge at Boynton's trial, because Boynton submitted to the king's will, or in relation to the power to pardon.

89. *The Oxford Edition of the Sermons of John Donne, Vol. 3: Sermons Preached at the Court of Charles I*, ed. D. Colclough (Oxford, 2013), 223. Donne rejects trial by jury and trial by peers, moving to trial by the king, but elides the king and God at this point.

90. Blakeway, *Regency*, 158. See also J. E. A. Dawson, Scotland Re-formed, 1488–1587 (Edinburgh, 2007), 40, and J. Wormald, Court, Kirk, and Community: Scotland 1470–1625 (Edinburgh, 1981), 14–15.

91. Smith, *Sir Edward Coke*, 199 and 203. See also BL, MS Lansdowne 211, fo. 141r.

92. For criticism, see *Nugae antiquae: Being a Miscellaneous Collection of Original Papers in Prose and Verse; Written During the Reigns of Henry VIII, Edward VI, Queen Mary, Elizabeth, and King James: By Sir John Harington, Knt. And by Others Who Lived in Those Times*, ed. T. Park (London, 1804), 180, and Francis Ashley's 1616 reading, where the executioner was identified as potentially being liable for the murder of the thief; Cambridge University Library (henceforth, CUL), MS Ee.6.3, fo.

119. The more extravagant claims made by the Venetian ambassador, that on James's progress from Scotland to London he ordered multiple executions, is not supported by any other evidence; Calendar of State Papers *and Manuscripts, Relating to English Affairs, Existing in the Archives and Collections of Venice, and in Other Libraries* of *Northern Italy*, 38 vols. (London, 1864–1947), vol. X, 25, no. 40.

93. See above, 97.

94. M. C. Bradbrook, 'Authority, Truth, and Justice in Measure for Measure', Review of English Studies, 17 (1941), 385–99, at 386. Bradbrook observes that some passages in the play were 'palpably meant for the ear of James' (ibid., 386).

95. P. Sidney, The Countess of Pembroke's Arcadia (The Old Arcadia), ed. K. Duncan-Jones (Oxford, 1985), 315.

96. Ibid., 324. As Duncan-Jones notes in her introduction, the Elizabethan *Arcadia* enjoyed 'enormous popularity' throughout the seventeenth century (ibid., ix).

97. See above, 94, for Coke.

98. J. Fortescue, De laudibus legum Anglie, ed. S. B. Chrimes (Cambridge, 1942), 23. This work was first printed in Latin in 1543, *Prenobilis militis, cognomento Fortescu ... de politica administratione, et legibus ciuilibus florentissimi regni Anglie* (London, 1543), and in English in 1567, *A learned commendation of the politique lawes of Englande* (London, 1567).

99. W. Staunford, Les plees del coron (London, 1557), fo. 54v. Staunford was therefore silent about the king judging in cases of misdemeanours, such as cases in the Star Chamber.

100. YB Mich. 20 Hen. VII, fos. 6–8, pl. 17, at 7 per Brudenell Sjt.

101. BL, Egerton MS 3376, fos. 24–24v.

102. James, 'Speach', 206. James's knowledge of Henry VII's practice is likely from the 'Liber intrationum', a collection of Council/Star Chamber papers from the reign of Henry VII; reproduced in *Select Cases in the Council of Henry VII*, eds. C. G. Bayne and W. H. Dunham (London, 1958), 6–47. This circulated in multiple early-modern collections on the Star Chamber; for the manuscripts see J. H. Baker and J. S. Ringrose, Catalogue of Legal Manuscripts in Cambridge University Library (Woodbridge, 1996), 304. The preface to the text highlights Henry VII's attendance in the Star Chamber; Bayne and Dunham, eds., *Select Cases in the Council*, 7.

103. J. Williams, Great Britains Salomon. A Sermon Preached at the Magnificent Funerall, of the Most High and Mighty King, James (London, 1625), 53.

104. Ibid., 53–5. Williams did praise the eloquence of James's speeches, including those in the Star Chamber (ibid., 41), but did not draw attention to the judicial nature of the speeches.

105. Of James's printed works, only the 'Speach' in the Star Chamber contains such material.

106. CSPS, vol. X, 523, no. 572.

107. What James means by the 'civil lawe' here is not clear. The rule he recounts does not reflect the *ius commune* tradition; see E. H. Kantorowicz, 'Kingship under the Impact of Scientific Jurisprudence', in M. Clagett, G. Post, and R. Reynolds (eds.), Twelfth-Century Europe and the Foundations of Modern Society (Madison, WI, 1966), 89–101, at 93–4, and M. Schmoeckel, 'The Mystery of Power Verdicts Solved? Frederick II of Prussia and the Emerging Independence of Jurisdiction', in G. Martyn, A. Musson, and H. Pihlajamäki (eds.), From the Judge's Arbitrium to the Legality Principle: Legislation as a Source of Law in Criminal Trials (Berlin, 2013), 110–45, at 115–19. I can find no mention in Scottish sources of this limitation on the king's judicial power. James had consulted with the Lords of Session about the law of evidence in relation to witchcraft and treason trials and in his speech referred to those rules of evidence as 'by the civill law' too, which suggests the source may be unreported remarks made by members of the Session to James; CSPS, vol. X, 522 and 525, no. 572.

108. See above, 90.

109. James, 'Speach', 207.

110. Ibid., 207.

111. *Prohibitions del Roy* 12 Co. Rep. 65. Julius Caesar's account of the dispute suggests something like Coke's remarks was said, as Caesar notes that 'The King but of six yeres standing in English Lawes and yet particeps rationis et ratio omnia legis'; BL, MS Lansdowne 160, fo. 427. This suggests that James acknowledged a lack of technical expertise in 1609 but did not regard that as a hindrance.

112. Acts of the Privy Council of England, 38 vols. (London, 1864–1947), vol. XXXIV, ed. J. R. Dasent, 600.

113. Williams, 'Developing a Prerogative Theory', 57–8.

114. Bodin, *Six Bookes*, 764.

115. James, 'Speach', 207.

116. Ibid., 207, and BL, MS Harley 1576, fo. 75v.

117. BL, MS Harley 1576, fo. 75v.

118. CSPS, vol. X, 524, no. 572.

119. Bodin, *Six Bookes*, 526. Bodin also discusses a prince who judges in his own cause, which he describes as 'contrarie unto the law of nature'; Bodin, *Six Bookes*, 514.

120. James, 'Speach', 207.

121. BL, MS Harley 1576, fos. 75v and 76.

122. Bodin, *Six Bookes*, 515.

123. MacDonald, *The Jacobean Kirk*, 40. For the context of Black's prosecution, see especially ibid., 66–9.

124. This aspect of the cases is particularly stressed in C. Larner, 'James VI and I and Witchcraft', in A. G. R. Smith (ed.), The Reign of James VI and I (London, 1973), 74–90, at 79. Bothwell, Francis Stewart, was the son of the illegitimate son of James VI's grandfather, James V.

125. On the religious sub-text to the scandal, see below, 110. Such sub-text was particularly problematic when James was engaged in negotiations for Prince Charles to marry a Spanish bride.

126. J. Goodare, State and Society in Early Modern Scotland (Oxford, 1999), 14 n. 9.

127. On the Overbury scandal, see Bellany, *Politics of Court Scandal*. The judicial investigation and trial are discussed at 218–20.

128. BL, MS Harley 1576, fo. 76.

129. CSPS, vol. X, 523, no. 572.

130. Ibid.

131. BL, MS Harley 1576, fo. 75v.

132. J. D. Ford, 'Conciliar Authority and Equitable Jurisdiction in Early-Modern Scotland', in Godfrey (ed.), *Law and Authority*, 140–69, at 160.

133. CUL, MS Kk.6.22, 2–3. Another copy is BL, MS Harley 6448, but the Cambridge manuscript is a superior presentation copy.

134. BL, MS Harley 1576, fo. 78v.

135. Ibid., fos. 76v–78.

136. James, *Trew Law*, 64.

137. Bellany notes that in the Lake affair 'accusations – many of them clearly recalling the Overbury affair – were hurled back and forth'; Bellany, *Politics of Court Scandal*, 253. On the reputational damage to James flowing from behaviour at his court, see M. Lee, Great Britain's Solomon: James VI and I in his Three Kingdoms (Chicago, IL, 1990), 132.

138. Bellany, *Politics of Court Scandal*, 138. This aspect of the case is highlighted in J. Rickman, Love, Lust, and License in Early Modern England: Illicit Sex and the Nobility (Aldershot, 2008), 83.

139. James, *Basilicon Doron*, 37.

140. Owen, ed., *Calendar*, 63 and 65.

141. James, *Basilicon Doron*, 37.

142. Owen and Anderson, eds., *Report*, 530.

143. CSPD, vol. CV, 14, no. 103.

144. J. Dod and R. Clever, A Godly Forme of Household Government: For the Ordering of Private Families, According to the Direction of God's Word (London, 1612), sig. A8v. For the importance of order, hierarchy and obedience in early-modern views of the family, and the parallels between family and government, see S. D. Amussen, An Ordered Society: Gender and Class in Early Modern England (Oxford, 1988), 34–66, esp. 35–42 and 54–60.

145. Owen, ed., *Calendar*, 63.

146. FSL, MS V.a.133, fo. 85v. The translation from law French is my own.

147. CSPD, vol. CV, 14, no. 103. Interference in the actions of her husband as lord treasurer was also a feature of the prosecution of the countess of Suffolk with her husband; A. Thrush, 'The Fall of Thomas Howard, 1st Earl of Suffolk and the Revival of Impeachment in the Parliament of 1621', Parliamentary History, 37 (2018), 197–211, at 201.

148. Bellany, *Politics of Court Scandal*, 254.

149. CSPD, vol. CV, 14, no. 104.

150. Owen and Anderson, eds., *Reports*, 626.

151. CSPS, vol. X, 524, no. 572.

152. BL, MS Harley 1576, fo. 77.

153. CSPS, vol. X, 523–4, no. 572.

154. Ibid., vol. X, 524, no. 572.

155. James, 'Speach', 207.

156. This suggests that the distinction James drew being acting judicially and declaratorily (see above, 95) was much less clear in practice.

157. BL, MS Harley 1576, fo. 76.

158. Ibid., fos. 76v–80v.

159. As William Lambarde noted of his model charge to be delivered at Quarter Sessions, one of the purposes of the charge was 'to instruct those that be ignorant, least they offende unawares'; W. Lambarde, Eirenarcha: Or the Office of Iustices of Peace (London, 1581), 311. On the charges generally, see Brooks, *Law, Politics and Society*, 87–92 and 157–60.

160. On the Jacobean campaign against duelling, see M. Peltonen, The Duel in Early Modern England: Civility, Politeness and Honour (Cambridge, 2003), 80–145.

161. Bellany, *Politics of Court Scandal*, 218–20.

162. See above, 108. It is possible that some of the allegations were deliberately crafted to resemble the earlier matter to attract James's attention.

163. Pitcairn, *Criminal Trials*, vol. I, part 2, 187–8.

164. For the remission of the penalty, see ibid., vol. I, part 2, 188 marginal n. 1.

165. CSPD, vol. XC, 450, no. 63.

166. Ibid.

167. Stat. 8 Eliz.1 c.4.

168. *AG* v. *Earl of Leicester* (1615), PRO E 126/2, fo. 62v. My thanks to David Foster for bringing this case to my attention.

169. *R* v. *Saunders* (1622), CUL, MS Ii.6.51, fo. 86.

170. *Stuart Royal Proclamations, Vol. I: Royal Proclamations of King James I, 1603–1625*, eds. J. F. Larkin and P. L. Hughes (Oxford, 1973), 153, 359, 407, 429, 539 and 540.

171. Owen and Anderson, eds., *Reports*, 247. Similar language is not present in Calderwood's account of the situation (above, 92), but Calderwood was interested in other aspects of the case.

172. James, *Basilicon Doron*, 22.

173. Ibid., 22.

174. Ibid., 23.

175. J. Stow, The Annales of England (London, 1605), 1431.

176. CUL, MS Ee.6.3, fo. 119. It is possible that the second pardon was conditional, but the surviving sources do not make this clear.

177. BL, MS Harley 1576, fo. 76v.

178. P. R. Seddon, Letters of John Holles 1587–1637, 2 vols. (Nottingham, 1983), vol. II, 222.

179. N. Millstone, Manuscript Circulation and the Invention of Politics in Early Stuart England (Cambridge, 2016), 262–3.

180. Ibid., 262–3.

181. Thrush, 'Fall of Thomas Howard', 206–9.

182. R. Zaller, The Parliament of 1621: A Study in Constitutional Conflict (Berkeley, CA, 1971), 83.

183. See above, 97.

184. BL, MS Harley 1576, fo. 77v. No closing parenthesis in the original.

185. A related point may be what Conrad Russell described as James's 'declining energy' in the early 1620s; C. Russell, James VI and I and his English Parliaments, ed. R. Cust and A. Thrush (Oxford, 2011), 177.

186. James, *Basilicon Doron*, 22. For the completion date, see J. Sommerville, 'Introduction', in Sommerville, ed., *Political Writings*, xviii. James's disappointment with the loyalty of his subjects is evident in *Basilicon Doron*, where he observed that 'I never found yet a constant biding by me in all my straites, by any that were of perfite aage in my parents dayes, but onely by such as constantly bode by them; I meane specially by them that serued the Queene my mother' (James, *Basilicon Doron*, 24). Examples of mercy followed by further offences would include David Black's seditious speeches and the behaviour of the earls of Bothwell and Huntly. Both earls were involved in the Brig O'Dee rebellion of 1589 and convicted of treason, but soon released and returned to court. Both then participated in further rebellious activity in the first half of the 1590s. For Bothwell, see R. Macpherson, 'Stewart, Francis, First Earl of Bothwell (1561–1612)', in Matthew and Harrison, *Oxford Dictionary of National Biography*, vol. LII, 668–9; for Huntly, see J. R. M. Sizer, 'Gordon, George, First Marquess of Huntly (1561/2–1626)', in Matthew and Harrison (eds.), *Oxford Dictionary of National Biography*, vol. XXII, 883–4.

187. For an example of the king's private involvement in the case of Thomas Ross, see above, 91.

188. Wormald, 'Two Kings', 197 and 204–5.

189. On judicial independence in the seventeenth century, see Hart, *The Rule of Law*, 67–70; A. F. Havighurst, 'The Judiciary and Politics in the Reign of Charles II', Law Quarterly Review, 66 (1950), 62–78 and 229–52; and A. F. Havighurst, 'James II and the Twelve Men in Scarlet', Law Quarterly Review, 69 (1953), 522–46.

190. Bedfordshire Archives and Record Services, MS St John J1386, unfoliated.

191. *Prohibitions del Roy* (1609) 12 Co. Rep. 63–5. The twelfth part of Coke's reports was printed in 1656; *The Twelfth Part of the Reports of Sir Edward Coke* (London, 1656).

192. Stat. 16. Car.1 c.10.

193. See Zaller, *Parliament of 1621*, 82–84, and C. G. C. Tite, Impeachment and Parliamentary Judicature in Early Stuart England (London, 1974), 112–13.

194. Zaller, *Parliament of 1621*, 84.

195. *Judicature in Parlement by Henry Elsyng Clerk of the Parliaments*, ed. E. R. Foster (London, 1991), 78–85.

04 THE COMPARATIVE LEGAL BACKGROUND OF THE FIRST ENGLISH TRANSLATION OF JUSTINIAN'S INSTITUTES, AS EXAMINED BY GEORGE HARRIS.

INTRODUCTION: AN OVERVIEW

Contemporary academic research on Roman law, along with other fields of legal history, places significant emphasis on the criticality of editions and translations of primary texts. Nevertheless, this phenomenon is not novel; it has been extensively documented since at least the 19th century. Examples encompass the unearthing of Gaius's palimpsest, the conventional editions of the Corpus iuris civilis and the Corpus iuris canonici, and the publication and editing of antiquated English yearbooks and legal reports. The diminishing understanding of Latin, which played a significant role in the initiation of translations, may be traced back to a minimum of one hundred years prior, specifically into the seventeenth century. [1] The increasing significance of national laws and languages has contributed to the gradual obsolescence of Latin. Due to this rationale, it became evident that a shift in the approach towards Roman law sources was necessary. Translations have become an indispensable instrument for the study of ancient law. George Harris translated Justinian's Institutes in the mid-eighteenth century, resulting in the English output. The significance of his work is multifaceted. To begin with, this translation is the initial comprehensive English rendition of any segment of Justinian's codification. Furthermore, Harris's scope extended beyond the mere creation of an English rendition of the ancient textbook. He incorporated numerous scholarly annotations, particularly significant given its numerous allusions to the English legal system. Due to this rationale, Harris's research might be regarded as a significant illustration of an early comparative legal analysis.

GEORGE HARRIS

George Harris was born in Westminster in 1721. [2] It seems that he spent part of his childhood in Wales with his father, John Harris, who was appointed bishop of Llandaff in 1729. [3] Shortly before his father's death, in June 1738, George was matriculated at Oriel College, Oxford. In 1745 he obtained the degree of Bachelor in Civil Law and five years later a doctoral degree. [4] Later the same year, on 23 October, Harris was admitted to the College of Advocates, and he began a legal practice. During his long-term membership, he performed many administrative functions: register (1763–4), librarian (1765–6) and treasurer (1767–70; 1781–2). [5] In addition, he was involved in the administrative and judicial organisation of many dioceses. It was noted in his obituary published in *The Annual Register* that Harris was chancellor of the dioceses of Durham, Hereford and Llandaff as well as the commissioner of Essex, Hertfordshire and Surrey. [6] This list can be supplemented with two more chancellorships in Bangor and Winchester. [7] It seems that most of these appointments were held by Harris almost until his death. [8]

It is possible to locate some traces of Harris's practice as advocate. Archival investigation indicates the survival of several legal opinions presented by Harris. Most of them concern ecclesiastical matters, primarily regarding staffing of offices. Lambeth Palace Library possesses three such opinions dated 1770/1, 1784 and 1787. [9] Another two opinions are held by the local archives in Yorkshire (1764) and Devon (1780). [10]

Like many other eighteenth-century civilians, Harris was also involved in judicial work. For many years he was a judge of the Prerogative Court of Canterbury. Through the press testamentary reports, it is possible to see that Harris was performing judicial duties as early as March 1759, when he proved the will and codicils of Henry Hawley. [11] He was still acting as a judge in 1790 when he proved the will of the well-known eccentric John Elwes. [12]

Besides the Prerogative Court, Harris was also acting as a judge while he was holding the diocesan offices. While he was a commissioner of Surrey, then part of the diocese of Winchester, Harris was engaged in an unusual case. At the time, the bishop of Winchester was visitor of Magdalen College, Oxford. He exercised his powers through the commissioner. In 1769 Harris was presiding over a hearing in a case regarding the deprivation of Ambrose Kent of his Doctor of Divinity degree and fellowship at Magdalen College. It seems that these hearings were partly informal since they were taking place in such different locations as Harris's chambers, the common-hall of Doctors' Commons and the bishop's home in Chelsea. [13]

Harris's judicial activity on behalf of the Winchester diocese was perpetuated by John Wentworth. By the end of the eighteenth century, this barrister and member of the Inner Temple published several volumes regarding judicial proceedings. The matters discussed were illustrated with actual examples from practice. During the analysis of the writ of prohibition, Wentworth included in his book a motion to grant a writ, the writ itself signed by George III, as well as Harris's declaration of admitting the writ, all concerning the 1777 case. [14]

Kent's was not the only university case in which Harris was involved. In 1793 Jesus College, Cambridge sent a request to the civilian for an opinion regarding an appropriate interpretation of the College statute. [15] The proceedings concern the publication of a treatise by William Frend entitled *Peace and Union Recommended to the Associated Bodies of Republicans and Anti-Republicans.* Although Harris was not called to appear in the Vice-Chancellor's Court, his opinion was used during the hearing. [16]

As a diocesan official, Harris was also acting widely as an administrator of different ecclesiastical legal matters. For example, as a commissary of Surrey, Harris was involved in the discussion regarding the dispute between the bishop of Winchester and the vicar general of the Province of Canterbury in issuing marriage licences (1765). [17] At another point, Harris was presiding on behalf of the archbishop of Canterbury over proceedings regarding applications for medical licences. [18]

Further, like many other civilians at the time, Harris did not limit his practice to ecclesiastical law. He was also an advocate in the Admiralty, where he gained an important position and held the post of Admiralty Advocate between 1764 and 1782. [19]

George Harris was professionally active until his death. The archives of Lambeth Palace possess documentation of a 1795 case pending in the Arches – the provincial court of the archbishop of Canterbury – wherein Harris was acting on behalf of the diocese of Winchester. [20] Harris died only a few months later, on 19 April 1796. [21] He left a last will in which he disposed of his huge wealth. [22] He created multiple trusts, including two significant ones on behalf of two hospitals in London - one valued at £20,000 and the other at £15,000. This observation is hardly unexpected, given Harris actively engaged in philanthropic endeavors during his career. The individual in question was affiliated with the Corporations of the Sons of Clergy, an organization that provided financial assistance to impoverished ecclesiastics and their families. [23]

TRANSLATION OF THE *INSTITUTES*: THE EDITIONS

As pointed out earlier, George Harris became an important part of the science of Roman Civil law in England as the first translator of Justinian's *Institutes.* It is often believed that the first edition of his translation was published in 1756 by the London printers C. Bathurst and E. Withers. [24] This assumption, however, is wrong. An anonymous translation of Justinian's first book of the *Institutes*, published in 1749, may in fact be the work of Harris. [25] At first glance the translations are different. The 1749 translation seems to be closer to a paraphrase than a translation as such. One indication of Harris's authorship is an introductory essay entitled 'A Brief Account of the Rise and Progress of the Roman Law'. The essay seems to be an earlier version of another one titled in the same way, which was later published as the beginning of the 1756 edition. It is not likely that Harris borrowed the title and the text itself from someone else. The later edition is an enlarged, rethought story of the history of Roman law. Furthermore, a closer comparison of the 1749 and 1756 translations shows a certain level of similarities. It can be assumed that Harris, still a candidate to the doctoral degree in law in Oxford, published the 1749 translation as a result of his teaching experiences.

A further edition was published during his lifetime, namely the London edition of 1761. [26] Finally, in 1811 another edition was published in Oxford. [27] All three editions of the entire *Institutes* were published without any changes. In 1814, a new version of the translation appeared, published without the original Latin text. [28] It was also deprived of all the valuable notes provided by the civilian, while the introductory essay was much shortened.

A much more interesting history of Harris's translation started at about the same time in the United States. In 1812, Thomas Cooper released a collection of several Roman law-related texts jointly titled *The Institutes of Justinian. With Notes.* [29] Cooper was an English-born lawyer and chemist who travelled to America, and at the time of the publication of the abovementioned set, he was a professor of chemistry at Carlisle College in Pennsylvania. Later, Cooper became a cofounder and second president of the University of South Carolina. [30] Cooper's collection contained several other works in addition to the translation of the *Institutes.* The first of them was an English translation of the Twelve Tables. It was extrapolated from Nathaniel Hooke's voluminous work devoted to the history of ancient Rome. [31] In addition, Cooper equipped his set of texts with an essay concerning the abbreviations used by the science of Roman law to indicate sources, as well as a list of famous Roman law scholars. Cooper's work gained much popularity in the United States. It was twice republished, first in 1841 [32] and again, in an enlarged version, in 1852. [33]

Cooper's knowledge about Harris's translation may have been twofold. Cooper, like Harris, was an Oxonian. It is possible that he learnt about the translation after matriculating at University College in 1779. He left the University, however, without any formal degree. He may also have learnt more about Justinian, his codification and Harris's work later, perhaps when he was admitted to the Inner Temple and became a barrister, or after his judicial appointment as a state judge in Pennsylvania.

The 1852 publication of Harris's translation was its last appearance. Interestingly, only a year later, Thomas Collett Sanders published the very first nineteenth-century rendition of the *Institutes*. In this way, he opened a new path for numerous new translations that were released variously in the United Kingdom, the United States and South Africa in the following one-hundred-and-fifty years. At the same time, Harris's translation began to fall into oblivion.

TRANSLATION OF THE *INSTITUTES*: CONTENT

Harris began his opus with an extensive dedicatory note addressed to Sir George Lee, then the dean of the Arches. [34] In a typical panegyric manner, the civilian praised the merits of the judge for the development of English law as well as for his intellectual qualities. It would not be an exaggeration to say that Harris packed the note with all possible flattery. As an illustration, two passages can be quoted: 'and, as I have the honor to attend those courts, in which you so eminently preside, I may hope to avail myself of the many opportunities of instruction, which must continually offer themselves' [35] and 'the benefits, conferred by you, are not confined to individuals; your conduct as a Lord Commissioner of the Admiralty, and the satisfaction it gave the public, are sufficiently known'. [36]

It seems that Harris here had a pragmatic purpose. Not only was George Lee, as the dean of the Arches, the presiding member of the College of Advocates, but he was also the head of the court before which the civilian appeared. It should not be ruled out that Harris's actions were parts of his efforts to obtain a judgeship in the Arches. If this really was the case, it may be that these efforts were successful. The dedicatory note was signed by Harris on 25 February 1756. Less than three years later, in March 1759, the lawyer was already a surrogate-judge for the dean of the Prerogative Court of Canterbury. It is true that at the time the Arches had a new dean, Sir Edward Simpson, but Lee had died only a few months earlier.

After the dedication, Harris placed the advertisement, where he pointed out his main aims in preparing his translation. He emphasised that his work should be treated as an introduction to the *Institutes*' edition and commentary written by Arnold Vinnius. [37] The second paragraph of the advertisement contains a short explanation regarding the notes added by Harris to the translation. He pointed out that the majority of them concern English law. He admitted also that they were not perfect but added that they should arouse the curiosity of a 'young reader'. He hoped that these notes could also rouse the desire of the readers to study more deeply their national law as well as the Civil law, described by Harris as 'the Master-work of human policy'. [38]

Finally, the introductory part is crowned with the already-mentioned 'A Brief Account of the Rise and Progress of the Roman Law'. [39] Starting from the earliest stages of Roman legal history, Harris presented first the semi-legendary stories of the legislative activity of Romulus, a gathering of the *leges regiae* by Sextus Papirius and finally the exile of Tarquinius Priscus from Rome. In the opinion of Harris, the subsequent events that led to the creation of the republic were the times of 'great incertainity in respect to law'. Arbitrary decisions of the magistrates brought widespread discontent among the people. As a consequence, the patricians succumbed to the plebeians and decided to appoint the ten men – *decemviri* – who would eventually propose a project to enact a law that would be partially based on Greek laws and partially on previous Roman laws. Next, Harris presented the circumstances that led to the appointment of another *decemviri* committee and to shape the final version of what would be known as the law of the Twelve Tables. [40]

The story told by Harris is focused on the republican period. He noticed that shortly after the enactment of the *lex duodecim tabularum*, its provisions started to be changed due to their severity. In his opinion, the Senate was primarily responsible for these changes, as well as the plebeians who voted during their assemblies. It is curious, from a modern point of view, that he did not mention the role played by the far more important legislative body of the republican period, the popular assembly, and their statutes (*leges*). Instead, Harris pointed out the important role played by the learned jurists, by what he calls 'auctoritas prudentum'. [41] Harris went on to state that after the promulgation of the law of the Twelve Tables, the Roman system of *actiones* was constituted. At first, they were unknown to the public until Flavius made them public. Shortly thereafter, Sextus Aelius introduced a newer, much improved system of the legal actions. [42]

Harris then suddenly changed the course of his arguments to focus on the pretorian edict. He explained that although the edict lost its authority after the one-year term of office of the pretor, nevertheless 'many of them were so truly valuable for their justice and equity, that they have been perpetuated as laws'. [43]

After these extended deliberations regarding the republican period, Harris dealt with the principate in just one paragraph. He declared that after the 're-establishment of monarchy' by Augustus, the Roman law gained new types of sources – the imperial constitutions and the responses of the lawyers. [44] The details regarding their issuing were, however, not interesting to him. Instead, he skipped about three-hundred years and proclaimed that at that time the number of the imperial constitutions was so great that it was necessary to codify them. He listed the names of the lawyers Gregorius and Hermogenes (*sic*), who compiled private collections of the constitutions during the reign of the emperor Constantine. Next, he emphasised, an official collection was promulgated on the command of Emperor Theodosius. Harris summed up this part of 'A Brief Account' by saying that all the foregoing attempts to fix the state of imperial legislation were imperfect. Due to this, the great work of Justinian's codification was necessary. [45]

In the following paragraphs, Harris presented the stages of the works of codification carried out by the forces appointed by the emperor. He mentioned that the laws created on behalf of the emperor should be unchangeable and that they should not be summarised or excerpted. [46] In a separate paragraph, Harris pointed out that Justinian had continued his legislative efforts by issuing novels and edicts which were written in Greek rather than Latin. He explained that it was a consequence of the greater popularity of Greek language in the Eastern Empire. He finished these deliberations by mentioning the release of the *Basilica*. [47]

Harris devoted the last part of 'A Brief Account' to the problem of later knowledge of the codification in Western Europe. He explained that it was not commonly known in the former Western Empire, and after the Lombard invasion it was nearly forgotten. Both *Code* and *Pandects* were missing until their rediscovery in the twelfth century, respectively in Ravenna and Amalfi. Since that time, however, they have been a subject of constant studies. [48]

There are no doubts that the history of Roman law and its sources presented by Harris is disputable, especially when compared with twenty-first-century knowledge of Roman legal science. Harris's knowledge, especially about the archaic and pre-classical Roman law, is rather simplified and based more on conjectures and legends than scientific arrangements. Other matters, like the rediscovery of the *Digest* in Amalfi were still unverified. It is important to remember, however, that 'A Brief Account' was only a short introduction and should precede further reading of Vinnius's commentary.

After 'A Brief Account', the main section of Harris's book starts: the translation equipped with numerous notes. His pattern is as follows: he first gives the original Latin text, followed by the English translation typed in italics. Where he believed it was necessary, he included a short commentary and the explanation of the pivotal terms at the end.

One of the characteristic features of Harris's translation was his inclusion of a reference to the parallel segments in other parts of Justinian's codification at the start of every title in the *Institutes*. For example, beneath the name of the first title of the first book of the *Institutes* (*De iustitia et iure*) Harris indicated the designation 'D. 1 T. 1' that redirects the reader to the first title of the first book of Justinian's *Digest*, which bears the same name. In another place, beneath the eighteenth title of the second book of the *Institutes* (*De inofficioso testamento*) the translator indicated the parallel places both in the *Digest* [49] and the *Code*. [50] Such practice was characteristic for English civilian literature in the eighteenth century. It can be observed in various places throughout the century. Francis Dickins, the Regius Professor of Civil Law in Cambridge (1714–55) used it, for example, in his lecture notes. [51] In the 1770s the same method was exploited by Samuel Hallifax in his textbook. [52]

Another characteristic of Harris's work was the addition of informal subtitles clarifying the content of the following segment of the *Institutes*. A good example is the already-mentioned title *De inofficioso testamento*. It was divided into the following subtitles: *Ratio huius querelae* (I. 2, 18, pr.); *Qui de inofficioso agunt* (I. 2, 18, 1); *Qui alio iure veniunt, de inofficioso non agunt* (I. 2, 18, 2); *De eo, cui testator aliquid reliquit* (I. 2, 18, 3); *Si tutor, cui nihil a patre relictum, pupilli nomine legatum acceperit* (I. 2, 18, 4); *Si de inofficioso nomine pupilli agens succubuerit* (I. 2, 18, 5); *De quarta legitima partis* (I. 2, 18, 6–7). Although the addition was unique in comparison with other civilian works of the epoch, it was not Harris's independent idea. The names of the subtitles were borrowed from Vinnius's commentary.

The publication of the English translation of Justinian's *Institutes* was a very important event in the history of the English science of Roman Civil law. A crucial component of that translation was the notes. In fact, they were arguably the most significant element of the translation. Close analysis of them shows that Harris was a very well-read independent scholar who knew both older and more recent legal literature well. His reading was not restricted to Civil law. On the contrary, Harris also reveals extensive knowledge of the English legal system. It is noteworthy that the works to which Harris referred very often represented other disciplines and are a good manifestation of the lawyer's comprehensive knowledge.

These legal sources are quoted by Harris on many different occasions. He had an extensive orientation in all parts of Justinian's codification. In many notes it is possible to find direct references to parallel passages of the *Digest*, *Code* and *Novels*. Quite often he based his argumentation also on Theophilus's *Paraphrase*. [53] The Theodosian Code, by contrast, was used infrequently. Harris also quoted non-legal sources. Besides the Cicero orations, [54] he also referred to Tacitus's *Annales*, [55] Suetonius [56] and Aulus Gellius. [57] Among the Greek authors, he used the works of Dionysius of Halicarnassus, [58] Herodotus, [59] Plutarch [60] and the Homeric epics. [61]

As for the scholarly works, Harris referred to a great number of Roman Civil law authors who represent different traditions. It is possible to find in the notes citation of the following authors: Bartolus, [62] Philibert Bugnyon, [63] Diego de Covarrubias y Leyva, [64] Cujacius (Cujas), [65] Jean Domat (quoted both in the original version [66] as well as in the English translation by William Strahan), [67] Jean Doujat [68], Claude-Joseph de Ferrière, [69] Simon van Groenewegen van der Made, [70] Johann Friedrich Gronovius, [71] Grotius, [72] Heineccius, [73] Joachim Hoppe, [74] François Hotman, [75] Gilles Ménage, [76] Joachim Mynsinger von Frundeck, [77] Matthew Wesenbeck [78] and, naturally, Arnold Vinnius. [79] In addition to these Continental scholars, Harris referred to only three English civilians, all of whom were living in the eighteenth century, namely Robert Eden, [80] John Taylor [81] and Thomas Wood. [82]

A separate group, much more interesting than the English civilians, is made up of writers on English law, whom he used extensively. This is a rather surprising occurrence, especially given that Harris had never been trained in Common law. It can be assumed, however, that he was quite well self-educated in this field of knowledge. Besides the oldest English legal treatises, i.e. *Glanvill* [83] and *Bracton*, [84] Harris referred also to another medieval text – *Britton*. [85] The lawyers of later epochs cited by Harris are: Matthew Bacon, [86] Thomas Blount, [87] Edward Coke, [88] John Cowell, [89] Anthony Fitzherbert, [90] John Fortescue, [91] Matthew Hale, [92] William Hawkins, [93] Thomas Littleton, [94] John Rastell, [95] Thomas Smith, [96] Christopher St German [97] and Thomas Wood. [98]

Harris was also keen to refer to English ecclesiastical lawyers, including Edmund Gibson, [99] John Godolphin [100] and Henry Swinburne. [101] In addition, in one of the notes, Harris referred to a work entitled *Ordo iudiciorum* [102] but did not insert the name of the author. The context of Harris's statement, however, suggests that he was referring to the work published in 1728 by Thomas Oughton. [103] Pre-Reformation literature was not exploited by Harris, except that he referred three times to Gregory IX's *Liber extra*. [104] The 'ecclesiastical' context was strengthened by Harris referring to passages from the Bible as well as the theological literature. It is interesting that among that last type of references it is possible to find a citation of the Catholic theologian, Peter Faber, a Jesuit priest and the disciple of Ignatius of Loyola. [105]

As to English law, it has to be emphasised that Harris devoted much of his attention to the problems of legislation and court practice. [106] This last feature of the translation is especially fascinating. The oldest law reports quoted by Harris date back to the sixteenth century. These are the reports of the judge Sir James Dyer, [107] those known as *Keilway's Reports* [108] as well as those of the lawyer Edmund Plowden. [109] From the late sixteenth and early seventeenth centuries come another three law reports: Sir Edmund Anderson's, [110] Sir Edward Coke's [111] and Sir George Croke's. [112] The seventeenth century is represented by the reports by Thomas Hardres, [113] Thomas Siderfin [114] and John Vaughan [115] and the collection known as *Levine's King's Bench and Common Pleas Reports 1660–1697*. [116] The turn of the seventeenth and eighteenth century is represented by the reports series *Modern Reports* [117] and the reports collected by William Salkeld, [118] whilst the eighteenth century is witnessed by the reports authored by Sir Jeffrey Gilbert, [119] Lord Raymond [120] and Sir John Strange. [121] The activity of the Chancery is attested by Harris through the quotation of four reports series: an anonymous *A General Abridgement of Cases in Equity, Argued and Adjudged in the High Court of Chancery etc.*, [122] the *Chancery Cases* [123] and the *Chancery Reports*, [124] as well as the reports of Thomas Vernon. [125] The ecclesiastical judgments are quoted only once, when Harris referred to the reports collected by Edward Stillingfeet. [126]

Quite unique are the references to the experience of Scottish institutional writers – Sir George Mackenzie [127] and Lord Stair. [128] In both cases Harris referred to their *Institutions*. Also, in one place, it is possible to find a mention of Norman customs of the Channel Islands. [129]

Obviously, Harris was also using some secondary, auxiliary literature. Among these works, it is worth mentioning the historical pieces Basil Kennett's *Antiquities of Rome* [130] and John Potter's *Archaeologia Greca or the Antiquities of Greece.* [131] Besides, Harris was using philosophical works, like *Tetrachordon* by John Milton [132] and Montesquieu's *De l'esprit des lois.* [133] Among the dictionaries can be mentioned *Thesaurus linguae latinae* by Robert Estienne [134] and *Thesaurus eruditionis scholasticae* by Basil Faber. [135]

Following the translation of the *Institutes*, Harris added a single supplement to his work. It was an English translation of the *Novel* 118, decreed by Justinian in 543. The imperial constitution was part of the famous changes that the emperor introduced in the field of the intestate succession. The reason for its attachment to the translation of the *Institutes* is not clear, as Harris did not explain his action in this regard. It seems natural, though, that the translation could have been dictated by practical reasons. After all, ecclesiastical courts – the domain of the civilians' activity – were mainly preoccupied with testamentary inheritance cases. The *Novel* and its translation cover a little over ten pages. The text was presented in three ways. First, Harris presented the Greek version of the constitution. Second, the Latin translation of the constitution was added. Finally, beneath these two versions, an English translation was included.

Just as with the *Institutes*, the lawyer equipped the *Novel* with extensive commentaries. The apparatus is varied again. Among the civilian works it is possible to find the two pieces already mentioned before – written by Domat [136] and Ferrière. [137] In addition, Harris also used two other civilian treatises authored by Petrus Gudelinus (Pierre Goudelin) [138] and Johannes Voet. [139] English law is again represented by *Glanvill,* [140] Littleton [141] and Coke, [142] and in addition by the work on criminal law written by Sir Michael Foster. [143] Finally, the law reports were used by Harris. Only the reports of Lord Raymond [144] were reused. In addition, another three were used by Harris for the very first time: the reports prepared by Sir John Holt, [145] Sir Bartholomew Shower [146] and William Peere Williams. [147]

What were the origins of such a wealth of literature? The translation was published in 1756. Even, if it is assumed that this project was initiated by Harris while still at Oxford, the 1749 edition of the translation does not reveal much about Harris's interest in constructing elaborate notes. It seems plausible that the notes were mostly already written after Harris's graduation, while he was a member of the College of Advocates. Besides a private library which was definitely continually expanded by Harris, [148] it is most likely that his main supplying source was the library of the Doctors' Commons. This conclusion can be partially confirmed by juxtaposing the list of works used by Harris with the library catalogue of Doctors' Commons published in 1818.[149] Although not all the works to which he referred can be found in the catalogue, many of them were in the College's possession. While he was living in London, it is possible that Harris also had access to Lambeth Palace Library as well as the libraries of the Inns of Court. Finally, it is plausible that he used bishops' or cathedrals' libraries while he was travelling around the country to fulfil his professional duties.

ASSESSMENTS OF HARRIS'S TRANSLATION

The first English translation of the entirety of Justinian's *Institutes* predictably met with some response from the scholarly and literary worlds. Harris's translation became a subject of three reviews. The first one appeared in July 1756 in *The Monthly Review.* [150] The time of preparing the review was exceptionally short given that Harris dated his dedication note on 25 February 1756.[151] The book had to have been published in March or April the same year. The review was anonymous, signing as 'W.'. In the introduction, the reviewer emphasised his admiration of Roman culture, warfare, policy and government, concluding that nothing illustrates Roman greatness better than its legal order. He believed that the importance of Roman law had much exceeded Rome's military achievements.[152] In this way, 'W.' started to present the content of Harris's work. He valued 'A Brief Account' highly, stating that the introductory essay was 'very authentic, improving, and agreeable'.[153]

The reviewer gave several quotations taken from Harris's work,[154] which he then commended, and indicated that the translator coped well with the complexities of the Latin language and 'elucidated with equal propriety and clearness'.[155] He also expressed his appreciation for all the notes added by Harris to his translation. 'W.' believed that they served as an expression of particular ideas and were added 'without the vain frippery of superfluous learning'. The notes themselves were called by 'W.' 'instructive and judicious'.[156] In a further part of the review, 'W.' quoted over a dozen exemplary notes,[157] and he emphasised their comparative character. In the closing of the review, it is stated of Harris's book: 'a work peculiarly adapted for the improvement of the young Student in Law, for whose service it seems principally to have been intended; but worthy also the perusal of every Gentlemen, who would form a just notion of the civil policy of the Romans, and obtain, at the same time, a comparative view of our own'.[158]

About a year later, in April 1757, a second review was published in Leipzig.[159] German interest in an English translation may be at first sight surprising, but in fact it shows the importance of translating Justinian's *Institutes* into English. In addition, one of the central arguments in favour of the edition, according to the reviewer, was its discussion of the comparative character of Roman and English legal institutions. In his opinion, the translation undertaken by Herr Harris would benefit both Englishmen and foreigners, who would like to learn more about the barely known, but extensive English legislation. [160] It can be mentioned that the reviewer's knowledge about the condition of English civilian literature had to be relatively good. At the beginning of his review he noticed that Harris's edition was released only a year after Taylor's exegetical analysis of the imperial constitution *Imperatoriam maiestatem*. [161]

The last review was published in February 1761 in *The Critical Review, or Annales of Literature*. [162] The late date of publication of the review was explained at once. The first edition of the translation preceded the creation of *The Critical Review*. For this reason, an opportunity to write a review was the publishing of the second edition of Harris's work. Almost the entire first two pages of the review served as a presentation of the significance of Justinian's codification for Roman law, as well as its aftermath in Western Europe. It can be assumed that the reviewer used as a template for his own considerations a seventeenth-century book written by Sir Arthur Duck – *De usu et authoritate Iuris civilis Romanorum in dominiis principum Christianorum*. The reviewer briefly described different European legal systems and their use of Roman law (though he omitted Central and Eastern Europe, which were included by Duck in his book).

The reviewer proclaimed that 'the public is greatly obliged to the learned translator, for clearing the channels to the foundation of justice, before obstructed by the difficulty and ambiguity which always attends a dead language'. [163] The translation was evaluated as 'just and not inelegant', and the notes were once more highly praised. Again, the reviewer emphasised the importance of Harris's comparisons between Common law and Civil law. Still, according to the evaluator, some notes (especially those related to the law of nations and natural law) were inaccurate. [164] As an example, the reviewer pointed out Harris's notes regarding the legal status of black slaves coming from colonies to the metropole. Nevertheless, the reviewer resumed his assessment by saying that 'our author is a free, sensible, and judicious translator'. [165]

CONCISE SUMMARY

Harris's extensive utilization of sources, literature, and legal reports leaves a profound impact on the reader. The method he employed greatly surpassed the norms of mid-eighteenth-century literature, and certainly surpassed the norms of an author who was not engaged in academia. Harris's bibliography encompasses a comprehensive collection of over ninety titles. The purpose of these resources was not to compose a cohesive monograph, but rather to enhance the translation by incorporating acquired annotations. Harris's intention also conceals the distinctive nature of the piece. As indicated in the promotional material of his publication, the author's commentary was not intended to serve as a comprehensive elucidation of the terminology employed in Roman Civil law. However, Harris aimed to stimulate interest in the field of English law. The objective was successfully attained. The evaluators of Harris's work unanimously highlight the English character of the notes. The diverse range of legal treatises employed by him on this topic is remarkable. However, of greater significance is Harris's tendency to cite excerpts from legal reports as a response to the issues under consideration. During the mid-eighteenth century, lawyers did not completely embrace the notion of precedent. While they held a high regard for and eagerly consulted previous legal rulings, these rulings were not infallible. Lord Mansfield's judicial activism concluded the process of establishing the doctrine of precedent in Common law. [166] The frequent utilization of law reports by civilians in their professional endeavours can be regarded as an exemplification of shifts in judicial practice. [167] Harris's limited utilization of his ecclesiastical experience is peculiar. Ecclesiastical law is infrequently mentioned in his notebooks. However, it is not an overstatement to assert that Harris's notes possess a really comparative nature.

Footnote

1. Concerning non-legal sources, this can be traced back even a century or two earlier. Since at least the mid-sixteenth century it is possible to observe constant efforts to render ancient classical works into English. Some of them were rather close to a paraphrase, but some others were direct translations; see J. E. Sandys, A History of Classical Scholarship, 3 vols. (Cambridge, 1903–8), vol. II, 239–43. It is interesting, however, that among these works are no legal texts. One of the early attempts to translate a Latin legal text into English is Clement Barksdale's translation of *De iure belli ac pacis* authored by Hugo Grotius; see M. Barducci, Hugo Grotius and the Century of Revolution, 1613–1718: Transnational Reception in English Political Thought (Oxford, 2017), 99–101.
2. See e.g. T. A. B. Corley, 'Harris, George (bap. 1721, d. 1796)', in Oxford Dictionary of National Biography (Oxford, 2004), available at www.oxforddnb.com/view/10.1093/ref:odnb/9780198614128.001.0001/odnb-9780198614128-e-12386?rskey=lHXxYn&result=2.
3. L. Thomas, 'Harris, John (1680–1738), Bishop of Llandaff', in *Dictionary of Welsh Biography*, available at https://biography.wales/article/s-HARR-JOH-1680.
4. C. L. Shadwell, Registrum Orielense: An Account of the Members of Oriel College, 2 vols. (London, 1893–1902), vol. II, 94.
5. G. D. Squibb, Doctors' Commons: History of the College of Advocates and Doctors of Law (Oxford, 1977), 192.

6. *The Annual Register for the Year 1796. Chronicle*, 2nd edn (London, 1807), 14–15.
7. 'Chancellors of the Dioceses of Bangor', *Old Wales*, 1 (1905), 218–19.
8. Ibid.
9. Lambeth Palace Library (LPL), MS 3416, fos. 10–12v, 20v–22v, 30v–35v and 39v–40.
10. East Riding of Yorkshire Archives and Local Studies Service, DDRI/27/17; Devon Archives and Local Studies Service, 2994A/PW 58.
11. *The Annual Register, or a View of the History, Politics, and Literature, of the Year 1759* (London, 1760), 348–51.
12. *The Lady's Magazine*, March 1790, 129.
13. For more about the case, see *The Conduct of the Right Reverend the Lord Bishop of Winchester, as Visitor of St Mary Magdalen College, Oxford, Fully Stated. With Brief Observations on Visitatorial Power. Addressed to His Lordship* (London, 1770).
14. J. Wentworth, A Complete System of Pleading, 10 vols. (London, 1797–9), vol. VI, 242–5.
15. W. Frend, An Account of the Proceedings in the University of Cambridge, Against William Frend, M.A. (Cambridge, 1793), xv–xvii.
16. Ibid., 226.
17. LPL, MS 1119, fos. 150–52.
18. LPL, VX IA/10/525/1-2 (2 June 1757); VX IA/10/527/1-2 (29 February 1768); VX IA/10/526/1-2 (10 December 1768).
19. J. Heydn and H. Ockerby, The Book of Dignities; Containing Lists of the Official Personages of the British Empire (London, 1890), 423. For Harris's admiralty cases see D. E. C. Yale, 'A Historical Note on the Jurisdiction of the Admiralty in Ireland', Irish Jurist, 3 (1968), 146–52, at 150, and D. Syrett, The Royal Navy in European Waters During the American Revolutionary War (Columbia, SC, 1998), 97–8.
20. LPL, Arches Aa 90/2, 3, 5, 10, 2; Arches AAa 35a; Arches Bb 102/3; Arches D 1572; Arches E 45/91; Arches F 12 fos. 176–183.
21. There was only one obituary published, in *The Annual Register for the Year 1796*, 14–5. Besides, a short note regarding Harris's death was published in the German journal *Intelligenzblatt der Allgemeinen Literatur-Zeitung*, 76 (1800), 627.
22. London, The National Archives, PROB 11/1275/118.
23. His name can be found among the organisers of the Feast of the Sons of Clergy in 1768. See G. Mathew, A Sermon Preached at the Anniversary Meeting of the

Stewards of the Sons of the Clergy (London, 1815), 15; The Royal Kalendar: Or, Complete and Correct Annual Register for England, Scotland, Ireland, and America for the Year 1796 (London, 1796), 207.

24. G. Harris, D. Justiniani Institutionum Libri Quatuor. The Four Books of Justinian's Institution, Translated into English, With Notes (London, 1756). A year before Harris's translation, John Taylor published his well-known book *Elements of Civil Law*. Its second chapter contains exegetical analysis of Justinian's constitution *Imperatoriam maiestatem*, the one which promulgated the *Institutes*; see J. Taylor, Elements of Civil Law (Cambridge, 1755), 29–39.

25. *D. Justiniani Institutionum Liber Primus. The First Book of Justinian's Institutes, With English Version, and Notes* (London, 1749). The translation was almost unnoticed. Only one note was released by the press soon after the translation's publishing: *The Gentleman's Magazine, and Historical Chronicle*, 19 (1749), 192.

26. G. Harris, D. Justiniani Institutionum Libri Quatuor. The Four Books of Justinian's Institutions, Translated into English, With Notes, 2nd edn (London, 1761).

27. G. Harris, D. Justiniani Institutionum Libri Quatuor. The Four Books of Justinian's Institutions, Translated into English, With Notes, 3rd edn (Oxford, 1811).

28. Dr [G.] Harris, Institutions or Elements of Justinian. In Four Books. Translated from the Original Latin (London, 1814).

29. The Institutes of Justinian. With Notes, ed. T. Cooper (Philadelphia, PA, 1812).

30. T. Cooper, 'Cooper, Thomas (1759–1840)', in L. Stephen (ed.), Dictionary of National Biography, vol. XII (New York and London, 1887), 151–2. For a detailed biography of Cooper, see D. Malone, The Public Life of Thomas Cooper, 1783–1839 (New Haven, CT, London and Oxford, 1926).

31. N. Hooke, Roman History, From the Building of Rome to the Ruin of the Commonwealth, 4th edn, 4 vols. (London, 1738–71), vol. II, 314–32.

32. T. Cooper, The Institutes of Justinian. With Notes, 2nd edn (New York, 1841).

33. T. Cooper, The Institutes of Justinian. With Notes. With Additional Notes and References, 3rd edn (New York, 1852).

34. W. P. Courtney, 'Lee, Sir George (1700–1758)', in S. Lee (ed.), Dictionary of National Biography, vol. XXXIII (New York and London, 1893), 353–6.

35. Harris, *D. Justiniani* (1756), iv.

36. Ibid., v.

37. Harris was referring to Vinnius's *In quatuor libros Institutionum imperialium commentarius academicus & forensis*, which was published first in the Netherlands in 1646. Until the nineteenth century the work enjoyed great popularity. The total

number of the editions reached 154. See L. Beck Varela, 'Vinnius: Commentary on the Institutes', in S. Dauchy, G. Martyn, A. Musson, H. Pihlajamäki, and A. Wijffels (eds.), The Formation and Transmission of Western Legal Culture: 150 Books that Made the Law in the Age of Printing (Cham, 2016), 197–200, at 198.

38. Harris, *D. Justiniani* (1756), viii.
39. Ibid., ix–xv.
40. Ibid., ix–x.
41. Ibid., ix.
42. Ibid.
43. Ibid., xii.
44. Ibid.
45. Ibid.
46. Ibid., xii–xiv.
47. Ibid., xiv.
48. Ibid., xv.
49. D. 5, 2 (*De inofficioso testamento*).
50. C. 3, 28 (*De inofficioso testamento*).
51. Cambridge, Trinity Hall, Old Library, MS 31.
52. S. Hallifax, An Analysis of the Roman Civil Law, 2nd edn (Cambridge, 1775).
53. In one place Harris pointed out that he worked on the *Paraphrase* edition by Willem Otto Reitz published in The Hague in 1751.
54. Harris, *D. Justiniani* (1756), book 1, 16, 70; book 4, 39.
55. Ibid., book 1, 38; book 4, 55.
56. Ibid., book 1, 38, 50, 66; book 4, 55.
57. Ibid., book 4, 3, 25.
58. Ibid., book 1, 66.
59. Ibid., book 1, 67.
60. Ibid., book 1, 32.
61. Ibid., book 3, 76–77.
62. Ibid., book 1, 43.
63. Ibid., book 4, 81.
64. Ibid., book 4, 4.

65. Ibid., book 1, 13; book 2, 91; book 3, 43; book 4, 60.
66. Ibid., book 2, 26, 44, 47, 86.
67. Ibid., book 1, 14; book 2, 26, 44, 47, 86.
68. Ibid., book 3, 6.
69. Ibid., book 1, 64; book 2, 10, 70, 91; book 3, 69.
70. Ibid., book 3, 40.
71. Ibid., book 1, 9; book 2, 120; book 4, 81.
72. Ibid., book 2, 16; book 4, 5.
73. Ibid., book 1, 3, 68; book 2, 21; book 3, 18, 50, 60; book 4, 15, 26, 39, 55.
74. Ibid., book 1, 9.
75. Ibid., book 4, 60.
76. Ibid., book 4, 76.
77. Ibid., book 1, 7, 40, 43; book 2, 70; book 3, 12, 19, 27, 40–41, 56.
78. Ibid., book 3, 27.
79. Ibid., book 1, 20, 32, 33, 35, 38, 40, 66, 68; book 2, 58, 79, 81, 100, 119, 120; book 3, 3, 10, 12, 13, 20, 21, 25, 27, 35, 36, 41, 44, 61, 64, 65, 66, 78, 80, 88, 89; book 4, 26, 30, 33, 81, 92.
80. Ibid., book 1, 9, 66.
81. Ibid., book 3, 29.
82. Ibid., book 2, 20, 23, 25.
83. Ibid., book 2, 16; book 4, 31.
84. Ibid., book 1, 25, 35; book 2, 16; book 4, 31, 36, 74, 84.
85. Ibid., book 4, 74.
86. Ibid., book 1, 61; book 2, 15; book 3, 16, 71; book 4, 9, 19, 21, 30, 31, 34.
87. Ibid., book 4, 31.
88. Ibid., book 1, 35, 50; book 2, 15, 16, 19, 27; book 3, 24; book 4, 1, 4, 66, 87, 88, 89, 92.
89. Ibid., book 1, 65; book 2, 19, 25, 29, 46, 69, 79; book 3, 40, 61; book 4, 15, 34, 40, 42, 51, 56, 74.
90. Ibid., book 4, 40, 85.
91. Ibid., book 1, 15, 50.
92. Ibid., book 1, 8; book 4, 4, 5, 8, 9, 12, 13, 16, 56, 87.

93. Ibid., book 1, 25; book 3, 86; book 4, 14, 16, 56, 87.
94. Ibid., book 1, 15, 27, 34, 43, 44, 47, 48; book 2, 29; book 3, 65; book 4, 30, 33, 61, 66, 84.
95. Ibid., book 3, 24; book 4, 84, 85.
96. Ibid., book 1, 12.
97. Ibid., book 4, 51.
98. Ibid., book 2, 19, 29; book 3, 82; book 4, 7.
99. Ibid., book 1, 25.
100. Ibid., book 3, 24.
101. Ibid., book 1, 55; book 2, 44, 47, 49, 54, 56, 57, 58, 59, 68, 86, 87, 109, 119; book 3, 24.
102. Ibid., book 4, 80.
103. See e.g. Ł. J. Korporowicz, 'Was the Roman Catholic Canon Law Studied in Eighteenth Century England?', Studia Prawno-Ekonomiczne, 108 (2018), 83–102, at 96–7.
104. Harris, *D. Justiniani* (1756), book 2, 46; book 4, 80, 91.
105. Ibid., book 3, 27.
106. Harris referred both to pre-1066 and post-1066 legislation. The Anglo-Saxon legislation was known to him through the work by D. Wilkins: *Leges Anglo-Saxonicae, Ecclesiasticae & Civilis* (London, 1721).
107. Harris, *D. Justiniani* (1756), book 1, 12; book 2, 57; book 4, 31.
108. Ibid., book 1, 25.
109. Ibid., book 4, 5.
110. Ibid., book 2, 57.
111. Ibid., book 1, 44, 61; book 2, 19; book 4, 16, 22, 23, 92.
112. Ibid., book 1, 57, 58.
113. Ibid., book 1, 71.
114. Ibid., book 1, 71; book 2, 57.
115. Ibid., book 1, 30, 32, 44, 61, 71.
116. Ibid., book 1, 55; book 4, 92.
117. Ibid., book 2, 87; book 3, 21.
118. Ibid., book 1, 71; book 3, 23.
119. Ibid., book 2, 56.
120. Ibid., book 1, 44; book 2, 57; book 4, 7, 91.

121. Ibid., book 2, 50.
122. Ibid., book 1, 55, 71; book 3, 16.
123. Ibid., book 2, 15.
124. Ibid., book 1, 71.
125. Ibid., book 1, 56.
126. Ibid., book 1, 71.
127. Ibid., book 2, 80.
128. Ibid.
129. Ibid., book 2, 16.
130. Ibid., book 1, 31.
131. Ibid., book 1, 50.
132. Ibid., book 1, 28.
133. Ibid., book 1, 13.
134. Ibid.
135. Ibid., book 1, 7.
136. Ibid., Nov., 5, 11.
137. Ibid., Nov., 5.
138. Ibid.
139. Ibid., Nov., 6.
140. Ibid., Nov., 5.
141. Ibid.
142. Ibid., Nov., 10.
143. Ibid., Nov., 5.
144. Ibid., Nov., 3.
145. Ibid.
146. Ibid., Nov., 11.
147. Ibid., Nov., 3, 5.
148. Harris's name frequently appears in the subscribers' lists of many books, e.g. T. Richards (ed.), Antiquae linguae Britannicae thesaurus (Bristol, 1753), xxix; J. Thorpe and J. Thorpe, Registrum Roffense: Or a Collection of Antient Records, Charters, and Instruments of Divers Kinds (London, 1769), 8.

149. *Catalogue of the Books in the Library of the College of Advocates in Doctors' Commons* (London, 1818).
150. *Monthly Review*, 15 (1756), 1–18.
151. Harris, *D. Justiniani* (1756), vii.
152. *Monthly Review*, 15 (1756), 2.
153. Ibid., 3.
154. Ibid., 3–7.
155. Ibid., 8.
156. Ibid.
157. Ibid., 8–18.
158. Ibid., 18.
159. *Neue Zeitungen von Gelehrten Sachen*, 31 (1757), 273–5.
160. Ibid., 275.
161. Ibid., 273.
162. *The Critical Review, or Annales of Literature*, 11 (1761), 99–103.
163. Ibid., 100.
164. Ibid.
165. Ibid., 103.
166. J. Oldham, 'Lord Mansfield, Stare decisis, and the Ratio decidendi 1756 to 1788', in W. H. Bryson and S. Dauchy (eds.), Ratio decidendi: Guiding Principles of Judicial Decisions, vol. I: Case Law (Berlin, 2006), vol. I, 137–50, at 138–44.
167. In fact, Lord Mansfield was appointed as a chief justice of the King's Bench a few months after Harris's translation was published.

05 LEGAL SCIENCE AND COMPARATIVE LEGAL HISTORY IN BLACKSTONE'S COMMENTARIES: AN EXAMINATION OF THE ESSENCE OF CUSTOM

When seen from a particular perspective, William Blackstone's Commentaries exhibit a dual focus on the organization of English law and the examination and harmonization of its ideas with the entirety of legal history. [1] Blackstone's interpretation of John Selden sheds light on this supplementary and potentially unnoticed worry. [2] Blackstone demonstrated a keen interest in Selden's works and meticulously recorded references to the majority of them in the margins of the Commentaries. Significantly, Blackstone was a reader who held the same opinion as Selden regarding the essential coherence of legal experience. It may seem contradictory, yet both Selden and Blackstone focused their historical and jurisprudential examination on the wide range of legal decisions made in the past and present. However, these various and perhaps conflicting decisions were all influenced, maintained, and ultimately regulated by the same legal authority: will. The will contemplated by Selden and Blackstone was not devoid of substance or lacking in purpose. It mostly aligned with the divine wisdom of God's will. The principles of natural law were determined by God's eternal word, and His will served as the ultimate authority that governed the human determination of positive laws. Selden and Blackstone held a similar perspective on customary and statutory standards, which was based on religious principles. They believed that human laws were interpreted, implemented, and elaborated upon in various historical legal systems, referred to as the 'eternal' and 'immutable laws of good and evil'. 3 As a result, both individuals were affiliated with an academic lineage that had entrusted jurisprudence with the responsibility of recognizing historical distinctions among distinct legal systems, evaluating the legal consequences of these differences, and harmonizing individual instances of the law with the entirety of legal history through comparative analysis and the application of fundamental principles. [4]

These seem to be the common premises that united Selden and Blackstone in their investigation of legal history and, by extension, elevated history to the summit of English legal education. When seen from this perspective, it was the legal interpretation of history that preserved, explained and reconciled the singularities of law. [5] Not only had it been in the course of history that the multiple sources of English law had emerged and combined – often at a high price – in one organic body, it had also been history itself that, in time, had been recognised as the crucial source of the English legal tradition. Hence, one of the central problems raised in Blackstone's *Commentaries* is that of determining the authority of the English legal tradition and of ascertaining the nature of its primary normative source: custom. [6]

Blackstone himself had invoked the authority of Selden at the very beginning of his examination of custom, and sided with his understanding of its nature, over the older one presented by Sir John Fortescue, and more recently restated by Sir Edward Coke:

> Our antient lawyers, and particularly Fortescue, insist with abundance of warmth, that these customs are as old as the primitive Britons, and continued down, through the several mutations of government and inhabitants, to the present time unchanged and unadulterated. This may be the case as to some; but in general, as Mr Selden in his notes observes, this assertion must be understood with many grains of allowance; and ought only to signify, as the truth seems to be, that there never was any formal exchange of one system of laws for another: though doubtless by the intermixture of adventitious nations, the Romans, the Picts, the Saxons, the Danes, and the Normans, they must have insensibly introduced and incorporated many of their own customs with those that were before established: thereby in all probability improving the texture and wisdom of the whole, by the accumulated wisdom of divers particular countries. [7]

The organic nature of English legal history summarised in this passage would seem sufficient to justify the comparative outlook that Blackstone was to adopt in his treatment of general custom. And yet, though the *Commentaries* repeated the trope according to which customs had originally been oral and ancestral habits retained by memory and usage alone, the customs that Blackstone identified as actual sources of English law had lost all ancestral qualities, and belonged instead to a highly formalised body of recorded customary law. [8] Moreover, Blackstone presented a sophisticated interpretation of English customary law that depended on the systematic use of external authorities, which he drew from a comparative history of European sources of law. [9]

Building on these considerations, I would like to propose a twofold argument. First, I would like to suggest that the place in which comparative legal history played its role in the *Commentaries* was in the relationship between text and authority. This at least seems to be the case judging from Blackstone's treatment of general custom, where sensitive questions concerning the legal nature of custom were addressed by including in the *Commentaries*' analysis comparative references to external authorities. The careful placement of these external points of reference offered to the student of English law valuable signposts and lent a greater sense of direction to Blackstone's investigation. But it also fulfilled a subtler purpose: it shaped the interpretation of English law and transformed the comparative history of European legal sources into one of the interpretative means by which the *Commentaries* organised English law. To put it succinctly, comparison supplemented the law, not because Blackstone considered external authorities to be formally normative and coercive, but because these authorities belonged to the substance of legal thought as it unfolded 'in the seamless web of legal history', thus proving vital in guiding his interpretation of English law. [10] Accordingly, and here is my second point, the effect of Blackstone's use of comparative legal history seems to have gone beyond simply clarifying contentious points of the law. It would seem to have uncovered the inner reasons of English laws, the reasons why history had given to these municipal norms their particular shape. And in doing so, it looks as if Blackstone's comparative perspective drew, out of the history of these norms, those first principles which the ascending degrees of systematic thinking present in the *Commentaries* deemed responsible for integrating the municipal laws of the English kingdom into a coherent body of internal law, and this body of internal law into the larger whole of the European legal tradition. Hence, my intent is to verify whether it might have been through such a process of comparison and integration that the *Commentaries* sought to understand the historical singularities of English law and dialectically reconcile them to the whole of legal experience.

The *sedes materiae* of Blackstone's treatment of customary law was the third section of his general introduction to the *Commentaries*. This section presents a systematic account of English legal sources and is opened, after a series of preliminary remarks on the fundamental partition between sources of English law, by a discussion on customs. In testing the argument that I have just outlined, I will follow Blackstone's comparative treatment of general custom and consider in turn the three defining issues he examined to determine its nature: supremacy, relation to case law and constitutional authority.

General customs known as Common law stood supreme among the sources of English law. [11] They were 'the first ground and chief corner stone of the laws of England'. [12] As such, Blackstone considered them to be among the core embodiments of English sovereignty. Yet, the exact scope of their supremacy and the normative rationale justifying their pre-eminence were complex issues that engaged Blackstone's labours throughout crucial portions of the *Commentaries*. This is why I will begin by drawing together the several strands of an argument developed by Blackstone to explore and explain the legal foundation of the Common law's primacy.

Within the municipal system of law's written and unwritten sources, Common law took precedence over unwritten laws that were either local or had acquired authority by virtue of their incorporation into English law. Blackstone called these latter norms 'particular laws' and included amongst them 'the civil and canon laws', i.e. that body of the *utrumque ius*, or *ius commune*, that had been adopted in England 'by custom' and 'used only in certain peculiar courts and jurisdictions'. [13] It was primarily in relation to this body of law that the Common law enjoyed preeminence.

Determining the relationship, within the English legal order, between the Common law and the *ius commune* was certainly not a new challenge. Unsurprisingly, therefore, Blackstone addressed it according to the settled opinion of English jurisprudence and adopted the view that had been restated only a century earlier by Matthew Hale: 'all the strength that either the papal or imperial laws have obtained in this realm, or indeed in any other kingdom in Europe', wrote Blackstone, 'is only because they have been admitted and received'. [14] As so often happens in the *Commentaries*, Blackstone gathered and abridged in a short turn of phrase the condensed outcome of a vast doctrinal debate. Beneath this statement lay, in fact, a principle that had been both developed and transformed over several centuries in a Europe-wide conversation. Well before the eighteenth century, this principle had been invoked to justify the independence of national laws and establish, by extension, their superiority over the *ius commune*. By the time Blackstone reverted to its authority, its use had become virtually ubiquitous, as jurists across Europe found in the creative consistency to its underlying rationale the explanation needed to establish a proper hierarchy of sources. Moreover, because of its foundational character, Blackstone never tired of restating it, so the principle reappeared countless times throughout the *Commentaries*. I would argue, however, that its most important formulation occurred in book 1, chapter 7, for it was here that Blackstone explicitly identified this European maxim and retraced its municipal authority to a correspondingly English source. The identification came amid Blackstone's analysis of royal prerogatives and was meant to explain why two Tudor statutes, enacted during the Reformation – 24 Hen. VIII c. 12 and 25 Hen. VIII c. 28 – had styled the English Crown as 'imperial' and the English kingdom as an 'empire':

Formerly there prevailed a ridiculous notion, propagated by the German and Italian civilians, that an Emperor could do many things which a king could not, (as the creation of notaries and the like) and that all kings were in some degree subordinate and subject to the Emperor of Germany or Rome. The meaning therefore of the legislature, when it uses these terms of *empire* and *imperial*, and applies them to the realm of England, is only to assert that our king is equally sovereign and independent within these his dominions, as any Emperor is in his empire; and owes no kind of subjection to any other potentate upon earth. [15]

There is an irresistible *concinnitas* to this passage that belongs only to Blackstone at his finest. Nothing stands in between text and authority. The two seamlessly blend together and coalesce in their illustration of the inner life of English law. Their harmonisation is such an essential part of Blackstone's legal reasoning that the presence of one of the most pervasive and consequential maxims of the *ius commune* goes almost unnoticed and appears to be integral – because Blackstone shows that it is – to the municipal logic of English law. [16] And yet, the passage does indeed select the principle according to which 'rex superiorem non recognoscens, in regno suo est imperator' ('the king, recognising no superior, is emperor in his kingdom') as the axis on which Blackstone hinged the legal justification of English sovereignty. This justification was essential to determining the proper order of sources under English law, since it was because England was subject to none that its main body of law stood supreme. [17]

Despite its integration into the text, however, the maxim still needed to be adequately grounded in the English legal tradition. Blackstone did so in the second edition of the *Commentaries*, where he completed thc passage just quoted by adding a . This addition allowed him to cite the *rex in regno suo* maxim according to the formula that had been supposedly spoken in the eleventh century by William II and later recorded by the thirteenth-century Benedictine monk Matthew Paris in his *Chronica majora*: 'Rex allegavit, quod ipse omnes libertates haberet in regno suo, quas imperator vendicabat in imperio' ('The king alleged that he should possess all the rights in his kingdom as the emperor was claiming in his empire'). [18] By so doing, Blackstone offered evidence that this principle had enjoyed municipal authority even before it had been adopted by the two Tudor statutes and could indeed be traced back to the earliest days of the Common law. At that time, the formula had enjoyed an extraordinary success throughout Europe and continued to designate, well into the heart of modernity, that supreme synthesis of powers later known by the name of sovereignty. Over time, however, the implications that jurists drew from the formula became increasingly radical. Francesco Calasso has so effectively summarised them that it is worth translating his observations in full:

[A]t first [the formula] had merely meant to say this: those powers that according to the spirit of the time belonged to the emperor, as *dominus mundi*, over the universal empire had to be recognized as belonging to each free monarch within the limits of his own kingdom. It did not take long for the formula to extend its meaning far beyond the circle of free kings and encompass within its orbit all the particular jurisdictions that, by holding within themselves the innermost reason of their individual life, possessed the powers necessary to develop it. Moreover, the formula did not fail to reproduce its effects on the order of law's sources by overturning the original notion of an absolute *ius commune*, ruling out all inconsistent expressions of particular law, to affirm in its place the primacy of the *ius proprium*, now understood to be the spontaneous and free – therefore legitimate – expression of life running through individual jurisdictions, that effectively assigned to the *ius commune* only the subsidiary function of supreme regulator and coordinator. [19]

Now, this line of reasoning seems to explain why Blackstone reverted so decisively, in his interpretation of English sovereignty, to a maxim belonging to a world that had long since died out: because it had been the jurisprudence developing around that maxim that had prepared and accelerated an inversion of authority that had first overturned the relationship between the *ius commune* and the *iura propria*, and then pressed legal thought to develop a new conception of municipal law. By proving that the *rex in regno suo* principle had continuously operated in English law, and that the combined effect of those forces animating its legal and historical vitality had been to elevate municipal law above the *ius commune*, Blackstone was trying to establish a systemic point of connection between the history of English law, the supremacy of its primary source and the scientific authority deposited in the European legal tradition. After all, this conclusion was an easy one to draw since it had been widely maintained by modern jurisprudence. And Blackstone knew it, if for no other reason than because it had been confirmed by his main source on the matter: John Selden. [20] Along with Hale, Selden guided Blackstone in his exploration of the Common law's preeminence and provided him with the references to crucial normative and doctrinal sources quoted in this section of the *Commentaries*. Not only did the references to Paris and the two Reformation statutes come from Selden, but it had been Selden who had explained the European scope and English authority of the *rex in regno suo* principle in his major work on comparative public law, *Titles of Honor*. Rich and subtle as it is, Selden's long review of the matter deserves extensive quotation. [21]

Although Selden was perfectly aware that emperors in both the East and West of Europe had claimed the title for themselves alone, excluding its application to all lesser rulers, he had no hesitation in recognising that 'Kings of other Nations' had also adopted the same title 'as no less proper to their own greatness'. [22] The 'Kings of England', for instance, had 'justly used' the title of emperor, 'and that from antient Ages'. [23] The claim was supported by precise historical evidence: 'For our Edgar frequently in his Charters called himself *Albionis & Anglorum Basileus*'. [24] This certainly did not represent an isolated case, for even though the title was 'not directly used in the following times, yet the substance of it was sufficiently challenged in that of William the Second, when he so confidently told Archbishop Anselm that *ipse omnes libertates habebat in Regno suo quas Imperator vindicabat in Imperio*, as the words in Matthew Paris'. [25] At this point, Selden moved briskly forward and, building on these historical premises, observed that

also under King Henry VIII the whole Parliament conceived, and so expressed themselves [Selden's marginal note: 24 Hen. VIII c. 12, 25 Hen. VIII c. 21] that *by diverse and sundry old authentique Histories and Chronicles it is manifestly declared and expressed that this Realm of England is an* Empire *and so hath been accepted in the World, governed by some supreme Head and King, having dignity and Royal Estate of the* Imperial *Crown of the same.* [26]

Having thus proven that the title of emperor had been in use in the kingdom of England, Selden moved to similar investigations concerning the kingdoms of France and Spain, among others. Now, once his historical evidence had been collected, Selden began considering its legal significance: [27]

Neither is the use of this Title of Emperor in the stile of other Princes any injury to the Emperor of Germany, who is commonly so known by that name as if it were only proper to him. Indeed divers Civilians, especially of Italy and Germany, which profess the old Laws of Rome, tell us, that the Emperor is at this day, of right, Lord of the Whole World or Earth ... But it is most clear that neither anciently nor at this day there is any such title, as Lord of the whole World, really due to him, and that diverse other Princes, as the Kings of England, Scotland, France, Spain, beside others, have their supremacy, acknowledging no Superior but God himself, and may every way as justly (as the Emperor of Rome) be stiled Emperors, or by any other name which expresses the fullest height of Honor and Dignity.

WHY? BECAUSE

besides the States of Asia, Afrique, and America, the greatest Kings of Europe have from many Ages been absolutely supreme, without any kind of colour of subjection to the Empire. As for the Kings of Spain, those great Lawyers of that Country, Valdesius, Burgo de Paz, Diego Perez, Ferdinando Vasques, Convaruvias, Hieronymo de Zevallos, and such more make it clear, that the King of Spain is from ancient right free from all colour of this kind of subjection. The same in the Kingdom of France, is justified by those French Lawyers, Bodin, Chassanaeus, Bignon, Carolus de Grassaliis, and divers others. ... But for this matter (which is indeed of itself most clear) whosoever shall be troubled with the obvious opinions and arguments of the Civilians, as especially of that Neopolitan Marta, Zoannettus, and the like, who attributed all temporal supremacy to the Empire of Germany, as it hath succeeded to Rome, let them more fully by particulars satisfie themselves out of those learned and judicious Lawyers that live under the Empire, Henningius, Arnisaeus, and Bernardus Zieritzius, besides the Spanish Zevallos, Albericus Gentilis, and some more of the discreeter Civilians, who have both singularly disputed this question, and have also vindicated the rights of supreme Majesty to other Kings of Europe, nothing at all derogating from the true Dignity of the Empire.

This entire passage elaborated a specific interpretation of the *rex in regno suo* principle, which turned on its head the traditional understanding of *imperium*. For the jurists belonging to the long tradition of the *ius commune*, the belief in the universal jurisdiction of the empire amounted to the belief in the existence of a supreme principle of justice embodied by the emperor, who, as the living law, secured the legitimacy of all subordinate acts of power exercised by inferior rulers. Being the pinnacle of justice on earth, the empire was entrusted with the task of securing order in human affairs. Consistently, the Emperor possessed exclusive powers that no lesser ruler could rightly claim as his own. Whereas Blackstone spoke only of the power to establish notaries, the chief power that the emperor possessed was the power to enact and interpret laws. However, as the historical institution of the Holy Roman Empire entered into crisis, a number of doctrines elaborated within the very experience of the *ius commune* began claiming that kings enjoyed, within their necessarily limited jurisdiction, the same powers that were held by the emperor universally. Thus, even within those doctrines that accompanied and sustained the rise of national jurisdictions and the establishment of municipal bodies of law, the paradigm of sovereign power was primarily understood by ascribing to kings the same *regalia* that had been traditionally recognised to the emperor alone. In this sense, the notion of the emperor became the keystone necessary to define municipal sovereignty well beyond the Middle Ages and the reach of the Holy Roman Empire. [28]

It may seem odd to consider Blackstone's use of the *rex in regno suo* maxim as an instance of comparative legal history. And yet, although Blackstone's comparison might have been mostly silent in this case, he did acknowledge that English law settled the relationship between its sources and the *ius commune* exactly like the rest of the contemporary European systems. As he stressed, the notions entertained by English jurists on this point had not been 'singular' in any way:

The Civil and Canon Laws, considered with respect to any intrinsic obligation, have no force or authority in this kingdom; they are no more binding in England than our laws are binding at Rome. But as far as these foreign laws, on account of some peculiar property, have in some particular case, and in some particular courts, been introduced and allowed by our laws, so far they oblige, and no farther: their authority being wholly founded upon that permission and adoption. In which we are not singular in our notions; for even in Holland, where the imperial law is much cultivated and its decisions pretty generally followed we are informed by Van Leeuwen that 'it receives its force from custom and the consent of the people, either tacitly or expressly given: for otherwise, he adds, we should no more be bound by this law, than by that of the Almains, the Franks, the Saxons, the Goths, the Vandals, and other of the antient nation.' Wherefore, in all points in which the different systems depart from each other, the law of the land takes place of the law of Rome, whether ancient or modern, imperial or pontifical. [29]

Yet, Blackstone went frequently beyond silent comparison. And he did so repeatedly when discussing general custom. Let me turn to the second issue concerning customary law examined in the *Commentaries* and illustrate how Blackstone relied on comparative legal history to explain the authority behind judicial decisions proving the existence of general customs.

Determining the exact relationship between customs and court decisions was among the most pressing problems facing Blackstone in this section of the *Commentaries.* [30] Blackstone was writing at a time when customs appeared to be viewed through the lens of two different sources. [31] On the one hand, there was the source of custom's legal authority. And this source consisted in immemorial usage and general reception. On the other, there were the sources recording and proving the existence of living customs, and these sources were court decisions. While Blackstone certainly did not confuse sources of authority with sources of evidence, he did argue that the latter absolved interpreters from the burden of independently determining the existence of customs: 'judicial decisions', he wrote, 'are the principal and most authoritative evidence ... of the existence of such a custom as shall form part of the common law'. [32] So, at least at first instance, Blackstone seems to have believed that 'judicial consent alone' shaped 'the common law'. [33] In fact, the *Commentaries* considered the evidence gathered by case law to be so conclusive that they treated it almost as if it were on the threshold of becoming binding and acknowledged that 'an established rule' compelled one 'to abide by former precedents, where the same points come again in litigation'. [34] But, in so doing, because the *Commentaries* did not ultimately overcome the distinction between sources of authority and sources of evidence, they did claim that the Common law was based on something more than mere practices settled by professional usage. In fact, Blackstone concluded that, according to the 'doctrine of the law', 'precedents and rules must be followed', given that: 'positive law, fixed and established by custom, which custom is evidenced by judicial decisions ... can never be departed from by any modern judge without a breach of his oath and the law'. [35]

In other words, as weighty as the evidence provided by court decisions might have been, precedents were not in themselves formally binding. [36] Their authority to determine a custom emanated from elsewhere, and Blackstone identified its source by relying on a comparative analogy: 'We may take it as a general rule, "that the decisions of courts of justice are evidence of what is common law": in the same manner as, in the civil law, what the Emperor had once determined was to serve for a guide for the future.' [37] This clarifying comparison was further integrated by a citation of Justinian's Code, the *lex Si imperialis maiestas* recorded at C. 1.14.12: 'If the Imperial Majesty has examined a case judicially and has given a decision with the parties at hand, then all judges who are under Our rule shall know that this is a law not only for the case for which it was given, but for all similar cases.' [38]

The absence of any commentary other than the few lines quoted above could suggest that the reference was little more than ornamental, and in any case extrinsic to Blackstone's argument. And yet, at closer inspection, the citation of the *lex Si imperialis maiestas*, along with Blackstone's succinct annotation, coupled with his quest to determine the source conferring authority to judicial assessments of general customary law points to the same essential problem: defining the instances in which qualified forms of legal interpretation enjoyed degrees of normative authority. Even taken by itself, the text of the *lex Si imperialis maiestas* suggests a proximity between the emperor's power to interpret the law and his power to enact the law. What justifies this proximity is the compulsion by which all magistrates are bound to uphold the same legal principles determined by the emperor while exercising his judicial capacity. Some of the most far-reaching pages of Ennio Cortese's *La norma giuridica* have been devoted to a detailed investigation of the convergence that early glossators perceived between this *interpretatio principis* and the intrinsically similar activity of enacting new law. The overall aim pursued by Cortese has been to prove that, beginning with Irnerius, glossators called upon the legislator to both promulgate the law and illustrate its meaning. Consequently, jurists fashioned 'the two processes of *condere* and *interpretari legem* as different manifestations of a unitary phenomenon, or at least as manifestations of the same power': *imperium*. [39]

By recalling the textual authority at the root of this conception, and drawing an analogy to the authority of court decisions in England, Blackstone seems to have been restating the principle by which certain forms of interpretation were upheld by – and almost seemed to possess a degree of – normative authority. In the case of England, the interpretations of existing customary law sustained by such normative authority were the ones settled by court decisions. Why? Blackstone did not spell out the answer to this question. But the legal reasoning suggested by his particular use of the *lex Si imperialis maiestas*, as fitted within his overall treatment of the distribution of sovereign power, suggests that he considered the courts to be participants in the English *imperium*. Courts received, in fact, their jurisdiction directly from the king, so much so that Blackstone described their authority as being delegated. Because of this, once he had established that 'all jurisdiction implies superiority of power', Blackstone adopted a fluvial metaphor, frequently employed in the literature, to link explicitly *imperium* and *iurisdictio*. The 'course of justice', he wrote, flows 'in large streams from the king, as the fountain, to his superior courts of record' and is then 'subdivided into smaller channels, till the whole and every part of the kingdom' is 'plentifully watered and refreshed'. [40]

As fountain of all jurisdiction, a title that the king enjoyed as emperor in his own kingdom, the monarch imbued his courts with a degree of *iurisdictio* and thus allowed them to partake in his *imperium*. This 'ideology of royal-dominated justice', rooted in the long tradition of English jurisprudence, rendered the office of the courts an emanation of sovereign power. [41] It is this partly implicit (certainly systematic) line of reasoning, I think, that explains Blackstone's comparison between the power of the emperor to set the law while solving disputes and the power of the English courts to provide near-conclusive evidence of existing customary law. Although it is clear that the two powers differed from each other, it is no less clear that Blackstone saw in both of them instances in which qualified forms of legal interpretation demanded to be followed. It is this similarity between the two that made them comparable. And because of their kindred nature, Blackstone appears to presume that the two powers belonged, if not to the same, at least to a conceptually similar form of authority, which would seem to be identifiable in the *imperium*.

Blackstone drew a further corollary from this conception. He argued that judges were the true 'depositary of the laws' and acted as their 'living oracles'. [42] What he meant was that the law spoke through its interpreters. Judges fulfilled their office by uttering the law and infusing life into its text precisely because it was judicial interpretation that brought to completion the process of law-making. So, it is clear that, in his view, law needed interpretation to operate fully. Montesquieu and Coke before him had argued a similar position, claiming, on the basis respectively of the *Digest* and of Cicero, that the judges were the true *mouths of the law*.

In book 11, chapter 6 of *De l'esprit des lois*, significantly dedicated to 'La constitution d'Angleterre', Montesquieu had stated that judges were 'la bouche qui pronounce les paroles de la loi', the mouth pronouncing the words of the law. [43] This claim has conventionally been interpreted by Continental readers as meaning that judges should yield to the legislature and merely repeat its prescriptions by mechanically applying them as the major premise of the judicial syllogism. [44] Yet, this is not the interpretation given by Blackstone to the same notion. For Blackstone, judges could truly act as oracles of the law only if they were able to relate the settlement of the particular disputes entrusted to their cognisance to 'the spirit of the laws and the natural foundations of justice'. [45] Judges, in other words, had 'to show the rational connection between' the particular facts under their scrutiny and 'the whole frame of the universe', [46] because it was through their judgments alone that the individual statutory and customary rules were related to each other, carried into effect and thus brought into the organic life of the law. Montesquieu himself had stated as much in a lesser known passage of his *œuvre*, written while commenting on the first title of the first book of the *Digest*, namely D. 1.1.8. Here, where the Roman compilation plainly stated 'Nam et ipsum ius honorarium viva vox est iuris civilis' ('indeed, the magistrate law is itself the living voice of Civil law'), Montesquieu wrote: 'Le droit du préteur est la voix du droit civil', by which he meant that it was the casuistic law issued by the *praetor* that gave voice to the Civil law. [47] I do not know whether these claims were made by Montesquieu primarily under the influence of a celebrated Ciceronian maxim, according to which the magistrate was the speaking law, while the law was only a silent magistrate ('magistratum esse legem loquentem, legem autem mutuum magistratum'), or whether they also reflected the influence of the *Glossa ordinaria*, which Montesquieu could have read in the margin of D. 1.1.8, where he would have found stated that, just as the inclinations of the heart were expressed by the human voice, so the science of Civil law was given voice by the *praetor* ('ut enim voce exprimitur cordis intentio, ita per praetorem iuris civilis scientia'). [48] Whatever the case, the point seems to be that for Montesquieu, and certainly for Blackstone, laws as such were merely abstract enactments that could fulfil their purpose and effectively order society only when they had been embodied in the rulings of judges, who were, in turn, the true 'depositary of the laws' precisely because they had sworn to uphold and interpret them according to the principles of justice. [49] Following the interpretation suggested by Karel Schönfeld, Montesquieu – and I would add Blackstone – drew this notion from one of the most important sources in English legal history: Sir Edward Coke's report of *Calvin's Case*. It is there, in fact, that both Montesquieu and Blackstone could have read that 'books and book-cases' acted as the 'eyes of the law', 'reporters' as the 'ears of the law', 'records of pleadings, cases, and judgments' as the 'stomach of the law', and 'Judges' as the 'mouth of the law (for *judex est lex loquens*)'. [50]

Looking back to the early modern sources of this conception one is reminded of a richly suggestive passage in Jean Bodin's last chapter of *Les six livres de la République*. Bringing to an end an insightful meditation on the authority of judicial interpretations, which had taken its cue from the *lex* opening the same title of Justinian's Code quoted in the abovementioned passage of Blackstone's *Commentaries*, Bodin argued in words not too dissimilar from the ones chosen by Blackstone himself that 'la droite interpretation de la loy n'est rien autre chose que la loy mesme'. [51]

Let me now conclude by turning to the third and final issue concerning customary law examined in the *Commentaries*. By relying on comparative legal history to determine why the Common law enjoyed preeminence and normative authority, Blackstone had laid the foundations to explain the constitutional function of English courts. It had been their historical responsibility to secure the living force of general custom. And it was their office to guarantee that general custom remained vital and was not silenced by the law-making authority of Parliament. A similar reductionism was certainly not inconceivable, given Parliament's newly acquired supremacy. But Blackstone was unyielding in his assertion that, even after the Revolution and the establishment of Parliamentary sovereignty, English law maintained its plurality of written and unwritten sources.

This latter consideration did not diminish the centrality of Parliamentary sovereignty. It did, however, highlight that Parliamentary sovereignty did not operate in a vacuum: it was part of a system that balanced written and unwritten law, as well as obedience and interpretation of the law. Preserved within this compound architecture, the ensuing independence of general custom – confirmed, safeguarded, and transformed into Common law by courts – represented for Blackstone one of the characteristic features of English constitutionalism. And it was this bond between custom and constitutional freedom that urged Blackstone to undertake his final comparison.

The authorities he now called to the stand told a cautionary tale taken from Roman jurisprudence. Their reference was meant to witness the authoritarian contortion that classical Roman law had suffered once its acknowledgement of custom's authority (D. 1.3.32) had been replaced by the proclamation of the emperor's exclusive power to legislate (D. 1.4.1). Thus, the section devoted to custom ended with Blackstone's effort to read Roman law's paradigmatic authorities on the *voluntas populi*, enacted through custom, and the *voluntas principis*, enacted through imperial legislation, in light of English constitutional history. [52] This comparison amounted to a stern warning emphasising how constitutional freedom was guaranteed by the orderly coexistence of diverse sources enacting the separate will of the kingdom's several constituent bodies. As Blackstone acknowledged: it is 'indeed one of the characteristic marks of English liberty, that our common law depends upon custom: which carries this internal evidence of freedom ... that it probably was introduced by the voluntary consent of the people':

The Roman law, as practiced in the time of its liberty paid also a great regard to custom; but not so much as our law: it only then adopting it, when the written law is deficient. Though the reasons alleged in the digest will fully justify our practice, in making it of equal authority with, when it is not contradicted by, the written law. 'For since, says Julianus, the written law binds us for no other reason but because it is approved by the judgment of the people, therefore those laws which the people hath approved without writing ought also to bind every body. For where is the difference, whether the people declare their assent to a law by suffrage, or by a uniform course of acting accordingly?' [D. 1.3.32.] Thus did they reason while Rome had some remains of her freedom; but when the imperial tyranny came to be fully established, the Civil laws speak a very different language. *'Quod principi placuit legis habet vigorem, cum populus ei et in eum omne suum imperium et potestatem conferat* [A decision given by the emperor has the force of law, because the people commits to him and in him its own entire authority end power]' says Ulpian [D. 1.4.1]. '*Imperator solus et conditor et interpres legis existimatur* [the emperor alone is considered maker and interpreter of the law]' says the code [C. 1.14.12]. And again, '*sacrilegii instar est rescripto principis obviare* [it is a sacrilege to oppose the mandate of a prince]' [C. 1.23.5]. [53]

Although the comparison between English law and classical Roman law immediately revealed how both traditions acknowledged the authority of customary law, it is clear that Blackstone's main interest in this passage was to emphasise the Common law's greater commitment to custom. This commitment was such that it had overturned the relationship between statutory and customary law, fixed in the second century by one of the greatest representatives of classical Roman jurisprudence, Julian. Whereas Roman law resorted to custom only when the written law was 'deficient', English law had established its foundations by asserting the equal authority, but greater antiquity, of customary vis-à-vis statutory law. This enhanced position of customary law overturned much more than classical Roman jurisprudence. It toppled the traditional definition of custom offered by the *Decretum* (c. 5, D. I). Although it is true that the *Commentaries* did not cite this definition, it would seem nonetheless to have been in the back of Blackstone's mind, since he phrased his examination of the authority enjoyed by customs under Roman law according to its text. In the words of the *Decretum*, in fact, custom was an expression of law established by usage that enjoyed the same authority of a statute 'cum deficit lex', or as Blackstone would appear to have translated 'when the written law is deficient'. [54]

Blackstone certainly had no need to insist on the relatedness of Canonical and Civil bodies of law. The *utrumque ius* had become apparently so connatural that even thinking of Roman law historically implied for Blackstone some form of silent association to the later canonical tradition. Nor did Blackstone need to emphasise how important strands of modern jurisprudence had overturned, at least since Machiavelli, the relationship between written law and custom presented in the *Decretum*. [55] He could easily retrace and abridge the arguments by which custom had been elevated by sixteenth- and seventeenth-century schools of historical jurisprudence to a position of primacy, and written law had been conversely construed as an essentially integrative source of law.

Blackstone's primary focus was on emphasizing a crucial aspect that added a sense of urgency to an otherwise scholarly passage and provided a rationale for this comparative conclusion. This aspect involved a dual consideration: English law could not be simplified to the legislative power of Parliament, as although this authority may appear absolute in theory, it is constrained by the presence of an autonomous body of customary law. Customary law encompassed the inherent manifestation of liberty, ensuring that the fundamental principles of English law were established and upheld via the voluntary agreement of the populace. [56] We have arrived at the central point in Blackstone's comprehensive analysis of general custom. The Commentaries undertook a comparative endeavor to interpret general custom in relation to sources derived from the European legal heritage, with the aim of upholding the constitutional authority of the Common law. If the preeminence and normative authority of Common law were the factors that gave it its position against the law-making authority of Parliament, then Blackstone's comparative effort can be seen as crucial to his successful treatment of English law as a distinct universality, despite its seemingly secondary nature. Contrary to advocating for the isolation of individual components, Blackstone actively promoted the comprehensive comparison of these components by ensuring their integration within the broader framework of the entire system. In doing so, he effectively condensed the extensive European legal heritage into a systematic interpretation of English law. [57]

Footnote

1. The last few years have seen a resurging interest in the work of William Blackstone led by the scholarly efforts of Wilfrid Prest. See W. Prest, William Blackstone: Law and Letters in the Eighteenth Century (Oxford 2008); along with W. Prest (ed.), Blackstone and his Commentaries: Biography, Law, History (Oxford and Portland, OR, 2009); W. Prest (ed.), Re-interpreting Blackstone's Commentaries: A Seminal Text in National and International Contexts (Oxford and Portland, OR, 2014); W. Prest (ed.), Blackstone and his Critics (Oxford and Portland, OR, 2018).
2. See M. Lobban, A Treatise of Legal Philosophy and General Jurisprudence, vol. VIII: A History of the Philosophy of Law in the Common Law World, 1600–1900 (Dordrecht, 2007), 100
3. W. Blackstone, Commentaries on the Laws of England, Book I: The Rights of Persons, eds. W. Prest and D. Lemmings (Oxford, 2016), [Int., sec. 2], 34. See also H. J. Berman, Law and Revolution, II: The Impact of Protestant Reformations of the Western Legal Tradition (Cambridge, MA, 2003), 245–8.
4. See G. Capograssi, Il problema della scienza del diritto (Milan, 1962), 220–1: 'the role of science in the history of law is precisely this: to make such history possible, to make the history of legal experience possible. Law's action, which tends to lose itself in the mixture of reality and in the inexhaustible diversity

of history, finds in science the strength that, not only fixes its essence in corresponding concepts, but proves that such diversity is always predicated on a profound unity of life, principles and needs, which explain and support the innumerable differences of historical forms. Science welcomes the differences of history as differences, but retraces them to the unity of experience, it gives them a precise meaning: illuminating and revealing them through the inherent conception that resides within experience and from which diversities arise; ... it therefore discovers the profound juridical meaning that diversities possess. Hence, it can be argued that science makes history possible, because science is entrusted with the office of placing, affirming, remembering the profound continuity of life and the course that, beneath all the leaps, the precipices and the discontinuities of reality, legal history reveals.' All translations are my own.

5. See M. D. Couzinet, Histoire et méthode a la Renaissance. Une lecture de la Methodus ad facilem historiarum cognitionem de Jean Bodin (Paris, 1996), 104. Bodin's historical comparativism had significant consequences for the history of legal thought beyond the Channel, see D. Quaglioni, 'Le comparatism historique d'Alberico Gentili (1522–1608)', Revue des Sciences Philosophiques et Théologiques, 102 (2018), 251–62.
6. See A. Cromartie, 'The Idea of Common Law as Custom', in A. Perreau-Saussine and J. B. Murphy (eds.), The Nature of Customary Law: Legal, Historical and Philosophical Perspectives (Cambridge, 2007), 203–27, along with the bibliography cited therein.
7. Blackstone, *Commentaries*, I. 51.
8. It is useful to keep in mind, while reading Blackstone, the traditional concerns raised, in the so-called Romanist tradition, around custom and customary law. A compelling illustration of them is provided in L. Mayali, 'La coutume dans la doctrine Romaniste au Moyen age', in J. Gilissen (ed.), La coutume – Custom, 2 vols. (Brussels, 1990), vol. II, 11–31.
9. By using these authorities, even as mere comparators, Blackstone showed them to be perhaps external to the norm he was interpreting, but not to the tradition in which he was operating.
10. J. Hudson, The Oxford History of the Laws of England, Volume 2: 871–1216 (Oxford, 2012), 14.
11. See Blackstone, *Commentaries*, I. [Int., sec. 3] 51.
12. Ibid., I. [Int. sec. 3] 55.
13. Ibid., I. [Int., sec. 3] 58. After discussing the history and authority of the Civil and Canon laws, highlighting the particular vicissitude of their English reception and usage, Blackstone further observed: 'There are four species of courts in

which the civil and canon laws are permitted under different restrictions to be used. 1. The courts of the arch-bishops and bishops and their derivative officers ... 2. The military courts. 3. The courts of admiralty. 4. The courts of the two universities'. See ibid., I. [Int., sec. 3] 62.

14. Ibid., I. [Int., sec. 3] 59. See M. Hale, The History of Common Law in England, ed. C. M. Gray (Chicago, IL and London, 1971), 18–20.
15. Blackstone, *Commentaries*, I. [Ch. 7] 157. See also the now classic article by W. Ullmann, 'This Realm of England is an Empire', Journal of Ecclesiastical History, 30 (1979), 175–203.
16. Harmony has been recently seen as the key to both Blackstone's diction and his doctrine. See K. D. Temple, Loving Justice: Legal Emotions in William Blackstone's England (New York, 2019).
17. Because it stood supreme, it was this body of law that limited sovereign power. The juristic significance of this interpretation is highlighted in K. Pennington, The Prince and the Law, 1200–1600: Sovereignty and Rights in the Western Legal Tradition (Berkeley, CA, 1993), 101.
18. Blackstone, *Commentaries*, I. 347. Insights concerning the legal learning of Matthew Paris may be gathered from M. T. Clanchy, 'Did Henry III Have a Policy?', History, 53 (1968), 203–16.
19. F. Calasso, I glossatori e la teoria della sovranità (Milan, 1957), 23. See also B. Tierney, 'Some Recent Works on the Political Theories of the Medieval Canonists', Traditio, 10 (1954), 612–19.
20. See Blackstone, *Commentaries*, I. [Ch. 7] 157, where Blackstone expressly references Selden's *Titles of Honor*, book I, chapter 2.
21. See J. Selden, Titles of Honor, 2nd edn (London, 1631), 18–23. During his lifetime, Selden compiled two editions of *Titles of Honor*. See G. J. Toomer, John Selden: A Life in Scholarship, 2 vols. (Oxford 2009), vol. I, 126–68. The first edition was published in 1614, the second in 1631. I am inclined to believe that, while discussing the principle *rex ... in regno suo est imperator*, Blackstone had in mind and cited the second edition of *Titles of Honor* rather than the first. I base this assumption of the similarity of Blackstone's language with the relevant passages in Selden. A more cogent reason is that, like Selden, Blackstone too called Italian and German civilian doctrines supporting the superior lordship of the emperor 'ridiculous'. See Blackstone, *Commentaries*, I. 157. The same expression recurred in the 1631 edition of *Titles of Honor* and specifically in the title given to book I, chapter 2, par. 6: 'The Supremacy of those and other Kings free from the subjection of the Empire of Rome against the common, but ridiculous, opinion of many Civilians.' Unless I am mistaken, this qualification does not appear in

the earlier 1614 edition, which – in any case – does not have titled paragraphs. A comparison between the two versions is highly interesting. Let me note, incidentally, that while the 1614 version seems more interested in refuting the notion of *dominus mundi* put forth by Bartolus – somewhat repeating the same arguments that had been outlined earlier by 'Tramontan Doctors' such as Bodin (*Republique*, I, 9) and that would eventually be reprised, eleven years after the first publication of *Titles of Honor*, by Grotius (*De iure belli ac pacis*, II, 22, 13) – the 1631 version was more focused on 'discreeter' civilian jurisprudence. Here, although Selden did indeed criticise the more conservative opinions of jurists like Marta, he also emphasised and relied on the doctrines of 'some more of the discreeter Civilians', such as 'Albericus Gentilis', who had recognised the full majesty of free kings. See Selden, *Titles of Honor*[2], 23. See also J. Selden, Titles of Honor, 1st edn (London, 1614), 26; J. Bodin, Les six livres de la République (Paris, 1583), 189; and H. Grotius, De iure belli ac pacis, ed. B. J. A. de Kanter-van Hettinga Tromp, R. Feenstra, and C. E. Persenaire (Aalen, 1993), 560.

22. Selden, *Titles of Honor*[2], 18.
23. Ibid., 18.
24. Ibid., 18.
25. Ibid., 19.
26. Ibid., 19 (italics in original).
27. Ibid., 20–23.
28. See D. Quaglioni, 'Empire et monarchie: aspects du débat juridique', in F. Cremoux and J. L. Fournel (eds.), Idées d'empire en Italie et en Espagne: XIVe–XVIIe siècle (Rouen, 2010), 37–46.
29. See Blackstone, *Commentaries*, I. [Int., sec. 1] 16.
30. See ibid., I. [Int., sec. 3] 52.
31. See Cromartie, 'The Idea of Common Law', 222, where the influence of Hale is also discussed.
32. Blackstone, *Commentaries*, I. [Int., sec. 3] 52.
33. N. Doe, Fundamental Authority in Late Medieval English Law (Cambridge, 1990), 26.
34. Blackstone, *Commentaries*, I. [Int., sec. 3] 52.
35. Ibid., I. [Int., sec. 3] 53.
36. See N. Duxbury, The Nature and Authority of Precedent (Cambridge, 2008), 8.
37. Blackstone, *Commentaries*, I. [Int., sec. 3] 53.

38. The Codex of Justinian: A New Annotated Translation with Parallel Latin and Greek Text, ed. and trans. B. W. Frier, 3 vols. (Cambridge, 2016), vol. I, 265. See the quotation in Blackstone, *Commentaries*, I. 53: 'si imperialis majestas causam cognitionaliter examinaverit, et partibus cominus constitutis sententiam dixerit, omnes omnino judices, qui sub nostro imperio sunt, sciant hanc esse legem, non solum illi causae pro qua producta est, sed et in omnibus similibus'.
39. E. Cortese, La norma giuridica. Spunti teorici nel diritto comune classico, 2 vols. (Milan, 1962–4), vol. II, 369.
40. W. Blackstone, Commentaries on the Laws of England, Book III: Of Private Wrongs, eds. W. Prest and T. P. Gallanis (Oxford, 2016), [Ch. 4] 20. See also D. Quaglioni, 'Il diritto comune pubblico e le Leggi di Roncaglia. Nuove testimonianze sulla *l. Omnis iurisdictio*', in G. Dilcher and D. Quaglioni (eds.), Gli inizi del diritto pubblico. L'età di Federico Barbarossa: legislazione e scienza del diritto. Die Anfänge des öffentlichen Rechts. Gesetzbung im Zeitalter Friedrich Barbarossas und das Gelehrte Recht (Bologna and Berlin, 2006), 47–63.
41. J. Hudson, The Formation of the English Common Law: Law and Society in England from King Alfred to Magna Carta, 2nd edn (London and New York, 2018), 201. See also The Treatise on the Laws and Customs of England Commonly Called Glanvill, ed. G. D. G. Hall (Oxford, 1993), 2.
42. Blackstone, *Commentaries*, I. [Int., sec. 3] 52.
43. C. Montesquieu, De l'esprit des lois, ed. R. Caillois (Paris, 1951), 404.
44. For a review of the relevant literature and an attempt to problematise conventional interpretations, see A. Merlino, Interpretazioni di Montesquieu (Foligno, 2018).
45. Blackstone, *Commentaries*, I. [Int., sec. 1] 28.
46. O. W. Holmes, *The Profession of the Law*, quoted in H. J. Berman, Law and Revolution: The Formation of the Western Legal Tradition (Cambridge, MA, 1983), vii.
47. C. Montesquieu, *Collectio juris*, ed. I. Cox and A. Lewis (Oxford and Naples, 2005), 1.
48. The first hypothesis has been advanced in K. M. Schönfeld, 'Montesquieu et la bouche de la loi: Jacques Ier, Edward Coke et l'antithèse rex-judex', in L. Desgraves and P. Botineau (eds.), La fortune de Montesquieu – Montesquieu écrivain (Bordeaux, 1995), 207–23. More on the jurists as the mouth of the law may be read in E. H. Kantorowicz, The King's Two Bodies (Princeton and London, 2016), 154.
49. Blackstone, *Commentaries*, I. [Int., sec. 3] 52.

50. See Schönfeld, 'Montesquieu et *la bouche de la loi*', 221. See also *Calvin's Case*, 7 Coke Report 1a.
51. Bodin, *République*, 1024.
52. See Cortese, *La norma giuridica*, vol. II, 101–67.
53. Blackstone, *Commentaries*, I. [Int., sec. 3] 55. Italics in original. The translations are a combination of my own and those of the editors.
54. Ibid., I. [Int., sec. 3] 55. In the second edition, Blackstone changed the verb tense to 'was'. See ibid., I. 321. The relevant passage of the *Decretum* is c. 5, D. I: 'Consuetudo autem est ius quoddam moribus institutum, quod pro lege suscipitur, cum deficit lex.'
55. See N. Machiavelli, 'Discorsi sopra la prima deca di Tito Livio', in N. Machiavelli, Opere, ed. C. Vivanti (Turin 1997), vol. I, 208: 'E dove una cosa per se medesima sanza la legge opera bene, non è necessaria la legge; ma quando quella buona consuetudine manca, è subito la legge necessaria'. See also, N. Machiavelli, Discourses on Livy, eds. H. C. Mansfield and N. Tarcov (Chicago, IL, 1996), 15: 'When a thing works well on its own without the [written] law, the [written] law is not necessary; but when some good custom is lacking, at once the [written] law is necessary.'
56. Blackstone, *Commentaries*, I. [Int., sec. 3] 55.
57. W. Benjamin, *Origin of the German Trauerspiel* (Cambridge, Mass., 2019), 27.

06 THE EXAMINATION OF ENGLISH COMMON LAW FROM THE PERSPECTIVE OF THE GÖTTINGISCHE GELEHRTE ANZEIGEN (EIGHTEENTH CENTURY): A CRITICAL ANALYSIS

INTRODUCTION: AN OVERVIEW

During the nineteenth century, there was a growing interest among German legal specialists in English law. Their viewpoints and preferences differed. While certain individuals, influenced by the teachings of the Historical School of Law, sought out legal sources or concepts that were genuinely Germanic, others were motivated to acquire knowledge through comparative analysis. Additionally, there were those who were not interested in reflecting on their own legal system through a comparative approach, but rather in comprehending a specific foreign legal system. [3] An illustrative instance of this inquisitive examination of foreign affairs is the deliberation on 'Geschworenengerichte', or juries, which was vigorously led in the 1840s by notable figures such as Friedrich August Biener (1787–1861), Joseph Ignaz Gundermann, Rudolf von Gneist (1816–95), and Heinrich Brunner (1840–1915), who emerged a generation later. [7] Individuals who possessed a strong inclination for constitutional or administrative law were captivated by the intricate dynamics between the king, parliament, and the populace of Great Britain, among other factors. An exemplary illustration of this methodology can be found in the work of Rudolf von Gneist, while Georg Friedrich Wilhelm Hegel's (1770–1831) reflections on the British constitution, which were published in 1831, can also be cited. Lastly, Felix Liebermann (1851–1925) is a German academic who demonstrated Anglophilia through his work in editing, translating, and analyzing early and high medieval English legal materials. 10 These discussions were not limited to Germany, but were frequently observed by British researchers and contributed to British conversations. Jacob Grimm (1785–1863) provided inspiration to John Mitchell Kemble (1807–57), and Frederick William Maitland and Thomas Frederick Tout held Liebermann's efforts and person in high esteem. There are just two cases, namely [11, 12] However, despite the widespread recognition of these nineteenth-century debates, areas of investigation, legal academics, and their written works, their historical origins are relatively obscure. Limited knowledge exists regarding the perspectives of German academics throughout the eighteenth century regarding English and other British legal systems. [14] This is particularly lamentable considering that this century appears to be the era of initial interaction within a legal academic framework. [15] The occurrence of this event during the eighteenth century is not unexpected. From a cultural and academic perspective, it can be argued that Great Britain held a peripheral position in the perception of German social, political, and academic elites during the seventeenth century. Nevertheless, a significant shift occurred when the Hanoverian dynasty assumed control of the British throne in 1714. The Holy Roman Empire facilitated the dissemination of information regarding Great Britain, namely England, through various means such as travel reports and translations of significant books on British history. [16]

GELEHRTE ZEITSCHRIFTEN

One of the often-overlooked features of this process of legal academic rapprochement is that it needed cultural midwives – translators. Until well into the latter half of the eighteenth century, very few people in the German territories read or spoke English. Translations of British literary products into better-known languages – Latin, French, Dutch, Italian and, of course, German – were vital. [17] Besides this, for an academic exchange to take place, this literature needed to be inserted into the academic discourses of the day, as is still the case. Both purposes were served not only by more or less professional translators [18] and by German publishers and booksellers distributing publications, [19] but also by *gelehrte Zeitschriften* – academic or learned journals.

From the late seventeenth century on, a plethora of such journals saw the light of day in Germany, with their creation and sometimes also their layout and emphases inspired by their foreign predecessors, especially the Parisian *Journal des sçavans* and the *Philosophical Transactions of the Royal Society*, both of which were first published in 1665. Beginning with the *Acta Eruditorum* (Leipzig, 1682–1732), edited by Gottfried Wilhelm Leibniz (1646–1716) himself, the following decades witnessed a fast growth and diversification of this new type of media. Some of the more resounding names are Christian Thomasius's (1655–1728) *Monatsgespräche* (Monthly Discourses, 1688–90, Halle/Saale), the first learned journal in German; the *Neuen Zeitungen von gelehrten Sachen* (News about Academic Matters, 1715), published in Leipzig; the *Hamburger unpartheyischer Correspondent* (Hamburg

Impartial Correspondent; 1721–1934); and the *Göttingische gelehrte Anzeigen* (Göttingen Learned Advertisements).

THE *GÖTTINGISCHE GELEHRTE ANZEIGEN*

The *Göttingische gelehrte Anzeigen* (henceforth, the *Anzeigen*) is the oldest German learned journal still being published. [20] It was initially established as a review journal: even though it did contain some short articles, essays and news sections about cultural life in Europe's metropolises, obtained from correspondents abroad or sieved from journals, magazines and pamphlets imported to Germany, the bulk of the roughly 1,100 pages per yearly volume was made up of literary reviews, varying widely in length, intensity and style. [21] All texts were written in German, but the reviewed works covered the whole range of European literary products deserving of the attention of scientific minds or of those with a sense of culture. Thus, the *Anzeigen* offered a mixture of eighteenth-century academia: theology, philosophy, literature, medical science, politics, history, maths, economics, geography, travels, agriculture, physics, biology and botany – and, of course, law.

The first issue of the *Anzeigen* was published in 1739, only a few years after the founding of the Georgia Augusta, the University of Göttingen (formal inauguration: 1737). From the very beginning, the journal was closely connected to the University and, a few years into its existence, also became tied to the Akademie der Wissenschaften zu Göttingen (Göttingen Academy of Sciences). [22] The Academy was founded in 1751 by the British king George II – who was, of course, also the elector of Hanover and the founder of Göttingen University. Seen from the perspective of this article, both bonds proved to be decisive influences: the *Anzeigen* not only maintained close ties with one of the hubs of academic life in eighteenth-century Germany, the Academy, [23] but could also make full use of the well-stocked shelves of the university library. Due to the close connections with Great Britain, the library of Göttingen University soon gained a reputation for maintaining the best collection of books from or on Great Britain in all the German-speaking territories. [24] Thus, the *Anzeigen* became one of the principal means of transmission for knowledge about Britain in eighteenth-century Germany.

ENGLISH LAW IN THE *ANZEIGEN*

From the start, the Göttingen journal featured not only the regular reports from London and Oxford, but also a healthy dose of reviews of British books, taking up about 5–10 per cent of each volume. [25] Some of these deal with legal literature. In the 1742 issue, for example, we find three reviews of English law books:

- 'Bibliotheca Legum: or a new and compleat list of all the Common and statute Law Books of this Realm, from their first Publication to the Year 1740. under proper Heads: compiled by John Worrall' (5th edition) [26]

- 'Repertorium iuridicum, or an Index to all the Cases in the Rear-Books [sic], Entries, Reports and Abridgments in Law and Equity, with an alphabetical Table of the Titles referring to the Cases, by a Barrister of Middle Temple' (1741) [27]
- 'Iura Ecclesiastica, or a Treatise on the ecclesiastical Laws and Courts, by a Barrister of the Middle Temple' (1742). [28]

These three articles from the 1742 issue are not quite representative of other issues of the 1740s, 1750s and 1760s; most contain fewer. Nevertheless, measured against the overall number of English books imported into Germany in those years – 155 books by 1769, [29] of which only a fraction would be dedicated to legal subjects – quite a substantial number of those books coming to Germany in any given year and dealing with English law would probably have been reviewed in the *Anzeigen*.

This leads to another observation for which the 1742 issue stands as *pars pro toto*: the reviews are usually dedicated to quite recent literature. The three English law books reviewed in the 1742 issue had been published between 1740 and 1742. This not only illustrates the review policy of the *Anzeigen*, aiming at timeliness, but also bears witness to the reviewers' access to the very latest literature – an observation which is true not only for reviews of English books but also in general.

All the texts were published anonymously, and it is not always possible to identify with precision the author of a particular review in the early issues of the *Anzeigen*. However, there are two important tools for lifting the veil of anonymity: contemporary ascriptions and hints in the reviews themselves.

The first of these tools – contemporary ascriptions – can be found in a particular set of *Anzeigen*-volumes held by the Göttingen Academy. The early issues (1760–1803) of what used to be an archival or working copy have handwritten annotations in the margins. A series of later commentators scribbled authors' surnames next to most reviews. [30] In the vast majority of cases the marginal glosses are correct, as these notes were meant to supplement the text of the *Anzeigen* for the administrative and archival purposes of the Academy, and were in all likelihood compiled using accounting books detailing not only the authors' fees but also their names. [31] Furthermore, in many instances these names can be double-checked using respective notes in other personal copies of leading staff members of the *Anzeigen*. [32] Even if any doubts should remain, at the very least these ascriptions offer hints at the persons whom contemporaries thought were capable of writing the review in question. [33]

If these entries are to be trusted, then, for example, the review of William Blackstone's *Commentaries on the Law [sic] of England*, published on 23 January 1769, [34] is ascribed to a certain 'Seybert' – that is, Phillip Heinrich Seybert (1743–69), professor of law in Göttingen, who was, at the time of publication, twenty-five or twenty-six years old and not yet known as an aficionado of English law. [35] The review is a relatively long one, comprising sixteen pages, and it is the longest one on British legal literature in the *Anzeigen* issues between 1739 and 1775. [36]

Two other names deserve a mention as mid-eighteenth-century reviewers of works on English law: Christian Hartmann Samuel Gatzert (1739–1807) [37] and Justus Claproth (1728–1805). [38] Both illustrate the second approach for identifying authors of reviews – clues in the texts themselves – while at the same time showing the limitations of such deductions.

In October 1765, a longer review was published in the *Anzeigen*, dealing in some detail with Gatzert's work *De iure communi Angliae.* [39] Unusual for a treatise by a German, it bore an English subtitle – *Of the Common Law of England* – and, according to an explanatory addition to the title, Gatzert's work was a historical-literary commentary of foreign law (*Commentatio iuris exotici historico-litteraria*). [40] The book had been published in Göttingen in the same year as its review – 1765 – and was written in Latin. It explains the sources of English Common law, then dedicates about a quarter of its 103 pages [41] to its history, followed by an account of the applicability of 'jus Romanum' in England, and lastly points to some helpful bibliographical tools. Along a double track of a historical 'Who's who' of English jurisprudence – from Glanvill and Bracton via Littleton and Coke to Blackstone – and a diachronic bibliographical cross-cut, Gatzert's treatise travels through six-hundred years of English legal history. It concludes by addressing some of the institutions of English law, such as the 'scholae et Collegia Iureconsultorum' [42] and the serjeants-at-law. [43] *De iure communi Angliae* is a bird's eye view of the contemporary English legal system and its sources, along with an *äußere Rechtsgeschichte.* Substantive and procedural law are scarcely mentioned.

Gatzert can thus be credited with the first comprehensive treatise on English law from a German quill. [44] At the time of publication, Gatzert was professor of law in Göttingen. In late 1762, he had spent some time in England. [45] The biographical-bibliographical part of his treatise in particular suggests that he had used this time to access libraries and to study English legal literature. Still, little can be said about Gatzert's knowledge of substantive and procedural English law; in all probability it remained uncertain at best.

Given the author's assumed modest knowledge of English law, his choice of topic seems strange, maybe even unfortunate. From the point of view of English jurists – and the English subtitle was probably meant as an advertisement directed at them as well as a display of linguistic skills – it merely was a miscellany of well-known facts, biographical-bibliographical data and a summary of Common law *Wissenschaftsgeschichte.* As such, it must have been of no concern to them. At the same time, it lay far off the dogmatic ambit of German legal academia and forensic practice, as it was especially remote from the *ius commune* and the regional *ius particulare.* Only its account of legal sources, methods and the applicability of Roman law could have interested a wider readership. Nevertheless, Gatzert's *De iure communi Angliae* is more than a mere product of leisure time during his stay in England. Its aim and the readership he had in mind are discernible from Gatzert's further activities in Göttingen, announced by the university calendar for the winter term 1764/5 as published in the *Anzeigen*:

Herr Doctor Gatzert will read *privatissime* for the English residing here the pure jurisprudence of Roman private law, along with the necessary antiquities, in the Latin language; and in doing so he will, as far as possible, point to the most important deviations of English and Scottish private law; the particulars of the structure of which lecture he will announce in a special *Programmate.* [46]

Thus, Gatzert attempted to establish a form of lecture or seminar on English Common law at Göttingen University. The book was meant as a primer or a textbook supporting this lecture. [47] Taking into account its aim to lay foundations in the novel field of English Common law, together with the comprehensive guide to English legal literature, it can also be read as an encouragement and manual for further research in that area. Gatzert gave the lecture only once, as announced in the winter term of 1764/5, shortly before he published his *De iure communi Angliae.* But contrary to the announcement in the university calendar, he gave it 'anglicano sermone', that is, in English, as he himself noted in the introduction to his *De iure communi Angliae.* [48] Perhaps due to the choice of classroom language, no German was attracted by the *ius exoticum*, to quote the sub-title of Gatzert's book: his only two students were British – 'Anglo altero, altero Scoto,' that is, 'an Englishman the one, the other a Scotsman'. [49]

The lecture-plans failed, as had the book. Soon after publication, Gatzert's *De iure communi Angliae* seems to have been all but forgotten. When, at a later point in the nineteenth century, the study of English law in Germany gathered momentum, none of the authors then involved was acquainted with Gatzert's work. [50]

Nevertheless, in 1765 this was all still in the future, and Gatzert seems to have been quite intent on giving his *De iure communi Angliae* all the publicity he thought it deserved: the anonymous review published in the *Anzeigen* is a concise summary of *De iure communi Angliae.* It describes its structure and repeats its main findings, all the while stressing the novelty of Gatzert's work. Not only that, but it is full of praise for the book and even goes on to repeat the expression of gratitude contained in the first pages of *De iure communi Angliae* for Gatzert's noble patron: 'the grace, which can never be praised enough, and the tireless munificence of our illustrious and gracious Curator, his excellency, the *Herr* prime minister Freyherrr von Münchhausen'. [51] It is highly unlikely that anyone but Gatzert himself wrote the review of his book. This assumption is confirmed by a commentary in the annotated *Anzeigen* copy of the Academy: in the margin next to the head of the review there is a note stating 'Gatzert'.

Much the same can be said of the work and career of Justus Claproth. Claproth was not only a professor of law in Göttingen – where he would spend the rest of his academic career – from 1761, but he took a deep interest in foreign literature and its translation. Aside from his more well-known work on Voltaire, he partially translated William Blackstone's *Analysis of the Laws of England* (4th edition, 1759) into German. [52] The review of Claproth's translation was published in the *Anzeigen* in July 1769, [53] and thus coincides with the publication of the translation. It repeats parts of Claproth's introduction to the translation verbatim. Claproth limited his translation to those passages from Blackstone's 'Analysis', which must have been most relevant to Continental jurists, as the passages related to the study of English law, the history of Roman law in England and the opinions English jurists had of Roman law. Very much like Gatzert's *De iure communi Angliae*, Claproth guided Continental jurists towards the more easily digestible parts of the English legal system. The anonymous reviewer addresses the reasons for this careful approach:

As this treatise [i.e. Blackstone's *Analysis of the Laws of England*] is a woven fabric of English artificial terms, which, moreover, wholly depart from the language of Roman, Longobardic and German law, it will, for a foreigner, be quite difficult to produce a good translation. ... Out of such important considerations, *Herr* Professor Claproth has drafted both pieces in our native tongue in a very natural manner; has, quite a few years ago, read these in our local German society; and now ... has had them printed. [54]

Again, the review shows such intimate knowledge of the translation and is so full of praise that it, too, smacks of the translator himself merely giving it an *interpretatio authentica*. Nevertheless, according to the marginal note in the *Anzeigen* copy held by the Göttingen Academy, this is not an instance of Claproth imitating Gatzert's attempt at self-advertisement. Rather, the reviewer is identified as Philipp Heinrich Seybert. The similarities between the review itself and the work under review are therefore misleading; but perhaps, at the same time, a nascent review-circle begins to emerge.

Seybert, Gatzert and Claproth would have all had different motives for reviewing books on English law. Perhaps they even represent different types of importers of legal knowledge in the German-speaking area around the mid-eighteenth century. Seybert's reasons for reviewing Blackstone's *opus magnum* are, as of now, not discernible, although the following notice in the *Anzeigen* of 16 October 1769 could contain a hint:

On 14 October, Prof. Juris extraordinarius, Philipp Heinrich Seybert, has died of a haemorrhage, after having returned only shortly earlier from a learned journey. It is he who has, in this year, penned all, and in the year before some of the legal contributions of our *Anzeigen*. And our readers will now for themselves judge his merits, and what could have been expected from him, had providence granted him a longer life. [55]

Perhaps this journey had led Seybert to, among other destinations, Great Britain, and perhaps he had acquired there the necessary academic equipment to engage in an English–German legal dialogue after his return to Göttingen.

Claproth, however, combined legal expertise with linguistic skills and an enthusiasm for translation. The third, and perhaps the most knowledgeable person with regard to the English legal system, Gatzert, followed a more ambitious scheme of introducing English Common law as a subject into the curriculum at Göttingen. The review of his 'course material', so to speak, can be viewed as a means of propaganda. As a side note, this propaganda piece ended with a cliffhanger: 'By the way, whether Hr. Pr. will continue to work on this arduous path of the British law in the future, we cannot say at this point of time.' [56]

Despite differing motivations, Seybert, Claproth and Gatzert had some things in common. Firstly, and rather obviously, they were all working in Göttingen. Even though the *Anzeigen* drew their reviewers from other academic centres of the German territories as well, most of the contributors worked in Göttingen or nearby. [57] Secondly, their main areas of academic interest lay elsewhere: Claproth published on procedural law, insolvency law and contract law; Gatzert, although he later held state offices in Hesse, penned his academic works primarily on the fields of *ius publicum*, *deutsches Privatrecht* and feudal law; [58] Seybert had written on tontines. [59] The opportunities of Göttingen thus united legal scholars from very different paths and directed some of their efforts towards English law.

It is clear that at least Claproth and Gatzert discussed their respective views of English law. Their common approach of choosing comparatively easily intelligible topics – aspects of the foundations and framework of the English legal system, like sources, institutions and scholars – as well as, by and large, leaving out substantive and procedural English law suggests as much. A clearer indication can be found in Gatzert's *De iure communi Angliae*: in a to William Blackstone's works Gatzert thanks his 'Fautor et Collega aestumatissimus [patron and highly esteemed colleague] ... Claprothius noster' for 'benevolent talks'. [60]

We can imagine that for a short period of time Seybert, Gatzert and Claproth discussed their peculiar visions of English law over a puff on the pipe and a glass of port. But after this brief survey of reviews of English legal literature, it is to be suspected that around the middle of the eighteenth century there were not many more Anglophile circles in Germany debating the hitherto rather unknown legal world of the British Isles.

That the enthusiasm of a small number of individuals, like the academic trefoil Seybert, Gatzert and Claproth, started to fill a blank space, may be illustrated by flipping through the pages of the most important German encyclopaedia of the eighteenth century, *Zedlers Universal-Lexicon*, which fills four metres of shelf-space. A quick search for those *lemmata* behind which one could reasonably expect entries on English law produces a meagre harvest: there are very short entries under 'Bracton', 'Juries', 'King's Bench' and 'court', [61] but nothing on, for example, 'englisches Recht', 'writ', 'Common law', 'Legibus', 'chancery' or 'equity'. Thus, even the most ambitious encyclopaedic project of the day had little interest in English law. Humble as Seybert's contributions as a reviewer, Claproth's translation of Blackstone and Gatzert's *De iure communi Angliae*, along with the latter's review of his own work may be, all three Göttingen academics were, in their own ways, trailblazers for a broader German academic interest in English Common law.

After this glance at their authors, some light shall now be cast on the reviews themselves. A few common aspects come to light regarding language, use of literature and contents. Reading the reviews, it soon becomes obvious that English proved to be a formidable linguistic barrier for many German scholars. The reviewers stress the need for translations time and again, and their comments on linguistic issues highlight their difficulties: the jumble of then-modern English on the one hand and law French on the other – a professional terminology not based on the Latin legal *lingua franca* of the *ius commune* – added to some Latin texts on English law for spice, all taken together became too much for German scholars. For example, in his treatise *De iure communi Angliae*, Gatzert complained about the 'unfortunate mixture of Latin, Norman and Saxon words' [62] that he had to confront – a complaint repeated in his review of *De iure communi Angliae* by pointing to the 'adventurous and un-English English legal language, the barbarism of which had already with our forebears brought about the saying that an English legal academic stops being an academic outside of England'. [63] Gatzert continued: 'The barbarism of the language must, even with the help of many and good dictionaries, cause in each and every one revulsion against this labyrinth of law, that ... he has to enter without any guidance.' [64]

What kind of English legal texts are referenced in the *Anzeigen*? The answer is a collection which can perhaps best be described as the 'catch of the day'. If one looks at the time roughly between 1739 and 1775, one will see Blackstone's commentaries next to a bundle of judgments on the reprinting of books, [65] Gatzert's treatise *De iure communi Angliae*, collections of reports, works on ecclesiastical law in England and *The Statutes at Large*. [66] The subject receiving the largest proportion of reviews was constitutional law, alongside related areas; [67] criminal law is rarely touched upon. [68] A common feature is the rather recent publishing date of the texts. Apart from that, it is hard to make out any consistent guidelines for choosing reviews; even the lengths vary considerably. [69] The library of Göttingen University offered a decent but limited collection of British books, and due to a lack of English skills, the circle of potential reviewers would have been small. Therefore, it is quite probable that the *Anzeigen* was not picky and published reviews on any English legal material offered. [70] This impression is supported by the particular culture of discussion: the works under review are never placed into a legal discourse. They lack references to other books, legal developments, judicature or protagonists, and are thus denuded of their context. It is therefore likely that the reviewers worked with very limited literary sources at hand and would rarely, if at all, have consulted any other book than the one under review. [71]

Content-wise, all reviews remain superficial. It is quite apparent that the reviewers do not really know their way around contemporary English law. [72] Their contributions are restricted to – albeit sometimes almost metaphorical – descriptions of an utterly foreign landscape. Claproth, for example, is obviously confused by the English system of legal education. Instead of clearly explaining the function of the Inns of Court in English legal education, he awkwardly calls them 'collegial orders' and 'juristic monasteries', [73] and does not explain the relationship of the education provided by these Inns to that provided by the universities of Oxford or Cambridge, which offered degrees in Civil or Canon law.

Gatzert's *De iure communi Angliae* shows that he had a far clearer idea of the English legal education and a career in law in England. Nevertheless, it is highly unlikely that many German readers, even those educated in law, would have understood what Gatzert meant when, in all brevity, he informed them about the importance of the Vinerian endowment: 'Thus, Carl Viner ... by these means attempted to remedy the shortcomings of the university. Because regularly, the Englishman will learn his law at London from the practice in the Temple.' [74]

A similar reservation can be felt when English courts are mentioned in the reviews: courts of Common law are sometimes spoken of, though not very often, and they are almost never explained. If one consults the review of the *Repertorium iuridicum*, one can read the following:

The author has taken pains to note all court cases, from the times of Edward I until the present day, which he has been able to find – partly in the laws [*Gesetzen*], partly in the cases, partly in a tremendous amount of books – and to attach their decisions, distinguishing between those reached according to the laws, and those according to equity [*Billigkeit*]. He has compiled around 40,000 quarrels, and with this he has put on the market English pandects. [75]

Referring to the pandects, the author uses a legal format familiar to all *ius commune* lawyers to describe the book at hand. Willingly or not, he would thus have stifled any appreciation of the peculiarities of English law and could have evoked a picture of the pandects not as one possible way among others to organise and structure legal sources, but rather as a literary constant of the legal world – to be found in England, too, if one only looked closely enough. [76] Furthermore, the different branches of English law, that is, Common law in a stricter sense and equity, are interpreted as legislative acts (*Gesetze*) and equity (*Billigkeit*) – in all probability mirroring a *ius commune* understanding of strict law and *aequitas* rather than being a clear grasp of English law. [77]

One focus of attention looms large, however: William Blackstone, or 'Wilhelm Blackstone'. [78] An issue of the *Anzeigen* published in December 1758 mentions the endowment of the Vinerian chair as well as the fact that the 'erste Vinerische Professor, Wilhelm Blackstone' had held his first lecture on 25 October 1758. [79] Why was there now such detailed news from Oxford in Göttingen? It is not unreasonable to view Claproth's 'juristic monasteries', as well as the news about the Vinerian chair and the reception of Blackstone's writings in the *Anzeigen*, as an attempt to bridge a deep chasm between English and German legal culture of the eighteenth century. German legal scholars of the eighteenth century were not only ignorant about substantive and procedural English law but also, perhaps more importantly, did not comprehend the English system of legal education. [80]

Neither the insight that jurisdiction established important ley lines for legal developments nor that it was a driving force behind the differentiation and the development of law was a novelty in the land of the *Reichskammergericht* (Imperial Chamber Court), nor was the fact that collections of cases and court decisions played an important part and had established themselves as a legal literary genre – a glance at the popular collections of decisions of the *Reichskammergericht* is proof of that. Even though English Common law also took into consideration acts, statutes and books of authority, the role of precedents and thus of case law was of a completely different quality. Therefore, even if the individual components of the English legal system were not foreign to Continental jurists, their respective importance, their role and their interaction followed, in the English context, very different rules. In the absence of introductory literature which did not set too high a linguistic barrier, and for want of first-hand experience gained within the English legal system, most German jurists of the mid-eighteenth century would neither have expected nor noticed this. German legal academics thought about law – be it their own or foreign law – by using the tools and concepts of their own legal education: universities, curricula, relatively static and accepted corpora of authoritative texts and learned efforts to systematise or at least to order the sources and rules of *ius commune* as well as *ius particulare*. It seems that against this backdrop, the institutional mooring of the university teaching of English law by way of the Vinerian chair had become a point of interest for German legal scholars. It was perhaps understood as a move towards Continental academic conditions and would certainly have facilitated understanding of the English legal system. The same holds true for William Blackstone's most impressive literary achievement as Vinerian professor, his *Commentaries on the Laws of England.* [81] The ordering of the Common law material in four volumes, bearing titles which would have seemed familiar to *ius commune* jurists, offered a comprehensive textual focal point for the study of English law – in all of his Majesty's domains.

GERMAN LEARNED JOURNALS AND ENGLISH LAW

The Anzeigen provides valuable insights into the process of legal learning, although it is worth noting that the subjects examined in this period (1739-1775) only provide a limited amount of knowledge on English law and its literature. However, the restricted caliber and the unique viewpoints of these contributions should not mislead two crucial aspects. The trickle of information was primarily facilitated by a strong current. During the eighteenth century, the Anzeigen served as a significant multidisciplinary source of information for scholars in the German-speaking regions, mostly because of its timeliness. Despite the potential for improvement in the intensity of scholarly analysis of English law, the level of engagement in the conversation was exceptional. Furthermore, while English attorneys and legal scholars had possessed comprehensive knowledge of ius commune and other Continental legal systems and laws since the Middle Ages, the converse was not necessarily accurate. During the mid-eighteenth century, German legal academia made initial and cautious efforts to familiarize themselves with English law. Therefore, we engage in the examination of legal terra incognita. In this context, the Göttingische gelehrte Anzeigen is employed as an illustrative case. During the eighteenth century, there existed other significant publications that played a crucial role in the dissemination of knowledge pertaining to English law across German-speaking regions. In addition to the aforementioned, certain specific literary domains and works associated with genuine Anglophilia appear to be highly promising subjects for further investigation. These include the Brittische Bibliothek (1756–67), the Britisches Museum für die Deutschen (1777–81), and the Annalen der Brittischen Geschichte (1789–1800). 82 A comprehensive examination of a larger quantity of these writings could perhaps reveal an initial reception of English law that occurred before to the more rigorous, precise, and well-informed scholarly endeavors of the nineteenth century, potentially serving as a precursor to their development.

Footnote

1. On such early undertakings by the Germanistic branch of the Historical School of Law, see F. Ranieri, 'Eine frühe deutsche Übersetzung der "Commentaries on the Laws of England" von William Blackstone. Zugleich ein Beitrag zur Instrumentalisierung des Common law in der deutschen Germanistik des 19. Jahrhunderts', in T. J. Chiusi, T. Gergen, and H. Jung (eds.), Das Recht und seine historischen Grundlagen. Festschrift für Elmar Wadle zum 70. Geburtstag (Schriften zur Rechtsgeschichte, 139; Berlin, 2008), 875–99. The academic framework of the nascent *Deutsches Privatrecht* is analysed by D. Klippel, 'Das deutsche Privatrecht in der zweiten Hälfte des 18. Jahrhunderts', in H. P. Haferkamp and T. Repgen (eds.), Usus modernus pandectarum. Römisches Recht, Deutsches Recht und Naturrecht in der Frühen Neuzeit. Klaus Luig zum 70. Geburtstag (Cologne, Weimar and Vienna, 2007), 63–74, and K. Luig, 'Die Anfänge der Wissenschaft vom deutschen Privatrecht', Ius Commune, 1 (1967), 195–222. One of the earliest attempts at what can be called comparative Germanistic legal science is Johann Carl Heinrich Dreyer's De usu genuine iuris Anglo-Saxonici in explicando iure cimbrico et saxonico, liber singularis (Kiel, 1747); reviewed in GGA 1747, 582–3 (abbreviation explained below in n. 20). All translations in the present essay are by the author.
2. J. I. Gundermann, Richteramt und Advokatur in England mit Vergleichung continentaler Zustände (Munich, 1870).
3. See, for example, J. I. Gundermann, Englisches Privatrecht, 1. Theil: Die Common Law (Tübingen, 1864); vol. II ('2. Theil') was never published.
4. F. A. Biener, Das englische Geschwornengericht (Leipzig, 1855); F. A. Biener, 'Die Criminaljury in England und ihre Zukunft', Kritische Zeitschrift für Rechtswissenschaft und Gesetzgebung des Auslandes, 25 (1853), 200–8; F. A. Biener, Begründung des Criminalrechts und Processes nach historischer Methode (Abhandlungen aus dem Gebiete der Rechtsgeschichte, 2; Leipzig, 1848), 9–183; F. A. Biener, 'Zur Geschichte der englischen Jury', Zeitschrift für deutsches Recht, 11 (1847), 57–65; F. A. Biener, Ueber die Einführung der Geschwornengerichte in England (Abhandlungen aus dem Gebiete der Rechtsgeschichte, 1; Leipzig, 1846), 7–54.
5. Biographic data not available; J. I. Gundermann, Ueber die Einstimmigkeit der Geschwornen. Beitrag zu Geschichte und Verständnis des Schwurgerichts (Munich, 1849); J. I. Gundermann, Geschichte der Entstehung der Jury in England und deren leitender Gedanke. Ein germanistischer Versuch (Munich, 1847).

6. R. (von) Gneist, Die Bildung der Geschworenengerichte in Deutschland (Berlin, 1849).
7. H. Brunner, Die Entstehung der Schwurgerichte (Berlin, 1872).
8. R. (von) Gneist, Das heutige englische Verfassungs- und Verwaltungsrecht, 2 vols. (Berlin, 1857–60); R. (von) Gneist, Englische Verfassungsgeschichte (Berlin and Heidelberg, 1882). Gneist's views of England have recently been analysed by A. Thier, 'Magna Carta in the German Discourse about English Constitutional Law between the Eighteenth and Early Twentieth Centuries', in C. Macmillan and C. Smith (eds.), Challenges to Authority and the Recognition of Rights, from Magna Charta to Modernity (Cambridge, 2018), 205–22, esp. 214–18, and F. L. Müller, 'Before "the West": Rudolf von Gneist's English Utopia', in R. Bavaj and M. Steber (eds.), Germany and 'the West': The History of a Modern Concept (Oxford, 2015), 152–66.
9. G. W. F. Hegel, 'Über die englische Reformbill' (1831), in Georg Wilhelm Friedrich Hegel: Werke, vol. XI: Berliner Schriften 1818–1831, eds. E. Moldenhauer and K. M. Michel (Frankfurt am Main, 1986), 83–128.
10. See especially his *magnum opus*, Felix Liebermann, ed., Die Gesetze der Angelsachsen, 3 vols. (Halle/Saale, 1903–16).
11. On Liebermann, his work and its impact, see the contributions in S. Jurasinski, L. Oliver and A. Rabin (eds.), English Law Before Magna Carta: Felix Liebermann and Die Gesetze der Angelsachsen (Leiden, 2010).
12. For a bigger picture, see S. Berger and P. Lambert, 'Intellectual Transfers and Mental Blockades: Anglo-German Dialogues in Historiography', in S. Berger, P. Lambert and P. Schumann (eds.), Historikerdialoge, Geschichte, Mythos und Gedächtnis im deutsch-britischen kulturellen Austausch 1750–2000 (Veröffentlichungen des Max-Planck-Instituts für Geschichte, 179; Göttingen, 2003), 9–61.
13. On early German legal academic views on Great Britain and especially on English law, see for example C. Fischer, 'The Reception of Magna Carta in Early Modern Germany, c. 1650–1800', The Journal of Legal History, 37 (2016), 249–68; Thier, 'Magna Carta'; H. Dippel, 'Blackstone in Germany', in W. Prest (ed.), Blackstone and his Commentaries: Biography, Law, History (Oxford and Portland, OR, 2009), 199–214; H. C. Kraus, Englische Verfassung und politisches Denken im Ancien Régime 1689 bis 1789 (Munich, 2006), esp. 552–3; W. Pöggeler, Die deutsche Wissenschaft vom englischen Staatsrecht: Ein Beitrag zur Rezeptions- und Wissenschaftsgeschichte 1748–1914 (Comparative Studies in Continental and Anglo-American Legal History / Vergleichende Untersuchungen zur kontinentaleuropäischen und anglo-amerikanischen Rechtsgeschichte, 16;

Berlin, 1995); and the contributions in H. Coing and K. Nörr (eds.), Englische und kontinentale Rechtsgeschichte: ein Forschungsprojekt (Comparative Studies in Continental and Anglo-American Legal History / Vergleichende Untersuchungen zur kontinentaleuropäischen und anglo-amerikanischen Rechtsgeschichte, 1; Berlin, 1985). Regarding civilian common ground see H. Coing, 'Das Schrifttum der englischen Civilians und die kontinentale Rechtsliteratur in der Zeit zwischen 1550 und 1800', Ius Commune, 5 (1975), 1–55. Medieval and early modern civilian encounters with English law are analysed by T. Rüfner, 'Continental Jurists and English Common Law', Glossae. European Journal of Legal History, 13 (2016), 627–35.

14. Along the same lines, see Ranieri, 'Eine frühe deutsche Übersetzung', 876–7. A notable exception in this regard is Kraus, *Englische Verfassung*, thoroughly analysing the constitutional discourses.

15. For sporadic earlier Continental views see Rüfner, 'Continental Jurists and English Common Law', 627–35.

16. On Anglophilia, access to information about Great Britain and German views of Great Britain in the course of the eighteenth century, see Fischer, 'Reception of Magna Carta', 252–3; J. Willenberg, Distribution und Übersetzung englischen Schrifttums im Deutschland des 18. Jahrhunderts (Archiv für Geschichte des Buchwesens – Studien, 6; Munich, 2008), 19–94; W. J. Mommsen, 'Das Englandbild der Deutschen und die britische Sicht seit dem Ende des 18. Jahrhunderts', in H. Süssmuth (ed.), Deutschlandbilder in Dänemark und England, in Frankreich und in den Niederlanden (Schriften der Paul-Kleinewefers-Stiftung, 3; Baden-Baden, 1996), 215–34; S. Haikala, 'Britische Freiheit' und das Englandbild in der öffentlichen deutschen Diskussion im ausgehenden 18. Jahrhundert (Studia Historica Jyväskyläensia, 32; Jyväskylä, 1985), 31–38. On German Anglophilia on the eve of the French Revolution, see ibid., 39–58; W. J. Mommsen: 'Zur Entwicklung des Englandbildes der Deutschen seit dem Ende des 18. Jahrhunderts', in L. Kettenacker, M. Schlenke and H. Seier (eds.), Studien zur Geschichte Englands und der deutsch-britischen Beziehungen. Festschrift für Paul Kluke (Munich, 1981), 375–97.

17. Regarding German as a language of science, this is of course a process which has been reversed.

18. According to Willenberg, the ability to read English, much less to speak it, only spread in Germany in the second half of the eighteenth century; Willenberg, *Distribution und Übersetzung*, 72–94. For example, E. Foss, An Abridgment of Blackstone's Commentaries (London, 1821) was partly translated into German by H. F. C. von Colditz and, together with an introduction by Niels Nikolaus Falck, published in Schleswig in 1822/3. Ranieri highlights the problems German

jurists had in translating English legal texts by examining the translation of a passage on the doctrine of consideration as well as Falck's thoughts on the use of precedents; Ranieri, 'Eine frühe deutsche Übersetzung', 894–8. For a case study of a linguistic intermediary, see C. W. Proescholdt, 'Johann Christian Hüttner (1766–1847): A Link between Weimar and London', in N. Boyle and J. Guthrie (eds.), Goethe and the English-Speaking World: Essays from the Cambridge Symposium for his 250th Anniversary (Studies in German Literature, Linguistics, and Culture; Rochester, NY and Woodbridge, 2002), 99–110.

19. Willenberg, *Distribution und Übersetzung*, 157–318.
20. The *Göttingische gelehrte Anzeigen* changed its title twice, from *Göttingische Zeitungen von Gelehrten Sachen* (1739–1752) to *Göttingische Anzeigen von Gelehrten Sachen* (1753–1801) and then in 1802 to its present name: *Göttingische gelehrte Anzeigen*. For convenience, its present name is used throughout the article; bibliographical references to the *Anzeigen* are abbreviated 'GGA', followed by the date and page range, and then the reviewer's surname in brackets, where it is known.
21. In the eighteenth century, each yearly volume, delivered to its subscribers in 150–250 instalments over the course of the year (3–5 per week), contained *c.* 1,100 pages, give or take 200.
22. Regarding the early years of the *Anzeigen* and the close connections with the University and particularly with the Academy, see J. Ringleben, 'Über die Anfänge der Göttingischen Gelehrten Anzeigen', in R. Smend and H.-H. Voigt (eds.), Die Wissenschaften in der Akademie. Vorträge beim Jubiläumskolloquium der Akademie der Wissenschaften zu Göttingen im Juni 2000 (Abhandlungen der Akademie der Wissenschaften zu Göttingen, Philologisch-Historische Klasse, 247 Dritte Folge; Mathematisch-Physikalische Klasse, 51 Dritte Folge; Göttingen, 2002), 345–55.
23. Ibid., 348–55.
24. F. Ranieri, 'Eine Begegnung mit dem Common Law an der Universität Göttingen Mitte des 18. Jahrhunderts. Zur "Commentatio iuris exotici-historica de iure communi Angliae. Of the Common Law of England" von Christian Hartmann Samuel Gatzert', in M. Wittinger, R. Wendt and G. Ress (eds.), Verfassung – Völkerrecht – Kulturgüterschutz: Festschrift für Wilfried Fiedler zum 70. Geburtstag (Berlin, 2011), 931–53, at 938.
25. Willenberg, *Distribution und Übersetzung*, 144. In the course of the eighteenth century, the *Anzeigen* reviewed probably as many publications in English as in French.

26. GGA 1742, 90–1. The year of publication is not given in the review; the fifth edition of the *Bibliotheca legum* was published in 1740.
27. GGA 1742, 250.
28. GGA 1741, 650–1.
29. Willenberg, *Distribution und Übersetzung*, 144.
30. On these commentators, see W. Schimpf (ed.), Die Rezensenten der Göttingischen Gelehrten Anzeigen 1760–1768. Nach den handschriftlichen Eintragungen des Exemplars der Göttinger Akademie der Wissenschaften (Arbeiten aus der Niedersächsischen Staats- und Universitätsbibliothek Göttingen, 18; Göttingen, 1982), 8–9.
31. Ibid., 9-10.
32. On these additional sources, see ibid., 7.
33. The ascriptions are gathered in two publications, which are therefore indispensable tools for working with the early issues of the *Anzeigen*: Schimpf (ed.), *Rezensenten*; O. Fambach (ed.), Die Mitarbeiter der Göttingischen Gelehrten Anzeigen 1769–1836. Nach dem mit den Beischriften des Jeremias David Reuß versehenen Exemplar der Universitätsbibliothek Tübingen (Tübingen, 1976).
34. GGA 1769, 89–104.
35. Philipp Heinrich Seybert is an elusive figure; there is no modern biography. For scattered biographical remarks, see *Archiv für Geschichte des Buchwesens*, 39 (1993), 35–6; H. J. Baumann, Die Seyberths. Bilder zur Geschichte einer Nassauischen Familie (Wiesbaden, 1989), 26. For contemporary remarks see GGA 1769, 561 (Michaelis) (Seybert made 'Professor juris extraordinarius' in Göttingen); GGA 1769, 1114 (Kästner) (short obituary).
36. On 14 October that same year, 1769, Seybert would pass away, and one cannot help but wonder whether he would have made more use of this, as it came to pass, singular advance into English Common law and whether he would have ventured deeper into the subject.
37. On Gatzert, see F. Knöpp, 'Gatzert, Hartmann Freiherr von', in Neue Deutsche Biographie, vol. VI (Berlin, 1964), 91–2, available at www.deutsche-biographie.de/pnd116466405.html#ndbcontent; J. R. Dieterich, 'Ein Gießener Professor als hessischer Staatsminister', Archiv für hessische Geschichts- und Altertumskunde, Neue Folge 5 (1907), 462–514; W. Huschke, 'Die Herkunft des hessen-darmstädtischen Staatsmanns Christian Hartmann Samuel von Gatzert (1739–1807)', Archiv für Familienforschung, 5(3) (2001), 164–77[1]; Ranieri, 'Eine Begegnung mit dem Common Law', 932–4; S. Jahns, Das Reichskammergericht und seine Richter. Verfassung und Sozialstruktur eines höchsten Gerichts

im Alten Reich, Teil II: Biographien (Quellen und Forschungen zur Höchsten Gerichtsbarkeit im Alten Reich, 26; Cologne, 2003), 1304–12.

38. Sometimes also spelled 'Clapproth'. On Claproth, see W. Henckel, 'Göttinger Lehrer des Konkursrechts im 18. Jahrhundert', in F. Loos (ed.), Rechtswissenschaft in Göttingen. Göttinger Juristen aus 250 Jahren (Göttingen, 1987), 100–22; B. Mertens, Gesetzgebungskunst im Zeitalter der Kodifikationen. Theorie und Praxis der Gesetzgebungstechnik aus historisch-vergleichender Sicht (Tübinger Rechtswissenschaftliche Abhandlungen, 98; Tübingen, 2004), esp. 288–90, 331–3, 337–9, 314 and 387–8, 442, 444, analysing the influence Claproth's draft legislation (*Ohnmasgeblicher Entwurf eines Gesetzbuches*, 3 vols. (Frankfurt am Main, 1773–6)) exerted on late eighteenth-century thinking about codification and the development of legislative techniques in Germany.

39. GGA 1765, 1017–26.

40. On this treatise, see Rüfner, 'Continental Jurists and English Common Law', 627–8, 634; Ranieri, 'Eine Begegnung mit dem Common Law'.

41. As well as an introduction (eight pages) and a table of contents (two pages).

42. C. H. S. Gatzert, De iure communi Angliae: Of the Common Law of England (Göttingen, 1765), 77–84.

43. Ibid., 84–6.

44. The few treatises by German authors on subjects of English law published earlier include, for example, J. A. Gerhard and O. Schulte, Discursus publicus de jura ac potestate parlamenti Britannici (Jena, 1660), and G. H. Ayrer, Orationes binae, [...]; iuncta est De sublimi sacri cognationis tribunali Anglis, The Court of the Lord High Stewart dicto, prolusio inauguralis (Göttingen, 1744); for a review of the latter, see GGA 1746, 684; a short notice concerning a reprint ('Ge. Henr. Ayreri D. Opuscula minora [...]', vol. II, 1747) can be found in GGA 1747, 373.

45. Gatzert, *De iure communi Angliae*, 94 n.: 'Memini in diurnis Londinensibus circa finem anni 1762'. The details of this stay in England are hazy, the duration uncertain.

46. 'Die reine Römische bürgerliche Rechtsgelartheit nebst den nöthigen Alterthümern wird Herr D. Gatzert den hier befindlichen Engelländern privatissime in lateinischer Sprache lesen; und dabey die wichtigsten Abweichungen des Englischen und Schottischen Privatrechts so viel als möglich anzeigen; von welchen Vorlesungen er die nähere Einrichtung in einem besondern Programmate bekannt machen wird'; GGA 1764, 852.

47. Ranieri, 'Eine Begegnung mit dem Common Law', 941–2.

48. Gatzert, *De iure communi Angliae*, Introductio, 3–4: 'Proximam scriptioni ansam Iuris Romani ab eoque diuersi Anglici Scoticique Collegium praebuit, quod anglicano sermone per elapsum semestre hibernum cum pari juuenum praeclarae indolis speique optimae, litteris apud nos laudabili opera vacantium, rogatus habui, Anglo altero, altero Scoto. Ea autem in re ita processi, ut ad Heineccii Institutionum librum, Bretonibus aeque magni ac nostratibus aestimatum, scholas meas instituerem, iisque semper in locis, ubi ipse doctrinae cujusuis usum Germanicum subjunxit, Anglicanum ego et Scoticum substituerem.'
49. Ibid., Introductio, 3–4.
50. Ranieri, 'Eine Begegnung mit dem Common Law', 952.
51. 'die nie genug zu preisende Gnade und unermüdliche Freygebigkeit unsers erlauchten und huldreichen Curators, des Hrn. Premierministers Freyherrn von Münchhausen Excellenz'; GGA 1767, 1026.
52. J. Claproth, Der neueste Zustand der Rechtsgelehrsamkeit in Engelland. Aus dem Englischen übersetzt von Justus Claproth [...] (Göttingen, 1767).
53. GGA 1767, 705–8.
54. 'Da diese Schrift [*sc.* Blackstone's *Analysis of the Laws of England*] ein Gewebe von englischen Kunstwörtern ist, die überdies von der Sprache des römischen, longobardischen und teutschen Rechts ganz abweichen; so wird es für einen Ausländer ziemlich schwer seyn, eine gute Uebersetzung zu liefern. ... Aus so wichtigen Gründen hat der Hr. Professor Claproth beyde Stücke, in unserer Muttersprache sehr natürlich abgefaßt, dieselben schon vor etlichen Jahren in der hiesigen teutschen Gesellschaft vorgelesen, und nun ... drucken lassen'; GGA 1767, 705–6.
55. 'Am 14ten October ist der Prof. Juris extraordinarius, Philipp Heinrich Seyberth, an einer Blutstürzung gestorben, nachdem er nur erst kurzens von einer gelehrten Reise zurückgekommen war. Er ist es, von dem in diesem Jahre alle, und vorhin einige juristische Artikel unserer Anzeigen kamen: und unsere Leser werden nunmehr selbst über seine Verdienste, und was von ihm zu erwarten gewesen wäre, wenn ihm die Vorsicht ein langeres Leben geschenkt hätte, urtheilen'; GGA 1769, 1114 (Kästner).
56. 'Ob übrigens der Hr. Pr. auf dieser mühsamen Bahn der Britannischen Rechte ferner zu arbeiten fortfahren werde, können wir noch nicht sagen'; GGA 1765, 1026.
57. The 1767 issue, for example, contains 597 contributions by 13 different authors (Johann Christoph Gatterer, Christian Hartmann Samuel Gatzert, Albrecht

von Haller, Christian Gottlob Heyne, Abraham Gotthelf Kästner, Gottfried Leß, Johann David Michaelis, Johann Andreas Murray, Johann Philipp Murray, August Ludwig Schlözer, Philipp Heinrich Seybert, Friedrich Wilhelm Stromeyer and Christian Wilhelm Franz Walch); see Schimpf (ed.), *Rezensenten*, 55–61. Out of these thirteen, eleven worked in Göttingen in 1767 (Gatzert left Göttingen for Giessen in the course of 1767). The remaining two also had very close connections to Göttingen: von Haller (Berne) had been a professor of medicine at the University of Göttingen (1736–53) and had also been the driving force behind the *Anzeigen* in its early years, while Schlözer, working in St Petersburg in 1767, would become a professor for the history of Russia in Göttingen two years later (1769). For an overview of their respective contributions to the *Anzeigen*, see Schimpf (ed.), *Rezensenten*, 80–97.

58. Ranieri, 'Eine Begegnung mit dem Common Law', 933 n. 7.

59. P. H. Seybert, De reditu annuo praesertim vitali tontina ac fiscis viduarum (Göttingen, 1767); review: GGA 1767, 1225–7 (Kästner).

60. Gatzert, *De iure communi Angliae*, 59 n. 2.

61. J. H. Zedler, Grosses vollständiges Universal-Lexikon, *vol. III:* King's Bench (Halle/Saale and Leipzig, 1733; repr. Graz, 1994), cols. 311–12; vol. IV: *Bracton* (Halle/Saale and Leipzig, 1733; repr. Graz, 1994), col. 796; vol. VI: *Court* (Halle/Saale and Leipzig, 1733; repr. Graz, 1994), col. 1487; vol. XIV: *Juries* (Leipzig and Halle/Saale, 1735; repr. Graz, 1995), cols. 1670–1.

62. Gatzert, *De iure communi Angliae*, 66 n.; further: 'linguae anglicanae juridicae barbarie' (91).

63. 'abentheuerliche und unenglische Englische Rechtssprache, deren Barbarey schon bey unsern Vorfahren das Sprüchwort verursacht hat, daß ein englischer Rechtsgelehrter ausserhalb England aufhöre, ein Gelehrter zu sein'; GGA 1765, 1022.

64. 'Die Barbarey der Sprache, so viele und gute Wörter-Bücher auch vorhanden sind, muß bey einem jeden doch einen Abscheu gegen dieses Rechtslabyrinth erregen, in das er sich noch dazu ohne Führer wagen muß'; GGA 1765, 1024–5.

65. GGA 1775, 346–50 (Kästner).

66. GGA 1759, 171–2: 'The Statutes at Large from magna Charta to the seventh Year of King George the Second'.

67. For example, GGA 1739, 631–4: 'An historical and political Discourse of the laws and Government of England from the first times, to the end of the reign of Queen Elizabeth. With a vindication of the ancient way of Parliaments in England. Collected from some Manuscript notes of John Selden, Esq. by

Nathanael Bacon, of Grays-Inn, Esq. the fourth edition, corrected and improved by a Gentleman of the Middle-Temple'; GGA 1740, 162–3: 'A collection of State-papers of John Thurloe, Esq [...]'; GGA 1741, 473–4: 'Ius Parliamentarium: or the ancient Power, Iurisdiction, Rights, liberties aud [sic] Privileges of the most High Court of Parliament [...] By W. Petyt [...] 1741'; GGA 1745, 293–4: 'Thomæ Rymeri Fœderibus & actis publicis Anglicanis' (parts 9 and 10); GGA 1746 (423–4): 'M. Samuel Squire Archidiaconus [...] a. 1745 [...] An enquiry into the foundation of the English constitution &c. oder Untersuchung der Anfänge der Englischen Staatsverfassung'; GGA 1747, 442–4: 'Histoire du Parlement d'Angleterre par M. l'Abbé Raynal'; GGA 1747, 572: 'the history and Proceedings of the house of commons during the last parliament'; GGA 1749, 629–30: 'The patriots miscellany'; GGA 1748, 554: 'Johann Strype [...] Abdrigment of the public treaties'. Many related titles focus more strongly on current politics or political history, for example GGA 1743, 417–18: 'Parliamentary Debates and Proceedings, both of the Lords and Commons' (21 vols.); GGA 1742, 618: 'Monarchy asserted to be the best, most ancient and Legal Form of Gouernment. 1742'; GGA 1743, 138–9: 'The History and Proceedings of the House of Lords, from the Restoration in 1660. to the present Time [...], voll. [sic] VII'; GGA 1747, 628–9: 'Liberty and Right'; GGA 1747, 506: 'Determinations of the honourable house of commons concerning Elections'; GGA 1747, 507: 'Orders, resolutions and determinations of the honourable house of Commons'; GGA 1748, 877: 'the whole proceeding and trial in the honse [sic!] of Peers against Simon Lord Lovat' (also in GGA 1748, 171); GGA 1748, 619: 'A comment on M. Warb. Alliance between church and state'.

68. GGA 1747, 572: 'The law of Arrests'; GGA 1772, 1266–7 (Feder): 'Principles of penal law. The second edition 1771'.

69. Seybert's review of Blackstone, for example, runs for a stunning sixteen pages, while the *Repertorium iuridicum* has to make do with fourteen lines.

70. For example, on matters as diverse as courts (GGA 1747, 611: 'Rules orders and notices in the court of Kings Bench'; GGA 1748, 629: 'Theodor Barlow, ein Rechtsgelehrter in Middle Temple, hat [...] drucken lassen The justice of peace'), bankruptcy (GGA 1743, 145–6: 'The Law for and against Bankrupts containing all the statutes, Cases at large, Arguments, Resolutions, Judgments and Decrees under the Head of Bankruptcy down to the present Time. By a late Commissioner of Bankrupts') and bills of exchange (GGA 1760, 679 (Selchow?): 'the law of bills of Exchange, promissory notes, Bank-notes and Insurances [...] by a Gentleman of the Middle Temple').

71. Gatzert's *De iure communi Angliae* is the one exception to the rule that in all probability the reviewers will have read few to no other works on English

law; see Ranieri's meticulous analysis of the books consulted by Gatzert while writing *De iure communi Angliae*: Ranieri, 'Eine Begegnung mit dem Common Law', 941–9.

72. Only a few books on Scottish law are treated: GGA 1742, 153: 'Thomae Cragii de Riccartoun [...], ius feudale, tribus libris comprehensum. Editio tertia, prioribus multo emendatior, opera & Iacobi Baillie, aduocati 1741'. Some are to be seen against the backdrop of the recent Jacobite rising, such as GGA 1747, 195: 'Hereditary right not indefeasible'; GGA 1747, 525: 'An ample disquisition into the nature of regalities and other heretable jurisdictions in Scotland'; GGA 1747, 611: a note stating that documents concerning current proceedings against the former lord provost of Edinburgh, Archibald Stewart, have been published – to be continued along with the proceedings.

73. GGA 1767, 707–8: 'collegialische Orden', 'juristische Kloster'.

74. 'Carl Viner vermachte, in seinem letzten Willen, der vom 29sten Dec. 1755 datirt ist, 12000 Pfund (72000 rthlr. [sc. *Reichstaler*] guten Geldes), eine Profeßion des gemeinen Rechtes davon zu stiften, auch Stipendiaten, die sich auf das Recht legten, davon zu unterhalten: und suchte auf die Weise einen bisherigen Mangel der Universität zu ersetzen. Denn ordentlich lernt der Engländer sein Recht zu London aus der Praxi im Tempel'; GGA 1758, 1479 (Gatzert).

75. 'Der Verfasser hat sich die Mühe gegeben, von den Zeiten Eduard I. an bis zu die jetzige Zeiten alle Gerichts-Händel zu bemerken, die er theils in den Gesetzen theils in den Gerichts-Handlungen theils in einer ungemeinen Menge von Büchern hat ausfündig machen können und ihre Entscheidungen theils nach den Gesetzen theils nach der Billigkeit beyzufügen. Er hat also auf 40 000 Händel gesammlet und Englische Pandekten des Rechts hierinnen zu Markte gebracht'; GGA 1742, 250.

76. A similar comparative use of Roman sources is found in GGA 1749, 268–9 ('The Grounds and rudiments of Law and equity'): 'It is the intention to bring the knowledge of the English Laws into a rule-based format, and to, so to speak, construct an English Digest for the advantage of teachers and students' ('Die Absicht ist, die Kenntniß der Enlischen [sic!] Rechte in eine Regelförmige Gestalt zu bringen, und so zu sagen einen Englischen Digest zum Nutzen der Lehrer und der Lernenden zu bilden').

77. Similarly GGA 1760, 680, on appeals to the 'Lord Canzler [...] who is the only judge in the whole realm entitled to decide a case without referring to a positive law, merely according to equity' ('Lord Canzler [...], welcher der einzige Richter im ganzen Reiche ist, so das Recht hat, ohne Anführung eines positiven Gesetzes bloß nach der Billigkeit zu sprechen [...]').

78. GGA 1758, 1480 (Gatzert).
79. GGA 1758, 1479–80 (Gatzert). In a footnote of his *De iure communi Angliae* (79, n.), Gatzert himself mentioned having written this notice in the *Anzeigen*, and he goes on to repeat much of its contents, informing the reader of the background to the Vinerian endowment and some of its particulars.
80. See Gatzert's complaint about 'difficultas studii'; *De iure communi Angliae*, 87–91.
81. 4 vols. (Oxford, 1765–70).
82. On these journals, see Willenberg, *Distribution und Übersetzung*, 148–53.

07 EXAMINING THE ORIGINS OF CONTINUOUS EASEMENTS IN ENGLISH LAW FROM A FRENCH PERSPECTIVE

The excitement of comparative law often arises from encounters with disparities; the resulting excitement is akin to the sensation felt by readers of George Orwell's Nineteen Eighty-Four when, in the opening line, they become aware that the other world is governed by rules that are either absent or inconceivable in their own. [1] Nevertheless, unforeseen parallels can be equally captivating.[2] The aforementioned rule, commonly referred to as the rule in Wheeldon v. Burrows, which is the focal point of this chapter, belongs to the latter classification. It is a well-known principle in English law that, around the middle of a land law course, one learns that an easement, which is the main type of servitude, can be implied when land owned by one person is divided by another person through a will, contract, or deed. [3] The central issue in the case of Wheeldon v. Burrows was whether a light easement was established when the owner of a plot with a building with windows sold the next plot without a building. Upon careful examination of the preceding sentences, it might be argued that the adjective 'enthralling' does not readily come to mind. However, beneath a seemingly mundane and obscure principle of English law is a vibrant narrative of broad importance to the fields of legal history and comparative law.[4] At its core lies the extraordinary transfer of a rather ordinary French legal concept to England.

A common lawyer will find a strikingly similar rule in articles 688 to 694 of the French Civil Code, which have not been altered since they were promulgated under the auspices of Napoleon in 1804. [5] The English and French rules are, prima facie, almost identical: the very same term, 'continuous and apparent', is found in both systems. Significantly, this similarity is entirely unexpected for two reasons. First, while French ideas influenced the development of many aspects of English private law in the nineteenth century, [6] land law was, generally, exempt from this phenomenon. [7] Secondly, while it has been said, justifiably, that 'the law of easements [is] perhaps the most Roman part of English law', [8] the rule which is the subject of this chapter is authentically French; it is not derived from Roman law.

This study recounts the remarkable story of a particular legal transplant: it examines the origins in French law, the donor system, of the rule on the creation of 'continuous and apparent' easements by implication; its transplantation [9] into English law, the donee system; and its fate thereafter in both systems. One part of this story has been told before. Over half a century ago, Brian Simpson published a landmark article on this subject; he described his contribution as 'a cautionary tale, containing several morals'. [10] Simpson's article was short – not even eight pages – and he used only English sources. [11] I argue here that many other 'morals' emerge from a deeper historical and comparative analysis of this reception, all of which are encapsulated in the central thesis, namely, that in the middle of the nineteenth century English lawyers adopted a French rule, oblivious, then as now, to the fact that it had already been recognised in France as profoundly problematic.

INTRODUCTION: AN OVERVIEW

A mere cursory perusal of the French rule on 'continuous and apparent' servitudes in the French Civil Code reveals a problem which contains two parts. The first is that articles 692 and 694 flatly contradict each other. Article 692 provides that only servitudes which are 'continuous and apparent' may be created by implication when land is divided, whereas article 694 says that a 'visible sign' and so only the apparent nature of the servitude are sufficient for this purpose. The second part of the problem concerns the categories of 'continuous' and 'discontinuous'. The term 'continuous' is defined in article 688: such servitudes can be exercised 'without needing an act of man', and drains and rights to light are given as two examples. [12] Article 688 also provides that 'discontinuous' is simply the antonym of 'continuous': a right of way is listed therein as one manifestation of a discontinuous servitude. When reading these provisions for the first time, one wonders why 'continuous' servitudes so defined are, according to article 692, given special treatment in the rule on the creation of servitudes by implication. The term 'continuous' is so firmly established in French law and in English law that this question has, in the past two centuries, been posed only once, in an unofficial but authoritative proposal for the reform of the law of property in France. [13] Yet retracing one's mental steps and rereading the relevant provisions again in search of the purpose underlying the distinction between continuous and discontinuous servitudes are of no avail; these categories seem to be devoid of any objective, still less a rational one. [14] How, then, can we account not only for the existence of the rule on the implication of servitudes in French law but also for its transplantation into and survival in English law?

This chapter focuses only on the adjective 'continuous'. [15] Its companion 'apparent' is equally significant in theory and in practice but the implications of this adjective are, principally, of interest to land lawyers: [16] the comparative lawyer and the legal historian may, therefore, pass them by with relative equanimity. The category of 'continuous' servitudes is, and always has been, a very problematic feature of English law: as we shall see in the following section, this concept has no stable meaning. One might be tempted to argue that it is then a failed transplant, a manifestation of what Gunther Teubner famously described as a 'legal irritant', a rule which is unsuitable simply because of its foreign origin. [17] It falls, after all, within the law of property, which, often and in various systems, has been considered to comprise material intrinsically unsuitable for transplantation or even for a comparative study of a purely speculative kind. [18] This chapter demonstrates that such a conclusion would be wrong. A deeper analysis of a comparative and historical nature reveals that the concept of 'continuous' servitudes is, and always has been, a problematic feature of French law too. The rule which is the subject of this chapter was, therefore, dysfunctional [19] from its very inception. This finding raises two particularly salient questions. First, why was the contemporary French dimension overlooked in English law when the rule was imported and subsequently developed? Secondly, when, why and how did English law move away from what Lewison LJ has recently called the 'rigid' definition of 'continuous' in the French Civil Code? [20] Answers to these questions are long overdue; after all, almost a century and a half has passed since *Wheeldon* v. *Burrows* decisively enshrined the rule on 'continuous' easements in English law. [21]

FRENCH RULE'S RECEPTION IN ENGLAND

The French rule on the creation of continuous servitudes by implication was planted in English soil in 1839 [22] when Charles Gale incorporated it into the first edition of what became a famous treatise on easements. [23] Holdsworth described it as a 'pioneer treatise' since '[o]n this subject there was very little English authority in 1839'. [24] Gale was, consequently, able to shape much of this area of English law by drawing principally on Roman and, notably for our purposes, French sources. His influence may be measured by the numerous cases on this rule in which his treatise (including subsequent editions thereof, edited by others) is cited: in the formative period between the publication of the first edition in 1839 and the seminal decision of *Wheeldon* v. *Burrows* four decades later, there are, at least, twelve such instances. [25]

Nonetheless, it is notable that Gale did not obsequiously copy French law in every respect when composing his treatise. Just before embarking on a discussion of the rule on 'continuous and apparent' easements, he emphatically rejected the distinction between rustic and urban servitudes, a legacy of Roman law, which is found in article 687 of the French Civil Code: he declared that it was not a 'practically useful distinction in the English law'. [26] While in Roman law certain consequences flowed from the classification of servitudes as rustic or urban, [27] this distinction was, actually, entirely otiose in French law when, in 1839, Gale's treatise was published. Indeed, in 1811, a mere seven years after the promulgation of the French Civil Code, Charles-Bonaventure-Marie Toullier, the author of a leading treatise, concluded that the distinction was 'of almost no use in practice'. [28] This is a withering assessment given that Toullier was writing in the exegetical tradition of reconciling and finding a rational purpose for every article in the French Civil Code; the adverb 'almost' appears simply to be a concession to the decorum of legal discourse as no use of any kind is even conceivable. Puzzlingly, the drafters of the Civil Code had overlooked the latter point entirely. [29]

While Gale had, therefore, exercised discernment in his discussion of rustic and urban servitudes, no such critical appraisal is evident in his discussion of the rule on continuous servitudes. There is no explanation of the purpose of the distinction between continuous and discontinuous easements and, in contrast to rustic and urban servitudes, Gale fails to consider whether the former categories are of any use in English law. Gale clearly had some affection for the French rule. He gave it prominence in the preface and devoted a substantial number of pages to it in a subsequent chapter. As Simpson notes, Gale 'seems to have been rather excited by the idea' that both the French rule and its English offshoot were based on pre-Revolutionary French law. [30] However, Gale's unsubstantiated claim in this respect [31] is not correct. As demonstrated in the following section of this chapter, this rule did not exist in France before the promulgation of the Civil Code in 1804. Furthermore, as Lord Blackburn observed, the distinction between continuous and discontinuous easements 'certainly is not to be found in any English law authority before Gale on Easements in 1839'. [32] The absence of any critical appraisal of the utility of this distinction may be the consequence of these emotions. However, Simpson too may have got carried away with his excitement for this topic: he thought that following the seminal case of *Wheeldon* v. *Burrows* in which the Court of Appeal held that the rule did not apply when the grantor – as opposed to the grantee – sought to create an easement by implication, the French rule was 'deprived thereby of its raison d'être in the common law'. [33] However, as the following section demonstrates, the rule never had a purpose in French law either.

The subsequent application of the rule on the creation of continuous easements by implication indicates that there has never been a stable interpretation of the categories of continuous and discontinuous easements in English law. [34] Sometimes the original – i.e. the French and, thus, Gale's – meaning is correctly understood. [35] One notable example is *Pearson* v. *Spencer*, where the creation of a right of way was expressly rejected on this basis: Blackburn J stated that 'there is a distinction between continuous easements, such as drains, &c., and discontinuous easements, such as a right of way'. [36]

In other cases, the original meaning is misunderstood or overlooked, and an interpretation which differs from the original is proffered. [37] The judicial seeds appear to have been sown in *Pearson* v. *Spencer* in 1863 when Wilde B interrupted counsel's argument to declare that '[a] path through a man's field may not be used once in six months, but a gravelled path up to his house may be used forty times in a day. On the other hand, a drain may be used only occasionally.' [38] The full story of the emergence of this indigenous (mis)interpretation will be recounted in the next section but one of this chapter. For now, it suffices to note that, since then, the term continuous has frequently been (mis)used to describe easements which are used often, and those which are used intermittently have been (mis)described as discontinuous. This new paradigm, which some judges considered to be the only one, generated an alternative (albeit bizarre) reason for the exclusion of rights of way from the rule on the creation of easements by implication. In 1884, Chitty J, for example, affirmed that 'a right of way ... is a discontinuous easement ... because a man is not always walking in and out of his front door'. [39] It is almost as if the French exegetical tradition, which encourages the pursuit of a rational and coherent explanation for every rule, was flowering in England just as it was wilting in France. [40]

Once this new (mis)interpretation of these terms spread, other truly discontinuous rights inevitably came to be classified as continuous by judges, who appeared to be oblivious to the fact that they were not actually continuous at all. Accordingly, in a case in which the claimant argued that an easement to discharge refuse into a stream had been created by implication, Channell B stated that '[i]n order to be continuous, the user need not be on every day in the week; and there was clearly a continuous user when the refuse was discharged into the stream, on an average, seven times a fortnight'. [41] The (mis)interpretation was still apparent almost a century later, when Ungoed-Thomas J declared that 'there has certainly been continuous user, in the sense the right has been in fact used whenever the need arose'. [42]

In 1916, it was said that 'the distinction between continuous and non-continuous easements has ... been considerably modified in favour of implying grants on severance even of non-continuous easements under special circumstances', [43] the special circumstances being that the right was used continuously, and as demonstrated in the previous paragraph, that could almost always be said to be the case and so the category became, effectively, meaningless. Therefore, there were also cases in which the original meaning was understood but then consciously disregarded. In *Brown* v. *Alabaster*, for example, Kay J stated that the right of way in issue in that case 'may pass, although in some sense it is not an apparent and continuous easement; or rather, may pass – because, being a formed road, it is considered by the authorities, in cases like this, to be a continuous and apparent easement – by implied grant'. [44] Strikingly, the terms continuous and discontinuous could thus be understood in the original French sense or (mis)understood in the new indigenously English sense: the conclusion would be the same in either case.

English law has, therefore, as Lewison LJ recently remarked, 'moved away from the rigid distinction in the French Code Civil'. [45] However, as the analysis in this section indicates, the terms continuous and discontinuous now appear to be otiose in England. They survive as labels which every student of law learns and many lawyers and judges invoke, but no case turns any more on their interpretation or (mis)interpretation. Indeed, this may be true of English law for, at least, the last ninety-one years. [46]

THE ORIGINS AND CURRENT SUCCESS OF THE RULE IN FRANCE

An examination of the French dimension yields three points of significance. First, the roots of the rule on continuous servitudes are not very deep. Its appearance in the final version of the Civil Code was a surprise since it was not mentioned in any of the three drafts which had been composed during the Revolutionary period. [47] Furthermore, it does not appear in the pre-Revolutionary law: where servitudes could be created by implication – essentially in the *pays de droit coutumier*, areas north of the Loire – it was not a requirement. [48] Gale claimed that the Civil Code 'merely recognised an ancient provision of the French law' and cited Robert-Joseph Pothier as authority for this proposition. [49] However, the terms 'continuous' and 'discontinuous' are entirely absent from Pothier's discussion of the creation of servitudes by implication; [50] in fact, there is no trace in his writings of the idea that only certain types of servitudes could be created in this way.

The second point of significance is that the problematic nature of the rule had been identified in France before 1839, when Gale's treatise was first published. From at least 1832, there were numerous conflicting decisions on whether discontinuous servitudes were excluded. [51] This uncertainty was the predictable consequence of the apparent conflict between articles 692 and 694 of the Civil Code: as we have already seen, the former, unlike the latter, appeared to exclude discontinuous servitudes from the rule on the creation of servitudes by implication. Significantly, this problem was discussed at the time in great detail in leading treatises, notably those which were composed by Toullier and Alexandre Duranton. [52]

Furthermore, it is important to note that this debate continued long after 1839. The question was described as 'one of the thorniest' in the law of servitudes and as 'really difficult' in commentaries on two separate cases published in 1840 and 1854 respectively. [53] It is clear that much intellectual energy was devoted to resolving the problem: as noted in a thesis published in 1885, more than 'seven theories' had been developed. [54] In 1863, a landmark decision of the Cour de cassation, the highest civil court in France, resolved the matter by adopting one of these theories: it held that discontinuous servitudes may be created by implication if the division of the land occurred in writing and there was no clause expressly excluding the servitude. [55] As writing is either required or almost systematically used in practice when land is divided, the exclusion of discontinuous servitudes has, thus, been heavily circumscribed: most servitudes which can be exercised 'without needing an act of man' are now capable of being created by implication.

Thus, like English law, French law was transformed in response to a clear desire to circumvent the rule on continuous servitudes. As explained in the preceding section, the meaning of 'continuous' was altered in English law in order to achieve this end. However, a different course was taken in France, as we have just seen. French courts decided to give precedence to a provision, article 694, which does not require the servitude to be continuous by greatly restricting the scope of another, article 692, which contains this very condition.

All these developments in French law were happening contemporaneously with the struggles in English law. Why did English law adopt one of the most problematic features of the French law of property, a body of rules which was described in 2008 by a large and important group of French scholars as 'not, by a long way, the best' part of the Civil Code? [56] Given the affection of the French for their Code, this is, really, a firm denunciation. Indeed, these scholars concluded that the rule on continuous servitudes was 'really of no practical use today'. [57] As demonstrated in this chapter, there is, in fact, no moment in time at which it was ever of practical use in France.

DISREGARDING THE CURRENT DISCOURSE IN FRANCE: AN EXCLUSION FROM ENGLISH PERSPECTIVE

One might legitimately wonder why this controversy was overlooked in England in 1839 and thereafter. After all, counsel and judges who sought to undermine the rule on continuous easements could have used this information to alter the rule earlier or even remove it altogether. This hypothesis is certainly not inconceivable. Indeed, a focus on the French roots of the part of the English rule which allowed an easement to be reserved in favour of the grantor helped to hasten its demise: Lord Westbury LC's observation in *Suffield* v. *Brown* that this part of the English rule was based on 'a mere fanciful analogy' with the French rule [58] was invoked by counsel in *Wheeldon* v. *Burrows*, the case which, as noted above, [59] excised this feature from the English rule. Two factors may explain why the contemporary debate in France was not known or used in legal discourse in England: first, there was a fateful focus in Gale's treatise on one particular French author, Jean-Marie Pardessus, who ignored the debate entirely; secondly, Gale's treatise was treated with such respect by those who edited subsequent editions and by judges and counsel that it may have seemed unnecessary to look elsewhere.

Pardessus, a contemporary French jurist, was cited liberally by Gale in the first edition of his treatise which was published in 1839. Indeed, Pardessus survived as a central feature of this treatise until the editor of the thirteenth edition decided, in

1959, to expunge him from the text. [60] Significantly, Pardessus did not mention the fact that the rule on continuous servitudes was controversial. He simply outlined his own theory of how the conflict between the relevant provisions in the Civil Code could be resolved. [61] Remarkably, while several contemporary cases are cited in his discussion, none addresses the tension between 692 and 694. [62] Yet, as noted above, from 1832 a series of (conflicting) decisions engaged directly with this very point.

In contrast, two of Pardessus's contemporaries in France discussed this debate in great detail before the cases on this point even began to emerge. In 1809, Toullier discussed several angles before concluding that 'we will have to wait for the courts to determine the true meaning of [article 694]' and its relationship with article 692. [63] Similarly, in 1827, Duranton highlighted the fact that articles 692 and 694 raised 'some difficulties', and he then outlined and assessed some views on how they could be resolved. [64]

Yet Gale focused almost exclusively on Pardessus. Only two other French writers, Pothier and Philippe-Antoine Merlin, are invoked and neither would have alerted Gale to this problem. Pothier was writing long before 1804 and, as noted in the foregoing section, there is nothing in his extensive oeuvre to support the idea that discontinuous servitudes ought to be excluded from the rule on the creation of servitudes by implication. [65] Merlin, who is cited in the second edition of Gale's treatise in 1849 but not in the context of this rule, is, in contrast to Pothier, a contemporary of Gale. Nonetheless, including Merlin's views on this point would not have been very illuminating since he simply notes the 'difference' between articles 692 and 694. [66]

Gale's decision to focus principally on Pardessus seems, at first sight, to have been sensible. Pardessus was a leading authority in France at the time. He was also held in high esteem in England and not only by Gale, who described him as 'an eminent French writer on servitudes'. [67] Even before Gale's treatise first appeared in 1839, Pardessus had been described by counsel as a 'writer of authority' in a case on easements. [68] Indeed, in the different context of bills of exchange, Pardessus's views had been cited by Joseph Chitty as early as 1818 in the fifth edition of his treatise on that subject. [69] Subsequent to this letter of introduction from Chitty, Pardessus was regularly invoked by counsel and judges in English cases on bills of exchange and shipping. [70] Therefore, Gale's reliance on Pardessus may have added weight and even lustre to the former's observations on the English law of easements. Nonetheless, it is likely that Gale's neglect of other sources led him to overlook the debate in France, in courts and amongst scholars, on the exclusion of discontinuous easements from the rule on the creation of servitudes by implication.

The second question which needs to be addressed is why other French sources which would have revealed the problem with the French rule were, seemingly, overlooked by others. The remarkable respect which judges had for Gale's treatise is a possible explanation. In 1847, Parke B described Gale's treatise as 'a very good one' [71] and eighteen years later Lord Westbury LC described Gale as '[a] learned and ingenious author' who had produced a 'work of great merit'. [72] Such esteem for scholarly work was, of course, not unprecedented, especially in land law: in 1854, Lord Campbell told the House of Lords that the works of Edward Sugden (Lord St Leonards) 'answered all the purposes of a code'. [73] Nonetheless, it is significant that Gale was one of only a few writers on whom accolades were bestowed so markedly in court. Furthermore, it seems that the editions of this treatise which were produced by legal minds other than Gale's were able to bask in the glow of the reputation earned by Gale. [74]

Gale is not exclusively to blame for failing to notice the controversy in France, of course; the editors who took over his treatise from 1862 and the judges and counsel in the cases failed to engage with alternative French sources which would have revealed that the rule in France was plagued by a similar problem. French sources on the Civil Code other than Pardessus were certainly not unknown to English lawyers at this time. Significantly, Toullier and Duranton, two eminent writers who, as explained in this section, had engaged in detailed discussion of the controversy surrounding the rule on continuous servitudes, were cited in English cases in the 1860s, and one of these cases was even on easements. [75] Had the discussions in these treatises relating to the rule on continuous servitudes been consulted by someone learned in English law, the problems with the French rule and their implications for its English progeny would have been immediately obvious.

EXAMINING THE ORIGINS OF THE ENGLISH (MIS) INTERPRETATION ANALYSIS

The story of this legal transplant would be incomplete without explaining how and why a separate meaning of the term 'continuous' emerged in England in the final decades of the nineteenth century. The impetus for the transformation came, initially, not from a case but from Gale's treatise. So far so unsurprising, except that it cannot be ascribed to Gale himself: the origin of the (mis)interpretation is a by William Henry Willes, a barrister who composed the third edition of Gale's treatise in 1862. [76] It is, though, a in form rather than in substance: it runs over four pages and there is space for merely two lines of the main text on two of these four pages.

Pearson v. *Spencer*, in which this (mis)interpretation first appears in law, was decided just one year after the publication of the third edition of Gale's treatise. [77] The reporter, in a , directs the reader to the relevant pages of Willes's edition, although not specifically to his fateful . Nonetheless, the influence of the is plain and striking. Wilde B's statement that 'a drain may be used only occasionally' echoes Willes's contention that '[e]ven in the case of drains ... the easement is not strictly "continuous" [since] the drain is not always flowing'. [78] Willes's (mis) interpretation was implicitly or, at least, unconsciously endorsed in 1865 by Erle CJ in *Polden* v. *Bastard*, the case which became the leading authority for the proposition that a discontinuous easement is one which is used intermittently. [79] During an unsuccessful attempt to argue that a right to take water from a well was continuous, counsel cited the precise page in Willes's edition of Gale's treatise on which the chapter on 'easements by implied grant' begins. It is, therefore, very likely that Willes's , which begins in the middle of that chapter, was the source of Erle CJ's declaration that easements which are 'used from time to time' are not continuous and, thus, are not created by implication on the division of land. [80]

At first sight, French law seems to have played no part in the development of Willes's innovation, but a closer inspection suggests that it was not entirely inconsequential. One passage contains clear but indirect evidence that Willes was aware of contemporary French debates. He states that no 'distinction [is] drawn between drains arising by act of man, and those from natural causes, as rain water'. [81] This rather esoteric point had never arisen in English law, but by 1862, when Willes's edition of Gale's treatise was published, much judicial and academic ink had already been spilled in France in pursuit of a resolution to this very question. [82] Furthermore, Willes's focus on the 'act of man', a crucial element in the French definition of the term 'continuous' according to article 688 of the Civil Code, is especially revealing here, given that the rest of the is devoted to the introduction of the very different criterion of frequency of use.

English law, on the other hand, is presented as the source of the novel meaning of 'continuous' which Willes proposed in the . However, *Glave* v. *Harding*, the one case which is examined in detail for this purpose in the , provides no support for his radical innovation. Having cited a significant portion of Bramwell B's judgment, Willes contends that it appears to be 'inconsistent' with Gale's definition of the term 'continuous'. [83] It is plain, however, that Bramwell B's reasoning focuses on the question of whether the easement is apparent and not whether it is continuous: his reference to the presence of 'excavations for foundations with openings, which were of a wholly uncertain character', which is reproduced in Willes's , makes sense only in the context of a discussion of the question of whether the easement is apparent. [84] Emptying the term 'continuous' of any content seems to have been a prelude to Willes's principal objective of recasting entirely the rule on the creation of easements by implication. Significantly, the term 'continuous' is silently dropped from Willes's alternative rule, which rests principally on *Hinchcliffe* v. *Kinnoul*, [85] a case which, tellingly, was decided in 1838, one year before the term 'continuous' was imported into English law via Gale's treatise.

How did a transform English law so dramatically? The status of Gale's treatise was, undoubtedly an important factor; as noted earlier, the prestige of the first two editions which had been composed by Gale himself was, seemingly seamlessly, extended to subsequent editions which were produced by others. [86] Moreover, Willes's edition of Gale's treatise was also considered to be of particular importance. This in Willes's edition was not the only one which was given unusual prominence in English law: in *Wheeldon* v. *Burrows*, a separate and much shorter by Willes is invoked by counsel on both sides. [87] It is especially notable that one argument in that case even relied on the precise date on which this was published. [88] Thus, as the author of the sixth edition of Gale's treatise noted, 'Mr. Willes' observations ... have often been quoted as authority'. [89]

Willes's on the meaning of the term 'continuous' was significant because it categorically contradicted the main text. There is an oblique acknowledgement of this inconsistency, but it is dismissed peremptorily and unconvincingly on the ground that it 'is only apparent'. [90] Willes's was consistently given more prominence as each edition of Gale's treatise succeeded another; subsequent authors were, therefore, consciously or unconsciously complicit in Willes's endeavour to circumvent the French interpretation of the term 'continuous'. In all editions from the fourth, in 1868, to the twelfth, in 1950, the label 'Mr Willes's opinion' was added to the margin. [91] Moreover, from 1888, Willes's views became even more conspicuous. In the edition of Gale's treatise which was published in that year, the was upgraded to the main text, although it was still placed in square brackets. [92] Willes's ideas finally broke free from all these textual restraints in 1916 when they were inserted in the main text of the treatise. [93] Yet, the contradiction was then even more patent. Indeed, it also emerged elsewhere in this edition of the treatise. In the first twelve editions of Gale's treatise, the terms 'continuous' and 'discontinuous' were expressly defined in a preliminary chapter by reference to article 688 of the Civil Code, but, in this 1916 edition, the English (mis)interpretation was added, incongruously, as a without any express recognition of a contradiction. [94]

The treatise was altered radically in 1959. The author of the thirteenth edition, which was published in that year, removed the definitions of the terms 'continuous' and 'discontinuous' which had featured in the early chapters of all previous editions; indeed, he removed all references to French law and Roman law on the ground that they are 'not now likely to influence the decision on any new point'. [95] The text of 'Willes's opinion' was also discarded at this point. As the author of this edition noted pungently in the preface, the chapter in which this section appeared was 'confused to the last degree ... [and] in places ... barely intelligible'. [96] Thus, from 1863, when Willes's edition was published, until 1959, Gale's treatise could be and, as we have seen, was invoked to support two entirely contradictory interpretations of the term 'continuous'. [97]

LESSONS FOR COMPARATIVE LAW AND LEGAL HISTORY: THREE KEY TAKEAWAYS

Drawing together the different threads of the story yields three significant insights of a comparative and historical nature. The first relates to legal transplants; the final two concern the sources of English law.

As for legal transplants, it seems that there may be, alongside the contested presumption of similarity, an unarticulated presumption of suitability in comparative law with respect to the rule in the donor system. [98] Thus, when a transplanted rule is not suited to the donee system, the social, cultural, political, economic and legal context of that forum are frequently examined minutely in the pursuit of explanations for the failure. The great comparative lawyer, Montesquieu, stated that laws 'should be so appropriate for the people for whom they are made that it is a very great coincidence if those of one nation are capable of suiting another'; [99] significantly, his premise was not that laws *are* always appropriate for the people for whom they are made. The story of the rule on 'continuous' servitudes shows that looking backwards at the donor system can be especially illuminating: it has revealed that the rule was unsuitable in the donor system before it migrated to the donee system.

One might call such a rule a 'legal irritant', extending a familiar idea in comparative law to the rule in the donor system too. [100] However, casting one's gaze further afield and borrowing from sociology, where the theory and method of functional analysis has been examined with rigour, produces more incisive insights into the rule on 'continuous' servitudes. In the language of the fecund model devised by Robert Merton, it is clear that this rule has always been 'dysfunctional' in both systems. [101] Neither the English nor the French varieties have ever had any discernible purpose. [102] Furthermore, the logical consequences of the application of the rule as originally formulated in the Civil Code were resisted in both systems: the French and English versions have been modified, in substance but not in form, to include almost all servitudes and easements respectively. Thus, as Merton's model predicts, in both systems, the 'stress, strain and tension' caused by the dysfunctional consequences ultimately led to changes which made the rule less dysfunctional. [103] Therefore, a transplanted rule may be dysfunctional not because it is not suited to conditions in the donee system but because it is dysfunctional in every place and in every time. The inception of the rule on 'continuous' servitudes in France in 1804 and its trajectory thereafter in both France and England indicates that it is such a rule: it was dysfunctional *ab initio*.

The second lesson concerns the significance of the French Civil Code as a source of English law. Harry Lawson, who once held the chair of comparative law at Oxford, said that he was 'certain' that the Civil Code had never influenced English law, and he added, emphatically, that '[i]t would be [a] sheer waste of time to look for any such thing'. [104] Although, the Civil Code has, unquestionably been less influential than certain French treatises, [105] Lawson's claim is far too sweeping. It is clear, for example, that the Civil Code formed an important part of the reasoning in *Hadley* v. *Baxendale*, a foundational case from 1854 on the measure of damages in English contract law. [106] Furthermore, the Civil Code was one of the factors which inspired the momentum for reform in land law in the first half of the nineteenth century. It featured prominently in several parts of the famous speech delivered by Henry Brougham in the House of Commons in 1828; perhaps most notably, the strong connection between the Civil Code and Napoleon was used to great effect in the conclusion, when members were exhorted to '[o]utstrip him as a lawgiver, whom in arms [they] overcame!'. [107] Thus, even before reverting to the rule on 'continuous' easements, which, unquestionably came from 'the French Code Civil', [108] it is plain that Lawson's claim can be refuted. However, his claim appears to be even more unsustainable now that the comparative and historical context of the rule on 'continuous' easements has been unravelled and reconstructed. In terms of longevity and enduring controversy, there seems to be no comparable example in English law to this transplantation from the Civil Code. [109] Perhaps only the reception of Pothier's views on mistake of identity in contract law comes close. [110]

The role of English treatises as sources of law in England is the subject of the final lesson. An English treatise played the principal role in the transplantation of the rule on 'continuous' easements: the importation and marketing of the plant, to continue the metaphor, was undertaken by Gale and the authors who published several subsequent editions of his treatise. Significantly, counsel and judges relied on Gale's treatise rather than the Civil Code itself. Even where the text of the French provisions is examined, the source is Gale's translation and not the Civil Code itself. [111] An important nuance must, therefore, be added to the position outlined in the preceding paragraph: the source of the English rule is the French Civil Code via Gale's treatise. This finding is wholly unsurprising: almost half a century ago, Simpson showed that English treatises were responsible for the propagation of French legal ideas on contract law in the English courts. [112] It is now clear that this phenomenon was not limited to contract law and that the survival of the rule on 'continuous' easements can be ascribed not just to Gale but to the authors who preserved his legacy in later editions of the treatise.

Conversely, a focus on English treatises as sources of English law leads to a separate finding which is wholly surprising. It is generally thought that, in the nineteenth century, these treatises were centripetal rather than centrifugal forces: they presented 'a chaotic common law' as consistent by marginalising or even omitting evidence to the contrary. [113] However, the various editions of Gale's treatise which are discussed in this chapter do not fit this model. In sharp contrast to other treatises, Gale's, with Willes's additions, were a cause of inconsistency. This inconsistency subsequently leaked into the cases, contaminating the law, since counsel and judges relied heavily on this secondary source. The problem was compounded by the reluctance of subsequent authors to alter the text until 1959, when, in the thirteenth edition, the contradictions were finally expunged.

CONCISE SUMMARY

In relation to Orwell's novel Nineteen Eighty-Four, it appears that the concept of the clock striking thirteen holds significance in both England and France. The English principle about 'continuous' easements appears unusual even when examined separately from its French origin, and the opposite holds true as well. However, the significance of these laws becomes much more evident when the complete historical and comparative aspects are revealed. Both the French and English interpretations of the terms continuous and discontinuous lack a clear rational reason. Furthermore, it remains unclear why discontinuous servitudes, regardless of their definition, should be exempt from the rule regarding the creation of servitudes by implication. The practical obsolescence of both the English and French varieties serves as evidence that the exclusion of specific servitudes was widely regarded as undesirable in both systems. This conclusion is further supported by the independent evolution of each rule in this regard.

Footnote

1. G. Orwell, Nineteen Eighty-Four (London, 1949), 1.
2. It is named after the eponymous case in the Court of Appeal which confirmed its status (and its limits); *Wheeldon* v. *Burrows* (1879) 12 Ch D 31. See the text from n. 32 to n. 33 and n. 57 to n. 60.
3. *Pheysey* v. *Vicary* (1847) 16 M. & W. 484; *Borman* v. *Griffith* [1930] 1 Ch 493.
4. There are important implications for (modern) English land law too, but they deserve a separate analysis in another forum.
5. Lewison LJ refers to articles 688 and 689 in *Wood* v. *Waddington* [2015] EWCA Civ 538, [15], but these provisions simply define the concepts; the subsequent provisions embed these concepts in the rule on the creation of servitudes by implication.
6. On contract law, see A. W. B. Simpson, 'Innovation in Nineteenth Century Contract Law', Law Quarterly Review, 91 (1975), 247–78. Simpson's article highlights only a part of this phenomenon. As discussed in the text (from n. 67 to n. 70), the views of J.-M. Pardessus appear in English cases on easements, bills of exchange and shipping. Furthermore, the very frequent citation of B.-M. Emerigon and R.-J. Valin in English cases on shipping is especially striking.

7. French land law was not entirely ignored in England, however. The provisions on this subject in the French Civil Code featured in the great political and legal debate in England on the merits of codification and the reform of land law in the early nineteenth century: see J. Humphreys, Observations on the Actual State of the English Laws of Real Property: With the Outlines of a Code (London, 1826). On the influence of the Civil Code more generally on the reform of English land law, see the text from n. 106 to n. 107.
8. B. Nicholas, An Introduction to Roman Law, 2nd edn (Oxford, 1975), 148.
9. Metaphors are especially conspicuous in comparative law. In this chapter, I consciously use the metaphor of transplantation to describe the movement of a legal idea from French law to English law. It is particularly apt here since, as explained in the section next but one, the French legal idea which is the subject of this chapter was deliberately adopted in, and so, figuratively, transplanted into, England. Furthermore, the presence in England of this legal idea was not ephemeral; as is evident in this chapter, it is still extant and, so, figuratively, embedded in English law.
10. A. W. B. Simpson, 'The Rule in Wheeldon v. Burrows and the Code Civil', Law Quarterly Review, 83 (1967), 240–7, at 240.
11. Simpson explains that he was not 'able to consult' a particular French treatise, but it is notable that no other French materials are cited either; ibid., 246.
12. This translation is mine, as are all other translations from French into English in this chapter.
13. See below, 194. Curiously, in its study of servitudes in 2011, the English Law Commission engaged in no critical analysis of the distinction between continuous and discontinuous easements; Law Commission, 'Making Land Work: Easements, Covenants and Profits à Prendre' (Law Com N° 327, 2011).
14. Indeed, it has been said that this distinction was transmitted to India 'more as a convenient method of classification than as a means of supplying *a logical and practical* division of the subject'; F. Peacock, The Law Relating to Easements in British India, vol. I (Calcutta, 1904), 19 (my emphasis). I am grateful to Professor Raymond Cocks for encouraging me to look at this treatise.
15. The concept of a continuous easement transcends the boundaries of the rule which is the subject of this chapter. There are, therefore, two other reasons for which it is important to understand fully the history of the term 'continuous'. First, even though the adjective 'continuous' is not mentioned in section 62 of the Law of Property Act 1925 or in the text of its predecessor, section 6 of the Conveyancing Act 1881, it has been held that only continuous easements can be created in certain circumstances on this statutory basis. This is a controversial

question, outside the scope of this chapter; the latest development is *Wood* v. *Waddington* [2015] EWCA Civ 538. Secondly, the term continuous may be used to describe an easement in an express grant. See, for example, *Wood* v. *Waddington* [2015] EWCA Civ 538, [12].

16. I intend to examine this aspect of the rule in a future article. In contrast to 'continuous', 'apparency' has not been controversial in either England or France.

17. G. Teubner, 'Legal Irritants: Good Faith in British Law or How Unifying Law Ends up in New Divergences', Modern Law Review, 61 (1988), 11–32.

18. On the latter, see S. Van Erp, 'Comparative Property Law', in M. Reimann and R. Zimmermann (eds.), Oxford Handbook of Comparative Law, 2nd edn (Oxford, 2019), 1031–57.

19. The use of this term is explained in the penultimate section.

20. *Wood* v. *Waddington* [2015] EWCA Civ 538, [15].

21. (1879) 12 Ch D 31, 48–60.

22. The French term 'continuous' (translated as 'continual' and 'continuable') and its antonym had been mentioned ten years earlier by Charles Purton Cooper, 'a lawyer and antiquary' (J. A. Hamilton, rev. B. F. Wood, 'Cooper, Charles Purton (1793–1873)', in Oxford Dictionary of National Biography (Oxford, 2004), available at https://doi.org/10.1093/ref:odnb/6213), in his evidence to the Royal Commission on Real Property, which had been established partly as a result of the publication of Humphreys's text (on which see n. 7): *Copy of the First Report Made to His Majesty by the Commissioners Appointed to Inquire into the Law of England Respecting Real Property* (London, 1829), 136. However, the context of this discussion was prescription rather than the creation of easements by implication. In French law, these categories are used in prescription too. See articles 690 and 691 of the Civil Code.

23. C. J. Gale and T. D. Whatley, A Treatise on the Law of Easements (London, 1839), 16, 47–54. Gale, a barrister of the Middle Temple, produced some of the named law reports and 'from 1846, or soon after the passing of the County Courts Act of that year, until about 1874, was a judge of county courts in the Southampton district'; M. Bowles, Gale on Easements, 13th edn (London, 1959), vii. Whatley, also a barrister of the Middle Temple, 'practised as an equity draftsman and conveyancer'; he does not appear in any subsequent edition of this treatise, and with respect to the first' '[t]he extent of his collaboration is not known'; ibid. The treatise is, generally, ascribed to Gale only. Further details on Gale and Whatley can be found in a note by E. Peters in J. Gaunt and P. Morgan, Gale on Easements, 19th edn (London, 2012), ix–xv.

24. W. S. Holdsworth, A History of English Law, vol. 15, eds. A. L. Goodhart and H. G. Hanbury (London, 1965), 295.

25. *Pheysey* v. *Vicary* (1847) 16 M. & W. 484, 488–9 (counsel); *Pyer* v. *Carter* (1857) 1 H. & N. 916, 918–19 (counsel); 922 (Watson B); *Worthington* v. *Gimson* (1860) 2 E. & E. 618, 234 (counsel); 234, 235 (Crompton J); *Pearson* v. *Spencer* (1861) 1 B. & S. 571, 579 (counsel); *Pearson* v. *Spencer* (1863) 3 B. & S. 761, 762 (counsel); *Dodd* v. *Burchell* (1862) 1 H. & C. 113, 117 (counsel), 121 (Martin B); *Hall* v. *Lund* (1863) 1 H. & N. 676, 681–2 (counsel); *Polden v. Bastard* (1863) 4 B. & S. 258, 263–4 (Crompton J); *Polden v. Bastard* (1865) L.R. 1 Q.B. 156, 159 (counsel); *Suffield* v. *Brown* (1864) 4 De G. J. & S. 185, 189 (counsel for both parties), *passim* (Lord Westbury LC); *Crossley & Sons Ltd v Lightowler* (1866) L. R. 3 Eq. 279, 282–3 (counsel), 293 (Sir W. Page Wood V.C.); *Watts v Kelson* (1871) LR 6 Ch App 166, 172 (counsel).

26. Gale and Whatley, *Easements*, 17.

27. W. W. Buckland, A Text-Book of Roman Law from Augustus to Justinian, 2nd edn (Cambridge, 1950), 262–8.

28. C.-B.-M. Toullier, Le droit civil français, suivant l'ordre du Code Napoléon, vol. III (Rennes, 1811), 507. Significantly, the principle underlying the distinction was 'uncertain' even in Roman law: Buckland, *Text-Book of Roman Law*, 262.

29. Unsurprisingly, a search of the database www.legifrance.gouv.fr reveals that servitudes have been described as rustic or urban in only two cases: Lyon, 19 May 2009 n° 08/00797 ('rustic servitude'); Cass civ 3, 25 October 1983 n° 81-15530 ('urban servitude'). For another (but, arguably, less egregious) example of Roman law being unthinkingly reproduced in the French Civil Code in 1804 and in the reformed text in 2016, see C. Kennefick, 'Violence in the Reformed Napoleonic Code: The Surprising Survival of Third Parties', in J. Cartwright and S. Whittaker (eds.), The Code Napoléon Rewritten: French Contract Law after the 2016 Reforms (Oxford, 2017), 109–33.

30. Simpson, 'Wheeldon v. Burrows and the Code Civil', 242–3.

31. No evidence is provided but in one passage the claim is qualified by the adjective 'probably'; Gale and Whatley, *Easements*, vi, 52. The statement that both rules are derived from 'ancient French law' (ibid., 52) was omitted from the sixth edition which was published in 1888, and it did not resurface in other editions; nonetheless, the claim survives in Gale's original preface which has appeared in every edition since the treatise was first published in 1839. Intriguingly, a similar claim, also without any evidence, was made in a French thesis in 1885; J. Latreille, De la destination du père de famille (Paris, 1885), 313–18. There is no reference to Gale in Latreille's study.

32. *Dalton* v. *Angus* (1881) 6 App. Cas. 740, 821. His comment is made in the context of prescription, but it does not appear to exclude the use of these categories in the rule on the creation of servitudes by implication.
33. Simpson, 'Wheeldon v. Burrows and the Code Civil', 244.
34. Moreover, the field in which they operate has never been stable: see n. 17.
35. Even then, there is, of course, room for dispute about whether certain easements need 'an act of man' and are, thus, discontinuous within the meaning of article 688 of the Civil Code. In French law, see, e.g. J.-L. Bergel, M. Bruschi and S. Cimamonti, Traité de droit civil: les biens, 2nd edn (Paris, 2010), 379–80.
36. (1861) 1 B. & S. 571, 583. The right of way was, however, created on the separate ground of necessity. Another clear example is *Pyer* v. *Carter* (1857) 1 H. & N. 916, 921–2 (Watson B). See too *Dalton* v. *Angus* where (the then) Lord Blackburn again correctly outlined the distinction albeit in the different context of prescription: (1881) 6 App. Cas. 740, 821.
37. See e.g. *Polden* v. *Bastard* (1865) LR 1 QB 156, 161 (Erle CJ); *Taws* v. *Knowles* [1891] 2 QB 564, 568, 570 (A. L. Smith J).
38. *Pearson* v. *Spencer* (1863) 3 B. & S. 761, 762–3.
39. *Bayley* v. *Great Western Railway Company* (1884) 26 Ch D 434, 442.
40. This tradition was in decline from 1880: J. Ghestin, G. Goubeaux and M. Fabre-Magnan, Traité de droit civil: introduction générale, 4th edn (Paris, 1994), 115.
41. *Hall* v. *Lund* (1863) 1 H. & N. 676, 685.
42. *Ward* v. *Kirkland* [1967] Ch 194, 225. Lewison LJ's description of this use of the term continuous as 'very unorthodox' in *Wood* v. *Waddington* [2015] EWCA Civ 538, [15], does not undermine the point in this paragraph since he was considering a different issue.
43. *Schwann* v. *Cotton* [1916] 2 Ch 120, 128 (Astbury J).
44. (1887) 37 Ch D 490, 507. See too *Thomas* v. *Owen* (1888) 20 QBD 225, 229 (Fry LJ); *Borman* v. *Griffith* [1930] 1 Ch 493, 499 (Maugham J).
45. *Wood* v. *Waddington* [2015] EWCA Civ 538, [15].
46. E. P. Hewitt and M. R. C. Overton, Dart's Treatise on the Law and Practice Relating to Vendors and Purchasers of Real Estate, vol. I, 8th edn (London, 1929), 489.
47. P.-A. Fenet, Recueil complet des travaux préparatoires du Code civil, vol. I (Paris, 1827), 45, 117–18, 251.
48. The distinction between continuous and discontinuous servitudes may have been used long before 1804 in the different context of the creation of servitudes

by prescription; P.-A. Merlin, Répertoire universel et raisonné de jurisprudence, vol. XXXI, 5th edn (Paris, 1828), 82–83. This is, of course, also the position in French law today. The distinction is certainly not Roman. Merlin ascribed it to Caepolla, a fifteenth-century jurist; ibid., 83. In contrast, Lord Blackburn stated that it was 'perfectly new; for though the difference between the things must always have existed, [he could not] find any trace of the distinction having been taken in the old French law'; *Dalton* v. *Angus* (1881) 6 App. Cas. 740, 821. It is not necessary, for the purposes of this study to resolve this debate in the context of prescription. The argument that the creation of servitudes by implication was not restricted to continuous servitudes before 1804 is substantiated in the text from n. 46 to n. 51.

49. Gale and Whatley, *Easements*, 52.
50. R.-J. Pothier, Coutumes des duché, bailliage et prévôté d'Orléans et ressort d'iceux (Paris and Orléans, 1780), 398.
51. Before 1839, the argument that discontinuous servitudes could not be created by implication had been rejected in several cases: see, e.g. Toulouse, 21 July 1836: S.37.2.155 and in the Cour de cassation, Cass 26 April 1837: S.37.1.916. This argument was, however, accepted in other cases: e.g. Lyon, 11 June 1831: S.32.2.123; Paris, 21 April 1837: footnote in S.37.1.916, 917.
52. Toullier, *Droit civil français*, 524–30; A. Duranton, Cours de droit français suivant le Code civil, vol. V (Paris, 1827), 576–84.
53. Cass 24 February 1840: S.40.1.97, 97 (anonymous author); Cass civ 30 November 1853: S.1854.1.679, 679 (anonymous author).
54. Latreille, *La destination du père de famille*, 10.
55. Cass req 7 April 1863: S 63.1.369. There is also a second reason for which this decision is a landmark. It was held that this rule applied to all modes of dividing land and was not restricted to 'contract' as article 694 suggests. This is also the position in English law; see the text from n. 1 to n. 2.
56. *Proposition de réforme du livre II du Code civil relatif aux biens* (which is known as the 'Avant-projet Capitant de réforme du droit des biens'), 3: www.henricapitant.org/storage/app/media/pdfs/travaux/Avant-projet_de_reforme_du_droit_des_biens_19_11_08.pdf.
57. Ibid., 3, 12.
58. (1864) 4 De G. J. & S. 185, 195.
59. See the text from n. 37 to n. 39.
60. Bowles, *Gale on Easements*, ix.

61. J.-M. Pardessus, Traité des servitudes ou services fonciers, vol. II, 8th edn (Paris, 1838), 121, 139–42. Pardessus produced several editions of this treatise, and it is not clear which edition Gale used. The decision to use the 1838 edition in this chapter is deliberate: this edition is, prima facie, least likely to be advantageous to the argument as the cases on the rule which begin in 1832 are more likely to feature therein than in previous editions.
62. Ibid., 139, 142.
63. Toullier, *Droit civil français*, 528.
64. Duranton, *Cours de droit français*, vol. V, 567, 576–84.
65. See the text from n. 55 to n. 57.
66. Merlin, *Répertoire de jurisprudence*, 76. It is clear that Gale was using this edition (see n. 46 for the details) of Merlin's work.
67. Gale and Whatley, *Easements*, vii.
68. *Peyton* v. *The Mayor and Commonalty of London* (1829) 9 B. & C. 725, 732.
69. J. Chitty, A Practical Treatise on Bills of Exchange, Checks on Bankers, Promissory Notes, Bankers' Cash Notes, and Bank Notes, 5th edn (London, 1818) 76, 78, 83.
70. Restricting the list to cases before 1839, see, e.g. *Cox* v. *Troy* (1822) 5 B. & Ald. 474, 476 (Chitty, counsel for the claimant, cited Pardessus in argument), 481 (Best J); *Mitchell* v. *Darthez* (1836) 2 Bing. N. C. 555, 562 (counsel); *Gould* v. *Oliver* (1837) 4 Bing. N. C. 134, 139 (counsel); *Shipton* v. *Thornton* (1838) 9 A. & E. 314, 335 (Lord Denman CJ).
71. *Pheysey* v. *Vicary* (1847) 16 M. & W. 484, 489.
72. *Suffield* v. *Brown* (1864) 4 De G. J. & S. 185, 193.
73. H. L. Deb., 9 February 1854, vol. CXXX, 356–7.
74. On this point but relating to English treatises more generally in the second half of the nineteenth century, see D. Sugarman, 'Legal Theory, the Common Law Mind and the Making of the Textbook Tradition', in W. Twining (ed.), Legal Theory and Common Law (Oxford, 1986), 26–62, at 52.
75. *Jones* v. *Tapling* (1862) 12 C.B.R. (N. S.) 829 (Toullier was cited by counsel in a case on easements); *Appleby* v. *Myers* (1867) L.R. 2 C.P. 651, 653, 655 (Duranton was cited by counsel).
76. W. H. Willes, A Treatise on the Law of Easements by C. J. Gale, 3rd edn (London, 1862).
77. (1863) 3 B. & S. 761, 762–763 (Wilde B).
78. Willes, *Easements*, 104.

79. *Polden* v. *Bastard* (1865) L.R. 1 QB 156, 161; *Taws* v. *Knowles* [1891] 2 QB 564, 566 (counsel); *Thomas v. Owen* (1888) 20 QBD 225, 228-9 (counsel); *Wood* v. *Waddington* [2015] EWCA Civ 538, [18].
80. Willes, *Easements*, 103–6.
81. Ibid., 105.
82. See, e.g. C. Demolombe, Traité des servitudes ou services fonciers, vol. II (Paris, 1855), 217–20. This issue arose, principally, in the context of prescription, but, of course, the answer had consequences for the creation of servitudes by implication. Contrary to Willes's view, expressed in 1862, the Cour de cassation affirmed three years later that there was a distinction and that drains carrying used water were discontinuous: Cass req 19 June 1865: D.65.1.478. The claimant had expressly invoked Demolombe's argument that both types of drains were continuous.
83. Willes, *Easements*, 104.
84. Ibid.
85. (1838) 5 Bing 1. Willes, *Easements*, 105–6.
86. See the text from n. 75 to n. 76.
87. (1879) 12 Ch D 31, 35, 36, 37. The reference is to a footnote on the creation of easements by implication in favour of the grantor in the edition of Gale's treatise which, at that point, had been published most recently: D. Gibbons, A Treatise on the Law of Easements: With the Notes of W. H. Willes, 5th edn (London, 1876), 102–3.
88. (1879) 12 Ch D 31, 36.
89. G. Cave, A Treatise on the Law of Easements: With the Notes of W. H. Willes, 6th edn (London, 1888), iii–iv.
90. Willes, *Easements*, 104.
91. In contrast to previous authors who had retained the structure of the first edition of Gale's treatise, Bowles, who published the thirteenth edition in 1959, deliberately reorganised the treatise on the ground that it had 'come to acquire a certain disjointedness and inconclusiveness'; Bowles, *Gale on Easements*, viii.
92. Cave, *Easements*, 108–12.
93. T. H. Carson, A Treatise on the Law of Easements by Charles James Gale, 9th edn (London, 1916), 135–9.
94. Ibid., 29–30.
95. Bowles, *Gale on Easements*, ix.

96. Ibid., viii.

97. See the text from n. 40. to n. 51.

98. Such a presumption is not limited to one side in the debate on legal transplants. See, e.g. A. Watson, Legal Transplants: An Approach to Comparative Law (Edinburgh, 1974); although the converse view appears in A. Watson, Society and Legal Change, 2nd edn (Philadelphia, 2001), 99; P. Legrand, Pour la relevance des droits étrangers (Paris, 2014).

99. C.-L. de S., de Montesquieu, De l'esprit des loix, vol. I (Geneva, 1748), 10. Montesquieu uses the verb 'devoir', which could mean 'must' rather than 'should', but the latter interpretation is more plausible given the context.

100. Teubner, 'Legal Irritants'.

101. R. Merton, On Theoretical Sociology: Five Essays, Old and New (New York and London, 1967), 73–138. I am grateful to Professor Mitchel Lasser for drawing my attention to Merton's work on functionalism.

102. Consequently, it is clear that it is not a 'malicious' transplant in the sense in which Siems has used that term; M. Siems, 'Malicious Legal Transplants', Legal Studies, 38 (2018), 103–19. I am grateful to Professor Paula Giliker for drawing my attention to this article.

103. Merton, *Theoretical Sociology*, 107. Notwithstanding the reduction of dysfunctional consequences, some, arguably, remain. However, this question calls for a critical examination of the modern law; it is, thus, outside the scope of a historical study.

104. F. H. Lawson, The Comparison: Selected Essays, vol. 2 (Amsterdam, 1977), 39.

105. On the latter, see n. 6.

106. (1854) 9 Ex. 341, 347 (Parke B).

107. H. C. Deb., 7 February 1828, vol. XVIII, 246.

108. *Suffield* v. *Brown* (1864) 4 De G. J. & S. 185, 193 (Lord Westbury LC).

109. As the litigation in *Wood* v. *Waddington* [2015] EWCA Civ 538 demonstrates, the meaning of 'continuous' is still contested.

110. The most recent episode is *Shogun Finance Ltd* v. *Hudson* [2004] 1 AC 919, 948 (Lord Millett). For a succinct overview of the history of this controversy, see J. Cartwright, Misrepresentation, Mistake and Non-Disclosure, 5th edn (London, 2019), 503–4.

111. *Pheysey* v. *Vicary* (1847) 16 M. & W. 484, 489 (counsel).

112. Simpson, 'Innovation'.

113. Sugarman, 'The Textbook Tradition', 54. Simpson's thesis, while different, is not wholly inconsistent with that of Sugarman. The former argues that, before the advent of treatises, 'it is certainly not always easy to identify and formulate the doctrine that is latent in the sources'; Simpson, 'Innovation', 251.

08 CASE LAW IN GERMANY: THE SIGNIFICANCE OF SEUFFERT'S ARCHIV

INTRODUCTION: AN OVERVIEW

The legal systems of Common law and Civil law can be considered as contrasting, with their primary distinguishing features being case law derived from specific judicial rulings and statutory law evaluated by legal academics. The incorporation of case law inside the Continental Civil law framework appears to be incongruous. While research emphasizes the recent merging of Common law and Civil law systems, it is commonly believed that two distinct legal cultures originated in the nineteenth century. 1 The well-defined English appeal stages facilitated rigorous adherence to the guidelines and conclusions of the higher courts, while the presence of several judiciaries in the German Confederation allowed for scholarly debates as long as Roman law was relevant. Nevertheless, in 1968, the legal historian John Dawson raised significant doubts regarding the distinction by designating the period from 1800 to 1945 as 'Germany's Case-Law Revolution'. 2 His research The Oracles of the Law conducted a comparative analysis of rational judgments in various legal systems, namely examining England, Rome, France, and Germany. The author conducted an analysis of the nature and scope of the impact that case law has had on them. 3 From the nineteenth century until the time of his writing, the author noted a consistent increase in the prestige and importance of the German judiciary, which he referred to as a significant indicator. 4 Dawson affirmed the increasing significance of the judiciary, which is linked to a more prominent role of case law, as a fundamental transformation. This research aims to analyze the aforementioned idea within the context of the mid-nineteenth century, utilizing a prominent collection as a case study. Starting in 1847, 'Seuffert's Archiv' published a large number of chosen rulings from the top regional courts for an audience across the entire country. This article primarily centers on the notion of precedents in case law, which serve as determinants of the outcomes of subsequent cases of a similar nature. I examine the conflict in German law between the explicit principle that previous rulings lack legal enforceability and the empirical evidence indicating that past cases have influenced subsequent rulings. The analysis of this renowned compilation from the nineteenth century offers valuable insights into the historical dimensions of the seemingly contradictory nature.

THE IMPORTANCE OF PROVIDING JUSTIFICATIONS FOR JUDICIAL RULINGS

According to Dawson, the aforementioned 'revolution' started around 1800, when laws in Germany obliged courts to explain to litigants the reasons for their decisions. Until the eighteenth century, courts kept the reasons for their decisions a secret. But the legal rules were not identical in every region that would later become Germany. Laws in some areas explicitly forbade publication of the court's reasons, whereas in other areas jurists interpreting Roman law simply did not recommend making reasons accessible. [5] Allegedly, transparency as to reasoning would show the parties the way to attack the court's judgment with a legal remedy and would therefore undermine its authority. This argumentation gradually changed. Modern authors stood up for reasoned decisions. They argued that reasons could quieten the parties by showing the accuracy of the court's judgment. [6]

This changed point of view during the Age of Enlightenment stimulated lawmakers to prescribe reasoned judgments in the different territories, and later the states of the German Confederation. This began with Saxony in 1715, Bavaria then introduced the obligation between 1804 and 1820 and Prussia gradually obliged its judges to reveal their reasoning between 1781 and 1832, to name just the largest territories. As we can see from these dates, the process of establishing new laws took over a hundred years. Moreover, the obligation often started with the lower courts and was only then extended to other parts of the judiciary. [7] In contrast to the English tradition of unofficial law-reporting, reasons had to be written by the judges of the court. Though it was possible for a clerk who was often a learned jurist to reconstruct the reasoning from notes, there was always an official version. It has been pointed out that these written reasons are a characteristic of European Continental law. [8] English law reporters are on the contrary not the authors of the published opinion.

Besides explaining the result to the parties, this new obligation enabled judges and scholars to access the reasoning in prior cases. Various forms of collections flourished. The number of reported cases escalated in the 1830s and 1840s. Simultaneously, the citation of prior decisions became more common. Since then, and to the present day, it is hard to find a decision of a higher German court without references to the judiciary itself. [9]

COLLECTIONS OF DECISIONS

Clearly, the new legal obligation to write down decisions' reasons changed the courts' everyday work: they had to make the reasons accessible for the parties. Various contemporary discussions can be observed, starting from the issue of how to convince the parties, and not only fellow judges, to propositions as to how much the parties should pay for a clear copy of the motives. [10] But, more importantly for this paper, a side-effect of the obligation to provide reasons for judgments was to establish new grounds for collections of legal decisions.

There had been a long tradition of juridical collections in Germany, stretching back to the Imperial Chamber Court, but in line with statutes it was strictly forbidden to publish reasoning. Nonetheless, the ambitious judges Andreas Gail (1526–87) and Joachim Mynsinger (1514–88) published internal reports in the sixteenth century. [11] These reports were only meant to be noticed by other judges of the same panel, to prepare correct decisions. They were strictly confidential. Though the statutes were not changed, these internal reports built an essential part of the so-called *Kameralliteratur*. Diverse forms of collections existed in the eighteenth century before the duty to justify decisions was established. [12] A final statement of the court as a panel was not formulated and therefore never included. Some lawyers simply published their assumptions as to what the court might have thought to justify its verdict and presented this as a collection of decisions. The confidentiality of the courts made it almost impossible to match the facts of a case and their legal interpretation. Thus, it was difficult to compare a current case to a prior one and then apply the same rules.

The new duty to justify every judgment to the litigants around 1800 changed collections fundamentally. Instead of being constrained by strict rules to hide reasoning, editors could now freely choose from numerous decisions. Though the reasons were supposed to explain the outcome to the parties, they were widely noticed amongst jurists. Different concepts of collections evolved. Some governments ordered official collections of the highest decisions. [13] Courts became editors themselves. Other jurists collected at their own financial risk and asked their ruler for permission. [14]

SEUFFERT'S INNOVATIVE COLLECTION

Some decades later, the first nationwide collection started. In 1847, the former appellate judge Johann Adam Seuffert first published his famous collection of decisions. He established a cross-regional collection of decisions and named it 'Archiv für Entscheidungen der obersten Gerichte in den deutschen Staaten' – 'Archive for Decisions of the Highest Courts in the German States'. Simply copying extracts from existing collections, Seuffert assembled reasonings of almost every German High Court of Appeal side-by-side, structured by topics. Thus, the reasonings in his collection were modified twice compared to the original version, in being extracts and in being summarized again. In 1857, his son, Ernst August Seuffert, continued the collection. From 1858 onwards the name 'J. A. Seuffert' preceded the title, to honour the deceased founder. In quotations and colloquial usage, the collection was called 'Seuffert's *Archiv*'. A former judge took over the editorship in 1863, but in the foreword he promised to stick to the principles that the Seuffert family had established. [15] The collection was printed until 1944.

The founder, Johann Adam Seuffert (1794–1857), was a professor of history, the pandects and Bavarian Civil law in his hometown Würzburg, where he became a member of the Assembly of Estates (Ständeversammlung). In this position, he fought against censorship in 1831. As a punishment, he lost the permission to teach at Bavarian universities and was transferred to different mid-level courts in the state. In 1839, he asked for early retirement and settled down in Munich, publishing political essays and poetry under a pen name. Above all, he was a private scholar and wrote legal textbooks and commentaries. Among his works, his collection of decisions was immensely successful. [16]

The volumes of Seuffert's *Archiv* follow a simple structure. Some volumes open with an informative introduction, such as the first volume, which gives the collection's purpose, or a later volume, which tells of the change of editors. Originally, four booklets were sold separately, as we can see from four separate coversheets per volume. They were later compiled in hardback books. The core parts are the entries of decisions. The length of the entries differs, but on average they cover one page. Every entry has a number for ease of reference. At the beginning, every entry lists similar decisions in previous volumes, by volume and entry number. The decision itself is reduced to the main issue and rarely repeats the parties' names. At the end, every entry specifies the source, for example a regional collection. A volume of Seuffert's collection assembles around two-hundred-and-fifty shortened decisions. To make all this information accessible, the collection used a structure well known to its readers, that is the order of material in legal textbooks at the time. This order, also called the Pandektensystem, goes back to Georg Arnold Heise, a professor from Göttingen, who used this structure in the early 1800s to teach Roman law to students. The Pandektensystem starts with a general part containing aspects such as sources of law or general principles. They are valid for the coming four parts unless an exception is stated there. The next parts contain property law and law of obligation. The last two parts are dedicated to family law and inheritance law. Detailed subsections enable jurists to find answers quickly. However, the abstract order is hard to understand at first sight. Up to today, Heise's Pandektensystem is the basis of the *Bürgerliches Gesetzbuch*, the German Civil law code. [17] Seuffert, the founder of the archive, was one of Heise's students. He first adapted this system for his own textbook in 1825. [18] In the *Archiv*, he did not refer to the Pandektensystem explicitly. However, the structure of every single booklet follows it, as does the register at the end of every compiled hardback book.

In the foreword to the first volume Seuffert explained that he started the collection to enable the integration of theory and practice. According to Seuffert, the connection between theory and practice was weak due to the Historical School of Law (*Historische Rechtsschule*). [19] Theorists would not notice collections of decisions anymore. [20] So Seuffert 'felt the need' to establish this cross-regional collection. Perhaps influenced by the Romanticism of his time, his argumentation was not purely rational. By establishing a collection covering decisions from all over Germany, he carefully contributed to the national movement on the eve of the 1848/9 German revolution. He hoped to support the unification of Civil law.

His work was a great success, as we can see from the remarks of contemporaries. August Ludwig Reyscher, a famous scholar and politician of the time, showed his appreciation for the collection in a journal. He, although not Seuffert himself, called the entries in the collection 'Präjudizien'. He was convinced that the given cases would not prevent courts from gaining better insight into a new case, but – I quote from Reyscher's review – 'in a certain manner' they would prevent a different opinion. Reyscher assumed it could be more 'convenient' to stick to the other court's point of view rather than establishing a different one. [21] Another writer, Johannes Emil Kuntze, observed a change in the method of jurists around 1850 and saw Seuffert's *Archiv* replacing the *Zeitschrift für historische Rechtswissenschaft*, the main journal of the Historical School of Law. [22] Rudolf von Jhering, in his later years a famous critic of abstract jurisprudence, [23] called Seuffert's *Archiv* a mirror of and a reliable guide to the judiciary. [24]

PRECEDENTS ACCORDING TO NINETEENTH-CENTURY GERMAN DOCTRINE

However, would this quantity of reprinted decisions have any effect on future cases? The new availability of decisions encouraged a lively debate about the binding effect of prior decisions among scholars. [25] The keyword in German is 'Präjudiz', which describes the consequences of a prior case on upcoming ones. An adequate translation is hard to find. It is a combination of precedent and prejudice. It does not indicate on its own whether the previous decision is binding for future cases or simply deals with similar facts. [26]

Scholars debated whether prior decisions were already binding according to Roman law, which had been changed and adapted over centuries (*Gemeines Recht*). Past decisions would be legally binding if they had the quality of a source of law. Some argued that the usage of courts (*Gerichtsgebrauch*) could produce customary law (*Gewohnheitsrecht*), the main source of law according to the leading Historical

School of Law. Hence, the outcome would be binding for the future. But this theory had some discrepancies. A judgment was imposed on the parties by jurists and did not evolve over a long time like customary law. Consequently, the majority did not accept a legally binding effect of the usage of courts. [27] A decision was valid law only for the specific case. [28] Still, earlier decisions had some authoritative value if the solution was correct from a legal point of view. [29] Until today, German case law as private law [30] remains in this rather unclear position: judge-made rules are generally not binding but have a high persuasive value. [31] While judgments are theoretically not considered a source of law, practice widely considers and often adopts opinions of higher courts. Editors used the word 'Präjudiz' to stress the importance of collections, especially in their forewords, and in some states of the German Confederation the legislator passed so-called Präjudiziengesetze, trying to bind the lower courts to principles decided by higher courts. [32] This was, however, an exception and did not lead to a strict *stare decisis.* [33]

THE ONE AND ONLY DECISION

Even if higher courts follow a certain opinion, it could be wrong. German scholars of the nineteenth century, probably influenced by the philosophy of German idealism, assumed that there was only one true and right solution to every case. The task is to find it. A previous decision must not prevent the judge from searching for the right solution. This search for the truth implies that the law provides adequate results to every legal problem. But a court could have been wrong when deciding the case in the first place. [34] Hence, a prior case should not be legally binding. [35] This is probably the main difference from Common law countries, where, by acknowledging prior cases as binding law, the decision becomes a source of law itself. The Common law way is a practical approach that guarantees predictability of legal decisions. Yet, it is not compatible with the subliminal ideal of only one lawful decision which is independent from the current jurisdiction. [36] In that logic, the result of a legal dispute cannot replace the already existing law even if no one had ever thought about this ideal correct solution.

The search for a correct solution also had practical effects for other legal issues. For instance, it played a major role in the concurrent discussion as to who was to bear the costs of a legal dispute. [37] The old doctrine stated the losing party had to pay unless they could prove the outcome was unforeseeable. It seemed unfair to impose the burden of costs on someone who did not know better in advance. Litigants safeguarded themselves against the financial risk by expert reports. If legal experts assured them that they would surely win their case, a later loss was unforeseeable. This changed radically when Adolph Dietrich Weber published his book about the costs in legal disputes in 1788. He argued that the right solution to every case was fixed even before the dispute arose. This one and true decision was already hidden in the law. From now on, the losing party had to bear the costs with very few exceptions.

ISSUE AND METHOD

Despite scholars' reservations concerning case law, collections of the time made prior cases widely available. On the one hand, the doctrine is clear and does not see prior decisions as having a legally binding effect. On the other hand, current research assumes a huge impact of prior cases to future decisions. Surprisingly, until now, scholars have paid little attention to how this worked in practice. How did courts and collections argue using concrete cases decided in the past? In suggesting one approach to answer this question, the following part compares four different versions of a single case. They are different stages, from a handwritten report to a shortened entry in Seuffert's *Archiv*. First of all, a single judge gave his opinion in a report. Secondly, the committee of judges based its reasoned judgment on that report. Thirdly, the reasons were shortened for a regional collection which printed it. Finally, 'Seuffert's *Archiv*' published parts of this last version. The example given here reveals the degree to which prior cases predetermined future courts' decisions. Certainly, generalisations from this one case are dangerous. However, by choosing an example from an influential court reprinted in an influential collection, the instance is likely to represent a common and acknowledged technique of the time. This case is a suitable paradigm for at least three reasons: all four versions of the case are preserved; the case contains past judicial quotations in every version; and, finally, the reasoned judgment is quite short and may be examined as a whole, containing as it does only two legal problems.

A COURT FILE BECOMES AN ENTRY IN SEUFFERT'S ARCHIV

Let us have a closer look at Seuffert's *Archiv*. How did entries in it arise from a report or a decision? What role did prior decisions play in it? The following analysis focuses on the argumentation and the way the different versions mention prior cases and other authorities. The legal issue still plays a role, as the following example will show.

Let us examine a legal dispute that took place in the 1850s in the city of Hamburg. The plaintiff was a widow named Schäuffler. She was represented by a *curator ad litem*. This was necessary for her lawsuit. Although women in general had legal capacity in the nineteenth century, [38] the city of Hamburg had its own particular rules. [39] The statutes limited women's legal capacity, especially in court. [40] The represented plaintiff demanded that the defendants pay interest. The defendants were the heirs of an alleged debtor named Voigt. The legal relationship from which this interest derived is not named clearly. Yet, the defendants refused to pay further interest, arguing the debt never existed at all.

The High Court of Appeal residing in Lübeck decided the case in April 1856. This court was competent to rule in cases from Hamburg, Bremen, Frankfurt and Lübeck – the four last remaining free cities within the German Confederation. The court had a particularly good reputation due to its highly qualified and hardworking judges. [41] Incidentally, the abovementioned Georg Arnold Heise left university to preside over the court in 1820 and kept this important legal practitioner's position until his death in 1851. The High Court of Appeal in Lübeck was influential far beyond its time. For instance, it developed most of Germany's commercial law. [42]

The schema that appears at the end of this essay presents four versions in separate columns. [43] The left column shows the argumentation of the single judge, Hermann Friedrich Brandis, who prepared the decision in a report. The second column shows the official reasons presented by the court for the parties. A regional collection gave a summary of these reasons (third column), and finally Seuffert's *Archiv* provided a shortened version of this summary (right column).

The internal report of the judge served as a preparation for the panel of seven judges to decide the case. It took judge Brandis from 30 December 1854 to 9 April 1856 to hand in the report. This document is by far the longest of the four versions, containing aspects that the panel of judges later regarded as irrelevant for the official statement of reasons.

It is notable that the structure of the reasons in the second column is entirely the same as in the first. The judgment is therefore based on the report and repeats its structure, argumentation and most of the sentences. It was tempting simply to copy the report, though some laws of the time and scholars explicitly militated against this, [44] and the guidelines in legal textbooks proposed not simply copying the reasons from the report to prevent this exact scenario. [45] Yet it was highly likely that the group of judges would confirm the reporter's opinion without carefully looking at the issues, and the prestigious court in Lübeck followed the proposal. Nevertheless, the reasoned decision is shortened, and the language slightly differs in comparison to the report, as we shall see. While the report serves to make an adequate decision, the reasons aim at explaining them convincingly to the parties and the public.

In 1859, that is, three years later, a regional collection quoted as 'Hamburger Sammlung' (column three) made the decision available to a wider audience. [46] It repeated decisions made by the High Court of Appeal in Lübeck dealing with cases from the city of Hamburg. The whole volume is dedicated to decisions of the year 1856. A second regional collection also reprinted the case. [47] Temporarily, Hamburg had two regional collections with the highest court's decisions. However, the analysis focuses on the first one, since Seuffert's *Archiv* quotes this version.

It was not until 1863 that the case appears in Seuffert's *Archiv*. Even seven years after the judgment, the case was found to be worthy of being told to a readership beyond the court's jurisdiction. Therefore, the up-to-dateness of a decision was not the main aspect. The new editor of Seuffert's *Archiv* probably learned of the case from the Hamburg collection, which he quoted. A detailed examination of the attached schema demonstrates differences between the versions row by row.

HEADLINE AND GUIDING PRINCIPLES

To facilitate the readers' orientation in a legal document, a headline or a guiding principle may be used as an introduction. Guiding principles (*Leitsätze*) help readers from outside the court gain better insight. These principles can be official, that is proposed by the court, or unofficial, that is added by the publisher. In *Schäuffler* v. *Voigt's heirs*, the initial report and the judges' reasons for the decision do not contain a headline or a guiding principle. These two versions were not created to be printed. In contrast, the regional collection as well as Seuffert's *Archiv* indicated the main issues by a preliminary sentence. Thus, the editors who stood outside the judiciary freely chose the headlines. Other contemporary collections were influenced by the court if members of the court were also part of the editorial board. At the *Kammergericht* in Berlin, for instance, judges subsequently prepared the headlines themselves. [48] From 1865 onwards, the High Court of Appeal in Lübeck had its own collection edited by the court's members. [49]

The regional collection describes the problems and the court's solution in a quite detailed manner, using abbreviated sentences. It says: 'Perennial debt-payments. Presumption thereof for a primary debt? This presumption is not plainly substantial; it is rather to be determined according to the special circumstances. Opinions of scholars on this matter. Interpretation of L. 6. § 1 de usuris 22.1.'

Seuffert's *Archiv* copied from the regional collection but omitted the complicated introduction. It indicated the main problem by a short and precise question: 'Do perennial debt-payments constitute an acknowledgement of the primary debt?' [50] Moreover, Seuffert's *Archiv* referred to similar cases in previous volumes in the headline.

FIRST QUESTION OF LAW

The case *Schäuffler* v. *Voigt's heirs* provided two major questions of law: one concerned admissibility, the other the use of a legal presumption. Firstly, the reporting judge Brandis discussed whether the High Court was competent to decide the case at all. The question whether the court had to deal with a case depended on the regulations of the free city where the case was decided on lower instance. According to Hamburg's statutes, the admissibility of the case depended on the value in litigation. [51] The demanded interest of forty-eight marks was too low to lead to the High Court of Appeal's jurisdiction. As the defendants denied the overall entitlement of 1,190 marks, the reporting judge concluded, this was the real value in dispute and the court was therefore competent. This question of admissibility is abbreviated in the schema. However, the preserved introductory sentence shows a remarkable aspect. The reporting judge uses the acronym 'm.E.', standing for 'meines Erachtens', which can be translated as 'in my point of view'. Thereby Brandis phrases clearly that he is expressing his own legal opinion on this issue, which is not the only one, and not necessarily correct. In the reasons for the judgment in the second column there is no longer any notion of this opinion being that of a single person with his own questionable opinion. Self-confident, the court expresses that there is no doubt ('kein Zweifel') about this particular outcome. This change in presenting a legal opinion has been an issue in recent studies. [52] The regional collection for Hamburg reproduced this first question of law, starting with the same first sentence as the official judgment. As the attached schema indicates, Seuffert's *Archiv* left this part out and dedicated the entry completely to the other issue. This is an example of how Seuffert's cross-regional collection separated cases into their single problems, so that every entry dealt with only one legal question.

SECOND QUESTION OF LAW

The reporting judge Brandis explains the second question of law in a long and complicated manner: 'Regarding the matter itself, the success of the remedy, which aims at the restitution of the judgment in first instance, depends completely on the answer to the legal question, what influence a perennial debt payment has on the existence or the proof of the initial debt.' [53]

This introduction named the various conditions. The judgment repeated this explanation of the legal issue while the Hamburg collection abbreviated the original section. Seuffert, on the contrary, left it out completely. He had already indicated the issue precisely in the opening headline. The entry of roughly two pages in Seuffert's *Archiv* is well arranged so readers can easily access the important information.

THREE OPINIONS

After bringing up this issue, Brandis discussed the legal effects of past years' interest payments. He gave three opinions on this subject. The first claims that the payments of interest over a certain time constitute a debt in its own right, even if it did not exist before. Brandis assessed this point of view as fallacious, quoting eighteenth-century authors for this obsolete opinion. It was so far beside the point that it did not even appear in the courts' judgment.

The second opinion argues that past payments of interest create a legal presumption of the debt. It could still be possible to prove the contrary, but the burden of evidence would rest upon the debtor. Brandis quoted several authorities on this idea but classified it as a view rarely now advanced. The judgment as well as the two collections did not adopt all of the references.

The third opinion states that there is no such presumption of a debt. Therefore, the evidence has to be valued and assessed by the court according to the individual circumstances of the given case.

Besides scholars of the time, Brandis quoted two decisions of other German high courts of appeal. These were recorded within an older volume of Seuffert's *Archiv*. Writing his internal report, Brandis quoted from this cross-regional collection. This is apparently the only way in which he took notice of the decisions made by other high courts of appeal since he names Seuffert explicitly as a reference. Though the entries are shortened and slightly changed, as we have seen, Seuffert's *Archiv* was the principal source to consult for recent decisions.

Brandis's allegation refers to volume two of Seuffert's collection. The older entry contains only four lines stating: 'A ten-year payment of interest on its own does neither generate an obligation of those making the payment to keep paying in future, nor the obligation to repay the initial debt.' [54] This short statement does not contain any argument but simply repeats the outcome of the case. The quotation from Seuffert's *Archiv* refers in a to a journal that printed a 'Präjudiz' from Cassel with the exact same outcome for a thirty-year payment of interest.

This core part of Brandis's report is reproduced nearly word for word in the judgment and the two collections. Slight variation in spelling and abbreviations is presumably due to different bibliographic styles. The allegation of Seuffert's *Archiv* underlines the effort to unify the law. Though the High Court of Appeal in Lübeck was not legally bound by other high courts of appeals' decisions, it quoted and considered their opinions.

STATEMENT OF THE JUDGE

However, Brandis does not simply follow the newest or somehow best authority when stating his preferred opinion. He names these opinions but discusses the best solution for the problem by explaining a fragment of Roman law. This fragment had already been used as an argument for the first and second opinion several times. According to Brandis, Roman law did not qualify interest payments differently from a partial payment or an inquiry to an extension of time. [55] They were all indications for the existence of an initial debt but did not constitute a legal presumption or even a debt on their own. Both the court's presentation of its reasons and the two collections copied almost all of this elaborate statement. Again, the court removed the personal 'in my opinion' in the judgment. The court shows its decision as the only reasonable answer to the given problem. There is just a transcriptional error in Seuffert's *Archiv*, referring to twenty-two instead of thirty-two, and we can find different expressions for 'and so on' in the German of the time. [56]

The examination of the Roman law fragment goes on for several pages of the report. [57] Brandis compared the case solved by Roman lawyers to his problem. He claimed it would not establish a general principle but was only the adequate solution in this case from antiquity. The circumstances of the old case were not mentioned in the *Digest* in detail. Brandis's method is close to that of distinguishing of cases in Common law.[58] The fragment would deal only with a special problem of the dowry, he argued. Therefore, it was not comparable to the given case. A general presumption could not be included since it did not give any specific requirements such as the necessary duration of the debt payments. Brandis admitted that there were also contrary interpretations of the fragment by other authors. But he stuck with his strict interpretation. The beginning of the fragment also dealt with a different legal problem. There – for Brandis – the initial debt was acknowledged but the obligation to periodical debt payments was in question. Thus, Brandis consulted Roman law to solve his case in this part of the report, whilst carefully evaluating the similarities and differences between that law and his own case.

Brandis also quotes from textbooks and collections. Yet, these authorities are not sufficient to justify the outcome. Only a clear evaluation of Roman law could do so. Roman law was the only binding text for Brandis. For this method, Germany's scholars were admired at the time. [58] Roman law gave not only a directive for research at university but served as a tool to solve legal issues in practice. The fragment itself was open to interpretation. In the end, Brandis followed the authorities of his time based on his understanding of the *Digest.*

APPLICATION OF THE LEGAL RULE TO THE CASE

Only after he had decided this main issue did Brandis turn to the specific case of the widow who sued her alleged debtor's heirs for further payment of interest. Thus, he distinguished between a rule that he deduced from Roman law and the case to which it was applied. The outcome of the case was not a final judgment but a judgment in evidence, a so-called Beweisurteil. This was a typical form in deciding cases until the nineteenth century. The court ordered the plaintiff to prove that the defendants owed her money. If she succeeded, she would have won her case. The court agreed on this result, but the collections left it out. Even the local collection from Hamburg surprisingly omitted it, although it published the parties' names.

CONCISE SUMMARY

In essence, Seuffert's Archiv facilitated the exchange of judges' rational judgments among several German states, thereby streamlining the process of citing legal precedents. It has been characterized as an antecedent to contemporary internet databases, allowing users to access the most recent decisions.[59] Consequently, decisions acquired a position of authority above other academic opinions when it came to deciding fresh cases in court. According to current legal principles, a previous ruling alone was not enough to justify the result of a case. This could only be achieved by assessing the relevant (Roman) legislation. The term 'Präjudizien' functioned solely as references or authorities and was not subjected to scrutiny as legal sources akin to Roman law. The judges were not obligated to follow the opinions of other courts, but they were compelled to at least take into account the arguments presented. The court, in the instance of the widow Schäuffler, ultimately adhered to the two 'Präjudizien' of other high courts of appeal that it consulted through Seuffert's Archive. According to Reyscher's statement in 1847, it was more convenient to adhere to the established rule. Indeed, it is worth noting that there exist instances in which courts have diverged from the outcomes documented in Seuffert's Archive.[60] However, the entries served as a significant source of legal inspiration and guidance.[61] Dawson's concept of a 'Case-Law Revolution' elicits connotations of establishing obligatory legal precedents for subsequent cases. This statement is inaccurate for the mid-nineteenth century in Germany. Nevertheless, when examining the contrast between Civil law and Common law, it becomes evident that the impact of the German 'Präjudizien' during that era bears the closest resemblance to the compelling precedents observed in contemporary Common law jurisdictions. Previous rulings could serve as precedents that the court could adhere to. This highlights the German political framework of that era and the establishment of the judiciary. Each state possessed its own supreme court and was not legally obligated to adhere to the jurisdiction of any other courts. Nevertheless, the courts demonstrated their mutual respect by considering the rulings of other courts. The aforementioned process can be characterized as a deliberation among superior courts. The courts, without any motivation from the German Confederation or the individual states, operated in this manner to consolidate the Civil law.

Footnote

1. M. Reimann, 'Die Erosion der klassischen Formen – Rechtskulturelle Wandlungen des Civil Law und Common Law im Europa des 19. und 20. Jahrhunderts', Zeitschrift für Neuere Rechtsgeschichte, 28 (2006), 209–34, at 216. If one thinks of these idealised concepts, the nineteenth century approaches them as closely as possible in reality; ibid., 233.
2. I would like to thank the editors for the opportunity to contribute to the volume and the helpful comments and rephrasing propositions which I gladly adopted. All translations are my own.
3. J. P. Dawson, The Oracles of the Law (Ann Arbor, MI, 1968), 432.
4. Ibid., xi.

5. Ibid., 432.
6. H. Gehrke, Die privatrechtliche Entscheidungsliteratur Deutschlands, Charakteristik und Bibliografie der Rechtsprechungs- und Konsiliensammlungen vom 16. bis z. Beginn d. 19. Jahrhunderts (Frankfurt am Main, 1974), 26–31.
7. The discussion is analysed by S. Hocks, Gerichtsgeheimnis und Begründungszwang. Zur Publizität der Entscheidungsgründe im Ancien Régime und im frühen 19. Jahrhundert (Frankfurt am Main, 2002).
8. R. Sprung, 'Die Entwicklung der zivilgerichtlichen Begründungspflicht', in R. Sprung (ed.), Die Entscheidungsbegründung in europäischen Verfahrensrechten und im Verfahren vor internationalen Gerichten (Vienna, 1974), 43–62.
9. Reimann, 'Erosion der klassischen Formen', 232.
10. In the 1990s, around 96–99% of higher courts' decisions quoted previous decisions as precedents, counted for various German judiciaries by R. Alexy and R. Dreier, 'Precedent in the Federal Republic of Germany', in N. MacCormick and R. Summers (eds.), Interpreting Precedents (Aldershot, 1997), 17–64, at 23.
11. C. Günzl, *Eine andere Geschichte der Begründungspflicht. Sichtweisen des frühen 19. Jahrhunderts* (forthcoming, Tübingen, 2021).
12. P. Oestmann, Wege zur Rechtsgeschichte: Gerichtsbarkeit und Verfahren (Cologne, 2015), 176.
13. For categories of German collections in the early modern age see Gehrke, *Die privat-rechtliche Entscheidungsliteratur*.
14. A. H. Simon and H. L. von Strampff (eds.), Entscheidungen des Königlichen Geheimen Ober-Tribunals (Berlin, 1837), iii.
15. F. G. L. Strippelmann (ed.), Neue Sammlung bemerkenswerther Entscheidungen des Ober-Appellations-Gerichtes zu Cassel, part 1 (Cassel, 1842), iv.
16. *J. A. Seuffert's Archiv für Entscheidungen der obersten Gerichte in den deutschen Staaten*, 17(1) (1863), i (edited by A. F. W. Preusser).
17. For Seuffert's biography see A. Quentin, 'Johann Adam Seuffert (1794–1857)', in Oberlandesgericht Nürnberg (ed.), In Stein gehauene Rechtsgeschichte aus zwei Jahrtausenden (Nuremberg, 2008), 12–17.
18. M. Schmoeckel, 'Vorbemerkung Vor § 1', in M. Schmoeckel, J. Rückert and R. Zimmermann (eds.), Historisch-kritischer Kommentar zum BGB (Tübingen, 2003), 123–65, at 137–8 (Rn. 20f).
19. J. A. Seuffert, Praktisches Pandektenrecht, 3rd edn, 3 vols. (Würzburg, 1852), vol. I, vii reprints the foreword from his first edition in 1824 in which he refers explicitly to Heise.

20. For the Historical School of Law, see H.-P. Haferkamp, Die Historische Rechtsschule (Frankfurt am Main, 2018).
21. J. A. Seuffert (ed.), Archiv für Entscheidungen der obersten Gerichte in den deutschen Staaten, vol. I (Munich, 1847), iii.
22. A. L. Reyscher, 'IX. Archiv für Entscheidungen der obersten Gerichte in den deutschen Staaten, herausgegeben von J. A. Seuffert (Appellationsgerichtsrath). Ersten Bandes erstes Heft. München 1847', Zeitschrift für deutsches Recht und deutsche Rechtswissenschaft, 11 (1847), 312–16, at 312: 'aber sie hindert sie [eine spätere bessere Ueberzeugung] gewissermaßen doch, weil es bequemer ist, einen Vorgang anzuziehen'.
23. J. E. Kuntze, Der Wendepunct der Rechtswissenschaft (Leipzig, 1856), 7: 'Die Zeitschrift für historische Rechtswissenschaft verstummt, – und was vermag unsere neue Zeit dagegen einzusetzen? Seuffert's Archiv für Entscheidungen der oberen Gerichtshöfe hat es seit mehreren Jahren übernommen, den reichen Springquell einer immer sich verjüngenden Kasuistik über unsere nahrungsbedürftige dürre Doktrin mit schätzenswerther Emsigkeit ausströmen zu lassen.'
24. For a short summary in English, see H.-P. Haferkamp, 'Legal Formalism and Its Critics', in H. Pihlajamäki, M. D. Dubber and M. Godfrey (eds.), The Oxford Handbook of European Legal History (Oxford, 2018), 929–44, at 933–6.
25. R. von Jhering, Scherz und Ernst in der Jurisprudenz, 13th edn (Leipzig, 1924), 101.
26. Dawson, *Oracles of the Law*, 440. At the same time, England established binding precedents in their purest form. See Reimann, 'Erosion der klassischen Formen', 217; S. Vogenauer, 'Zur Geschichte des Präjudizienrechts in England', Zeitschrift für Neuere Rechtsgeschichte, 28 (2006), 48–78, at 64.
27. H.-J. Becker, 'Präjudiz', in A. Erler and E. Kaufmann (eds.), Handwörterbuch zur deutschen Rechtsgeschichte, vol. 3 (Berlin, 1984), cols. 1866–70.
28. J. Schröder, Recht als Wissenschaft 2nd edn (Munich, 2012), 200.
29. R. Ogorek, Richterkönig oder Subsumtionsautomat? Zur Justiztheorie im 19. Jahrhundert (Frankfurt am Main, 1986), 196.
30. Dawson, *Oracles of the Law*, 441: 'their products acquired authority by meeting the test of legal science'.
31. An exception is fields of law that consist merely of case law, such as employment law.
32. M. Payandeh, Judikative Rechtserzeugung, Theorie, Dogmatik und Methodik der Wirkungen von Präjudizien (Tübingen, 2017).

33. Ogorek, *Richterkönig oder Subsumtionsautomat?*, 193–6.
34. For a different view, see U. Müßig, 'Geschichte des Richterrechts und der Präjudizienbindung auf dem Europäischen Kontinent', Zeitschrift für Neuere Rechtsgeschichte, 28 (2006), 79–106, at 80.
35. Also suggested in ibid., 106.
36. T. Herbst, 'Die These der einzig richtigen Entscheidung', JuristenZeitung, 18 (2012), 891–900.
37. Ogorek, *Richterkönig oder Subsumtionsautomat?*, 196.
38. W. Sellert, 'Die Akzessorietät von Kostentragung und Prozeßerfolg, ein historisches Problem von aktueller Bedeutung', in H.-J. Becker (ed.), Rechtsgeschichte als Kulturgeschichte, Festschrift für Adalbert Erler zum 70. Geburtstag (Aalen, 1976), 509–37.
39. H. Coing, Europäisches Privatrecht, 2 vols. (Munich, 1989), vol. II, 291: 'Die Frau ist geschäftsfähig. Die im Mittelalter vorhandene und im älteren gemeinen Recht territorial aufrechterhaltene Geschlechtsvormundschaft existiert nicht mehr.'
40. E. Holthöfer, 'Die Geschlechtsvormundschaft. Ein Überblick von der Antike bis ins 19. Jahrhundert', in U. Gerhard (ed.), Frauen in der Geschichte des Rechts (Munich, 1997), 390–451, at 421.
41. *Der Stadt Hamburg Gerichts-Ordnung und Statuta* (Hamburg, 1842), 503.
42. For an overview in English, see P. Oestmann, 'Court Records as Sources for the History of Commercial Law: The Oberappellationsgericht Lübeck as a Commercial Court (1820–1879)', in H. Pihlajamäki, A. Cordes, S. Dauchy and D. De ruysscher (eds.), Understanding the Sources of Early Modern and Modern Commercial Law: Courts, Statutes, Contracts, and Legal Scholarship (Leiden, 2018), 364–85, at 369–71.
43. J. Rückert, 'Handelsrechtsbildung und Modernisierung des Handelsrechts durch Wissenschaft zwischen ca. 1800 und 1900' in K. O. Scherner (ed.), Modernisierung des Handelsrechts im 19. Jahrhundert, Abhandlungen aus dem gesamten bürgerlichen Recht, Handelsrecht und Wirtschaftsrecht (Heidelberg, 1993), 19–66; P. Oestmann, 'The Unification of Law via the Institution of Jurisdiction in the 19th Century: Commercial Law before the High Court of Appeal of the Four Free Cities of Germany', Juridica International, 16 (2009), 224–30.
44. For the schema, see below, 224–35.
45. See for instance, *Königlich-Baierisches Regierungsblatt*, 1813, col. 565.

46. For an example, see J. K. Gensler, Grundsätze der juristischen Vortrags- und formellen Entscheidungskunde (Jena, 1815), 57–8.
47. J. F. Voigt (ed.), Sammlung von Erkenntnissen und Entscheidungsgründen des Ober-Appellations-Gerichts zu Lübeck in hamburgischen Rechtssachen nebst den Erkenntnissen der unteren Instanzen, vol. III, part 1: Erkenntnisse aus dem Jahr 1856 enthaltend (Hamburg, 1859, 1864), 57–60.
48. Anonymous, Vollständige Sammlung der vom Ober-Appellations-Gerichte zu Lübeck im Jahre 1856 in hamburgischen Rechtssachen abgegebenen Urtheile sammt Motiven, mit den Vorentscheidungen der verschiedenen Unterinstanzen (Leipzig, 1859), 130–8.
49. Berlin, Geheimes Staatsarchiv Preußischer Kulturbesitz, I. HA Rep. 97a Nr. 443, 444, 446.
50. J. F. Kierulff (ed.), Sammlung der Entscheidungen des Ober-Appellationsgerichts der vier freien Städte Deutschlands zu Lübeck (Hamburg, 1865).
51. Original: 'Ist aus mehrjährigen Zinszahlungen eine Anerkennung der Capitalschuld zu folgern.'
52. H. Greb, Die Verfassung des Oberappellationsgerichts der vier freien Städte Deutschlands zu Lübeck (Göttingen, 1967), 94–5.
53. P. Oestmann, Zur Gerichtspraxis im 19. Jahrhundert, ein Schmuggeleiprozess am Oberappellationsgericht Lübeck (Cologne, 2019), 51–4.
54. Original: 'B. Soviel die Sache selbst betrifft, so hängt der Erfolg der aufgestellten alleinigen Beschwerde, welche auf Wiederherstellung des Erkenntnisses erster Instanz gerichtet ist, ganz u. gar von Beantwortung der Rechtsfrage ab, welcher Einfluß einer mehrjährigen Zinszahlung in Beziehung auf das Bestehen oder den Beweis einer Capitalschuld beizulegen sei.'
55. J. A. Seuffert (ed.), Archiv für Entscheidungen, vol. II (Munich, 1849), 339, no. 268: 'Eine zehnjährige Zinsenzahlung für sich allein begründet weder die Verbindlichkeit dessen, der sie bewirkte, zur ferneren Entrichtung dieser Zinsen, noch weniger seine Verpflichtung zur Zahlung des Capitals.'
56. Original: 'wie ein Gleiches auch durch andere Handlungen, z.B. eine Abschlagsbitte, Fristbitte pp. bekundet warden kann.'
57. i.e. 'pp.', 'etc.', 'u.s.w.'.
58. The following evaluation is not part of the schema below.
59. See S. Vogenauer, 'An Empire of Light? Learning and Lawmaking in the History of German Law', Cambridge Law Journal, 64 (2005), 481–500, at 481.
60. Quentin, 'Seuffert', 17.

61. M. Berger, C. Günzl, and N. Kramp-Seidel, 'Normen und Entscheiden, Anmerkungen zu einem problematischen Verhältnis', in U. Pfister (ed.), Kulturen des Entscheidens, Narrative – Praktiken – Ressourcen (Göttingen, 2019), 248–66.
62. Similarly, see Vogenauer, 'Zur Geschichte des Präjudizienrechts in England', 59, referring to England in the seventeenth and eighteenth centuries.

09 THE HISTORICAL SIGNIFICANCE OF LEONE LEVI (1821–1888) IN THE FIELD OF COMPARATIVE COMMERCIAL LAW

INTRODUCTION: AN OVERVIEW

Leone Levi, an Italian-born merchant, established himself as a jurist, statistician, and economist during the Victorian era in Britain. His diverse character, along with his unwavering dedication to a wide range of legal, economic, and statistical matters, is inherently captivating. [1] The current body of scholarly work mostly focuses on his significant contributions to the fields of economics and statistics, with relatively less attention given to his treatise on comparative commercial law within the realm of legal historiography. The objective of this essay is to elucidate Leone Levi's distinctive contribution to the field of commercial law throughout the nineteenth century, while also delving into a more comprehensive analysis of his comparative studies in commercial law. The significance of this matter lies primarily in the recognition by legal historiography of the necessity for adopting a comparative methodology when examining the historical development of commercial law. Furthermore, commercial law inherently leans towards comparison because to the global nature of trade and commerce. Scholars and practitioners in the field of commercial law frequently use a comparative and global perspective. This study aims to analyze the utilization of comparative legislation by Leone Levi, a unique commercial lawyer of the nineteenth century, in the context of commercial and company legal affairs. It is important to consider that Levi's research on comparative commercial law was interconnected with other significant legal matters, including codification. Leone Levi has made significant contributions to the disciplines of commercial law, comparative law, codification, and legal education for merchants. He has authored a substantial number of papers, pamphlets, lectures, and articles covering a wide range of legal subjects. Despite being perceived as a 'bizarre figure' by certain Englishmen, he possessed exceptional personality traits. [2] Born in 1821 to a Jewish family in Ancona, the individual in question had a conventional commercial education within his hometown and was subsequently unable to pursue classical studies, a decision that he would later come to lament. [3] The Jewish community in the seaport of Ancona, where he was raised, has experienced substantial growth and development since the Middle Ages, making it one of the oldest and most prominent communities in Italy. The Jewish community residing in Ancona, which was compelled to reside in a ghetto following the incorporation of the town into the Papal States during the latter half of the sixteenth century, played a significant role in engaging in commercial activities, trade, and financial transactions with the Levant region. In the nineteenth century, Ancona, despite the prominence of other maritime routes, continued to have a significant impact on commerce in the Mediterranean region, particularly with the Ottoman Empire. As a result, the town attracted merchants from various nations, with a particular emphasis on Greeks. [4] Undoubtedly, Leone Levi was born in a suitable location to develop a keen understanding of the requirements of commerce and trade in a multicultural setting.

Very soon, at the age of fifteen, he started working in his brother's business and travelled to England. In 1844 he moved to Liverpool, where he learned English and started his new challenging British life, in a country which had embarked upon the second industrial revolution and where the free trade movement was growing rapidly. [5] Within that political climate, Levi developed a passionate interest in the political campaigns and writings of Richard Cobden, the leader of the Anti-Corn Law League, [6] and the young Jewish merchant soon entered into contact with him.

Leaving aside battles over the abolition of the Corn Laws and free trade, historians are in agreement in concluding that the United Kingdom experienced a period of considerable prosperity between the mid-nineteenth century and the start of the 1870s, which extended to all forms of economic activity, including foreign trade. The country produced a broad variety of consumer goods, in addition to primary capital goods (coal, iron and steel) and investment goods destined for both British industry and foreign countries. In summary, the Victorian Britain that Levi found was acting as a catalyst for increasingly complex and sophisticated international trade, so much so that it was considered as 'the world's leading trader and manufacturer' or the 'workshop of the world'. [7]

Levi enjoyed the dynamic (and controversy-filled) atmosphere and the public debates. In 1847 he became a naturalised British subject. In particular, as regards the issue of most interest for our present purposes, during his first few years in Britain he dedicated his energies to campaigning in favour of the chambers of commerce: he is well known for having played an active role in the foundation of the Liverpool Chamber of Commerce. [8]

He also joined the Presbyterian Church, a denomination that bore the 'uniform' of respectability and rank in Victorian Britain. [9] Indeed, Levi became an active member of the Presbyterian Church of England and campaigned in support of Protestants in Italy through the Bible Society and the Evangelical Continental Society, a British missionary society. [10] In this sense, his conversion to evangelical Christianity and his commitment to the broad dissemination of the Holy Scriptures in pre- and post-unification Italy may be understood as a reaction to the conservative and obscurantist Catholicism that he had witnessed as a Jew in the Papal States.

Leone Levi, a self-made man, [11] ended up lecturing on commercial law at King's College London in 1853 and was called to the bar in 1859 at Lincoln's Inn. In 1861 he was awarded a doctorate in Political and Economic Sciences by the University of Tübingen. He was also an active member of the Council of the Royal Statistical Society and in 1887 attended the Congress of European Statisticians in Rome. That occasion was his final opportunity to visit Italy, only a year before his death. [12]

Despite his conversion and British citizenship, Levi maintained close relations with his city of birth. He returned to Ancona whenever he had the opportunity and, as far as is apparent, was always received with honour by his former fellow citizens. In 1881, now a famous man, he set up a fund to finance education for local merchants during a stay in the city. Later, in 1888, he bequeathed to the city the prizes and awards he had received along with the manuscript version of his treatise on comparative commercial law, published in two editions in 1851–2 and 1863, which will be considered in the following pages. [13]

After Leone Levi settled in Britain, his native country fulfilled its destiny with the successful conclusion of the *Risorgimento* and the unification of Italy in 1861, [14] and the emancipation of the Italian Jews followed in the new secular state. From that moment onwards, the Jews of Ancona, who had already played an active role in the *Risorgimento*, became actively involved in the government of the city and were appointed to leading positions in the local chamber of commerce. In 2001, the Ancona Chamber of Commerce established an arbitration court that was named after Levi himself. [15]

COMMERCIAL LAW OF THE WORLD

It was through his family business that Leone Levi became specifically interested in British mercantile law and in British judicial procedure. This occurred after he settled in Liverpool and after a series of misfortunes linked to the general financial circumstances of the country. [16] His subsequent path may be traced through his various initiatives calling for the creation of chambers of commerce with associated commercial courts, as well as the campaign for the unification of the commercial laws of England (and Wales), Scotland and Ireland. This was linked to the idea of collecting and documenting the commercial laws of various countries and imagining a uniform code of commercial law for 'civilised nations'. [17]

Considering each of these initiatives in order, in 1849 Levi was extremely active in promoting the Liverpool Chamber of Commerce. He also advocated the establishment of commercial courts attached to the chambers of commerce in order to simplify commercial procedure. This was a key point for him: he argued that commercial law litigation should be simplified, and, for this purpose, he also called for the reform of the law of arbitration. [18] His suggestions had an impact on the arbitration clauses of the Common Law Procedure Act of 1854. [19]

Levi corresponded with a number of politicians. For instance, in 1849 he wrote to Benjamin Disraeli concerning chambers of commerce. [20] However, his favourite correspondent was Lord Henry Brougham, former lord chancellor and head of the Law Amendment Society, who was a partisan of free trade. It seems that the two men were bound by a common spirit of reform. [21] A sample of Levi's correspondence with Lord Brougham over fifteen years, from 1850 to 1864, concerning commercial law reform and judicial statistics has been published and sheds some light on his tireless activity. [22]

Generally speaking, Levi's links and correspondence with leading political figures in Britain are valuable for assessing the reformist drive within British public life during that period. At the same time, his copious writings, coupled with the fact that he was able to operate immediately and with ease within the prevailing social context, confirms that it was becoming increasingly easy during those years to keep informed and correspond, even in relation to topical political issues. Daily newspapers and journals, along with popular publications, all of which were on sale at railway stations, were experiencing strong expansion due to falling production costs and the broadening of the reading public. [23]

That said, it was as the honorary secretary of the Liverpool Chamber of Commerce that Levi found himself in a strategic position to collect precise information in an official capacity concerning the rules of foreign chambers of commerce, and above all concerning foreign commercial law. Levi sent letters abroad through the consular network and Liverpool merchants, asking for foreign texts to be sent to him by foreign mercantile, consular and political authorities. He sought to do so because he was persuaded of the need to be aware of foreign legislation when doing business. He was also guided by his past experience as a merchant.

The collection and study of the precious documentation from various parts of the world soon convinced Levi of the similarities and analogies between the commercial laws of the different countries, despite differences in terms of drafting and form. This gave him the idea of drawing up a text containing comparisons between the various commercial laws in force. [24] His declared and recognised source was the similar work carried out by the French jurist Fortuné Anthoine de Saint-Joseph (1794–1853), who authored well-known volumes on legislative concordance between the French codes, including the Civil Code and the Commercial Code, along with several other nineteenth-century foreign codes. In particular, it was in the British Museum Library that Levi had the opportunity to read the *Concordances entre les codes de commerce étrangers et le code de commerce français,* [25] which was first published by de Saint-Joseph in 1844 [26] and later issued as a new edition in 1851. [27]

De Saint-Joseph was a learned jurist: a royal prosecutor who later became a judge. He compiled synoptic charts of French codes and foreign codes and legislation. He did so within a cultural environment that was keenly aware of comparative law studies; two French law journals were dedicated to this issue, the *Thémis* and the well-known *Revue Foelix.* [28] De Saint-Joseph was supported by a number of contributors in his work of collecting and translating foreign commercial legislation. Even the foreign minister of the French government helped him with his treatise on the concordance of the French Code de commerce with foreign commercial law. [29]

Levi's task was slightly different as his starting point was the uncodified British mercantile law. [30] With this in mind, he wrote that his work was 'an attempt, however imperfect, to reduce the mercantile law of Great Britain to the form of a code'. The goal was to compile 'a manual for constant use and reference to the mercantile classes'. [31] Moreover, Levi was not yet a lawyer when he first published his book on comparative commercial laws. Indeed, he had neither studied nor practised law and lacked any formal juridical qualifications, [32] even though a few years later he was to become a barrister. [33]

Nonetheless, inspired by a healthy dose of intellectual curiosity and secure in his eclectic talents, Levi applied himself with great diligence to writing his book *Commercial Law, Its Principles and Administration, or, The Mercantile Law of Great Britain Compared with the Codes and Laws of Commerce of the Following Mercantile Countries: Anhalt, Austria [...] Würtenburg and the Institutes of Justinian,* [34] the first volume of which was published in 1850, followed by the second in 1852. In particular, the first volume contained chronological tables of laws governing land and maritime trade in various countries and during various periods, as well as comparative tables presenting customary practices at the main commercial trading centres, starting from London and Paris. The treatise was divided into sections, which dealt specifically with merchants, books of commerce, partnerships, factors, contracts, bills of exchange, shipping, insurance, bankruptcy, commercial jurisdiction and so on.

On each topic, following the model of de Saint-Joseph, Levi proposed a kind of synopsis of the laws applicable in various countries. He listed his sources, which were mainly the same as those listed by de Saint-Joseph. This essentially involved the translation into English by Levi of the translations into French collected or arranged by de Saint-Joseph. Specifically, when translating into English the text of foreign commercial laws, Levi stated that he had personally supervised the translation work from French or other languages, depending upon whether or not the texts featured in de Saint-Joseph's work. [35]

This effort of translating translations is certainly of interest in assessing Levi's contribution to comparative law scholarship. There is no doubt that the authenticity of the original text was lost, which naturally made it harder to understand the foreign text with precision. However, during this phase, it was essentially through translation that national jurists were able to gain knowledge of texts written in languages other than their own. This complex phenomenon has been studied in depth: [36] as an instrument for the circulation of legal knowledge, translation must always be treated with the utmost caution, whether the translation is direct or second-hand. For Levi, translating legal texts was the core element of his work. Besides, he himself was not writing in his native language and always attributed major importance to having a knowledge of foreign languages.

The theorists listed by de Saint-Joseph amongst the guiding inspirations for his work included (alongside Jean-Jacques Gaspard Foelix) Karl Joseph Mittermaier for German law [37] and Edward Chitty for the law of England and Wales. [38] These authors were also cited by Levi as sources in the introduction to his book. In particular, de Saint-Joseph started his section on the correlations between commercial laws by quoting at length within a from a publication by the greatest expert in French commercial law during the first half of the nineteenth century, Jean-Marie Pardessus. [39]

A capable jurist, having cut his teeth in everyday practice, a theorist of commercial law, a pioneer in university teaching of this branch of the law in the wake of the adoption of the Code de commerce, Pardessus authored publications including, amongst others, a collection of ancient maritime laws as well as the fundamental *Cours de droit commercial.* [40] De Saint-Joseph referred to an article published by Pardessus in 1842 in the refined *Journal des Savans* – the journal of the Académie des Inscriptions et des Belles Lettres – in which he reviewed the eight volumes of the *Collection des lois civiles et criminelles des États modernes* by Victor Foucher (which appeared between 1833 and 1841). In his review, the renowned commercial lawyer argued that contemporary legal science should also be open to the historical and comparative dimension. [41]

The drafting of uniform laws in the form of national codes, which started during the eighteenth and nineteenth centuries, had sparked off a trend towards the simplification and harmonisation of the various laws in force within each legal system. The comparative study of codes, which was made possible thanks to the translation and collection of foreign laws, in turn became an instrument for correcting and improving individual national laws, which could be used also by lawmakers. At the same time, relations between citizens from different countries arising through travel and trade were starting to increase in number. National courts were thus required to rule on disputes for which a knowledge of foreign laws was essential; alternatively, court actions against foreign nationals had to be launched before the courts of their respective countries of origin. This was particularly the case in the area of commercial law. Thus, a collection of foreign laws translated into the national language was also a 'precious gift' for practical purposes, to use the expression of Pardessus, which was essentially reiterated by de Saint-Joseph. [42] For his part, Levi translated the words of Pardessus into English and incorporated them into the main body of his introduction, citing directly from the source of de Saint-Joseph's citations alongside an animated discussion of the history of trade and commercial law. [43]

Levi's treatise won him international prizes and medals. [44] It was soon reviewed abroad. For example, German commercial lawyer Karl Heinrich Ludwig Brinckmann reviewed Levi's work for the *Kritische Zeitschrift für die gesamte Rechtswissenschaft* in 1853: not surprisingly, it was presented as something very similar to de Saint-Joseph's *Concordance.* [45] De Saint-Joseph and Levi did not really compare laws; [46] rather, they collected foreign laws and chose a framework for presenting them. For de Saint-Joseph, this framework was drawn from the structure of the French Code de commerce. [47] The comparative work was left to one side, or to the readers. Furthermore, both de Saint-Joseph and Levi were persuaded of the supremacy of their national laws, respectively French and British, as Levi was operating within the horizon of the British Empire. However, Levi's work did promote a knowledge of foreign commercial laws which were translated into English. The same had been done by de Saint-Joseph, who made foreign legislation available in French. In fact, before comparing anything one has to know what the foreign laws are. That was what Levi did for the English-speaking world. [48]

To summarise, thanks to the materials he was able to collect and thanks also to the hard work of compilation carried out by him in the Advocates Library in Edinburgh, [49] Leone Levi published his comprehensive comparative treatise. Better known as *Commercial Law of the World*, it was genuinely ground-breaking. Nevertheless, Levi was already looking beyond the collection of foreign laws published by him and intended his work also as a step towards an international commercial code. [50] In fact, in the introduction to his first volume, Levi included an address to Prince Albert, the prince consort, in which he suggested the feasibility of an international code of commercial law for the whole world, [51] which could be discussed at the 1851 Great Exhibition in London. [52]

Over the following months Levi lectured and published extensively on the topic. [53] As mentioned above, Levi found support and patronage at the highest level: *Commercial Law of the World* was dedicated to the earl of Harrowby, a founding member and president of the Royal Statistical Society, who was another keen supporter of Levi's initiatives. [54] Following on from Levi's treatise, the earl organised a conference in 1852 along with Lord Brougham, which led to the enactment of the various Mercantile Law Amendments Acts in 1856 for England, Scotland and Ireland. [55] This outcome was regarded as unsatisfactory by Levi: whilst he had somehow managed to persuade his audience that it would be appropriate to consider aligning the various commercial laws in force in the United Kingdom, his ideas concerning an international commercial code fell on deaf ears. [56]

In the meantime, Levi continued to explore statistics and to study economics, subsequently publishing a second revised edition of his treatise on comparative commercial law, which appeared in 1863. That was a quite different version of his work and had a different title: *International Commercial Law: Being the Principles of Mercantile Law of the Following and Other Countries, viz.: England, Scotland, Ireland, British India, British Colonies, Austria, Belgium, Brazil, Buenos Ayres, Denmark, France, Germany, Greece, Hans Towns, Italy, Netherlands, Norway, Portugal, Prussia, Russia, Spain, Sweden, Switzerland, United States, Württemberg.* [57]

First of all, the two editions differ essentially in terms of graphic and editorial choices. As mentioned above, the first edition – *Commercial Law of the World* – followed the framework previously adopted by de Saint-Joseph. This involved a series of comparative tables situated in the middle of the page, referring to a particular text selected for comparison; Levi's texts were drawn specifically from British commercial law, which was presented following the structure of the French Commercial Code. For a British lawyer, the presentation might not have been self-explanatory, and would most likely have appeared complicated and somewhat cumbersome. For a Continental lawyer on the other hand, the tables summarising the various legislation presented by Levi were readily accessible, and were even of direct benefit: consider for example the widespread practice in Italy throughout the nineteenth century of publishing commentaries and comparisons between the various codes that had been enacted in the various territories over the space of a few years.

Returning to Levi's book, the second edition – *International Commercial Law* – by contrast endeavoured to overhaul the presentation in order to make it clearer and more fluent, and above all better suited to the needs and expectations of an English-speaking readership. The author thus abandoned the synoptic tables and incorporated references to foreign legislation into his discussion, using italics and subheadings in order to guide the reader through the comparative study of legislation. Moreover, the removal of the tables allowed him to present issues of interest and to better identify points of contact between them, thus striving to achieve that uniformity that he was seeking. As a result, the exploratory journey of Leone Levi through the field of commercial law, including both legal comparison *lato sensu* as well as wider issues, can be appreciated by considering these two editions of the treatise.

Levi had in fact expanded the horizons of his own knowledge, having nurtured a passion for statistics since the 1850s, [58] and subsequently focused on the study of wage conditions and the working classes, including also the issues of duties, taxes and wages. In addition, he pursued his legal studies in greater depth. To sum up, over the ten-year period falling between the two editions of his treatise, Levi had cultivated his various interests and was keen to reap the benefits of this study within his conception of the tasks of legal comparison.

Furthermore, between the middle of the century and the early 1870s, commercial law on the European continent underwent far-reaching changes, not least due to the progressive expansion of the industrial economy to countries such as France, Prussia and the German states. As a result, in France the Code de commerce appeared to have been superseded in many respects by the special legislation subsequently enacted, in particular in relation to capital companies and bankruptcy. [59] In the German area, on the other hand, the enactment of the General Law on Bills of Exchange in 1848 was followed by the entry into force of the General German Commercial Code (ADHGB) in 1861, a text that had many positive aspects, resulting from a desire to promote a capitalist economy, even to the detriment of the traditional rules of private law. [60] During the Restoration in Italy, Levi's unforgotten homeland, it was possible to observe a proliferation of commercial codes and regulations. Soon after unification, a few politicians struggled to reach consensus around a new commercial code and adequate rules on joint stock companies, even though the Italian economy was still in a pre-industrial phase. [61]

Levi was well aware of all of this, and so it was necessary to update his works. However, the most prominent feature of the book published in 1863 is the novel nature of his approach to comparison between the commercial laws of various countries, as well as the attention dedicated to the commercial law of the British colonies, which received much greater emphasis than it had in the first edition published in 1850–2. [62] At the same time, as noted above, he also attempted to present the contents of the various laws in a more homogeneous manner. Levi was now a British citizen who was attuned to the needs of the Empire and its colonies; he was no longer an 'outsider'. However, he remained a visionary. Drawing inspiration from the teachings of Emer de Vattel, whom he cited – 'Commerce is a law of nature and the right of trading is a natural right' – he pursued his idea of an international commercial code. [63]

Thus, Levi's thoughts evolved further in the direction of the emerging international law and writers in that field, [64] in which he became increasingly interested. 'Commerce can only be carried on safely and advantageously in times of peace', he wrote without any particular originality; and yet, once again he was fully in line with the spirit of the times, and in fact in some sense even pre-empted that spirit.

FROM THE COMPARATIVE LEGISLATION TO THE PROCESS OF CODIFICATION

The most significant aspect of Levi's contribution to commercial law seems to be his promotion of the alignment of commercial laws. He also lectured extensively regarding this matter. Thanks to his commitment and his treatise on the *Commercial Law of the World*, practical measures for harmonising the laws of the three jurisdictions of England (and Wales), Scotland and Ireland were discussed, resulting in the enactment of the Mercantile Law Amendments Acts in 1856. [65] Levi might be considered in some sense to be an influencer. He was a supporter of legislation on mercantile matters, [66] seeing legislation as an instrument for modernisation and simplification. It is perhaps possible to discern an echo of the influential thinking of Jeremy Bentham within his preference for legislation, although Levi never cited this author. [67] However, he chose to open his book with a citation in Italian concerning the quality of laws, taken from the first book of *Scienza della legislazione*, written by the eighteenth-century Neapolitan Enlightenment scholar Gaetano Filangieri. [68] It is evident that new horizons were opening up within Levi's thinking around the middle of the nineteenth century in relation to legislation, both within Britain and internationally.

During the age of codification, when commercial law was being codified in Continental Europe and entered into a new phase of overcoming its corporative origins and becoming part of the law of the state, Levi contributed to addressing the issue of codification in Victorian Britain. He did so from the viewpoint of the codification of mercantile law, which seemed to be an excellent place to begin. [69] Levi called for the alignment of commercial laws. In this sense, he was a man of his times. As regards substantive commercial law, one of his core calls was for the introduction of general limited liability for joint stock companies. [70]

Indeed, as mentioned above, he went even further in supporting the codification of commercial law by conceiving of the idea of an international code of commercial law, basing his arguments also on comparative law studies. His campaign for an international commercial code was somewhat unconventional. De Saint-Joseph had in fact been more cautious regarding that issue: the learned French jurist had merely suggested that common universal principles within commercial matters could be appropriate.

Levi's arguments in favour of an international commercial code were based on the fundamental principles of right and equity, which were acknowledged by all civilised countries, as well as the universal nature of the most important commercial customs. In his view, the principles of jurisprudence that constituted the basis for commercial law coincided with the fundamental precepts of natural law. The problems he discerned included a lack of uniformity between the various systems of commercial law and an ignorance of foreign commercial laws.

In the meantime, a commercial treaty was concluded between Britain and France in 1860: it was known as the Cobden-Chevalier Treaty.[71] This was a bilateral trade treaty which aimed to liberalise trade between the two countries. It was the first of its kind and would be followed by others, concluded between other European states. Levi for his part was an enthusiastic supporter of such trade treaties, regarding them as a significant step towards the creation of a free trade area that extended beyond the borders of individual countries. Levi was without doubt an optimist, and his pragmatic spirit led him to appreciate also initiatives that were not in keeping with the idea of an international commercial code.

Furthermore, as mentioned above, following the publication of the first volume of *Commercial Law of the World*, Levi became increasingly interested in economic and statistical studies. He contributed extensively to statistical science and economics, delivering a number of public lectures and writing a number of economic articles for journals and magazines. He became a strong supporter of judicial statistics, commercial statistics and agricultural statistics. He was regarded as an expert in the field: many of his related articles were published in the *Journal of the Royal Statistical Society*. It is important not to overlook the emergence and growing importance of judicial statistics in those years, especially in the fields of criminal law and prison law in many European countries as well as on the international stage.[72]

It therefore comes as no surprise that the second volume of *Commercial Law of the World*, published in 1852, was accompanied by a 'Statistical Chart of the Principal Commercial Countries of the World', which provided a synopsis of the respective populations and the geographical, tax and economic circumstances of a number of countries, focusing specifically on the aspects of public debt, imports and exports, as well as monetary systems and weights and measures, compared to those used in the United Kingdom. This chart, into which Levi condensed his ongoing research on statistics and economics, as well as on economic history, clearly reflects the practical and multi-disciplinary approach of the author, who was able to use the instruments offered by the nascent social sciences to engage with the issue of comparative legislation, including specifically a study of the feasibility of a supranational commercial code.

He thus envisaged a kind of international conference of lawyers, merchants and bankers hailing from different countries. In 1863, when he published the second edition of his treatise, *International Commercial Law*, Levi had specifically in mind the preparatory works for the General German Commercial Code of 1861, which had been written by the delegates who attended the conferences held under the auspices of the kingdom of Prussia, [73] although he did not propose a similar kind of political leadership. The path he saw involved stakeholders proposing reforms to governments, which would then promote public discussion and engagement. His idea of a code was that of a set of standard principles of commercial law common to the civilised world. He spoke of a Universal Code of Commerce of the civilised nations. [74] This wording used by Levi might sound familiar to scholars of the first comprehensive comparative law theories developed by Raymond Saleilles and Edouard Lambert at the turn of the century, albeit on very different scientific bases.

To sum up, Levi suggested the benefits of an international commercial code and always followed a pragmatic and informed approach, seeking to promote legislative reforms and uniformity within the commercial laws of all nations involved in international trade. It was a constant battle, pursued through various publications and even through one of his most important contributions to economic scholarship, namely his *History of British Commerce and of the Economic Progress of the British Nation 1763–1870*, which he originally conceived of as an 'account of one of the most important interests in the empire' as well 'as a manual for the British trader all the world over'. [75]

In his preface to the *History*, written in January 1872, ten years after the publication of *International Commercial Law*, Levi did not miss the opportunity to reiterate his ideas concerning commercial laws and economic relations, arguing specifically that the validity of economic laws was not limited either in space or in time, and adding that not even scientific achievements fall within the exclusive domain of any individual state. His was a cosmopolitan vision: Levi remained an enthusiastic supporter and promoter of economic liberalism, and exalted British law, which sought in all senses to liberalise trade and to provide security to commercial transactions. As usual, he drew upon a variety of sources, ranging from specialist literature to the reports of parliamentary committees and royal commissions, from the specialist press to reports written by British diplomats serving abroad, including embassy secretaries and consuls. Levi took great care to ensure that the data on which he based his reflections were accurate and never hid his admiration for the marvels of British commerce 'among civilised and incivile nations'. [76]

Furthermore, Levi was not only a supporter of free trade to promote British supremacy, but also of peace: international trade for international peace, or international peace for international trade. During those years, another jurist, the US lawyer Davis Dudley Field, wrote the *Outlines of an International Code*, which focused on the codification and improvement of existing rules of international law. Field was a preeminent figure within the American codification movement [77] who proposed that the law of nations be codified: [78] he presented his work in Manchester in 1866 at the meeting of the British Association for the Promotion of Social Sciences. [79] Levi for his part was familiar with Field's work. Moreover, even though his specific proposal had come earlier, he was ideally placed within the debate surrounding the codification of international law that was authoritatively supported by his American counterpart. [80]

CONCISE SUMMARY

Levi's scholarly analysis of commercial law provides valuable perspectives on the utilization of comparison arguments in the context of commercial law during the nineteenth century. During that period, there was a notable absence of a coherent theory or methodology in the field of comparative law. [81] Nevertheless, jurists from various European and non-European countries, including ancient Italian states[82], the German Confederation,[83] France[84], Spain[85], the United States, and Victorian Britain, engaged in comparative arguments within their legal debates. [86] The field of foreign and comparative legislation has garnered significant attention due to a multitude of reasons and objectives. Moreover, these jurists frequently possessed knowledge of one another's research and expressed admiration for each other's creations. 87 The development of comparative legal studies in the nineteenth century was undeniably influenced by the international exchange of legal knowledge and ideas. This is evident in the correspondence of renowned German jurist Karl Joseph Mittermaier and, at a later point in time, in the firsthand experiences of Leone Levi. It is worth considering the potential influence of Levi's work on the field of comparative law studies during the late nineteenth century. Undoubtedly, it addressed matters that would become increasingly significant in the early 1900s, with the establishment of national societies for comparative legislation. The first such society was the French Société de Législation Comparée, which was created in Paris in 1869. The establishment of the British Society of Comparative Legislation occurred in 1894 in London, with the primary objective of fostering collaboration among Common law nations and advancing the understanding of foreign legal systems inside the British Empire. The Journal of the Society of Comparative Legislation was produced by the Society starting in 1896. 89 In 1900, the inaugural congress of comparative law took place in Paris. In his report, Charles Lyon-Caen, a renowned French professor of commercial law, expounded upon the efficacy of comparative commercial law, particularly in enhancing domestic legislation and fostering harmonization across diverse national legal frameworks. The concept of an international commercial code, as proposed by Lyon-Caen, draws inspiration from Levi's previous notion. The recognition of the potential advantages of comparative law in establishing a standardized commercial law applicable to all developed nations was widely acknowledged during that period. Nevertheless, throughout the summer of 1900 in Paris, Lyon-Caen was acutely cognizant of the challenges that lay ahead. The primary hindrances he perceived were inherent national prejudices and a strong adherence to antiquated traditions. 90 In relation to the 1900 Paris congress, Jean-Luis Halpérin has recently highlighted the contentious relationship between the global aspect of the intellectual networks established by comparative law experts in the late 1800s and the national backgrounds of those legal scholars. This relationship is likely to result in nationalist prejudice and the expression of imperialistic aspirations. Another concern arose from the establishment of multinational institutes of comparative law after the First World War, such as the International Academy of Comparative Law in The Hague and Unidroit. These institutes were primarily concerned with the practical objective of aligning laws, thereby pursuing similar goals as Leone Levi during his era. 91 Levi's proposition for the worldwide consolidation of commercial law and his recommendation for the creation of an international code of commercial law were indeed ahead of their time, and the initiative ultimately failed. However, it does provide evidence that during this period, individuals were starting to contemplate the merits of a unified legal system, as noted by Harold Cooke Gutteridge. [92]

It is also necessary to make one last point concerning Levi's contribution to comparative commercial law: in 1853 he was appointed to the newly created chair of mercantile law at King's College in London, where his audience was made up of merchants and bankers. [93] Of particular interest in relation to this matter are his introductory lessons to the Evening Class Department courses taught by him in 'Principles and practice of commerce and commercial law' and later in 'Commerce and commercial law', which he taught in 1870 also as dean of the department. At this time, the aim of King's College in holding its evening classes was to provide a technical education to its students within the various departments in order to spread knowledge of the sciences that were most closely related to the country's industrial development. They thus sought to provide targeted teaching also to professionals within the commercial and trade sectors. In his introductory lecture held in October 1868 entitled 'Education of the merchant', Leone Levi listed the basic knowledge that British merchants would have to acquire should they wish to become competitive on the international markets. [94] First of all, he called for a working knowledge of foreign languages, including Italian, which was useful above all when trading with Greek markets in the East. He then turned to the need for a sound knowledge of mathematics and geography. [95]

In addition, in his view it was essential to acquire some familiarity not only with basic principles of British commercial law, but also with foreign laws, which should be regarded as being 'equally important as our own'. Moreover, if there was any increase in trade with a particular country, it was of the utmost importance to be familiar with the commercial code of that country. This was in fact necessary for extremely practical purposes, in order to avoid blunders and resulting economic losses, which could even be significant. Regarding the transnational nature of commerce, he also added that a knowledge of international law was also useful in order to be successful as a merchant.

Several years later, in 1876, Levi illustrated the importance of trade with Turkey on the borders of Europe, as the gateway to the Asian continent. He did so in an introductory lesson to the King's College evening classes dedicated to the issue of peace, entitled 'Peace: the handmaid of commerce'. His approach was vaguely Kantian in inspiration and undoubtedly was in full accord with the sentiments of the Victorian era that saw peace as a prerequisite for prosperity. [96] Insisting on the need to keep trade routes with the Sublime Porte open, especially in the run-up to the Russian-Ottoman conflict in the Balkans and the subsequent Congress of Berlin (1878), which forced the Ottoman Empire to relinquish some of its European territories, Levi was speaking not so much as a jurist but rather as an expert merchant, mindful of the value of East–West trade, and with considerable specific knowledge of political economy and international relations. [97]

Levi's approach was indeed decidedly pragmatic: attuned to the needs of everyday commercial activity, not particularly well disposed towards pure theory, whilst being open to other fields of sciences and knowledge gained empirically through concrete application. His view of the problems of commercial law was one in which a comparative inspiration was incorporated into legal discourse for purely practical purposes. Moreover, his engagement with issues of commercial law had increased over time in the light of his personal and professional experience.

Similarly, his interest in legal comparison as well as that specifically in comparative legislation and legal codification arose out of and was fuelled by his eclectic research interests: from statistics to economics and economic history, and from the tax system to working conditions, with which he was fascinated above all during the 1870s and 1880s. It was moreover during this period that he also developed an interest in issues relating to extreme poverty, having experienced the reality of life in London, and became a supporter of the so-called ragged schools, which were intended to provide an education to the children of the poorest workers. [98] For sure, the issue of education remained a constant feature on various levels within his experience as an autodidact.

In summary, Levi emerged as a trailblazer in various domains that he perceived as interrelated, encompassing comparative commercial law, statistics, and economic studies. In the realm of British mercantile law, he made significant contributions to the codification movement. Levi's origins can be traced back to Ancona, similar to Benvenuto Stracca, a renowned jurist of the sixteenth century who had a significant role in advancing scholarly research in the field of commercial law and guiding the focus of attorneys towards this area of study. 99 The correlation established between the two authors, Levi and Stracca, is evidently merely a proposition influenced by their mutual geographical background and their shared fascination with commercial law throughout pivotal periods in its development. However, the similarities and contrasts found in both instances are illuminating. Despite the temporal gap of three centuries between their experiences and words, both individuals were pioneers, and their works exerted a substantial and enduring influence. According to Stracca, a prominent Renaissance scholar, the development of a philosophy of commercial law and its secularization, thereby liberating it from the influence of Canon law and morals, should be the primary objective of a legal science grounded in Romanism. Levi, however, was a pragmatic individual who also fostered diverse scientific pursuits. In the mid-nineteenth century, a pivotal era for legal codification, he actively addressed the matter with innovative reasoning and authored treatises that continue to serve as a benchmark for comparative legal studies.

Footnote

1. 'Professor Leone Levi, LLD', *Journal of the Royal Statistical Society*, 51(2) (1888), 340–2; G. R. Rubin, 'Levi, Leone (1821–1888)', in Oxford Dictionary of National Biography (Oxford, 2004), available at www.oxforddnb.com/view/10.1093/ref:odnb/9780198614128.001.0001/odnb-9780198614128-e-16551?rskey=Llur0U&result=2.
2. A. Rodger, 'The Codification of Commercial Law in Victorian Britain', Proceedings of the British Academy, 80 (1993), 149–70, at 152 n. 13.
3. L. Levi, The Story of My Life: The First Ten Years of My Residence in England, 1845–1855 (London, 1888), 3.
4. M. Milano, 'Ancona', in Encyclopaedia Judaica, 6 vols. (Jerusalem, 1971–2), vol. II, 942–3. See also M. L. Moscati Benigni, Marche. Itinerari ebraici: I luoghi, la storia, l'arte (Venice, 1996), 23–43; L. Andreoni, Ebrei nelle Marche. Fonti e ricerche. Secoli XV–XIX (Ancona, 2012).
5. E. Pesciarelli, 'Leone Levi fra statistica e legislazione commerciale', Annali della Facoltà di Giurisprudenza, Università di Macerata, 4 (1978), 579–691. On the free trade movement, see also C. K. Harley and D. N. McCloskey, 'Foreign Trade: Competition and the Expanding International Economy', in R. Floud and D. N. McCloskey (eds.), The Economic History of Britain since 1700, 2nd edn, 3 vols. (Cambridge, 1995–7), vol. II, 56–61.

6. J. Morley, The Life of Richard Cobden (London, 1906); N. C. Edsall, Richard Cobden: Independent Radical (Cambridge, MA, 1986).
7. J. R. T. Hughes, Fluctuations in Trade, Industry and Finance: A Study of British Economic Development 1850–1860 (Oxford, 1960), 34–71; E. J. Hobsbawm, Industry and Empire: An Economic History of Britain since 1750 (London, 1968), 110–27; D. H. Aldcroft (ed.), The Development of British Industry and Foreign Competition 1875–1914: Studies in Industrial Enterprise (London, 1968). See also W. Cornish, S. Banks, C. Mitchell, P. Mitchell, and R. Prost, Law and Society in England 1750–1950, 2nd edn (Oxford, 2019), 6–10.
8. R. J. Bennett, Local Business Voice: The History of Chambers of Commerce in Britain, Ireland, and Revolutionary America, 1760–2011 (Oxford, 2011), 262–4.
9. J. Roebuck, The Making of Modern English Society from 1850, 2nd edn (London, 1982), 33–35.
10. D. Raponi, Religion and Politics in the Risorgimento: Britain and the New Italy 1861–1875 (London, 2014), 73 s. and 140 s.
11. Levi, *The Story*, 74–77. On the social structure of Victorian society, see P. Thane, 'Social History 1860–1914', in Floud and McCloskey (eds.), *The Economic History of Britain*, II. 198–224.
12. G. Bassi, 'L'opera di un giurista ed economista italiano in Inghilterra (Leone Levi)', Rassegna Nazionale, 15 (1918), 200–9. Bassi wrote his essay on Levi in 1917, when Italy and the United Kingdom were allied in the Great War: his purpose was to highlight the long-standing relationships between the citizens of the two countries. See also R. Fedecostante, Ebrei illustri anconetani (Ancona, 1992), 57–58.
13. The papers and other memorabilia of Leone Levi that were salvaged after Allied bombing during 1943 are now conserved at the Biblioteca Civica Benincasa in Ancona along with a large collection of his publications.
14. See L. Levi, 'The Economic Progress of Italy during the Last Twenty Years, since the Formation of the Italian Kingdom in 1861', Journal of the Statistical Society of London, 45 (1882), 1–36.
15. L. Guazzati, Storia della Camera di commercio di Ancona (Ancona, 2009), 121–2.
16. Levi, *The Story*, 19–21.
17. See J. Sloan, 'Civilized Nations', in Max Planck Encyclopedia of Public International Law (2011).
18. According to Rubin, 'Levi, Leone', 542, Levi was addressing a fundamental question, i.e. 'what significance did legal rules have for the development of trade and commerce in a nineteenth-century market economy?', and, in the

advocacy of commercial courts and of improved commercial arbitration laws, the former Italian merchant was challenging whether law was itself an ideal framework for regulating business affairs. This was in fact an issue also in Continental Europe in the age of codification of commercial law.

19. Pesciarelli, 'Leone Levi fra statistica e legislazione commerciale', 586–9. See also M. Graziadei, 'L'influenza del diritto privato italiano in Europa', Annuario di diritto comparato e studi legislativi (2014), 307–38, at 311–12.
20. See Levi's missive to Benjamin Disraeli of 1 August 1849, edited in Pesciarelli, 'Leone Levi fra statistica e legislazione commerciale', 621–4.
21. Rodger, 'The Codification of Commercial Law', 153ff.
22. Pesciarelli, 'Leone Levi fra statistica e legislazione commerciale', 625–47.
23. Roebuck, *The Making of Modern English Society*, 43–45.
24. L. Levi, Commercial Law, its Principles and Administration, or The Mercantile Law of Great Britain Compared with the Codes and Laws of Commerce of the Following Mercantile Countries: Anhalt, Austria [...], 2 vols. (London, 1850–2), vol. I, Preface, VII–XIV.
25. Levi had a good knowledge of French: Levi, *The Story*, 37–38. See also Levi, *Commercial Law*, I. Preface, IX–X.
26. A. de Saint-Joseph, Concordance entre les codes de commerce étrangers et le code de commerce français (Paris, 1844).
27. G.-R. de Groot and A. Parise, 'Antoine de Saint-Joseph: A Nineteenth-Century Paladin for the Development of Comparative Legislation', in B. van Hofstraeten et al. (eds.), Ten definitieven recht doende ... Louis Berkvens Amicorum (Maastricht, 2018), 71–92, esp. 75–77.
28. *Revue Foelix* was the publication's nickname. It was founded in 1833 as the *Revue étrangère de législation et d'économie politique*. From 1844, and until 1850, it took the title *Revue de droit français et étranger*. A. Mergey, 'Le réseau constitué autour d'Antoine de Saint-Joseph et de la Concordance entre les codes civils étrangers et le code Napoléon. Entre exaltation d'un nationalisme juridique modéré et promotion d'un fond juridique commun', in T. Le Yoncourt, A. Mergey, and S. Soleil (eds.), L'idée de fonds juridique commun dans l'Europe du XIXe siècle. Les modèles, les réformateurs, les réseaux (Rennes, 2014), 187–221.
29. de Saint-Joseph, *Concordance*, Avertissement, VIII–X.
30. See J. W. Smith, A Compendium on Mercantile Law, 10th edn, 2 vols. (London, 1890), vol. I, LXIII–LXXXIII.
31. Levi, *Commercial Law*, I. Plan of the Work.

32. See M. Lobban, 'The Education of Lawyers. 1. 1820–60', in William Cornish et al. (eds.), The Oxford History of the Laws of England, vol. XI (Oxford, 2010), 1175–222, at 1175–85.
33. P. Polden, 'Barristers', in Cornish et al. (eds.), *Oxford History*, vol. XI, 1018–62.
34. Levi listed fifty-nine 'countries' in alphabetical order.
35. Levi, *Commercial Law*, I. Plan of the Work.
36. Recently, M. Bassano and W. Mastor (eds.), *Justement traduire. Les enjeux de la traduction juridique (histoire du droit, droit comparé)* (Toulouse, 2020).
37. Referring to H. Mohnhaupt, 'Rechtsvergleichung in Mittermaiers Kritische Zeitschrift für Rechtswissenschaft und Gesetzgebung des Auslandes', in M. Stolleis (ed.), Juristische Zeitschriften. Die neue Medien des 18.–20. Jahrhunderts (Frankfurt am Main, 1999), 277–301. On Mittermaier's scholarly works, see L. Nuzzo, Bibliographie der Werke Karl Joseph Anton Mittermaiers (Frankfurt am Main, 2004).
38. de Saint-Joseph, *Concordance*, Avertissement, X.
39. J. Hilaire, 'Pratique et doctrine au début du XIXe siècle. L'œuvre de Jean-Marie Pardessus', in A. Deperchin, N. Derasse, and B. Dubois (eds.), Figures de justice. Études en l'honneur de Jean-Pierre Royer (Lille, 2004), 287–94, esp. 288–90; J. Hilaire, 'Jean-Marie Pardessus', in P. Arabeyre, J.-L. Halpérin, and J. Krynen (eds.), Dictionnaire historique des juristes français (XIIe–XXe siècle), new edn (Paris, 2015), 793–5. See also L. Moscati, 'Dopo e al di là del Code de commerce: l'apporto di Jean-Marie Pardessus', in C. Angelici et al. (eds.), Negozianti e imprenditori: 200 anni dal Code de commerce (Milan, 2008), 47–80.
40. J.-M. Pardessus, Cours de droit commercial, 6th edn (Brussels, 1833).
41. J.-M. Pardessus, 'Collection des lois civiles et criminelles des Etats modernes, par M. Victor Foucher, avocat général à la Cour royal de Rennes. 8 vol. in-8°, 1833 à 1841', Journal des Savans (1842), 625–38. See J. Hilaire, 'Le comparatisme en matière commerciale au XIXème siècle', Revue d'histoire des Facultés de droit et de la culture juridique, 12 (1991), 127–42.
42. In this publication, Pardessus considered in particular two commercial codes translated in the collection published by Foucher, specifically the Spanish Commercial Code of 1829 and the Dutch Commercial Code. These translations were subsequently used by Saint-Joseph himself: Pardessus, 'Collection des lois civiles et criminelles', 631–2.
43. Levi, *Commercial Law*, I. Preface, VIII–IX.

44. Levi, *The Story*, 53–62. See the letters edited and translated into Italian by Pesciarelli, 'Leone Levi fra statistica e legislazione commerciale', 652–3.
45. K. H. L. Brinckmann, 'Commercial Law [...] by Leone Levi. 1850–52. London [...]', Kritische Zeitschrift für die gesammte Rechtswissenschaft, 1 (1853), 281–91.
46. Hilaire, 'Le comparatisme en matière commerciale', 132–5.
47. For a summary of events surrounding the codification of commercial law, with specific reference to codification in France, see de Saint-Joseph, *Concordance*, Introduction, XI–XVII.
48. Brinckmann, 'Commercial Law [...] by Leone Levi', 290.
49. Levi was able to access the Advocates Library in Edinburgh thanks to John Shank More, professor of the Law of Scotland at the University of Edinburgh: Levi, *The Story*, 39–41 and 68–70.
50. Levi, *Commercial Law*, I. Preface, V–X. See Rodger, 'The Codification of Commercial Law', 152; Pesciarelli, 'Leone Levi fra statistica e legislazione commerciale', 589–90.
51. Levi, *Commercial Law*, I. Preface, XV–XVIII.
52. On this event, see Roebuck, *The Making of Modern English Society*, 15–18.
53. Levi, *The Story*, 44–52. Among his many contributions, see L. Levi, 'On Commercial Statistics, and an Attempt to a Universal Commercial Code', Journal of the Statistical Society of London, 15 (1852), 108–14.
54. Levi, *The Story*, 72–73.
55. Rodger, 'The Codification of Commercial Law', 154; Pesciarelli, 'Leone Levi fra statistica e legislazione commerciale', 591–2.
56. Levi, *The Story*, 78–82.
57. L. Levi, International Commercial Law: Being the Principles of Mercantile Law of the Following and Other Countries, viz.: England, Scotland, Ireland [...], 2nd edn, 2 vols. (London, 1863).
58. Pesciarelli, 'Leone Levi fra statistica e legislazione commerciale', 595–600.
59. A. Padoa-Schioppa, 'Franckreich, Handelsrecht', in H. Coing (ed.), Handbuch der Quellen und Literatur der neureren europäischen Privatrechtsgeschichte, vol. III, part 3 (Munich, 1986), 3152–87; J.-P. Allinne, 'Le développement du droit commercial en dehors du Code et l'influence des droits étrangers 1807–1925', in C. Saint-Alary-Houin (ed.), Qu'en est-il du Code de Commerce 200 ans après? Etats des lieux et projections (Toulouse, 2009), 75–104.

60. Recently, see M. Löhnig and S. Wagner (eds.), Das ADHGB von 1861 als gemeinsames Obligationenrecht in Mitteleuropa (Tübingen, 2018).

61. In English, see A. Monti, 'The Italian Destiny of the French Code de commerce', in M. Gałędek and A. Klimaszewska (eds.), Modernisation, National Identity and Legal Instrumentalism, 2 vols. (Leiden, 2020), vol. I: *Private Law*, 111–42, esp. 131–3.

62. Levi, *International Commercial Law*, I. Preface, VII–XII.

63. *Rights of commerce in time of peace and war*, in ibid., I. Introduction, XXXIX–LII, esp. XXXIX–XL; Levi cites E. de Vattel, Le droit des gens, ou principes de la loi naturelle, new edn, 3 vols. (Neuchatel, 1777), vol. I, book I, chapter VIII, 139–59.

64. W. Cornish, 'International Law', in Cornish et al. (eds.), *Oxford History*, vol. XI, 255–77. See also M. Koskenniemi, The Gentle Civilizer of Nations: The Rise and Fall of International Law 1870–1960 (Cambridge, 2001).

65. See above, n. 54.

66. Rodger, 'The Codification of Commercial Law', 149–70.

67. On the debate over codification and the influence of Bentham and Benthamites in early nineteenth-century England, see M. Lobban, The Common Law and English Jurisprudence 1760–1850 (Oxford, 1991), 185–94. Recently, see C. Riley, 'The Hermit and the Boa Constrictor: Jeremy Bentham, Henry Brougham, and the Accessibility of Justice', American Journal of Legal History, 59 (2019), 1–26. See also J. Bentham, 'Legislator of the World': Writings on Codification, Law, and Education, eds. P. Schofield and J. Harris (Oxford, 1998), XI s.

68. Levi, *Commercial Law*, I. VII. See G. Filangieri, La scienza della legislazione, 6 vols. (Milan, 1817–18), vol. I, lib. I.

69. On commercial law codes, which changed the form of commercial law, and on the needs of commerce in late nineteenth-century Britain, see R. B. Ferguson, 'Legal Ideology and Commercial Interests: The Social Origins of the Commercial Law Codes', British Journal of Law and Society, 4 (1977), 18–38.

70. 'It is a great pleasure to me to find that in this matter I was for years in advance of public opinion', as later stated by Levi, *The Story*, 84. See, for example, L. Levi, 'On Joint Stock Companies', Journal of the Statistical Society of London, 33 (1870), 1–41; L. Levi, 'The Progress of Joint Stock Companies with Limited and Unlimited Liability in the United Kingdom, during the Fifteen Years 1869–84 (In Continuation of a Paper Read before the Society in January, 1870)', Journal of the Statistical Society of London, 49 (1886), 241–72. On the topic, refer to R. Harris, Industrializing English Law (Cambridge, 2000), esp. 127–32, 273–4; M.

Lobban, 'Joint Stock Companies', in Cornish et al. (eds.), *Oxford History*, vol. XI, 613–73, esp. 625–31. See also Cornish et al., *Law and Society in England*, 246–52.

71. See Morley, *The Life of Richard Cobden*, 352–65; Edsall, *Richard Cobden*, 325–52.
72. Levi, *The Story*, 97–103.
73. For the attention paid in Scotland to the German codification of commercial law, see Rodger, 'The Codification of Commercial Law', 156–7.
74. Levi, *International Commercial Law*, I. Preface, IX–XII.
75. L. Levi, History of British Commerce and of the Economic Progress of the British Nation 1763–1870 (London, 1872). Levi's *History* is considered by many to be his chief work, even though it is regarded as 'rather too partisan': Pesciarelli, 'Leone Levi fra statistica e legislazione commerciale', 604–5.
76. Levi, *History of British Commerce*, Preface, VII–IX.
77. C. M. Cook, The American Codification Movement: A Study of Antebellum Legal Reform (Westport, CT, 1981), 186ff.
78. H. W. Briggs, 'David Dudley Field and the Codification of International Law (1805–1894)', in Institut de Droit International, Livre du Centenaire 1873–1973. Évolution et perspectives du droit international (Basel, 1973), 67–73; K. H. Nadelmann, 'International Law at America's Centennial: The International Code Committee's Centennial Celebration and the Centenary of Field's International Code', American Journal of International Law, 70 (1976), 519–29.
79. See also the Italian translation of Field's *Outlines of an International Code: Storia del diritto internazionale nel secolo XIX*, trans. A. Pierantoni (Naples, 1876), 485–90, and the French translation by Albéric Rolin, *Projet d'un Code international* (Paris, 1881).
80. E. Nys, 'The Codification of International Law', The American Journal of International Law, 5 (1911), 871–900.
81. H. C. Gutteridge, An Introduction to the Comparative Method of Legal Study and Research (Cambridge, 1946), 11ff.
82. C. Vano, 'Codificare, comparare, costruire la nazione. Una nota introduttiva', in C. Vano (ed.), Giuseppe Pisanelli. Scienza del processo, cultura delle leggi e avvocatura tra periferia e nazione (Naples 2005), XIX–XXIX.
83. A. Mazzacane and R. Schulze (eds.), Die deutsche und die italienische Rechtskultur im 'Zeitalter der Vergleichung' (Berlin, 1995).
84. Hilaire, 'Le comparatisme en matière commerciale', esp. 128–32.
85. C. Petit, 'Revistas españolas y legislación extranjera. El hueco del derecho comparado', Quaderni fiorentini, 35 (2006) vol. I, 255–338.

86. Comparative law had not yet emerged as a field of scholarship; J. W. Cairns, 'Development of Comparative Law in Great Britain', in M. Reimann and R. Zimmermann (eds.), The Oxford Handbook of Comparative Law (Oxford, 2006), 131–73, at 132–8.

87. Concerning Italy, Saint-Joseph's work was translated into Italian: A. de Saint-Joseph, Concordanza fra i codici di commercio stranieri ed il codice di commercio francese (Venice, 1855). On the contrary, Levi's treatise was not translated, but it circulated; for example, see G. Carnazza Puglisi, Il diritto commerciale secondo il Codice di commercio del Regno d'Italia, 2 vols. (Milan, 1868), vol. I, 21–23. See M. T. Napoli, La cultura giuridica europea in Italia. Repertorio delle opere tradotte nel secolo XIX, 3 vols. (Naples, 1987).

88. See A. Mazzacane, 'Alle origini della comparazione giuridica moderna: i carteggi di Karl Joseph Anton Mittermaier', in La comparazione giuridica tra Otto e Novecento (Milan, 2001), 15–38.

89. Cairns, 'Development of Comparative Law', 138–41.

90. C. Lyon-Caen, 'Rôle, fonction et méthode du Droit comparé dans le domaine du Droit commercial', in Congrès international de Droit comparé, Procès-verbaux des séances et documents, 2 vols. (Paris, 1905–7), vol. I, 343–7.

91. J.-L. Halpérin, 'Associations, réseaux et ambitions nationales des comparatistes de la fin du XIXe siècle à la Seconde Guerre mondiale', Clio@Thémis, 13 (2017), 1–14.

92. Gutteridge, *An Introduction to the Comparative Method*, 146. Among successive proposals, see for example W. Ward and M. S. Rosenthal, 'The Need for the Uniform Commercial Code in Foreign Trade', Harvard Law Review, 63 (1949–50), 589–92.

93. Levi, *The Story*, 88–90.

94. See also L. Levi, 'On the Progress of Commerce and Industry during the Last Fifty Years: An Introductory Lecture, Delivered at King's College [...] on 13th October, 1887', Journal of the Royal Statistical Society, 50 (1887), 659–68.

95. L. Levi, The Education of the Merchant: Introductory Lecture Delivered at King's College, London, on the 15th October 1868 (London, 1868).

96. L. Levi, Peace: The Handmaid of Commerce with Remarks on the Eastern Crisis: An Introductory Lecture Delivered at King's College London, 12th October 1876 (London, 1876).

97. The issue of trade with the Ottoman Empire had already been at the centre of public debate in Britain on various occasions over the previous decades: during the mid-1830s and subsequently at the start of the 1850s during the Russian-

Ottoman conflict that led to the Crimean War. One of the promoters of British non-intervention and of peace initiatives was Richard Cobden; see Morley, *The Life of Richard Cobden*, 303f., and Edsall, *Richard Cobden*, 269–90.

98. Levi, *The Story*, 90–94. See Pesciarelli, 'Leone Levi fra statistica e legislazione commerciale', 606–16.

99. B. Stracca, De mercatura, seu mercatore tractatus (Venice, 1553). In English, see C. Donahue, Jr, 'Benvenuto Stracca's De Mercatura: Was There a Lex Mercatoria in Sixteenth-Century Italy?', in V. Piergiovanni (ed.), From Lex Mercatoria to Commercial Law (Berlin, 2005), 69–120; S. Gialdroni, 'Tractatus de mercatura seu mercatore, 1553, Benvenuto Stracca (Straccha) (1509–1578)', in S. Dauchy, G. Martyn, A. Musson, H. Pihlajamäki and A. Wijffels (eds.), *The Formation and Transmission of Western Legal Culture: 150 Books that Made the Law in the Age of Printing* (Cham, 2016), 96–99.

10 THE CROWN'S RADICAL TITLE AND ABORIGINAL TITLE: NORTH AMERICA IN 1763, NEW SOUTH WALES IN 1788, AND NEW ZEALAND IN 1840

The concept of "radical title," which refers to the fundamental or ultimate ownership of all lands throughout Commonwealth countries, is believed to have originated from English Common law and was subsequently adopted by the majority of British colonies. This legal principle can be traced back to Anglo-Norman feudal concepts. The primary subject matter of this chapter pertains to the historical development of this ideology and its consequential influence on the acknowledgment or lack thereof of the sovereignty, laws, titles, and rights of indigenous populations. Australia, Canada, and New Zealand are three contemporary nation-states, with the former two possessing federal constitutions, which originated from various colonies within the British Empire. From the inception of colonial rule, European settlers gradually assumed control over many dimensions of political, social, cultural, and economic spheres in all of these colonies. Within the legal framework of the colonies, indigenous peoples, referred to by different names such as Natives, Indians, Eskimos, Aborigines, Maori (and occasionally as savages, primitive barbarians, and other racial labels), were deliberately excluded and marginalized through the implementation of legal provisions. The indigenous people experienced a variety of programs referred to as amalgamation, assimilation, adaptation, or integration, aimed at "civilizing" those who survived the significant fall in population that ensued after the entrance of European settlers.

When almost all the colonies, protectorates, protected states and other polities within that Empire became independent states in the United Nations during the decolonisation era after World War II, [1] the colonised peoples of British North America within what is now Canada, of New Holland in what is now known as Australia, and of New Zealand found themselves a small minority within constitutional monarchies and an electoral system based on a democratic franchise of one person, one vote. During the latter part of the twentieth century, however, an increasingly vocal and persistent number of movements and protest actions by indigenous peoples, with support from elements of civil society in the majority population, forced state institutions to search for ways and means to attend to their calls for justice and redress. One of the responses in each of the three legal systems was the development by the judicial branch of government of a doctrine usually known as aboriginal title. [2] In the enunciation of this doctrine by judges and scholars, a good deal of attention has been devoted to the notion of the radical title of the Crown to all lands.

A reasonably coherent account of legal history on this topic might seem possible, and even plausible, if one focused on the development of the Common law in just one of the three legal systems. The value of comparative analysis and historical contextualisation in this instance is that the semblance of coherence and clarity tends to evaporate when one investigates judicial pronouncements on this Anglo-Norman doctrine as a substratum element of aboriginal title rights in the three settler-dominated jurisdictions, and in the advice proffered to the sovereign by the Judicial Committee of the Privy Council in a small number of much cited decisions, including especially two appeals from African territories. This essay notes, in particular, the divergent judicial responses to the status and relevance of pre-colonial indigenous norms and values when evaluating aboriginal title claims. These range from outright rejection of their relevance based on 'waste lands' or *terra nullius* conceptions, to limited acceptance of usufructuary and possessory rights, to a broader acceptance more recently that aboriginal title must be understood in the light of prior and present indigenous understandings.

I begin with quotations from relatively recent appellate court judgments in each of the three jurisdictions. The first is from the decision of a full bench of the New Zealand Court of Appeal in litigation asserting Maori customary rights over foreshore and seabed lands in the Marlborough Sounds. [3] In her leading judgment Elias CJ wrote:

[30] The radical title of the Crown is a technical and notional concept. It is not inconsistent with common law recognition of native property, as *R v Symonds, Manu Kapua v Para Haimona* and *Nireaha Tamaki v Baker* make clear. Brennan J described such radical title in *Mabo v Queensland (No 2)* (1992) 175 CLR 1 at p 50 as:

'... merely a logical postulate required to support the doctrine of tenure (when the Crown has exercised its sovereign power to grant an interest in land) and to support the plenary title of the Crown (when the Crown has exercised its sovereign power to appropriate to itself ownership of parcels of land within the Crown's territory).'

[31] Any property interest of the Crown in land over which it acquired sovereignty therefore depends on any pre-existing customary interest and its nature, as the Privy Council in *Amodu Tijani v Secretary, Southern Nigeria* held. The content of such customary interest is a question of fact discoverable, if necessary, by evidence (*Nireaha Tamaki v Baker* at p 577). As a matter of custom the burden on the Crown's radical title might be limited to use or occupation rights held as a matter of custom (as appears to be the position described in *St Catherine's Milling and Lumber Co v The Queen* and as the tribunal in *William Webster's Claim* seems to have thought might be the extent of Maori customary property). On the other hand, the customary rights might 'be so complete as to reduce any radical right in the Sovereign to one which only extends to comparatively limited rights of administrative interference' (*Amodu Tijani v Secretary, Southern Nigeria* at p 410). The Supreme Court of Canada has had occasion recently to consider the content of customary property interests in that country. It has recognised that, according to the custom on which such rights are based, they may extend from usufructory [sic] rights to exclusive ownership with incidents equivalent to those recognised by fee simple title (see, for example, *Delgamuukw v British Columbia* [1997] 3 SCR 1010 at paras 110–119 per Lamer CJ). [4]

In 2014, many decades of expensive litigation by large numbers of indigenous plaintiffs on aboriginal title issues, going back to 1983, [5] finally culminated in the first declaration of aboriginal title by the Supreme Court of Canada in respect of land that had never been ceded nor been the subject of a historic treaty with the Crown. The declaration in favour of the Tsilhqot'in Nation covered a 1,900 square kilometre area of British Columbia. In her judgment for the entire court McLachlin CJ made these observations on radical title:

[69] The starting point in characterizing the legal nature of Aboriginal title is Dickson J.'s concurring judgment in *Guerin*, discussed earlier. At the time of assertion of European sovereignty, the Crown acquired radical or underlying title to all the land in the province. This Crown title, however, was burdened by the pre-existing legal rights of Aboriginal people who occupied and used the land prior to European arrival. The doctrine of *terra nullius* (that no one owned the land prior to European assertion of sovereignty) never applied in Canada, as confirmed by the *Royal Proclamation* of 1763. The Aboriginal interest in land that burdens the Crown's underlying title is an independent legal interest, which gives rise to a fiduciary duty on the part of the Crown.

[70] The content of the Crown's underlying title is what is left when Aboriginal title is subtracted from it: s. 109 of the *Constitution Act, 1867*; *Delgamuukw*. As we have seen, *Delgamuukw* establishes that Aboriginal title gives 'the right to exclusive use and occupation of the land ... for a variety of purposes', not confined to traditional

or 'distinctive' uses (para. 117). In other words, Aboriginal title is a beneficial interest in the land: *Guerin*, at p. 382. In simple terms, the title holders have the right to the benefits associated with the land – to use it, enjoy it and profit from its economic development. As such, the Crown does not retain a beneficial interest in Aboriginal title land.

[71] What remains, then, of the Crown's radical or underlying title to lands held under Aboriginal title? The authorities suggest two related elements – a fiduciary duty owed by the Crown to Aboriginal people when dealing with Aboriginal lands, and the right to encroach on Aboriginal title if the government can justify this in the broader public interest under s. 35 of the *Constitution Act, 1982*. The Court in *Delgamuukw* referred to this as a process of reconciling Aboriginal interests with the broader public interests under s. 35 of the *Constitution Act, 1982*. [6]

This signal victory for the Tsilhqot'in Nation still leaves a good deal of scope for ambiguity or ambivalence about the nature of radical title. As Ryan Beaton has written, Canadian judicial doctrine 'has long been torn between a nation-with-nation vision and a vision of perfected Crown sovereignty'. If recognition of prior occupation and pre-existing systems of indigenous law truly are burdens on underlying Crown title, then how is it that the Crown, unilaterally it seems, may invoke 'the right to encroach on Aboriginal title if the government can justify this in the broader public interest' as stated by the Chief Justice? [7]

The doctrine of radical title also played a large part in the reasoning of judges of the High Court of Australia when prior decisions declaring that aboriginal title was not part of Australian Common law were overruled. The most frequently cited statement is from the judgment of Brennan J (with which Mason CJ and McHugh J agreed):

51. By attributing to the Crown a radical title to all land within a territory over which the Crown has assumed sovereignty, the common law enabled the Crown, in exercise of its sovereign power, to grant an interest in land to be held of the Crown or to acquire land for the Crown's demesne. The notion of radical title enabled the Crown to become Paramount Lord of all who hold a tenure granted by the Crown and to become absolute beneficial owner of unalienated land required for the Crown's purposes. But it is not a corollary of the Crown's acquisition of a radical title to land in an occupied territory that the Crown acquired absolute beneficial ownership of that land to the exclusion of the indigenous inhabitants. If the land were desert and uninhabited, truly a terra nullius, the Crown would take an absolute beneficial title (an allodial title) to the land for the reason given by Stephen C.J. in *Attorney-General v. Brown* (1847) 1 Legge, at pp 317–318: there would be no other proprietor. But if the land were occupied by the indigenous inhabitants and their rights and interests in the land are recognized by the common law, the radical title which is

acquired with the acquisition of sovereignty cannot itself be taken to confer an absolute beneficial title to the occupied land. Nor is it necessary to the structure of our legal system to refuse recognition to the rights and interests in land of the indigenous inhabitants. The doctrine of tenure applies to every Crown grant of an interest in land, but not to rights and interests which do not owe their existence to a Crown grant. The English legal system accommodated the recognition of rights and interests derived from occupation of land in a territory over which sovereignty was acquired by conquest without the necessity of a Crown grant.

52. [...] In *Amodu Tijani*, the Privy Council admitted the possibility of recognition not only of usufructuary rights but also of interests in land vested not in an individual or a number of identified individuals but in a community. Viscount Haldane observed (1921) 2 AC, at pp 403–404:

The title, such as it is, may not be that of the individual, as in this country it nearly always is in some form, but may be that of a community. Such a community may have the possessory title to the common enjoyment of a usufruct, with customs under which its individual members are admitted to enjoyment, and even to a right of transmitting the individual enjoyment as members by assignment inter vivos or by succession. To ascertain how far this latter development of right has progressed involves the study of the history of the particular community and its usages in each case. Abstract principles fashioned a priori are of but little assistance, and are as often as not misleading.

Recognition of the radical title of the Crown is quite consistent with recognition of native title to land, for the radical title, without more, is merely a logical postulate required to support the doctrine of tenure (when the Crown has exercised its sovereign power to grant an interest in land) and to support the plenary title of the Crown (when the Crown has exercised its sovereign power to appropriate to itself ownership of parcels of land within the Crown's territory). Unless the sovereign power is exercised in one or other of those ways, there is no reason why land within the Crown's territory should not continue to be subject to native title. It is only the fallacy of equating sovereignty and beneficial ownership of land that gives rise to the notion that native title is extinguished by the acquisition of sovereignty. [8]

One might conclude from reading the above quotations that the radical title of the Crown and the feudal doctrine of tenures have happily accommodated recognition of indigenous peoples' aboriginal title rights in all three Commonwealth realms. There might be some variance as between recognition of usufructuary and possessory rights only, or a fuller recognition of native title rights, but those rights are not only cognisable but also justiciable and enforceable in ordinary courts. Nevertheless, it was not always thus, and comparative legal history tells a more complicated tale.

The starting point, indeed, is not legal history at all, but legal fiction. Brendan Edgeworth correctly observed that the radical title of the Crown and feudal tenure systems did not appear overnight following the Norman Conquest in 1066 and the replacement of English landholders with Norman feudal lords. Some centuries elapsed before 'the role of the Crown in the ownership of land came to be reconceived in much more expansive terms. Not only did leading feudal overlords owe their titles to grants from the monarch, but all landowners, including tenants lower down the pyramid, were now presumed to have received their titles from *grants subsequent upon* those original grants', though 'this pattern of creation of titles never occurred as historical fact'. [9] Edgeworth notes that while English legal historians have no doubt that 'this "wholly mythic", doctrinal revisionism took place', they do not pinpoint with precision when this modern dogma emerged. [10] Edgeworth also points to Brennan J's *Mabo (No. 2)* judgment in crediting William Blackstone's *Commentaries* as the first attempt to try to understand this 'modern' fiction. [11] Blackstone, despite his Tory connections, was not one who would want to emphasise the Norman yoke in eighteenth-century England. In that era of Whig hegemony Sir Edward Coke's equally fictitious 'ancient constitution', based on documents falsely attributed to the saintly Anglo-Saxon King Edward, still held sway as being basic to English liberties. [12] Blackstone made clear his adherence to the supposedly ancient constitution when describing the radical title of the Crown. For him,

> it became a fundamental maxim and necessary principle (though in reality a mere fiction) of our English tenures, 'that the king is the universal lord and original proprietor of all lands in his kingdom; and that no man doth or can possess any part of it, but what was mediately or immediately been derived as a gift from him to be held upon feodal services'. [13]

Invented fiction may be all well and good to account for the evolution of English land law on radical title and on tenures during a number of centuries of feudalism in the medieval period. The magisterial contributions of J. G. A. Pocock have identified some twists and turns as Tudor forms of late feudalism transitioned into the Common law patterns of reasoning that have prevailed since the seventeenth century. [14] But a feudal form of political economy as such was not part of the baggage transported when England, and later the United Kingdom, began to assert sovereignty over plantations and colonies in overseas continents and islands where there were long established indigenous populations . Mercantilist capitalism, not feudalism, prevailed in the early years of imperial expansion. Laissez-faire capitalism had taken centre stage by the time cartographers tinted a quarter of the world's map in British imperial pink. Triumphalist rhetoric waxed lyrical about the extent and strength of this empire: 'On her dominions the sun never sets; before his evening rays leave the spires of Quebec, his morning beams have shone three hours on Port Jackson, and while sinking from the waters of Lake Superior, his eye opens upon the Mouth of the Ganges.' [15] Yet, as Maya Jasanoff observed, 'the imperial map was little more than a rose-tinted fiction. It lied time and again. The uniform coloring falsely implied similarities across radically different kinds of domains.' [16] Further to that insight, in this chapter it will be argued that, even as between somewhat similar European settler domains, the doctrine of tenures evolved in radically different ways when judges were called on to assess what (if any) rights or title to land might have been retained by the indigenes after proclamations of British sovereignty.

The application by colonial judges and Privy Counsellors of another passage from Blackstone is an especially important context for understanding the diverging pathways in Australia, Canada and New Zealand. In *Commentaries*, Book I, Blackstone opined:

[O]ur more distant plantations in America, and elsewhere, are also in some respects subject to the English laws. Plantations, or colonies in distant countries, are either such where the lands are claimed by right of occupancy only, by finding them desart and uncultivated, and peopling them from the mother country; or where, when already cultivated, they have been either gained by conquest, or ceded to us by treaties. And both these rights are founded upon the law of nature, or at least upon that of nations. But there is a difference between these two species of colonies, with respect to the laws by which they are bound. For it is held, that if an uninhabited country be discovered and planted by English subjects, all the English laws are immediately there in force. For as the law is the birthright of every subject, so wherever they go they carry their laws with them. But in conquered or ceded countries, that have already laws of their own, the king may indeed alter and change those laws; but, till he does actually change them, the antient laws of the country remain, unless such as are against the law of God, as in the case of an infidel country.

Our American plantations are principally of this latter sort, being obtained by right of conquest and driving out the natives (with what natural justice I shall not at present enquire) or by treaties. And therefore the common law of England, as such, has no allowance or authority there; they being no part of the mother country, but distinct (though dependent) dominions. They are subject however to the control of the parliament. [17]

Unsurprisingly, none of the judgments quoted above and delivered in *Mabo (No. 2)* in 1992, *Ngati Apa* in 2003 and *Tsilhqot'in* in 2014 embraced Blackstone's notion that a territory might be lawfully occupied by British settlers if they found it desert and uncultivated so that it could be deemed to be 'an uninhabited country' in which all English laws, including of course the radical title of the Crown to all land, were immediately there in force. Quite rightly, from the retrospective comfort of contemporary points of view, judges in those cases have rejected the racism and enthnocentrism undergirding European imperialist thinking in the past that justified the acquisition of territories without even the pretence of obtaining consent from those upon whom colonial rule was imposed. It was not so, however, for many of their judicial forebears.

In considering Blackstone's formulae, it is not at all surprising that inconsistent policies were adopted by decision-makers at the point when British sovereignty was proclaimed, and later by judges scrutinising the basis for those assertions of sovereignty. Did English law (including radical title) automatically apply in new colonies as the birthright of British subjects – regardless, incidentally, of whether they hailed from England, Wales, Scotland, Ireland or other jurisdictions within the United Kingdom? Were the plantations of North America, and the later colonies in Australia and New Zealand, properly claimed by occupancy, by conquest or by treaty? That is not a question for which clear answers are available even to this day. When Blackstone wrote of an 'uninhabited country', did that mean a stretch of territory totally devoid of any human persons? Or rather, was the focus of British policy-makers' attention on whether the inhabitants whom British sailors had 'discovered' were capable of owning property – for which the test would be Lockean notions of cultivation and labour as the basis for private property rights, and without regard to indigenous conceptions of connections to land and country?

Of the three jurisdictions considered in this essay, the Canadian portion of British North America has the most complicated history of intrusions into indigenous territories by Europeans who claimed to have 'discovered' them. There, various indigenous nations controlled military forces, some of whom were allies (and some enemies) of Great Britain in wars against France and later against rebels in the thirteen colonies that became the United States of America. These nations engaged in trade for some centuries with both British and French interests and concluded a great variety of treaty and wampum covenant transactions with Europeans. Beyond the eastern seaboard, there were prairies and mountains where the Hudson Bay Company traded for a long time before gold seekers and settler migrants arrived in the nineteenth century to disperse and displace indigenous populations. Brian Slattery has identified the complexities of the legal instruments by which New France was incorporated into British North America following the Treaty of Paris in 1763. [18] For Paul McHugh the outcome by the nineteenth century was clear. The status of indigenous peoples had been 'moved from ally to subjects of the Crown'. [19] By the 1820s, 'their forms of political organization and representation were denied juridical standing before the courts of Upper Canada. Their relations with the Crown were rendered "political" in the sense of being non-justiciable or unrecognizable in the colonial courts except through the protective agency of the

Governor'. [20] When considering the radical title of the Crown and any aboriginal titles or rights that may have survived treaties, conquests and occupation policies, the complexities and the different histories in what are now the provinces of federal Canada were usually disregarded in favour of a primary focus on the Royal Proclamation 1763. [21] That was certainly the reasoning in the leading case from Canada that was appealed to the Privy Council in 1888: *St Catherine's Milling and Lumber Co.* v. *The Queen*. [22] The Proclamation dealt with a number of issues following the British defeat of French forces, subsequent capitulations and a treaty. Relevant to this paper is this recognition of indigenous interests:

And whereas it is just and reasonable and essential to Our Interest and the Security of Our Colonies, that the several Nations or Tribes of Indians, with whom We are connected, and who live under Our Protection, should not be molested or disturbed in the Possession of such Parts of Our Dominions and Territories as, not having been ceded to, or purchased by Us, are reserved to them, or any of them, as their Hunting Grounds. [23]

The Proclamation affirmed and extended the policy of Crown pre-emption. The Crown held a monopoly right to purchase lands from the Indian nations or tribes and to extinguish native title in the land ceded. Any land occupied by settlers prior to a Crown purchase remained lands reserved to the Indians, and settlers were bidden forthwith to remove themselves from such settlements.

Delivering the advice of the Privy Council in the *St Catherine's* litigation between the government of Canada and the government of Ontario province (from which the indigenous Salteaux nation, a party to the relevant Treaty No. 3, was entirely excluded), Lord Watson concluded that the Royal Proclamation 1763 was the primary instrument to identify whatever indigenous interests there might have been in the land in dispute between Ontario and Canada. Addressing the character of the interests that 'Indian inhabitants had in the lands surrendered' by a treaty, Lord Watson wrote:

Their possession, such as it was, can only be ascribed to the general provisions made by the royal proclamation in favour of all Indian tribes then living under the sovereignty and protection of the British Crown. It was suggested in the course of the argument for the Dominion, that inasmuch as the proclamation recites that the territories thereby reserved for Indians had never 'been ceded to or purchased by' the Crown, the entire property of the land remained with them. That inference is, however, at variance with the terms of the instrument, which shew that the tenure of the Indians was a personal and usufructuary right, dependent upon the good will of the Sovereign. ... There was a great deal of learned discussion at the Bar with respect to the precise quality of the Indian right, but their Lordships do not consider it necessary to express any opinion upon the point. It appears to them to be sufficient for the purposes of this case that there has been all along vested in the Crown a substantial and paramount estate, underlying the Indian title, which became a plenum dominium whenever that title was surrendered or otherwise extinguished. [24]

Some Canadian scholars detect in that reasoning support for the modern doctrine of aboriginal title – cognisable and enforceable *in the courts* – that has been developed by Canadian judges since *Calder* in 1973 leading to *Tsilhqot'in* in 2014. Disagreeing with McHugh for views that are said to be 'neither good history nor good law', [25] they assert that the post-*Calder* jurisprudence 'reassessment' of *St Catherine's* does not amount to 'a revision of the law' laid down in that case, but rather that modern case law is 'based on a better understanding of Indigenous societies, their relationship with land, and their cultures, including their legal orders'. [26] *St Catherine's* is accepted as an important precedent but criticised as a flawed precedent owing to factual findings that were 'riddled with prejudicial assumptions about the Salteaux that must have led the Privy Council to conclude that they were too primitive to have laws of their own or any land rights that had not been conferred on them by the Crown'. [27]

In my reading of Lord Watson's advice to Her Majesty, I would note the finding that Salteaux interests in Treaty 3 lands, as recognised by the 1763 Proclamation, were possessory only, were usufructuary only and were protected (if at all) only by 'the goodwill of the Sovereign' – not by judgments of the sovereign's courts. I have long argued that what is indeed 'good law' for the late twentieth and early twenty-first centuries has emerged from 'revisionist legal history'. Even if judges persistently disavow being revisionists – long a feature of Common law reasoning – that does not mean legal scholars should disregard the actual historical context of bygone precedents. [28] Judges in 1888 did indeed conclude that indigenous peoples in Canada were too primitive to have laws of their own – as the notion of 'law' was then understood by those judges. That did not mean that indigenous interests were entirely irrelevant to the colonisers' law. It did mean, however, that in the colonisers' law indigenous interests were not recognised as 'ownership' interests; all land was vested in the Crown as an estate 'underlying the Indian title', and vindication of those interests depended on the 'goodwill' (or otherwise) of the political branches of government, not the judicial branch of government.

There was a rather simpler legal history on the application of radical title in Australia. First named New Holland by Europeans who thought of themselves as 'discoverers', the Commonwealth of Australia now covers a continent that has been inhabited by numerous diverse indigenous peoples for many tens of thousands of years. Was that continent uninhabited, desert and uncultivated in 1788 – when a British penal settlement known as New South Wales was established on the continent's east coast, under a military dispensation that bore but a faint resemblance to ordinary English law? [29] Or in 1828 – when an imperial statute formally applied 'all Laws and Statutes in force within the realm of England' to the colonies of New South Wales and Van Diemen's Land (now Tasmania)? [30] The answer of Australian and Privy Council judges prior to 1992 was clear. The continent was indeed 'uninhabited' in law.

The most important pre-*Mabo (No. 2)* case in Australia on radical title was the 1847 New South Wales Supreme Court decision *Attorney-General (NSW)* v. *Brown.* [31] This was a dispute between the Crown and the lessee of land who mined for coal despite an explicit reservation in the Crown grant that rights to mine gold, silver and coal were retained by the Crown. The defendant challenged the Crown's title to the land. That defence was peremptorily dismissed. According to Stephen CJ 'the waste lands of this Colony are, and ever have been, from the time of first settlement in 1788, in the Crown; that they are, and ever have been, from that date (in point of legal intendment), without office found, in the Sovereign's possession'. He went on to aver that 'At the moment of its settlement the colonists brought the common law of England with them.' Waste lands of the Crown was a term that 'meant all the waste and unoccupied lands of the colony; for, at any rate, there is no other proprietor'. Furthermore, even though the radical title of the Crown was a fiction in English law, 'in a newly-discovered country, settled by British subjects, the occupancy of the Crown with respect to the waste lands of that country, is no fiction. ... Here is a property, depending for its support on no feudal notions or principle.' [32]

The invisibility and irrelevance of indigenous peoples in actual possession of large tracts of the continent within the boundaries of New South Wales could hardly be more striking to modern eyes, but the law laid down was abundantly clear. Similarly, the Privy Council in 1889 had no difficulty in identifying the law applicable to land rights in New South Wales. In *Cooper* v. *Stuart*, the self-same Lord Watson, who had delivered the Privy Council decision in *St Catherine's* the previous year, had this to say about New South Wales:

> The extent to which English law is introduced into a British Colony, and the manner of its introduction, must necessarily vary according to circumstances. There is a great difference between the case of a Colony acquired by conquest or cession, in which there is an established system of law, and that of a Colony which consisted of a tract of territory practically unoccupied, without settled inhabitants or settled law, at the time when it was peacefully annexed to the British dominions. The Colony of New South Wales belongs to the latter class. [33]

In support of this proposition, Lord Watson quoted the famous passage from Blackstone's *Commentaries*, Book I, that I quoted above. He then addressed what the relevant land law might be:

There was no land law or tenure existing in the Colony at the time of its annexation to the Crown; and, in that condition of matters, the conclusion appears to their Lordships to be inevitable that, as soon as colonial land became the subject of settlement and commerce, all transactions in relation to it were governed by English law, in so far as that law could be justly and conveniently applied to them. [34]

Even as late as 1971, in a test case seeking recognition of aboriginal title to land on the Gove Peninsula in the Northern Territory of Australia, Blackburn J in a lengthy judgment refused to shift from the orthodoxy of those precedents. He affirmed the view that 'the Crown is the source of title to all land', that all land is held mediately or immediately of the Crown and that on the foundation of New South Wales 'every square inch of territory in the colony became the property of the Crown'. [35] The Gove Peninsula, incidentally, is some 2,889 kilometres from Sydney. There are a large number of square inches between the location where a small penal colony was established at Botany Bay and Port Jackson in 1788 and the territory of the Yolngu people, who have occupied the Gove region for at least 60,000 years. This seems a very long stretch for a doctrine that, so it was said, 'is no fiction'.

Moving some 2,155 kilometres from Sydney in a different direction – across the Tasman Sea to New Zealand – legal history on the radical title of the Crown has followed a very different trajectory to that of either Canada or Australia. In Canada, there were multitudes of alliances, treaties and other legal transactions between indigenous peoples and the Crown in northern America prior to confederation pursuant to the British North America Act 1867. Then, post-confederation in western Canada, there were eleven 'numbered treaties' entered into between 1871 and 1921. All these treaties are important to the narratives on radical title and extinguishment of indigenous rights. In Australia, on the other hand, there were no authorised treaties at all between the Crown and the continent's prior inhabitants. There was an 1835 unratified document, often called Batman's Treaty, purporting to purchase a large tract of land from the Aboriginal people in the area that is now Melbourne. The story of that one and only Australian attempt to treat formally with the indigenous peoples prior to being dispossessed of their lands has been told well by Bain Attwood. [36]

In New Zealand, however, just one treaty signed at the outset of colonial rule in 1840 continues to define Maori–Crown relations. [37] In New Zealand's flexible and evolving Westminster-style constitutional arrangements, the Treaty of Waitangi is described now in the *Cabinet Manual 2017* as 'a founding document of government in New Zealand'. [38] There have been disputes as to the congruence of the Maori text, signed by a large proportion of Maori tribal leaders throughout the New Zealand islands in 1840, with an English text of the treaty. Both texts, though, are embedded in the schedule to the Treaty of Waitangi Act 1975, which created the Waitangi Tribunal to inquire into and report on issues between Maori and the Crown.

There has been significant debate also about whether or not the Treaty's provisions align with whatever protection a colonial court may have provided under what is now known as the Common law doctrine of aboriginal title. [39] In my view, Ned Fletcher is right to argue that policies based on the Treaty initially guaranteed a good deal more protection to Maori interests than any American or colonial common-law court would have permitted:

The principal conclusions of the thesis are that British intervention in New Zealand in 1840 was to establish government over British settlers, for the protection of Maori. British settlement was to be promoted only to the extent that Maori protection was not compromised. Maori tribal government and custom were to be maintained. British sovereignty was not seen as inconsistent with plurality in government and law. Maori were recognised as full owners of their lands, whether or not occupied by them, according to custom. [40]

That high level of protection for Maori interests, and the broad recognition of Maori property rights in all land, was anathema to the New Zealand Company – a private company seeking to bring settlers to New Zealand. The Company had friends in high places in Westminster. In 1844, a House of Commons select committee resolved that the conclusion of the Treaty of Waitangi 'was a part of a series of injudicious proceedings' and the recognition of Maori property in 'wild lands' was 'an error which has been productive of very injurious consequences'. [41] In support of their view that native title rights should be narrowed as much as possible so as to enable rapid emigration of settlers to the new colony, Company advocates – including Henry Chapman, the proprietor-editor of the *New Zealand Journal* (a newspaper subsidised by the Company) – called in aid the jurisprudence of Marshall CJ in a famous trilogy of cases from 1823 to 1832 on federal Indian law [42] and in Kent's *Commentaries.* [43] Company supporters argued for a 'fundamental principle of colonial law' that native rights should be admitted only when based on actual current occupation of small areas of land. [44] Opposing that view, and defending his Tory government's much more generous interpretation of the Treaty of Waitangi, a member of the Commons in 1845 declaimed:

I suspect I know the origin of this new fundamental principle of colonial law. It comes, I think, from the land in which the Black Man is a slave, and the Red Men of the forest are driven and hunted from their lands, as the Seminole and other Indians have been, according to certain adjudications that Indians have no property to the soil of their respective territories than that of mere occupancy. [45]

Not long after that debate, however, the Tory government lost a vote of no confidence and a new Whig ministry replaced it. Viscount Howick, who had chaired the 1844 select committee in the Commons, but was now the third Earl Grey, sitting in the Lords, became the Secretary of State for War and the Colonies in the Whig administration. [46] With that change of government in the United Kingdom, and also a change of governor in the colony, by 1847 the scene was set to bring a test case in the New Zealand Supreme Court. The new governor issued a Crown grant over land to one of his own officials who had no personal nor pecuniary interest in that land. This collusive piece of litigation was designed to obtain findings from the Supreme Court to reaffirm Crown pre-emption in dealing with Maori land (waived for a period by the previous governor). The governor sought rulings that the radical title to all land was vested in the Crown and only by Crown grants could settlers obtain a lawful title to land. In reaching this conclusion the Court was not called on to inquire exactly how (and with what justice) Maori customary interests had been extinguished prior to the Crown grant.

By now, Henry Chapman was a judge on the New Zealand Supreme Court bench. In the case concerning this grant, *R* v. *Symonds*, he and Martin CJ duly cited and relied upon the Marshall CJ decisions. Those American precedents, they held, laid down the settled law applicable in colonies such as New Zealand. The Treaty of Waitangi was now realigned to conform to them. According to Chapman J, in 'solemnly guaranteeing the Native title' and 'the Queen's pre-emptive right', the Treaty of Waitangi 'does not assert either in doctrine or in practice any thing new and unsettled'. [47] The reasoning in *Symonds* relied heavily on *Johnson* v. *M'Intosh* and quoted with approval Kent's summary of the decision that 'on the discovery of this continent by the nations of Europe, the discovery was considered to have given to the government by whose subjects or authority it was made, a title to the country, and the sole right of acquiring the soil from the natives'. [48] It should be noted, too, that Chapman J did not apply to New Zealand Marshall CJ's later recognition in *Cherokee* v. *Georgia* that the indigenous communities in that state should be recognised as being 'domestic dependent nations'. [49]

Colonial government policy in New Zealand, following *Symonds*, ruled out the possibility that Maori customary law would govern land transactions between Maori and Europeans. It was local statute law – not American law nor Common law nor *iure gentium* – that assessed the validity of land transactions, known as 'old land claims', entered into prior to 1840. A Land Claims Act 1840 was passed by the legislature of New South Wales (when New Zealand was a dependency of that colony) and was reenacted as the Land Claims Ordinance 1841 after New Zealand was erected as a separate colony. [50] This legislation assessed old land claims not by reference to Maori customary law, nor by assessing the intentions of Maori in entering into pre-Treaty land transactions, but rather by the amount paid to Maori in any purported purchase. A schedule to these statutes sets out a scale: 6 pence per acre would suffice to justify any transactions prior to the end of 1824; 8 pence per acre from 1824 to 1829; and so on, rising to between 4 and 8 shillings per acre in 1839. [51] In all cases, however, the commissioners appointed to inquire into old land claims could not make an award in excess of 2,560 acres. One who refused to accept this law was James Busby, who had served as British Resident from 1835 until the Treaty of Waitangi. He challenged the validity of the Land Claims Ordinance 1841, which treated his pre-Treaty of Waitangi land purchases as 'null and void'. For two decades he continued to maintain his claim to hold large areas of land under 'native title' as conferred on him by Maori. All his efforts came to nought in 1859. [52] Then, from 1862, the Native Land Court became the instrument for extinguishing customary title. Under its statute-bestowed jurisdiction, this court devised its own understandings of Maori customs and usages so as to extinguish them as rapidly as possible, and thus free up Maori land for the government to make it available for incoming settlers. [53]

Hence it was statute law – not the Common law and not the Treaty of Waitangi – that determined and governed Maori–Crown relationships. The statutory definition of 'customary land' was 'land vested in the Crown and held by Natives under the customs and usages of the Maori people'. [54] An explanatory memorandum for the Bill that became the Native Land Act 1909 explained the crucial role of Crown radical title, as understood in New Zealand law, in explicitly denying court enforceable rights to Maori (until *Ngati Apa* in 2003):

Customary land, since it has never been Crown-granted, belongs to the Crown. It is in a wide sense of the term Crown land, subject, however, to the right of those Natives who by virtue of Maori custom have a claim to it to obtain a Crown grant (or a certificate of title under the Land Transfer Act in lieu of a grant) on the ascertainment of their customary titles by the Native Land Court. This right of the Natives to their customary lands was recognised by the Treaty of Waitangi in 1840. In its origin it was merely a moral claim, dependent on the good will of the Crown, and not recognisable or enforceable at law. [55]

And yet there is a significant body of scholarship that has looked to legal history in order to bolster the claims of the modern Common law doctrine of aboriginal title as a coherent corpus of jurisprudence applicable to Canada, Australia and New Zealand alike where indigenous rights are enforceable in the ordinary courts and the source of those rights lie (or should lie) in indigenous law conceptions. This has been described by Mark Hickford as 'a golden thread of reasoning about native title independently actionable at Common law in the courts'. [56] Three Privy Council cases in particular are regularly cited in support of these claims: *Nireaha Tamaki v Baker* (1901); [57] *In re Southern Rhodesia* (1919); [58] and *Amodu Tijani v Secretary, Southern Nigeria* (1921). [59] The Canadian scholar Kent McNeil cites all three cases for the proposition that they 'make clear that Indigenous laws, when revealed by evidence, can give rise to legal land rights enforceable in common law courts'. [60] The

Australian scholar Ulla Secher cites all three cases for a proposition 'contrary to the conventional view' that 'the Crown does not have a present proprietary interest underlying Aboriginal title' and furthermore that *St Catherine's* is not authority for the view 'that the Crown's radical title is necessarily a full proprietary estate underlying *any* pre-existing title which is recognised by the common law'. [61] Whilst respecting the passion of these authors to advance indigenous peoples' rights, I submit that the facts of each case, the actual outcome following each decision, and the surrounding historical context of each case point to untidiness, ambiguity and a distinct lack of coherence in the Common law. Edward Cavanagh, on the other hand, is closer to historical veracity when he suggests that 'the jurisprudence of the highest imperial court of appeal at the time' led to decisions that 'often hung on the ad hoc response ... to a particular colonial political crisis. In this court, history and precedent alike never served, but were instead made subservient to a pragmatic ambition to bolster the constitution of the Empire Commonwealth.' [62]

The *Tamaki* litigation in New Zealand began with a number of orders of the Native Land Court in 1871 individualising the customary title of members of the Rangitane tribe. [63] Much of the land was immediately sold to the Crown and was proclaimed Crown land, but survey requirements of the Native Land Acts were not fully complied with. In 1893 the Crown offered the sold lands for on-sale to European settlers. Nireaha Tamaki, and other non-sellers awarded title in an adjacent block, then seized on the surveying irregularity to claim that their customary title had not in fact been extinguished by the 1871 court orders. Richmond J delivered the brief judgment of the Court of Appeal in 1894:

> The plaintiff comes here on a pure Maori title, and the case is within the direct authority of *Wi Parata* v. *The Bishop of Wellington*. We see no reason to doubt the soundness of that decision. ... There can be no known rule of law by which the validity of dealings in the name and under the authority of the Sovereign with the Native tribes of this country for the extinction of their territorial rights can be tested. Such transactions began with the settlement of these Islands; so that Native custom is inapplicable to them. The Crown is under a solemn engagement to observe strict justice in the matter, but of necessity it must be left to the conscience of the Crown to determine what is justice. The security of all titles in the country depends on the maintenance of this principle. [64]

An appeal was eventually heard by the Privy Council in 1901. The Judicial Committee humbly advised His Majesty that the appeal should be allowed. After quoting in full the English text of the Treaty of Waitangi and many statutes beginning with the Land Claims Ordinance 1841, Lord Davey was of the opinion that 'if the appellant can succeed in proving that he and the members of his tribe are in possession and occupation of the lands in dispute under a native title which has not been lawfully extinguished, he can maintain this action to restrain an unauthorised invasion of his title'. [65] Too much weight has been accorded by adherents of 'a golden thread of reasoning' to this successful appeal by a Maori plaintiff to the Privy Council. The actual outcome of the case was a settlement payment to Tamaki of £4,566 minus court costs and his agreement to the extinguishment by legislation of native title to the disputed land. [66]

As to the 1877 *Parata* precedent, their Lordships opined that dicta in that case, especially in relation to the interpretation of the Native Rights Act 1865, 'went beyond what was necessary for the decision' and were plainly wrong. Native title was indeed cognisable and had been recognised in statutes. Nevertheless, their Lordships saw 'no reason to doubt the correctness of the conclusion arrived at' by Richmond J and Prendergast CJ in refusing to annul a Crown grant that implied native title had been extinguished. [67] The colonial judiciary in a number of subsequent cases applied the *Parata* precedent so that customary title could not be enforced in the ordinary courts. [68] Maori would have their rights recognised in court but if, and only if, they could point to a statutory basis for their claims. [69]

Secher's criticisms of *Parata*, and of decisions that followed it, are in some respects seriously misconceived. For a start, she misunderstands a quotation from the *Parata* judgment as being a statement that New Zealand was acquired as a colony by cession. [70] On the contrary, the judges concluded that Maori were 'primitive barbarians' who lacked the capacity to enter into a treaty so that the Treaty of Waitangi was 'a simple nullity'. [71] Secondly, she asserts that there was a 'marked contrast' between the *Symonds* reasoning and that in *Parata*. [72] I would argue that, in all essential aspects of the actual decisions, *Symonds* and *Parata* are closely aligned, including, as expressed in *Parata*, that there is a duty on the sovereign 'as supreme protector of aborigines, of securing them against any infringements of their right of occupancy'. [73] Thirdly, Secher states that the Privy Council in *Tamaki* 'effectively overruled the decision' in *Parata*. [74] As noted above, the Privy Council did not doubt the correctness of the *Parata* decision, and it was followed on numerous occasions after 1901. [75]

It is likewise odd that the *Southern Rhodesia* case is invoked in support of a court enforceable doctrine of Common law aboriginal title rights. [76] In that case, legal arguments submitted by the Anti-Slavery and Aborigines' Protection Society asked the Judicial Committee to uphold the land rights of the native population rather than focus on the dispute between the British South Africa Company and the settlers' Legislative Council concerning 'unalienated lands'. [77] In his rejection of these submissions, Lord Sumner pronounced:

> The estimation of the rights of aboriginal tribes is always inherently difficult. Some tribes are so low in the scale of social organization that their usages and conceptions of rights and duties are not to be reconciled with the institutions

or the legal ideas of civilized society. Such a gulf cannot be bridged. It would be idle to impute to such people some shadow of the rights known to our law and then to transmute it into the substance of transferable rights of property as we know them. In the present case it would make each and every person by a fictional inheritance a landed proprietor 'richer than all his tribe.' On the other hand, there are indigenous peoples whose legal conceptions, though differently developed, are hardly less precise than our own. When once they have been studied and understood they are no less enforceable than rights arising under English law. Between the two there is a wide tract of much ethnological interest, but the position of the natives of Southern Rhodesia within it is very uncertain; clearly they approximate rather to the lower than to the higher limit. ...

Whoever now owns the unalienated lands, the natives do not. [78]

The crucial historical context for this decision was the pragmatic consideration that Southern Rhodesia was destined in the minds of Britain's rulers to be a territory dominated by European settlers and any extensive recognition of native title rights would be most inconvenient.

Southern Nigeria provided a very different historical context. This was a region where there was a large African population and a very high death rate for European residents from 'blackwater fever' (malaria) and other diseases. Tropical Africa did not attract European settlers who might one day claim the right to responsible self-government as was envisaged in Rhodesia. A tiny number of European colonial officials were called on to exercise political domination in tropical Africa colonies. The solution they arrived at to deal with what Mahmood Mamdani names as the 'native problem' in such colonies and protectorates was to institute a system of administration known as indirect rule. [79] The leading proponent of indirect rule was Sir Frederick Lugard (later Baron Lugard of Abinger), who spent a good deal of his career in Nigeria and later wrote up his ideas in *The Dual Mandate in British Tropical Africa.* [80] Under this policy, external, military and tax control was operated by the British, while most aspects of life were left to local traditional chiefs and their courts.

One such chief in 1921 was Amodu Tijani, Chief Oluwa of Lagos. He most certainly did win a case appealed to the Privy Council. It held that he was entitled to full compensation for land taken for public purposes on the footing that he had exercised full ownership rights in the land. In reaching that result, Viscount Haldane LC made an observation that was cited with warm approval in *Mabo (No. 2)* and *Ngati Apa*:

There is a tendency, operating at times unconsciously, to render [native] title conceptually in terms which are appropriate only to systems which have grown up under English law. But this tendency has to be held in check closely. As a rule, in the various systems of native jurisprudence throughout the Empire, there is no such full division between property and possession as English lawyers are familiar with. ...

To ascertain how far this latter development of right has progressed involves the study of the history of the particular community and its usages in each case. Abstract principles fashioned a priori are of but little assistance, and are as often as not misleading.

In the case of Lagos and the territory round it, the necessity of adopting this method of inquiry is evident. As the result of cession to the British Crown by former potentates, the radical title is now in the British Sovereign. But that title is throughout qualified by the usufructuary rights of communities, rights which, as the outcome of deliberate policy, have been respected and recognised. [81]

The current recognition of the Tijani decision as highly authoritative should not be seen as evidence supporting the existence of a cohesive body of Common law inside Privy Council case law. Contrarily, as emphasized by their esteemed peers, it is advisable to refrain from relying on "abstract principles" and instead focus on examining the historical context of the specific society. The Privy Council demonstrated a willingness to independently evaluate, without substantial evidence, and on an individual basis, whether indigenous peoples possessed legal conceptions that were 'neither less precise' than English property law concepts, or if they occupied a lower position in the hierarchy of civilization.

In conclusion, as I initially said, it is evident that a legal history of the idea of aboriginal title lacks coherence and clarity. The concept of a radical title might be likened to a chimera, consisting of diverse and distinct components. In Privy Council instances such as St Catherine's, Cooper, Tamaki, Southern Rhodesia, and Tijani, the prevailing factors that contributed to success were the policy and pragmatism considered suitable for the specific time, location, and historical circumstances of each case, rather than the principled reasoning based on Common law.

Footnote

1. K. Roberts-Wray, Commonwealth and Colonial Law (London, 1966).
2. P. G. McHugh, Aboriginal Title: The Modern Jurisprudence of Tribal Land Rights (Oxford, 2011); K. McNeil, Common Law Aboriginal Title (Oxford, 1989).
3. *Attorney-General* v. *Ngati Apa* [2003] 3 NZLR 643 (henceforth, *Ngati Apa*).
4. Ibid., 655–6.
5. *Calder* v. *Attorney-General of British Columbia* [1973] SCR 313 (henceforth, *Calder*). See H. Foster, H. Raven, and J. Webber (eds.), Let Right Be Done: Aboriginal Title, the *Calder* Case, and the Future of Indigenous Rights (Vancouver, 2007).

6. *Tsilhqot'in Nation* v. *British Columbia* [2014] 2 SCR 257 (henceforth, *Tsilhqot'in*), at 292–3.
7. R. Beaton, The Crown Fiduciary Duty at the Supreme Court of Canada: Reaching Across Nations, or Held Within the Grip of the Crown? (Waterloo, 2018), 14. See also J. Borrows, 'The Durability of *terra nullius*: Tsilhqot'in Nation v British Columbia', University of British Columbia Law Review, 48(3) (2015), 701–42.
8. *Mabo* v. *Queensland (No 2)* [1992] HCA 23 (henceforth, *Mabo (No. 2)*) (footnotes omitted).
9. B. Edgeworth, 'The Mabo "Vibe" and Its Many Resonances in Australian Property Law', in S. Brennan, M. Davis, B. Edgeworth and L. Terrill (eds.), Native Title from Mabo to Akiba: A Vehicle for Change and Empowerment? (Sydney, 2015), 75–98, at 78.
10. Ibid., 79, citing W. Holdsworth, A History of English Law, vol. II, 4th edn (London, 1936), 200–1, and A. W. B. Simpson, A History of the Land Law, 2nd edn (Oxford, 1986), 47.
11. Edgeworth, 'The Mabo "Vibe"', 79 citing the judgment of Brennan J in *Mabo (No. 2)*, at 16.
12. J. Greenberg, The Radical Face of the Ancient Constitution: St Edward's 'Laws' in Early Modern Political Thought (Cambridge, 2001).
13. W. Blackstone, Commentaries on the Laws of England, Book II: Of the Rights of Things (Oxford, 1766), 51, as quoted in S. Stern's edition, part of *The Oxford Edition of Blackstone*, ed. W. Prest (Oxford, 2016), 33.
14. J. G. A. Pocock, The Ancient Constitution and the Feudal Law: A Study of English Historical Thought in the Seventeenth Century. A Reissue with a Retrospect (Cambridge, 1987).
15. The British Newspaper Archive, 'The British Empire', *Caledonian Mercury*, 15 October 1821, 4.
16. M. Jasanoff, 'Hearts of Darkness: The Incoherence of the British Empire', The New Republic, 244(9) (2013), 48–53, at 49, a review of John Darwin, Unfinished Empire: The Global Expansion of Britain (New York, 2012).
17. W. Blackstone, Commentaries on the Laws of England, Book I: Of the Rights of Persons (Oxford, 1765), 104–5, as given in D. Lemming's edition, part of *The Oxford Edition of Blackstone*, ed. Prest, 75–6.
18. B. Slattery, 'Aboriginal Title and the Royal Proclamation of 1763: Origins and Illusions', working draft paper, 6 December 2019, available at www.researchgate.net/publication/337821333, 72–90. See also B. Slattery, 'Paper Empires: The

Legal Dimensions of French and English Ventures in North America', in J. McLaren, A. R. Buck and N. E. Wright (eds.), Despotic Dominion: Property Rights in British Settler Societies (Vancouver, 2005), 50–78. But see also E. Cavanagh, 'Possession and Dispossession in Corporate New France, 1660–1663: Debunking a "Juridical History" and Revisiting Terra Nullius', Law and History Review, 32(1) (2014), 97–125.

19. P. G. McHugh, Aboriginal Societies and the Common Law: A History of Sovereignty, Status, and Self-Determination (Oxford, 2004), 156.
20. Ibid., 156.
21. Ibid., 87–109.
22. (1888) 14 App Cas 46, [1888] UKPC 70 (henceforth, *St Catherine's*) on appeal from *St. Catharines* [sic] *Milling and Lumber Co.* v. *The Queen* (1887) 13 SCR 577 (SCC).
23. Slattery, 'Aboriginal Title and the Royal Proclamation of 1763', Appendix A, 162. Slattery's appendix most usefully sets out the Proclamation text in *British Royal Proclamations Relating to America, Volume 12: Transactions and Collections of the American Antiquarian Society*, C. S. Brigham (Worcester, MA, 1911), 212–18, which reproduces the original text of the Proclamation printed by the King's Printer, Mark Baskett, in London in 1763. This text, according to Slattery, is the most authoritative printed version of the Proclamation available.
24. *St Catherine's*, 54–55.
25. Slattery, 'Aboriginal Title and the Royal Proclamation of 1763', 56.
26. K. McNeil, *Flawed Precedent: The St Catherine's Case and Aboriginal Title* (Vancouver, 2019), 125. See also K. McNeil, 'The Source, Nature, and Content of the Crown's Underlying Title to Aboriginal lands', The Canadian Bar Review, 96(2) (2018), 273–93.
27. McNeil, *Flawed Precedent*, 187.
28. D. V. Williams, A Simple Nullity? The *Wi Parata* Case in New Zealand Law and History (Auckland, 2011), 199–233. See also D. V. Williams, 'Historians' Context and Lawyers' Presentism: Debating Historiography or Agreeing to Differ', New Zealand Journal of History, 48(2) (2014), 136–60.
29. B. Kercher, 'Perish or Prosper: The Law and Convict Transportation in the British Empire, 1700–1850', Law and History Review, 21(3) (2003), 527–84.
30. Australian Courts Act 1828, 9 Geo IV c. 83, s. 24, came into force on 25 July 1828.
31. *Attorney-General (NSW)* v. *Brown* (1847) 1 Legge 312.
32. Ibid., 316–18.

33. *Cooper* v. *Stuart* [1889] 14 App Cas 286, [1889] UKPC 1 (henceforth, *Cooper*), para 11.
34. Ibid., para 13.
35. *Milirrpum* v. *Nabalco Pty Ltd* (1971) 17 FLR 141, 245.
36. B. Attwood (assisted by H. Doyle), Possession: Batman's Treaty and the Matter of History (Carlton, 2009).
37. C. Orange, The Treaty of Waitangi (Wellington, 2011). Although, see R. Boast, 'Treaties Nobody Counted On', Victoria University of Wellington Law Review, 42(2) (2011), 653–70.
38. K. Keith, 'On the Constitution of New Zealand: An Introduction to the Foundations of the Current Form of Government', in Cabinet Manual 2017 (Wellington, 2017), 1.
39. M. Hickford, Lords of the Land: Indigenous Property Rights and the Jurisprudence of Empire (Oxford, 2011).
40. N. Fletcher, 'A Praiseworthy Device for Amusing and Pacifying Savages? What the Framers Meant by the English Text of the Treaty of Waitangi', unpublished PhD thesis University of Auckland (2014), iii–iv.
41. 'Report from the Select Committee on New Zealand together with the Minutes of Evidence, Appendix, and Index', *British Parliamentary Papers, Colonies New Zealand*, vol. II (Dublin, 1968), v–vi, xii (2d Resolution).
42. *Johnson* v. *M'Intosh* (1823) 21 US 543; *Cherokee Nation* v. *State of Georgia* (1831) 30 US 1; *Worcester* v. *State of Georgia* (1832) 31 US 515.
43. J. Kent, Commentaries on American Law, 3rd edn (New York, 1836), vol. III, part VI, lecture LI [51].
44. H. S. Chapman, The New Zealand Portfolio: Embracing a Series of Papers on Subjects of Importance to the Colonists (London, 1843).
45. M. Hickford, '"Decidedly the Most Interesting Savages on the Globe": An Approach to the Intellectual History of Maori Property Rights, 1837–53', History of Political Thought 27(1) (2006), 122–67, citing at 159 'A Corrected Report of the Debate in the House of Commons on the 17th, 18th, and 19th of June 1845 on the State of New Zealand and the Case of the New Zealand Company (London, 18 June 1845), 124'.
46. P. Burroughs, 'Grey, Henry George, Third Earl Grey (1802–1894)', in Oxford Dictionary of National Biography (Oxford, 2004), available at www.oxforddnb.com/view/10.1093/ref:odnb/9780198614128.001.0001/odnb-9780198614128-e-11540?rskey=5Y3XwE&result=4.

47. *R* v. *Symonds* (1847) NZPCC 387, 388–90; [1847] NZHC 1 (henceforth, *Symonds*).
48. Ibid. For critiques of the assumptions of 'discovery' by Europeans underlying aboriginal title law, see R. A. Williams, Jr, Like a Loaded Weapon: The Rehnquist Court, Indian Rights, and the Legal History of Racism in America (Minneapolis, MN, 2005); R. A. Williams, Jr, The American Indian in Western Legal Thought: The Discourses of Conquest (New York, 1990); S. J. Anaya, Indigenous Peoples in International Law, 2nd edn (New York, 2004); R. J. Miller, Native America, Discovered and Conquered: Thomas Jefferson, Lewis and Clark, and Manifest Destiny (Lincoln, NE, 2008).
49. A more accurate analysis, in my opinion, than that by Chapman J of the Marshall decisions and Kent's *Commentaries* is to be found in the 'infamous' judgment in *Wi Parata* v. *Bishop of Wellington* (1877) 3 NZJR (NS) SC 72 (henceforth, *Parata*). See Williams, *A Simple Nullity?*, 167–73, 225–6.
50. New Zealand Land Claims Act 1840 (NSW) 4 Vict No 7; Land Claims Ordinance 1841 (NZ) 4 Vict No 2.
51. Schedule D of the 1840 Act; Schedule B of the 1841 Ordinance.
52. B. Fletcher and S. Elias, 'A Collusive Suit to "Confound the Rights of Property Through the Length and Breadth of the Colony"?: Busby v White (1859)', Victoria University of Wellington Law Review, 41 (2010), 563–604.
53. R. Boast, Buying the Land, Selling the Land: Governments and Maori Land in the North Island 1865–1921 (Wellington, 2008); D. V. Williams, 'Te Kooti tango whenua': The Native Land Court 1864–1909 (Wellington, 1999).
54. Native Land Act 1909, s. 2. This remained the law in force until the passage of Te Ture Whenua Maori Act/Maori Land Act 1993, s. 129(2)(a): 'Land that is held by Maori in accordance with tikanga Maori [Maori custom law] shall have the status of Maori customary land.' This then relatively recent statutory amendment was in force by the time the *Ngati Apa* decision was delivered in 2003.
55. J. W. Salmond, 'Native Land Bill: Memorandum. Notes on the History of Native-Land Legislation', Number 87-3, Bill Books, 1909, 1, Parliamentary Counsel Office, Wellington; H. Bassett, R. Steel and D. V. Williams, Māori Land Legislation Manual (Wellington, 1994), Appendix C, 95.
56. M. Hickford, 'John Salmond and Native Title in New Zealand: Developing a Crown Theory on the Treaty of Waitangi, 1910–1920', Victoria University of Wellington Law Review, 38 (2007), 853–924, at 873.
57. [1901] AC 561; [1901] UKPC 18 (on appeal from the New Zealand Court of Appeal) (henceforth, *Tamaki*).

58. [1919] AC 211 (a matter specially referred to the Judicial Committee by an Order in Council under the Judicial Committee Act 1833, s. 4, for hearing and consideration) (henceforth, *Southern Rhodesia*).
59. [1921] 2 AC 399; [1921] UKPC 80 (on appeal from the Supreme Court of Nigeria) (henceforth, *Tijani*).
60. McNeil, *Flawed Precedent*, 124.
61. U. Secher, Aboriginal Customary Law: A Source of Common Law Title to Land (Oxford, 2014), 75–6. The foreword to this book is by Kent McNeil, vii–viii.
62. E. Cavanagh, 'Colonial History and the Language of the Judiciary: Aboriginal Rights Before and After *Tsilhqot'in*', unpublished paper, Department of Justice, Ottawa, 10 February 2014, 8.
63. Waitangi Tribunal, The Wairarapa ki Tararua Report, Wai 863, vol. II (Wellington, 2010), 395–554, esp. 466–70.
64. *Nireaha Tamaki* v. *Baker* (1894) 12 NZLR 483, 488.
65. *Nireaha Tamaki* v. *Baker* [1901] AC 561 (henceforth, *Tamaki* (PC)), 578.
66. Native Land Claims Adjustment and Laws Amendment Act 1901, s. 27; Waitangi Tribunal, *The Wairarapa ki Tararua Report*, 401. Relatives of Tamaki still wished to pursue the case in court: *Nireaha Tamaki* v. *Baker* (1902) 22 NZLR 97. Their action was discontinued by the Maori Land Claims Adjustment and Laws Amendment Act 1904, s. 4. More generally, a ten-year limitation period was imposed on any litigation designed to question findings of the Native Land Court: Land Titles Protection Act 1902. The Native Land Act 1909, ss. 84–87, codified the *Parata* precedent in stipulating that any claims by Maori that their customary title rights had not been properly extinguished prior to the issue of a Crown grant or a Native Land Court order were non-justiciable in the ordinary courts.
67. *Tamaki* (PC), 579.
68. *Hohepa Wi Neera v Bishop of Wellington* (1902) 21 NZLR 655.
69. *Tamihana Korokai v Solicitor-General* (1912) 32 NZLR 321; *Te Heuheu Tukino* v. *Aotea District Maori Land Board* [1941] AC 308, [1941] UKPC 6.
70. Secher, *Aboriginal Customary Law*, 69.
71. *Parata*, 77–78.
72. Secher, *Aboriginal Customary Law*, 70.
73. Williams, *A Simple Nullity?*, 170–2.
74. Secher, *Aboriginal Customary Law*, 75.

75. The *Parata* precedent was cited with approval by the New Zealand Court of Appeal as late as 1963: *In re the Ninety-Mile Beach* [1963] NZLR 461, 475.
76. Secher, *Aboriginal Customary Law*, 446.
77. E. Cavanagh, 'The Unbridgeable Gulf: Responsible Self-Government and Aboriginal Title in Southern Rhodesia and the Commonwealth', in S. Dubow and R. Drayton (eds.), Commonwealth History in the Twenty-First Century (Cham, 2020), 81–99; see also E. Cavanagh, 'Crown, Conquest, Concession, and Corporation: British Legal Ideas and Institutions in Matabeleland and Southern Rhodesia, 1889–1919', in E. Cavanagh (ed.), Empire and Legal Thought: Ideas and Institutions from Antiquity to Modernity (Leiden, 2020).
78. *Southern Rhodesia*, 233–5.
79. M. Mamdani, Citizen and Subject: Contemporary Africa and the Legacy of Late Colonialism (Princeton, 2018).
80. F. D. Lugard, The Dual Mandate in British Tropical Africa (Edinburgh, 1922).
81. *Tijani*, 403–4.

75. [illegible] was [illegible] by the [illegible] [illegible] Britain [illegible]

76. [illegible] Original Thought [illegible]

77. [illegible] Commonwealth, [illegible] Twenty First Century [illegible] also [illegible] Legal [illegible] and Legal Thought [illegible]

78. Ibid. [illegible]

79. [illegible] Africa [illegible] Legal [illegible]

[illegible]

11 CONCEALED FRUSTRATIONS, PRIVATE ADVOCACY, AND THE BREAK WITH ENGLISH LAW IN THE MID-CENTURY: AN ANALYSIS OF THE HIGH COURT OF AUSTRALIA

The High Court of Australia experienced a period of unhappiness throughout the 1940s, primarily due to the adverse effects of the World War on its members and their families. The decade was characterized by a lack of unity[1]. The Court experienced a decline in personal relationships among specific judges. Additionally, the Court had to endure extended periods with a reduced number of judges due to their engagement in diplomatic duties during wartime[2]. Furthermore, the majority's repeated obstruction of the Labor government's[3] postwar reconstruction program resulted in significant divisions both within and outside the Court. [4] However, during the 1940s, the Court officially expressed a nearly unified opinion regarding the significance of English law in the Australian jurisdiction. This perspective did not emerge as a reaction to the insecurity experienced during conflict. Instead, the Court appeared to be advocating for a broader call for cooperation between the judiciaries of England and Australia. [5] However, several judges and historians have interpreted the Court's perspectives during this era as indicative of a complete deference towards the English courts during the initial part of the twentieth century. This deference was only interrupted by exceptional instances like Parker v. The Queen (1963) at a later point in time. [6] According to this perspective, the High Court had a progressive increase in autonomy starting from 1968, as a result of legislative initiatives that ultimately eliminated all means of appeal from Australian courts to the Privy Council. [7]

This traditional account of the evolution of Australian judicial 'independence' warrants further study – particularly the circumstances surrounding the delivery of the High Court's judgment in *Parker* insofar as it represented an explicit break from following House of Lords precedent. *Parker* is all the more interesting because the author of its most celebrated passages, Chief Justice Dixon, was also one of the judges supportive of a unified Common law in the 1940s – even when unity came at the expense of following the High Court's own precedent. *Parker* has been variously described as an early, 'fatal crack' in the relationship between the Australian and English courts; [8] as a 'decisive landmark' in the evolution of a distinct Australian law; [9] and even as a 'Declaration of Judicial Independence'. [10] But *Parker*, landmark or not, is often characterised as a singular event, an aberration in a wider, enduring story of the Australian judiciary's long-standing, 'internalised imperialism' [11] and subservience to the superior courts of England. [12] It is only in more recent years that scholarship has emerged that suggests that the development of a distinct Australian Common law was evident in the early years following Federation. Early law reports reveal that even trial judges were prepared to diverge from English precedent where circumstances compelled it in private law cases; although it must be conceded that these judgments were usually expressed in a subtle, politic manner, far removed from the forthright prose of *Parker*. [13]

Parker was handed down less than a year before Dixon's retirement from the Court. [14] Dixon sought the approval of the other members of the Court before making his 'declaration' in his dissenting judgment; every other member of the Court willingly authorised him to make the remarks on their behalf. The Court had been invited to follow the precedent of the House of Lords in the criminal case of *Director of Public Prosecutions* v. *Smith*, [15] that an accused should be presumed to intend the natural and probable consequences of their acts. Dixon wrote unapologetically:

> Hitherto I have thought that we ought to follow decisions of the House of Lords, at the expense of our own opinions, but having carefully studied *Smith's Case* I think we cannot adhere to that view or policy. There are positions laid down in the judgment which I believe to be misconceived and wrong ... I wish there to be no misunderstanding on the subject. I shall not depart from the law on the matter as laid down in this Court and I think *Smith's Case* should not be used as authority in Australia at all. [16]

Parker can certainly be interpreted as a directive from the bench of a (domestic) apex court to the judges below that a degree of freedom had been granted to consider prevailing local conditions in developing the Common law, rather than to slavishly observe English precedent. But within the Court, the decision to make such a directive in such an extraordinary manner was not taken lightly. Rather, the decision reflected years of internal anguish about the 'Privy Council situation' in particular. Thus, the bench was not suddenly emboldened; the sentiments contained in *Parker* did not reflect grievances only freshly suffered. This essay attempts to tease out some of the private concerns of the judges of the High Court in the years leading up to the decision in *Parker*, and to provide some context for what is otherwise arguably perceived of as the most sensational judicial *volte-face* in Australian legal history. It tentatively concludes that, regardless of the Court's public avowals of adherence to English legal principle, there existed long-running tensions and failed attempts at private advocacy before the reluctant decision was taken to jettison aspirations of a unified Common law. To this end, the traditional account of an emerging Australian jurisprudence is affirmed: *Parker* does reflect a break with English ties, even if provoked not by a fervent sense of 'nationalism' but by growing concern at developments in the English Common law and the operations of the Privy Council. But *Parker* is by no means an anomaly: it is the inevitable endpoint of a judicial relationship that had been in decline for at least two decades.

Prior to continue, it is imperative to exercise prudence regarding the primary sources employed in this article. The availability of personal papers of High Court judges in Australian repositories is limited. The National Archives has recently taken steps to address the reluctance of judges to leave their papers for future scholars[17]. The institution now aims to promote the practice of retiring judges leaving their papers in Canberra upon retirement. 17th For this purpose, significant emphasis is placed on the public non-judicial writings of the judges, as well as the extensive and unique collection of Sir Owen Dixon's records. The documents authored by Dixon were deposited at the National Library in the year 2010, following his demise in 1972. [18] The core narrative in this chapter is Dixon's recounting of his interactions with colleagues judges and politicians in the years preceding Parker.

A UNIFIED COMMON LAW: AT WHAT COST?

The High Court personnel at mid-century were held in high regard internationally. Dixon, in particular, was viewed even beyond Australia as the preeminent antipodean jurist of his generation, with justices Windeyer and the late Fullagar following closely behind. Dixon's overseas diplomatic missions in the 1940s enabled him to cultivate friendly relations with a wide network of jurists and statesmen, some of whom became his lifelong correspondents. These included United States Supreme Court Justice Felix Frankfurter and, in Britain, the eminent jurists Simonds, Pearce, Reid and Denning. [19] These correspondents wrote to him privately, and at length, to express their admiration for his work, and to inform him of their reliance on his judgments in drafting their own. Dixon was no mere apostle of the classical, nineteenth-century, English approach of strict logic and high technique in developing the law (much as he admired the era): his brand of 'legalism' was particularly nuanced and acknowledged the incursions that legal realism was making into the study of law. [20] Thus it is somewhat surprising to find that Dixon, and later Windeyer, became frustrated over time at what they perceived to be a routine ignorance of High Court jurisprudence in the English courts. [21] The unity of the Common law, it seemed, flowed mainly in one direction: the High Court declared its commitment to working with English principles, but no corresponding assurance was consistently evident in the written judgments from London.

A careful examination of the three early cases in which the Court reaffirmed its commitment to English precedent bear this out. Despite these cases sometimes being taken as examples of judicial obsequiousness towards England, another conclusion may be drawn. That conclusion is not that Dixon et al. had an enduring faith in the infallibility of English jurisprudence, but rather that the *maintenance* of the unified Common law was of paramount concern in Australian decision-making. This largely reflects a pragmatic view held not just by judges, but by some of the judges' political contemporaries at this time. (As shall be discussed, those political contemporaries were unyielding in this view, thus being of little support to the later Dixon Court as it sought to abandon its initial stance.)

In the first case, *Waghorn* v. *Waghorn*, decided in 1942, the High Court heard a matter which ultimately required a decision to be made about the application of directly analogous High Court precedent or English precedent: not Privy Council or House of Lords precedent, but English Court of Appeal precedent. The case, falling within the (then) fault-based matrimonial causes jurisdiction, explored whether the High Court might make a decree for the dissolution of a marriage on behalf of a husband on the basis of his wife's desertion. [22] The husband had committed adultery; but the wife had not been aware of this particular betrayal when deciding to leave. The husband was now living with another woman. Three of the five judges indicated they would have preferred to adopt the High Court's own directly applicable precedent, which would have permitted them to reject a finding of 'wilful' desertion on the part of the wife. [23] However, as puisne Justice Dixon noted, it appeared that in England the Court of Appeal had not had the benefit of reading the Australian precedent on point, and had subsequently decided an analogous case in favour of a husband. Dixon concluded that even though the majority judges were confident of the correctness of their previous decision, there were wider matters to consider. Without wishing to defer to the Court of Appeal on a wholesale basis, Dixon nevertheless suggested that at the very least, in cases involving *general* propositions, the High Court should be wary of embarking on 'needless divergences' from English law. [24]

A year later, with Dixon away from the Court on diplomatic duties, in *Piro* v. *Foster* the Court reaffirmed its position of deference to English law at the expense of direct High Court precedent, this time in relation to principles of contributory negligence established by the House of Lords. [25] Chief Justice Latham observed that while the Court was not 'technically' bound by the decisions of the House of

Lords, there were 'convincing reasons' to proceed as if the decisions were binding – namely, uniformity of principle across the Empire. [26]

In 1948, with Dixon having returned to the bench, he made his strongest statement yet about the necessity of following English precedent. In *Wright* v. *Wright* – yet another matrimonial causes matter – the Court considered the applicable standard of proof in adultery cases, noting that the Court had previously preferred the *Briginshaw* v. *Briginshaw* standard. [27] Nevertheless, a recent Court of Appeal decision had adverted to a criminal standard of proof being required. Dixon observed that it would be

> better that this Court should confirm to English decisions which we think have settled the general law ... than that we should be insistent on adhering to reasoning we believe to be right but will create diversity ... Diversity in the development of the common law ... seems to me to be an evil. Its avoidance is more desirable than a preservation here of what we regard as sounder principle. [28]

Dixon nevertheless went on to find that, given the high level of uncertainty across England in various aspects of matrimonial jurisprudence, he preferred to follow Australian precedent on this occasion. [29]

While all three cases expressed the need for a unified Common law in similar terms, Dixon's judgments are of particular interest. In *Waghorn*, Dixon reluctantly forgave the Court of Appeal for ignoring the High Court's precedent; in *Wright*, he forgave both the Court of Appeal and the House of Lords for widespread inconsistencies in principle across the matrimonial jurisdiction. Perhaps at this point he saw these difficulties as par for the course on the basis of the physical distance between the jurisdictions or, at the very least, on the basis that discrepancies of opinion were to be expected in any judicial hierarchy. Yet these rationalisations did not hold for Dixon or his colleagues as time went on.

By the 1950s, developments in other areas of law also frustrated the High Court judges. The first of these concerns did not relate to any specific disjuncture of Australian and English law, but rather to judicial personnel. Dixon had been following the renewed interest in promissory estoppel in the English courts, as first advanced by Lord Denning in the *High Trees* case of 1947. [30] Dixon began to take an interest in Denning himself. Dixon questioned not only Denning's methodologies, but also his extra-judicial communications with the wider public. Dixon's relationship with Denning had begun on friendly footing: the judges became acquaintances by the early 1950s, and Denning wrote delightedly to Dixon to advise him that his reading of the Australian case law on estoppel indicated it was moving in the same direction as England. 'It would be very good if we could all advance on the same broad point – and learn from each other', remarked Denning. [31] Here, indeed, was an English judge willing to study developments from the Australian jurisdiction. But Dixon, who received updates on Denning's endeavours from his close friend Viscount Simonds, soon took a dim view of the man he began to regard as a '*deliberate* innovator'. Denning and his followers, it seemed, would be willing to cut across the basic contract principles of offer, acceptance and consideration in favour of advancing the *High Trees* principles – that is, allowing a remedy in the case of a promise relied upon and later withdrawn, even if consideration was never furnished. [32] Dixon's view of the law, and of the impropriety of judges speaking candidly about the indeterminacies of judicial law-making, could not have been further from Denning's position. Dixon thought a model judge ought to *believe* in a discernible set of external standards that could be applied in most situations; this positivistic faith in external law was essential to principled decision-making. Writing to another of his correspondents, Frankfurter, Dixon bemoaned Denning's repeated public statements that emphasised the creative aspect of the judicial function. 'He (Denning) ought to appear to believe that he has some external guidance, even if in his ignorance he regards it as untrue', Dixon remarked. [33] Dixon seemed concerned that Denning would produce judicial acolytes who would bring the English courts into disrepute. In 1955 Dixon proudly told an American audience that there was no such evidence of judicial innovation on the High Court bench. [34]

The second concern, unsurprisingly, related to developments (or lack thereof) in criminal law, and certainly directly presaged the decision in *Parker*. The High Court had sought, since its decision in *Stapleton* in 1952, to distance itself from rigidly narrow English precedent on the interpretation of the M'Naghten rule on the defence of insanity (specifically, the rejection of evidence of 'irresistible impulse' as relevant to a defence of insanity). [35] The Court in *Stapleton* had remarked that a rule whereby the criminally accused is presumed to intend the natural consequences of their acts was 'seldom helpful and always dangerous'. [36] Dixon took the opportunity in a public lecture to opine that the failure to expand the M'Naghten rule, or at least make some acknowledgement of medical developments in the understanding of mental illness, had rendered certain English cases a 'discreditable chapter of the law'. [37] In 1959, the Privy Council overruled the High Court's *Brown* decision, in which an order of retrial had been made for a case in which the trial judge specifically informed the jury that 'uncontrollable impulse' was no defence to murder. [38] No doubt this frustrated the members of the High Court, but the final straw appeared to occur in 1961 – not in an appeal of the Australian case, but in an English case itself. The House of Lords in *Smith* again affirmed the presumption that an accused intended the natural consequences of their acts, the very presumption that the High Court had questioned the utility of nine years earlier in *Stapleton*. [39] It appeared no headway had been made in developing this area of the law. One of Dixon's associates recalled Justice Fullagar entering Dixon's chambers upon hearing of the result, saying 'Well, Dixon, they're hanging men for manslaughter in England now'.[40] In these circumstances, it seems not too controversial to surmise that the Court resolved to take the next opportunity that arose to decry the application of *Smith* in Australia. That opportunity arose two years later, in *Parker*.

Although this is by no means an exhaustive list of the Court's 'frustrations' over Common law developments in England at mid-century, it may suffice to provide a backdrop to some of the Court's more pragmatic concerns that probably further propelled Dixon towards making the statement in *Parker*. For, while the decision in *Parker* seemingly related only to the development of a unified Common law, it appears that matters quite separate to Common law principle also operated as motivating factors in the drafting of the judgment. These matters related primarily to the operation of the Privy Council.

THE PRIVY COUNCIL'S UNWITTING ROLE IN *PARKER*

The Privy Council was the highest appellate court in Australia until 1986. While later-twentieth-century objections towards that court remaining at the apex of the Australian judicial system are well known – they relate just as much to nationalistic aspirations as to a growing confidence in the competency of the High Court being able to work independently of London – it is worth observing that objections to the Privy Council's role in Australian law have existed since well before Federation. Early sentiments were assuaged to some extent by the British Colonial Office's modest concession, during federation negotiations, towards the Privy Council having at best an irregular role in conducting judicial review (that is, permitting the High Court itself to decide whether to grant leave to appeal to the Privy Council on matters involving the limits *inter se* of the constitutional powers of the states and the Commonwealth under section 74 of the Constitution). Of course, this did not stop the first Chief Justice of the High Court, Samuel Griffith, stating in the 1907 case of *Baxter* v. *Commissioners of Taxation* that at the time of Federation 'the eminent lawyers who constituted the Judicial Committee were not regarded either as being familiar with the history of conditions of the remoter part of the Empire, or having any sympathetic understanding of the aspirations of the younger communities which had long enjoyed the privilege of self-government'.[41]

In practice, the Privy Council's interventions into constitutional matters were more regular than anticipated, and, according to various members of the Court, these interventions revealed little understanding of the practical complexities of the Australian constitutional arrangements. The Privy Council variously held that matters involving the interpretation of section 92 (freedom of interstate trade) and section 109 (inconsistency between state and federal laws) of the Constitution were not usually *inter se* matters, opening up a further avenue for disgruntled litigants to sidestep High Court precedent. It is the Privy Council's 'section 92 cases' that brought particular consternation in the late 1940s, reaching a crescendo by the time that *Parker* was handed down. As the entry on the Privy Council in the *Oxford Companion to the High Court of Australia* observes, 'the Privy Council never had a sufficient flow of Australian constitutional cases to develop a proper understanding of the Australian Constitution, but did have enough to do considerable damage'. [42] The Privy Council had already overruled the High Court's understanding of section 92 in *James* v. *Cowan* in 1932 and in *James* v. *Commonwealth* in 1936, [43] but the low point was the *Bank Nationalisation* case of 1947, in which the Privy Council acknowledged that while it did not have jurisdiction to hear the case (as it involved an *inter se* question), given the efforts of the parties to put their case in London, an opinion on the matter would nevertheless be proffered. [44] Dixon was incensed, even if the advisory opinion endorsed his own views. He wrote to Frankfurter of the 'ingenious paradoxes' contained in the labyrinthine prose: 'I find myself quite at sea because I cannot understand the reasons given for a view which was supposed to be mine.' [45] Several years later, in *Hughes & Vale* v. *New South Wales*, the Privy Council ironically enough *endorsed* an approach Dixon had already abandoned on account of the directives given by the Privy Council in earlier section 92 judgments. [46] Taken together, this series of cases appears to have pushed Dixon to commence the process of consensus-building in the Court to advocate collectively for Privy Council change, as will be discussed shortly.

Yet the Court's concerns about the Privy Council did not begin and end with its section 92 jurisprudence. The Privy Council's constituency and collective ability were also raised as a source of apprehension. For Chief Justice Latham (as he then was) and Justice Starke, some of the received case law was a source of puzzlement. [47] For others, such as Justice Menzies and Dixon, the evidence indicated that the members of the board did not 'have a clue'. [48] Windeyer and Fullagar were more temperate in their public remarks, but even Windeyer adverted to the possibility that the law lords were ignoring precedent from other Commonwealth jurisdictions in considering the matters before them. [49]

For Dixon, the problems of the Privy Council were an acute source of anguish. Dixon's attachment to Britain was particularly strong: he described his visits to London as akin to coming home. On Australian soil, this feeling presented itself as what we now regard as a particular narrow-mindedness. He was a supporter of the White Australia policy; he became overtly concerned at the 'Americanisation' of postwar society; [50] he was unsettled about immigration from the north. [51] He had spoken proudly of the fact that Australia was '97 per cent British', noting that the relationship between Britain and Australia was one of interdependence and mutual reliance. [52] The disappointments emerging from the Privy Council must have been particularly hard to bear given Dixon's cultural loyalties. Thus two developments in particular gave Dixon pause for thought in the years leading up to the decision in *Parker*. The first was the news that discussions were afoot to staff the Judicial Committee with several Dominion representatives: Dixon worried that Africans might be appointed to oversee appeals from the High Court. The second was the news that the Judicial Committee might begin hearing appeals in the Dominions, which was further cause for alarm. His objection was not on nationalistic grounds, but rather that it afforded smaller jurisdictions little of the autonomy supposedly championed by Britain. 'For a body to come from London to Australia and superintend the administration of justice here would be much resented and I think rightly so', Dixon wrote to Pearce in 1959. 'It completely loses the sight of the position in Australia.' [53] Adding to Dixon's growing resentment of the Privy Council was the fact that this news had not been conveyed to him personally (he had been appointed to the Privy Council some years earlier, though he never sat on a case). He heard of the potential reforms on the wireless. [54]

To some extent, this Anglophilic sentiment explains why Dixon and indeed other members of the Court bore their disappointments privately during the course of most of the 1940s and 1950s. Even *after* the decision in *Parker* was handed down, other judges were keen to maintain a respectful deference towards the English judiciary in extra-legal communication, if not in their judgments. Whether this was done as a self-protective measure or as a genuine expression of fidelity to a single Common law is not known. Note, for instance, Justice Menzies' impassioned defence of a unified law in 1968. In 1954, he had privately expressed his dismay at section 92 jurisprudence in a lengthy conversation with Dixon. In 1963, he consented to Dixon making the well-known remarks in *Parker* on his behalf. By 1968, however, he suggested that he ultimately *supported* the Privy Council's section 92 jurisprudence, and that it reflected prevailing legal opinion. Not only that, but Menzies was saddened by the divergence of the Common law between the jurisdictions:

> The decisions of the House of Lords, the High Court and the Privy Council together have had the unfortunate consequence of tearing the fabric of the common law even though the rent is but small ... the Privy Council [has now recognised] ... that the common law may not be the same in Australia as it is in England. [55]

Windeyer was more candid. He was a scholarly judge who was held in particularly high esteem by Dixon (the same could not be said of some of his colleagues). Windeyer was by no means an 'innovator' but was more of a realist than Dixon. [56] Three years after the decision in *Parker*, Windeyer delivered a speech at the Thirteenth Dominion Law Conference in New Zealand on the topic of unity in the Common law. [57] Another invited speaker was Denning. Windeyer's speech is interesting not only for its generous appreciation of judicial creativity at large, [58] but because it reveals that Windeyer was never of the view that the High Court's proper role involved the consideration of English law at the expense of other helpful precedent. He nevertheless surmised that there was 'misgiving and apprehension' at the idea of the Common law being developed differently in other jurisdictions because for many people in Britain, Australia and New Zealand ... there is a sentiment born of the past and of the greatness and pride of the past – a feeling of reverence for the law as the law of our peoples, a remembrance of the great days of Empire ... [but] The Australian method is, on final analysis, somewhat different from that of the English Courts. They are inflexibly bound by the decisions of the House of Lords ... From its earliest days the High Court has said that it is its duty to proceed as a national Court of final appeal, for that is the duty that was cast by Imperial Parliament. ... [I]t is desirable to preserve uniformity in our law, [and] decisions of the House of Lords are regarded as of the highest persuasive authority ... But when an English Court has proceeded upon a consideration of English cases only, and seemingly to meet conditions prevailing in England and ignoring what has been said on the matter elsewhere, its decision may have less weight with us. [59]

This passage seems to reflect Dixon's private views as much as Windeyer's. Indeed, it provides a frank expression of the sentiments which underscored the decision in *Parker*. (There should be no surprise at the effortless summation of the mood of the era: Windeyer was a talented legal historian in his own right.) What precedes these observations in the speech, however, is utterly curious. Windeyer knew that these statements were not uncritical of the English courts, so he self-consciously sought to assure the audience that his remarks should not be construed as an 'unseemly assertion of independence or as a strident expression of Australian nationalism'. [60] There is a sense of discomfiture in finding that Windeyer then thought it necessary to give the particulars of his own family history ('despite my Swiss name, my family have been British subjects for two hundred and thirty years or thereabouts') to allay any hint of subversiveness. [61]

What might be concluded at this point is that at least several of the judges appeared to have been pulled in two directions in deciding how to proceed in both dealing with the Privy Council and in maintaining a unified Common law. None of this cohort appeared to want to 'take on' the English courts because of their personal fervour for nationalism. The frustrations were evident: the Court felt that its work was not always taken seriously in London; and it had doubts as to the collective capability of the Privy Council. It was no judge's first instinct to deal with these concerns in the most public of ways, that is, through communicating with London via High Court judgments. Instead, alternative, private channels of communication were considered first.

FAILED ADVOCACY

Dixon, acting on behalf of the Court, initiated efforts to promote change in London through three distinct avenues, prior to resorting to the public announcement in Parker. Notwithstanding his endeavors, the modifications he pursued in a private capacity did not come to fruition: internal improvements pertaining to the appeal process were declined; and Dixon's criticisms regarding the efficacy of the Privy Council and the 'deliberate innovators' were disregarded.

The first of these efforts was to press domestically for a curtailment of appeals to the Privy Council. Dixon was close friends with Australia's prime minister, Robert Menzies, whose second term in office spanned the years 1949 to 1966. Menzies had been Dixon's pupil at the bar, and both shared a common bond in their appreciation of the 'civilising influence of England' in Australian society. [62] As early as 1952, and well before Dixon's elevation to the chief justiceship, Dixon had expressed concerns privately to Menzies about the performance of the Privy Council – namely, its lack of expertise in handling questions of federalism, and its propensity to grant leave to appeal indiscriminately in other matters. Menzies, who would be visiting London the following year, undertook to raise these concerns diplomatically with the lord chancellor (in that period, coincidentally, the lord chancellor was Dixon's friend, Simonds). There is no evidence to suggest that Menzies pressed the case with any zeal, however. In 1954, Dixon had the opportunity to discuss the Privy Council again with a senior barrister, future High Court justice and the prime minister's cousin, Douglas Menzies. Douglas Menzies was convinced the judges did 'no work behind the scenes'; perhaps, he remarked, they considered it poor form to be engaged in any form of preparatory work before hearing Australian appeals. Dixon likely took this as an encouragement. [63] He decided to counsel the Prime Minister again to consider his position. This time, rather than press for careful diplomacy in London, Dixon suggested a local solution. The Federal Parliament could take legislative action, as permitted by section 74 of the Constitution, to restrict appeals to the Privy Council – on constitutional matters at the very least. Dixon prepared his own draft of the legislation and arranged for a meeting in which the prime minister could canvas the entirety of the High Court bench at once in order to understand the gravity of the problem. Again, it appeared that the draft was not taken further by the prime minister. Later in life, Menzies explained that he did not object to proposals to restrict appeals on constitutional grounds, but that breaking ties with the Privy Council in Common law cases would be to abandon 'a common inheritance which has much to do ... with true civilisation'. [64] Perhaps Menzies' commitment to that common inheritance had left him in stasis when Dixon implored him for help.

At around the same time, Dixon decided to take matters into his own hands and press both Simonds (as lord chancellor) and Pearce, then a lord justice of appeal, directly. To Simonds, he wrote to express his concern over the Privy Council's ever-increasing interventions in constitutional affairs, but added that the bench seemed to fail to appreciate unique Australian conditions when hearing appeals more generally. [65] Dixon hinted of the possibility of a transformation in the Australian political climate following the decision in the *Bank Nationalisation* case, suggesting that the Labor party might well seek to abolish all Privy Council appeals imminently.

This, he presumably hoped, might cause sufficient embarrassment to Simonds as to provoke him to counsel the members of the Privy Council bench to take more care with Australian matters. Dixon wrote that he appreciated that deciding cases for a faraway jurisdiction was an 'Aristotelian' task, but he nevertheless pressed for the quality of judgments to be improved. The Australian reader, he suggested, had a fear that: 'unfamiliarity with Australian conditions, institutions and circumstances and the general background will lead to misunderstandings and misinterpretations, ... [and] mere remoteness and distance will increase the chance of things generally going wrong'. [66] Whether Simonds put Dixon's concerns to his colleagues is not known. Simonds responded some time later, not directly addressing Dixon's concerns but reassuring him that at least one of the upcoming cases to be heard by the Privy Council would likely be dismissed on account of it falling within the *inter se* restrictions. [67]

Dixon's correspondence with Simonds continued on friendly terms despite this outcome, but it appears that, some time around the point that *Brown* was decided in the Privy Council, Dixon decided to direct his apprehensions to Pearce in separate correspondence. (Pearce did not sit on the appeal in *Brown*.) Pearce at least confirmed that he would take up Dixon's concerns with the new lord chancellor. Dixon by this point appeared uncharacteristically intemperate in his expression:

The plain fact is that the dominant consideration with me is to preserve every tie with England, ... [b]ut the difficulties in doing it grow. ... '[F]ederalism' is exotic and you must live under it to understand the problems to which it gives rise. As to care in giving special leave, I suppose it comes down to wisdom of 'legal statesmanship'. [The Privy Council] is not now guided by the principles [in granting leave] which Haldane expounded. [68]

Again, there appears to have been no response that satisfied Dixon. His entreaties to the Privy Council having thus failed, Dixon turned back to the issue of judicial innovation in the general law. In respect of this, there was only one further course of diplomatic action that Dixon considered: to plead with the 'source', Denning, directly. As discussed earlier, the relationship between Dixon and Denning had begun on a firm footing, but as Denning became more vocal about the creative aspects of the judicial function, so did Dixon's cautioning against innovation for its own sake. Dixon decided to use the opportunity given to him, as a recipient of a prize at Yale in 1955, to deliver a lecture containing a call for a return to the time-honoured methods inherent in 'strict and complete legalism'. [69] He spent much of the lecture on a hypothetical case in which he showed the principles of contract law could be adapted to novel facts without the need for recourse to an amorphous form of estoppel – a topic chosen quite deliberately. He later told colleagues that he had meant to direct those comments to Denning. [70] Much to Dixon's disbelief,

Denning later wrote to tell him that he agreed with everything he had said in the lecture. [71] Undeterred, Dixon took up the topic again in 1958, this time in person at a visit to Denning's home: he offered criticism of those English judges who treated case law 'otherwise than as a stream of authority'. [72] This did not chasten Denning, who instead affably reaffirmed his confidence in the High Court. Denning and Dixon did not meet again. Denning's hubris (or obliviousness) had proved yet another stumbling block for Dixon.

DENOUEMENT

Dixon had become fatigued with using private means of lobbying to express his and his colleagues' concerns about the situation in England by the end of 1960. He regarded his endeavors as a futile exercise. The individual's melancholic disposition became apparent in his correspondence with Frankfurter, wherein he expressed that his inclination towards maintaining the integrity of the common law, as reflected in both Privy Council appeals and endeavors to align with the evolving legal landscape in England, has been overshadowed by an excessive influence of British sentiment.

[It is] too much for me ...'. [73] The Parker proceedings provided an opportunity for a more public expression of those concerns. Upon careful examination of the comprehensive circumstances preceding the Parker case, it becomes evident that Dixon's ruling does not warrant immediate jubilation as a significant milestone in the annals of Australian legal history. The impact of Parker is significant, as it enabled the High Court and lower Australian courts to expand their scope in shaping the Common law. It enabled those courts to prioritize the evaluation of local circumstances. However, the ruling did not demonstrate a courageous judicial decision; instead, it was solely driven by need. The available avenues for engaging a London audience had been fully explored. When seen through the lens of the twenty-first century, Parker is occasionally lauded as a pivotal figure in the formation of Australian nationhood. However, it is probable that Dixon, along with some of his colleagues judges, perceived this as the conclusion of a very somber era in the legal history of England and Australia.

Footnote

1. Chief Justice Latham, for instance, lost his eldest son in overseas military service in 1943.
2. Justice Dixon, for instance, found himself at odds with Latham's approach; Justice Starke, who had a history of falling out with his fellow judges, was particularly critical of Justice McTiernan during this decade.

3. Chief Justice Latham, for instance, spent time as Australia's minister (ambassador) to Japan; Justice Dixon was asked to take leave to become minister to Washington; Justice Webb acted on postwar international tribunals.
4. See, e.g. *Attorney-General (Vic)* v. *Commonwealth* (1945) 71 CLR 237; *Bank of New South Wales* v. *Commonwealth* (1948) 76 CLR 1 ('*Bank Nationalisation* case'); *British Medical Association* v. *Commonwealth* (1949) 79 CLR 201.
5. See, e.g. *Waghorn* v. *Waghorn* (1942) 65 CLR 289; *Piro* v. *Foster* (1943) 68 CLR 313; *Wright* v. *Wright* (1948) 77 CLR 191.
6. (1963) 111 CLR 610 ('*Parker*').
7. See, for example, the essays reflecting on the state of the law at the time of the Australian bicentenary in M. Ellinghaus, A. Bradbrook and A. Duggan (eds.), The Emergence of Australian Law (Oxford, 1989); B. Kercher, An Unruly Child: A History of Law in Australia (Crows Nest, 1995), 188; A. Mason, 'Future Directions in Australian Law', Monash University Law Review, 13 (1987), 149–63; M. Gleeson, 'The Privy Council: An Australian Perspective', speech delivered to the Anglo-Australian Lawyers' Society, The Commercial Bar Association and The Chancery Bar Association, London (18 June 2008), 24, available at www.hcourt.gov.au/assets/publications/speeches/former-justices/gleesoncj/cj_18jun08.pdf.
8. Kercher, *An Unruly Child*, 177.
9. T. Blackshield, 'Parker v The Queen', in T. Blackshield, M. Coper and G. Williams (eds.), The Oxford Companion to the High Court of Australia (Oxford, 2001), 523.
10. M. Kirby, 'The Old Commonwealth – Australia and New Zealand', in L. Blom-Cooper, B. Dickson and G. Drewry (eds.), The Judicial House of Lords 1876–2009 (Oxford, 2009), 339–50, at 341.
11. Kercher, *An Unruly Child*, 166.
12. See, for instance, former Chief Justice of the High Court Murray Gleeson's observation that 'the early Australian attitude' towards appeals to the Privy Council in civil and criminal cases was positive: 'Australians recognised and greatly valued the legal capacity of the senior United Kingdom judges. They expected it would continue to be available to them'; Gleeson, 'The Privy Council: An Australian Perspective', 8. Gleeson later added that there was no comparable 'intensity of feeling' about the constitutional role of the Privy Council in Australia as there was, say, in Canada in the mid-twentieth century; at 11.
13. It is not possible to provide an exhaustive list of this work in this volume, but for the most recent examples, see, e.g. the work of Mark Lunney with respect to

the development of an Australian law of tort: M. Lunney, A History of Australian Tort Law 1901–1945: England's Obedient Servant? (Cambridge, 2018). See also A. Loughnan, Self, Others and the State (Cambridge, 2019), esp. ch 4 ('The "Birth" of Australian Criminal Law'), and M. Finnane, 'Irresistible Impulse: Historicising a Judicial Innovation in Australian Insanity Jurisprudence', History of Psychiatry, 23 (2012), 454–68.

14. *Parker* v. *The Queen* (1963) 111 CLR 610.
15. *Director of Public Prosecutions* v. *Smith* [1961] AC 290 ('*Smith*').
16. *Parker* v. *The Queen* (1963) 111 CLR 610, 632.
17. National Archives of Australia, 'Records Authority 2010/00663993 – High Court of Australia' (Records Authority, 22 November 2010), [9]. This provision was inserted into the Authority in 2010. See generally T. Josev, 'Judicial Biography in Australia: Obstacles and Opportunities', University of New South Wales Law Journal, 40 (2017), 842–61.
18. O. Dixon, *Papers of Sir Owen Dixon*, in National Library of Australia (henceforth 'NLA'), MS Acc.09. The papers are not yet processed. The references that follow in this chapter therefore use box numbers, followed by the informal annotations made on the corner of each document (believed to have been made either by Dixon's former associate, the late Jim Merralls QC, or Dixon's biographer, Philip Ayres).
19. Viscount Simonds was, at the time of his correspondence with Dixon, a lord of appeal in ordinary and sat on the Privy Council. He was lord chancellor from 1951 to 1954 before returning to his previous judicial role. Baron Pearce was, at the time of his correspondence with Dixon, a lord justice of appeal and sat on the Privy Council. In 1962, he was made a lord of appeal in ordinary. Baron Reid was a lord of appeal in ordinary at the time of corresponding with Dixon. Baron Denning was, at the time of his correspondence with Dixon, a lord justice of appeal (appointed 1948) and later a lord of appeal in ordinary (from 1957) before being appointed master of the rolls in 1962.
20. M. Coper, 'Concern about Judicial Method', Melbourne University Law Review, 30 (2006), 554–75; K. Hayne, 'Sir Owen Dixon', in J. Gleeson, J. Watson and E. Peden (eds.), Historical Foundations of Australian Law, 2 vols. (Alexandria, 2011), vol. I, 372–407.
21. See Dixon J's judgments in *Waghorn* v. *Waghorn* (1942) 65 CLR 289 and the discussion below in relation to *Attorney-General (SA)* v. *Brown* [1960] AC 432 and *Director of Public Prosecutions* v. *Smith* [1961] AC 290.

22. *Waghorn* v. *Waghorn* (1942) 65 CLR 289. See also V. Windeyer, 'Unity, Disunity and Harmony in the Common Law', in B. Debelle (ed.), Victor Windeyer's Legacy: Legal and Military Papers (Alexandria, 2019), 114–28.
23. Starke J, although agreeing with the majority that the wife's appeal should be allowed, thought the previous Australian authority on point was wrongly decided: *Waghorn* v. *Waghorn* (1942) 65 CLR 289, 294.
24. Ibid., 297.
25. *Piro* v. *Foster* (1943) 68 CLR 313.
26. Ibid., 320.
27. *Briginshaw* v. *Briginshaw* (1938) 60 CLR 336. The '*Briginshaw* principle' is the civil standard of proof (i.e., on the balance of probabilities).
28. *Wright* v. *Wright* (1948) 77 CLR 191, 210 (Dixon J).
29. Ibid., 211.
30. *Central Property Trust Ltd* v. *High Trees House Ltd* [1947] KB 130. Dixon's estoppel jurisprudence can hardly be regarded as an impediment to the continued development of the area either: his decision on estoppel *in pais* in *Grundt* v. *Great Boulder Pty Gold Mines Ltd* (1937) 59 CLR 641 is still routinely referred to by judges seeking to extend the reach of equitable principles today: see, e.g. *Sidhu* v. *Van Dyke* (2014) 251 CLR 505 and *ASPL* v. *Hills Industries Ltd* (2014) 253 CLR 560.
31. Letter from T. Denning to O. Dixon, 15 July 1953, from NLA, MS Acc.09, Box 5, PP12.34.
32. O. Dixon, 'Concerning Judicial Method', Australian Law Journal, 29 (1956), 468–76, at 472 (emphasis added).
33. Letter from O. Dixon to F. Frankfurter, 14 January 1959, from NLA, MS Acc.09. Box 3. PP7.73.
34. Dixon, 'Concerning Judicial Method', 472.
35. *Stapleton* v. *The Queen* (1952) 86 CLR 358, referring specifically to *R* v. *Windle* [1952] 2 QB 82. Note too that Dixon had been particularly concerned since the 1930s with how courts might appreciate new medical understandings of insanity; see, e.g. *R* v. *Porter* (1933) 55 CLR 182 and *Sodeman* v. *The King* (1936) 55 CLR 192 (which was taken on appeal, with the Privy Council rejecting Dixon's formulation). Dixon took a particular interest in medical understandings of insanity, and he was a member of the Medico-Legal Society of Victoria for some time.
36. *Stapleton* v. *The Queen* (1952) 86 CLR 358, 365 (Dixon CJ, Webb and Kitto JJ).

37. O. Dixon, 'A Legacy of Hadfield, M'Naghten and Maclean', Australian Law Journal, 31 (1957), 255–66, at 261.
38. *Attorney-General (SA)* v. *Brown* [1960] AC 432.
39. *Director of Public Prosecutions* v. *Smith* [1961] AC 290.
40. P. Ayres, Owen Dixon (Melbourne, 2003), 276.
41. *Baxter* v. *Commissioners of Taxation (NSW)* 4 CLR 1087, 1111–12.
42. T. Blackshield, M. Coper and J. Goldring, 'Privy Council', in Blackshield et al. (eds.), *Oxford Companion to the High Court of Australia*, 560–4, at 561 (quoting constitutional scholar Geoffrey Sawer).
43. James v. Cowan (1932) 47 CLR 386; [1932] AC 542; *James* v. *Commonwealth* (1936) 55 CLR 1; [1936] AC 578.
44. *Commonwealth Bank* v. *Bank of New South Wales* [1950] AC 235.
45. Letter from O. Dixon to F. Frankfurter, 30 October 1952, from NLA, MS Acc.09, Box 3, 63A.
46. *Hughes & Vale Pty. Ltd.* v. *New South Wales* (1954) 93 CLR 1.
47. See, e.g. Ayres, *Owen Dixon*, 80.
48. Ibid., 246.
49. Windeyer, 'Unity, Disunity and Harmony in the Common Law', 126.
50. Letter from O. Dixon to E. Pearce, 10 December 1959, from NLA, MS Acc.09, Box 5, PP12.52.
51. See, e.g. letter from O. Dixon to G. Simonds, [undated] 1953, from NLA, MS Acc.09, Box 3, PP7.60.
52. O. Dixon, 'An Address by Sir Owen Dixon, Australian Minister to Washington before the Tulane University of Louisiana, to be delivered on Thurs Feb 10 4pm', 10 February 1944, from NLA, MS Acc.09, Box 8, MISC3.84.
53. Letter from O. Dixon to E. Pearce, 30 December 1959, from NLA, MS Acc.09, Box 5, PP12.54.
54. Ibid. Dixon was appointed to the Privy Council in 1951.
55. D. Menzies, 'Australia and the Judicial Committee of the Privy Council', Australian Law Journal, 42 (1968), 79–87, at 85.
56. A. Mason, 'Foreword', in Debelle (ed.), *Victor Windeyer's Legacy*, i–xiv, at vi.
57. Windeyer, 'Unity, Disunity and Harmony in the Common Law'.
58. Ibid., 119.
59. Ibid., 125–6.

60. Ibid., 124.
61. Ibid.
62. As adopted from a letter from O. Dixon to J. Latham, 15 September 1950, from NLA, MS Acc.09, Box 3, PP7.27.
63. Ayres, *Owen Dixon*, 245.
64. R. Menzies, Afternoon Light: Some Memories of Men and Events (London, 1967), 324–5.
65. Letter from O. Dixon to G. Simonds, [undated] 1954, from NLA, MS Acc.09, Bx 3, PP7.60A.
66. Ibid.
67. Letter from G. Simonds to O. Dixon, 25 April 1956, from NLA, MS Acc.09, Bx 4, PP11.21.
68. Letter from O. Dixon to E. Pearce, 30 December 1959, from NLA, MS Acc.09, Box 5, PP12.54.
69. Dixon, 'Concerning Judicial Method'.
70. Ayres, *Owen Dixon*, 253.
71. Ibid.
72. Ibid., 269.
73. Letter from O. Dixon to F. Frankfurter, 20 December 1960, from NLA, MS Acc.09, Box 5, PP13.14.

12

THE COMPREHENSIVE SLAVE LAWS OF THE BRITISH WEST INDIES CAN BE TRACED BACK TO THE ORIGINS OF ENGLISH SOCIETAL LAWS.

INTRODUCTION: AN OVERVIEW

The rate at which British West Indian colonial slavery became indispensable to the functioning of society was unsurpassed, rendering it the fundamental aspect of British Caribbean history. [1] From 1665 to 1833, there was a significant surge in the slave population in the West Indies. [2] In the year 1643, Barbados was home to a population of 18,600 European colonists and 6,400 African slaves. By 1724, the population had undergone a significant transformation: there were 18,300 Caucasians and 55,206 African enslaved individuals. [3] In 1807, the slave population in the British West Indies was over 775,000, and it had declined by just 100,000 by 1834, marking the official conclusion of the slave trade. [4] The location possesses the perhaps questionable distinction of being the initial in the Americas to initiate the sugar revolution, which subsequently relied on the institution of slavery and had a role in the dissemination of American colonial slavery. Caribbean slavery exhibited a unique characteristic whereby the amalgamation of slavery, sugarcane, and the plantation system exerted a more systematic and profound impact than any other region. [5] The colonial government and planter class, cognizant of their minority status, employed institutional measures to maintain their dominance by enacting rules and regulations pertaining to the legal and economic dimensions of slavery. The establishment of the slave regime and the corresponding legal framework facilitated the integration of the diverse colonies across the Atlantic world, so serving as a rationale for the forced displacement of millions of individuals. [6]

West Indian colonial enslavement involved three interrelated aspects of law that were transformed with the introduction of African chattel slavery: firstly, defining slaves as property; secondly, establishing forms of control over slaves; and thirdly, developing legal definitions of race, which distinguished the African enslaved and their descendants from the rest of the population. [7] This essay examines the origins of the comprehensive slave codes and slave treatment within the British West Indies. It delves into pre-colonial English society to identify various laws and regulations adopted and adapted in the colonies. It argues that transplantation was central to development within colonial legislation. This stands not just for the legal transplants from England to the colonies but within and throughout the colonies themselves. The transplants came in particular forms of property law, laws of villeinage, police law, martial law and various vagrancy regulations.

This essay contributes to the extant scholarship by Edward Rugemer, [8] Christopher Tomlins [9] and David Barry Gaspar [10] on colonial West Indian plantation societies, their fallout and their legacies, by tracing their legal origins and legal ramifications. Furthermore, the research follows on from and adds to such North American scholarship by signifying the legal foundations of the slavery regime and its Atlantic connectivity. It provides a comprehensive analysis of the origins debate, specifically the importance of the Barbadian Code as the progenitor of legislating colonial enslavement, a feat not yet completely tackled within Caribbean legal history. Its claim is not that the English were innovators but rather improvisers within a region that was already conducive for their colonising tactics. [11] The English were latecomers to the West Indies in comparison with their European counterparts, and in many ways these other powers provided a blueprint on how to create a successful slavery regime. The essay begins, though, with an examination of a particular piece of Caribbean slave legislation.

THE BARBADOS SLAVE CODE INTRODUCED IN 1661

Barbados will be my main point of reference. It was the richest settler island for the majority of the seventeenth and eighteenth centuries. The need for the development of comprehensive slave legislation was in a large part due to the success of the cash crop sugar. The growing demand for the crop necessitated the increase in importation of African slaves, requiring a proper mechanism for their regulation; by the 1650s, large, capital-intensive sugar plantations dependent on imported slave labour dominated Barbados. [12] Following years of unrest, resistance from slaves and problems with indentured servants, the Barbados legislature decided it was time to attend to these issues.

In 1661, the Barbadian Assembly passed the first comprehensive slave code in the English Americas, to 'better manage its profitable but unruly slave society'. The Act was entitled 'An Act for the better ordering and governing of Negroes'. [13] The code consisted of provisions that dealt with issues concerning order and governance of 'Negro slaves', since their 'heathenish, brutish and volatile proud manner' rendered prior laws unsuitable. The colonial Assembly acknowledged that although they had to enact laws which conformed to the laws of England, those English laws gave 'noe track to guide ... where to walk nor any rule set up how to govern Slaves'. [14] Therefore, in light of this deficiency the Assembly decided to 'revive whatsoever wee have found necessary and usefull' in the former laws and to then create their own laws where English ones were lacking. [15]

The Act covered the four crucial issues concerning slaves: firstly, their growing numbers; secondly, their status as property; thirdly, their difference in culture; and lastly, their innate rebellious nature. The code's twenty-three articles covered a variety of issues pertaining to slave relations with the English colonials as a whole. Above all, it was concerned with all elements of slave control and coercion, including their criminal and non-criminal punishments. Of the twenty-three articles, approximately ten focused on prohibiting the mobility of slaves, whilst others also in some way tackled the potentiality of slave flights. The legislature thus created a superstructure of slave laws that consisted primarily of a precise criminal law of slavery, specifying categories of slave crime and appropriate trial and punishment. The Barbados Code gave masters and slaves demarcated rights and obligations; it left the masters with near complete dominion over the life and death of their slaves. Slave owners, overseers and even the layman-indentured servant were required to act as police officers, and in effect to manage slaves with a whip constantly in hand. The code did not address legal issues like purchase, sale, mortgaging or other financial transactions involving the enslaved; control, not commoditisation, was the legislators' paramount concern.

The Assembly also used the opportunity to address two other crucial issues. The first concerned the ambiguity over the status of indentured servants, linked to their treatment, and the second addressed the joint rebellions of those servants and slaves. The Servant Act and the Militia Act thereby came into fruition. [16] These three Acts marked the deliberate attempt of the legislature to control and maintain the order of the underclasses: poor whites, vagabonds and the enslaved.

The Barbadian slave code was the 'premier slave code in the English colonies' by the early eighteenth century, due to its central role in initiating slave codes throughout the English slave-holding territories. [17] This codified legislation was an amalgamation of English property law, laws of villeinage, police law, [18] martial law and various vagrancy regulations. It is important to examine these influences to decipher what exactly was adapted, borrowed or transplanted into colonial slave laws.

ENGLISH PROPERTY LAW: SLAVES AS CHATTELS

There was no initial codified treatment of slave status as chattels, although such a notion was embedded in the colonial custom and mind-set from the outset of colonial slavery. A variety of such rules, practices and attitudes, as we have seen, underlay the region's first comprehensive code. [19] However, it was property law that lay at the core of English legal concepts and practices. It is therefore to be expected that the development of colonial organised societies would require protection specifically through property laws for newly acquired territories and peoples; one might 'assume that colonial Englishmen would apply English notions and rules of property to slaves'. [20] English property law provided a wide range of options and principles applicable to commoditising the enslaved. [21]

The institution of African slavery within the English Americas became dependent on ownership of humans as chattels. [22] The Barbados Code's preamble stipulated that the enslaved would be protected as 'other goods and chattels'. [23] A chattel under English property law was any property other than freehold. [24] This legal concept was simple to make fit the instance of slaves, restricting any immediate need for colonial legislators to create statutes classifying slaves as property. Chattel property conceptions under English law conferred enormous power on the slave-owners. These included the right to destruction. [25] As chattels, slaves could be used as mortgage, hired, sold up for debts, disposed of in accordance with inheritance laws, bequeathed, distributed in estate settlements, entailed and subject to a widow's right of dower; and they could be valued in currency or sugar, all while having no property rights themselves. [26] Their chattel status remained for life, and passed on to their children (specifically through the matrilineal line), continuing as long as the institution existed. Furthermore, English personal property law included a doctrine of deemed ownership. [27] Within colonial slavery persons had the legal right to punish slaves who did not belong to them but were found on their land. This meant that slaves were goods capable of giving relative titles to possessors. [28]

However, the Barbadian Assembly eventually defined slaves as real estate, though seven years after the 1661 Code. This meant that the heirs and widows of slave owners would not lose their property in slaves to creditors upon the owners' death: 'Two provisos made clear that slaves could still be bought and sold by the living, but the law protected a planter's investment in slaves as if they were a landed estate, to be preserved for his descendants.' [29]

Claim to a property right, i.e. a legal right in a 'thing', was deemed as 'nothing but a permission to exercise certain natural powers, and upon certain conditions to obtain protection, restitution, or compensation by aid of public force'. [30] Slave-owners did what was necessary to preserve their property right in the enslaved. This usually involved seeking compensation for slave deaths or for dismemberment, as well as demanding the return of fugitive slaves, by offering rewards and threats. Issues did arise, however, when trying to interpret the law on slavery; for example, by trying and convicting the enslaved for various crimes, lawyers and judges inadvertently acknowledged their humanity. In addition, some saw owners as having the right to the slave services in addition to their obedience but did not purport to own the 'soul' of the slave. [31]

VILLEINAGE'S SIGNIFICANCE

Jamaican planter and historian Edward Long spoke of the correlation between villeinage and colonial slavery legislation within colonial Jamaica:

> The Negroe code of this island appears originally copied from the model in use at Barbadoes; and the legislature of this latter island, which was the first planted by the English, resorted to the English villeinage laws, from whence they undoubtedly transfused all that severity which characterizes them, and shews the abject slavery which the common people of England formerly laboured under. [32]

Long contended that the harshness and general nature of West Indian slavery laws undoubtedly came from villeinage laws, to which they bore 'so near an affinity'. [33] He believed that the first settlers to the island colonies brought with them the prejudices of the villeinage system so much that it transferred to governance of African enslaved labourers. Long did cite other regulations as sources of colonial slavery legislation; however, he highlighted villeinage as the cornerstone.

There exists a multitude of discussions concerning the role played by villeinage in constructing colonial slave law. The connection was raised in discussions of chattel slavery and in litigation, despite arguments that neither time nor place could connect slavery and villeinage. [34] The central link between the two forms of bondage was the lack of liberty, followed closely by the tie to the land and forced labour. Villeins in medieval England were by law unfree and in theory subject to the will of their lord who governed them through various rents and exactions 'all of which are usually assumed to have impacted negatively on their economic well-being and by extension the efficiency of the agrarian economy at large'. [35] A distinction could be drawn between two types of villeins. Villeins *regardant* were annexed to the property of the lord, whilst villeins *in gross* were annexed to the person of the lord and so transferable by deed from one owner to another. [36] Villeins *regardant* appeared to correspond with the argument related to the enslaved being real estate and attached to the property of their owner, whereas villeins in gross were themselves sellable and therein correspond simply to chattels. [37]

Villeinage principles served as a model for colonial slavery for several reasons, making it very suitable as the basis for what Alan Watson has called the process of legal transplant. [38] Villeinage was never officially abolished, and cases pertaining to it continued up until the start of English Atlantic settlement. It was the primary example of a form of servitude which cemented bondsmen and their labour to the land of their lord. Akin to slaves, villeins were saleable, were unaware of their futures and were subjected to beatings and punishments. Lord Chief Justice Sir Edward Coke held in reporting on *Combes's Case* that 'the lord may beat his *villain* for cause or without cause and the *villain* shall not have any remedy'. [39] However, there were also major differences. Female villeins, according to Coke, 'had an appeal of rape, in case the lord violated them by force'. [40] Such protection was not given to the colonial slaves. Law also prohibited the maiming and killing of villeins, which differentiated their position from that of colonial slaves. [41] This was because the law recognised villeins as 'the king's subjects' (unlike slaves) and protected them 'against atrocious injuries of the lord: for he might not kill, or maim his villein, though he might beat him with impunity'. [42] The colonial enslaved could be beaten, mutilated and even killed without any judicial recourse. The only ramification was the owner's compensation for the loss of property, which the colonial treasury bore. [43] There were also distinctions in that villeins had at least a limited capacity to acquire property, and the passing on of status regarding the enslaved was simpler than that regarding villeins: children of enslaved persons simply inherited the status of the mother, at least within the English colonised territories. By contrast, though generally children of villeins inherited the status of their parents, where the male parent was a free person, the child would also acquire that free status.

Blackstone regarded villeins to rank legally somewhere between indentured servants and unfree chattel slaves. Lords tied villeins to themselves for a specified number of days each year, and on those days they coerced them to do whatever labour was required. [44] He also agreed with his predecessors that slavery did not exist in England and the laws of master and servant therefore were not synonymous with those of slavery. Blackstone contended that the colonies of North America were not English settlements but instead conquests, so they were not governed by English Common law but by the royal prerogative. Hence, he believed that the law pertaining to slavery in England (predominantly case law) was distinct from the law on slavery in the colonies (predominantly statutory law).

In terms of colonial enslaved persons, it was only upon entering the realm of England that they could ascertain their status and resist actions seeking their recovery. Within the colonies there was not a court where an enslaved person could seek redress either regarding status or ill-treatment. Actions of recovery of the enslaved in the colonies comprised of offers of rewards and/or fines for either aiding or precluding their return. Within England, actions of either trover or trespass were used where an enslaved fled the premises of their owner; trover was an action in Common law that would lie for recovery of damages for the wrongful taking and detaining of specific chattels in which the plaintiff had a property right. [45]

The case of *Chamberline* v. *Harvey* (1697) [46] was one of the first to examine the possibility of colonial slaves being analogous to these categories of villeins. It concerned an enslaved person brought to England from Barbados. In the words of William M. Wiecek:

The slave in question had been owned originally in Barbados, where a slave was legally a part of real estate, rather than a chattel. He had been brought to England and baptised there. Counsel seized on these circumstances to explore the law of slavery and to begin unravelling the implications of the imperial relation. [47]

The plaintiff sought the recovery of his property, i.e. the enslaved, through the remedies of either trespass or trover. His counsels argued that colonial slavery was an extension of villeinage and therefore baptism should not deprive an owner of his property in the enslaved. Wiecek has succinctly summarised their arguments as follows:

slavery could nonetheless exist there, legitimated by a quasi-contract under which the master derived 'power' over the slave in return for providing him with food and clothing ... The peculiar feature of Barbadian law making a slave realty, counsel insisted, made a Barbadian slave the legal equivalent of a villein regardant (a villein attached to the manor, as opposed to a villein in gross, who was attached to the person of his lord). A villein regardant had to be formally manumitted (freed) by his lord, and this slave had not been. Any manumission here would have to be implied or constructive; from the slave's having been brought either to England or having been baptised. [48]

The enslaved's counsels, on the other hand, argued that there was no connection between villeinage and slavery because villeins held more legal rights than colonial slaves. An enslaved person could not be a villein *in gross* because he was not at large but rather born of parents belonging to the plantation. They also contended that the enslaved could not be a villain *regardant* either, since such a category required that the plaintiff and his ancestors be seised of this 'negro and his ancestors time out of memory of man'. Moreover, the enslaved did not possess the hereditary aspect that the lord and villein had. This was because 'villeinage rested on an ancestral tie to the land shared by the lord and the villein from time out of memory of man'. Villeinage and slavery were distinct.

Sir John Holt in *Chamberline* rejected the precedent of the case *Butts* v. *Penny* (1677), which stated that enslaved people were recoverable through trover. [49] Holt opined that neither trover nor an ordinary action in trespass were suitable for the recovery of an enslaved person. He proposed that the appropriate remedy was trespass *per quod servitium amisit*, 'an old declaration claiming loss of the services of a servant'. [50] The differences between the available actions were highly specialised. Whereas an action in trover would equate the enslaved to a chattel, thus 'a thing so utterly unfree that it was vendible', an action in trespass *per quod servitium amisit* would liken the enslaved to a bound or apprenticed labourer, 'a slavish servant, a human being whose freedom was restricted but not annihilated'. [51]

Lord Hardwicke, in addressing the link between villeinage and colonial slavery in relation to actions of trover, stated in *Pearne* v. *Lisle* in 1749 that 'There were formerly villains or slaves in England, and those of two sorts, regardant and in gross; and although tenures are taken away, there are no laws that have destroyed servitude absolutely.' [52] Hardwicke's opinion concerned the adjudication of a debt owed for the rent of fourteen black slaves. The defendant entered a rental contract for the services of enslaved persons for a two-year period but refused to pay the fee or return the enslaved. The plaintiff brought an action for their recovery when the defendant threatened to take the enslaved with him to Antigua. Hardwicke's decision used the words of villein and slave interchangeably. As Dana Rabin has contended, Hardwicke's 'elision of villeinage and slavery sanctioned chattel slavery and recognised the legitimacy of colonial legislation pertaining to slavery in the metropole'. [53]

Further cases throughout the seventeenth and eighteenth centuries reveal differing assessments regarding the relationship between slavery and villeinage. Lord Chief Justice Holt, in the case of *Smith* v. *Brown and Cooper* (1706), held that one may be a villein in England but not a slave. This reasoning was rooted in the idea that slavery did not exist within England. [54] However, just a couple of decades later, in 1729, it was reported that Attorney General Philip Yorke (1690–1764) and Solicitor General Charles Talbot (1685–1737) took a different view. They contended that the presence of enslaved persons within England, in the words of Rabin, 'had no liberating effect and no impact on a master's rights to his property'. [55] When he became lord chancellor, Yorke (now the first earl of Hardwicke) pronounced in *Pearne* v. *Lisle* that a slave 'is as much property as any other thing'. [56]

Other arguments arose in the late eighteenth century in the landmark case of *Somerset* v. *Stewart* concerning slave status in England. [57] The case concerned James Somerset, a Virginian slave of a Bostonian customs officer, Charles Stewart. Somerset was bought from his Virginia plantation by Stewart and commenced his servitude to his new master in Massachusetts. Stewart took Somerset to London with him in 1769 where he was supposed to remain for a limited time for business purposes. After two years in Stewart's custody, Somerset fled from his master. Stewart then arranged his recapture and placement on the ship of Captain Knowles, headed to Jamaica, where Somerset would be resold into slavery there. [58] Thereby the issue arose regarding the status of slaves in a jurisdiction where slavery allegedly had no legal basis.

When news of Somerset's abduction reached three abolitionists – Thomas Walkin, Elizabeth Cade and John Marlow – they successfully applied to Lord Mansfield for a writ of *habeas corpus* to Knowles the ship owner. Knowles was ordered to return Somerset so that his case could be heard before Lord Mansfield. Acording to William R. Cotter, 'Mansfield was not especially sympathetic to Somerset and in fact required him, even though he was the plaintiff, to produce sureties for his appearances in court.' [59] The abolitionist Granville Sharp heard of the case and encouraged leading barristers to appear on behalf of Somerset, *pro bono*.

Somerset's lawyers contended that villeinage was not a precedent for trans-Atlantic slavery. English barrister William Davy stated that villeinage was 'confined to complexion ... and to a particular quarter of the world'. He further argued that from as far back as 1640, judges in the Star Chamber ruled that 'England was too pure of air for slaves to breathe.' [60] Villeinage in England consisted of English people with ties of family, transmitted only through ancestry, whiteness and place. [61] Granville Sharp and his co-counsels further argued that colonial enslavement could not operate within England and that villeinage no longer existed at the time of the case, and hence no new family could confess to such a status. Nevertheless, Sharp and his counsels did concede, as did Mansfield, that slavery contracts outside of England were still valid. [62]

The *Somerset* case promulgated the ideal that slavery had no place within eighteenth-century English society. It also held that Englishmen never tolerated the institution. Simply touching the soil of England made men free. However, if this principle had been generally accepted, cases such as *Somerset* would not have required such lengthy deliberations. The constant movements (of persons, goods, ideas, laws and more) due to the slave trade and the fact that a number of plantation owners resided in England or at least visited regularly meant that there was necessarily some form of connection between the laws regarding blacks in the colonies and blacks in England. Comparing villeinage and slavery thus also signified a different but related issue: the question of jurisdictional boundaries and the connection between colonial and metropolitan laws. Case law as guidelines were particularly murky, exacerbating the entangled bonds of centre and periphery. [63]

LAW PERTAINING TO POLICE CONDUCT, VAGRANCY, AND MARTIAL LAW

In Watson's account of slave laws in the English Americas, he described slavery as not simply concerned with the relationship between planter and slave but between both parties and the plantation societies of which they were a part. [64] To understand why slavery and its related laws became such a public domain and why police laws acted as the basis of such laws, one must look at public order in early modern England. In the words of Bradley J. Nicholson:

Ex-soldiers, rogues, 'sturdy beggars' and vagabonds were a preoccupation of the ruling elite. Such 'idlers' were anathema to the Tudor elitist concept of society, a chain of ruling authority reaching down from the King and Queen, to the father of the household, or the master. Everyone was supposed to be subsumed with this hierarchy. Bond labour, especially apprenticeship for long periods, was a salient feature of English life, for the lower classes. The hierarchical ideal ... was sought aggressively through a long line of legislation which developed a strict and often brutal police law outside common law for society's lower strata. [65]

The English colonials sought to regulate indentured servants and slaves in ways highly similar to those used for the unemployed and vagabonds in England. In fact, many of the rogues and vagabonds became colonial indentured servants. The colonial elite, i.e. the planter class and administrators, strove for 'good government' analogous to that of the metropole. In so desiring this, they made attempts to replicate English society in the colonies, requiring that each member of the lower class have a master responsible for them. Anyone who fell outside this standard became perilous to the order of that colonial society. Therefore, to maintain order, colonials adopted and adapted English police laws. [66]

The police law of slavery borrowed some of the English vagrancy laws and therefore resembled or appeared to authorise provisions therein. The English believed that if such people were not controlled there would be a spread of vagrancy or vagabondage, which was, in Nicholson's words, the most 'intractable of social problems'. [67] The 1547 Vagrancy Act provided that vagabonds could be enslaved for two years and those vagabond slaves were allowed to be bought and sold. Additionally, vagabond children became 'apprentices', which was arguably another term for child labour and slavery. The Act further provided for the enslavement of those who did not submit to the authority of a master as punishment. This provision was applicable to the unemployed, the homeless and the ill. In addition, a master could 'cawse the said slave to worke by beating, cheyninge or otherwise in such worke and Labour how vyle so ever it be'. [68] A master could also place iron rings on the neck and feet of the enslaved. Those who absconded faced lifelong enslavement. Despite the Act being repealed soon after, it provided an example of how coerced labour laws could be constructed and directed towards those idle and restless members of society needing control. The Act thus illustrated, in Thomas Morris's words, that the 'English were quite capable of conceptualizing human beings as slaves', once a strict perception on the status of slavery was not taken. [69]

The West Indian slavery legislation, pioneered by Barbados, followed this example. In the words of Gaspar:

The police laws of slavery in Barbados ... came to be composed of practices well known in England, and based on England's previous experience with problems of social order in the sixteenth century. The colonists found the sixteenth century experience valuable because the legal dimension of slavery was foreshadowed by the problem of masterless men in England during the previous century. [70]

The Barbadian Code stipulated that a slave was to be 'severely whipped, his nose slit and bee burned in the face' if he ran away or misbehaved. [71] Such a provision followed the English Act, which recommended the branding of vagabonds with the letter 'R' for various misdemeanours including absconding, thereby identifying and proclaiming status. [72]

The laws of the metropole also paved the way for the requirement that slaves carry passes when they had to leave a plantation. [73] Both servants and slaves alike had to carry passes whenever outside their plantation, even if only to do tasks required of them by their masters. The 1563 Statute of Artificers dictated that workers were to carry passes if leaving the master's service. Letters from the Privy Council in 1569 and 1571 and a Royal Proclamation in 1590 also endorsed the pass requirement for workers in England. [74]

Martial law, in the words of Albert Dicey, is essentially the 'suspension of ordinary law and the temporary government of a country or parts of it by military tribunals'. [75] It was usually decreed either in a time of war or through acts of necessity in response to an immediate threat to peace. It was borne out of the courts of constables and marshals of the king's armies and via ambulatory courts by travelling marshals trying, convicting and executing those who were guilty of treason. [76] The notion emerged during the period from about 1300 to 1628, the epoch that marked, in J. V. Capua's words, the 'establishment of custom governing the situations in which it might be invoked'. [77] Such law, the object of much controversy, [78] was invoked by those who, as David Dyzenhaus has noted, 'maintained the British Empire, as they sought to defend imperial interests in the midst of an often very hostile local population'. [79] This situation obviously was applicable to the slave holding territories of the West Indies.

Martial law justice was akin to the summary proceedings applicable to the adjudication of slave trials, where such proceedings became the norm in tribunals set up particularly for such matters and separate from the common-law courts. The Barbadian Code prescribed that less than a full English jury of peers should try the enslaved who were accused of crimes. [80] This clause also imitated the Statute of Artificers, mentioned above, which laid down that slaves be tried by two justices of the peace or a town mayor and 'two others of the discreetest persons' of the relevant town. [81]

Reports likened Jamaica to a great garrison or army, and it was the only island colony that utilised martial law prior to the plantation economic boom. The Jamaican judiciary adapted English legal discourses to widen the range of martial law. Threats, conspiracies or rumours of attacks, rebellions and invasions were frequent around the period that England took Jamaica from the Spanish. Soldiers and sailors who failed to conform to English law during times of war were disciplined using martial law. The governor and the council of war then used their discretionary power in the aftermath of their battle with the Spanish to institute martial law. They thought this necessary to curb not just threats from the Spanish but also privateers, buccaneers and pirates. However, Charles II decided in 1661 to limit the powers of the Governor via a Crown order. This allowed the establishment of an elected council and civilian courts to carry out 'justice based upon a non-repugnancy principle'. [82]

The slavery legislation of Barbados prescribed martial law in the event of any slave rebellion or uprisings. Clause 17 of the 1661 Code indicated that such are acts of insurrection or rebellion: to make preparation of arms, or offensive weapons, or hold any council or conspiracy for raising mutinies or rebellion in the island 'are immediately grounds for the enactment of martial law with the punishment of death or other pains as their crimes deserve'. Still fearful of its vulnerability for attacks, being so far removed from other English colonies, Jamaica enacted a Militia Act in 1664 along with their Slave Code. This Act was justified on the basis that the island was in the 'midst of a subtile, rich and potent enemy', referring to the fugitive slaves and eventually the Maroon community. [83] The Act was used in the next year to quell insurrections by the slave and fugitive slave populace. Martial law provisions became part of the Jamaican slavery regime, which was marked by constant slave uprisings and absconding. Beyond Jamaica, martial law was not as popular during the peak of plantation society, apart from the summary judgment proceedings aforementioned. The only occasions that warranted martial law's use in other islands were much later: the Demerara and the Barbados 'Bussa' slave rebellions quashed in the 1810s and 1820s.

CONCISE SUMMARY

The fundamental principle underlying the regulatory systems pertaining to slavery in the English West Indies was the imperative to exert control over the continuously expanding population by the minority controlling authority. The West Indian slave legislation has a wide range of underpinnings. Gaining a comprehensive comprehension of the individual contributions to the slave codes is exceedingly challenging. The purpose of examining the foundations of the slave codes is to demonstrate the functioning of transplanted legal aspects within a system that was not replicated or existing in England. The legislators were able to adapt and utilize these valuable principles as a structure to create a complete law that was unparalleled in the metropole. The legal prohibition of slavery in England prompted legislators in the West Indies to seek a concept that closely resembled a system of bondage, so establishing the significance of villeinage. Nevertheless, this association gave rise to a multitude of unresolved matters pertaining to the connection between villeins and colonial slaves, the social standing of villeins, and the question of villeins being considered as chattels and so interchangeable with slaves. Moreover, the code was primarily shaped by English society restrictions against vagabonds, police legislation related to criminal activities, and anti-revolutionary measures that were part of martial law. The fact that slavery endured for more than two centuries suggests that these modified restrictions were largely effective and well-suited for upholding the slavery system.

Footnote

1. B. L. Solow, Slavery and the Rise of the Atlantic System (Cambridge, 1991), 21–22. I will use the terms the Caribbean and the West Indies interchangeably.
2. B. Dyde, R. Greenwood and S. Hamber, Emancipation to Emigration, 3rd edn (New York, 2008), 33.
3. http://discoveringbristol.org.uk/slavery/routes/places-involved/west-indies/plantation-system/.
4. B. W. Higman, 'Population and Labour in the British Caribbean in the Early Nineteenth Century', in Stanley L. Engerman and Robert E. Gallman (eds.), Long-Term Factors in American Economic Growth (Chicago, IL, 1986), 605–39.
5. W. D. Jordan, White Over Black: American Attitudes towards the Negro 1550–1812 (Chapel Hill, NC, 1968), 3–4.
6. S. E. Hadden, The Fragmented Laws of Slavery in the Colonial and Revolutionary Era (Cambridge, 2008), 253.
7. A. L. Hartfield, Atlantic Virginia Intercontinental Relations in the Seventeenth Century (Philadelphia, PA, 2004), 155.
8. E. Rugemer, Slave Law and the Politics of Resistance in the Early Atlantic World (Cambridge, MA, 2018).
9. C. Tomlins, 'Transplants and Timing: Passages in the Creation of an Anglo-American Law of Slavery', Theoretical Inquiries in Law, 10(2) (2009), 389–421.
10. D. B. Gaspar, 'Rigid and Inclement: Origins of Jamaican Slave Laws of the Seventeenth Century', in C. Tomlins and B. H. Mann (eds.), The Many Legalities of Early America (Chapel Hill, NC, 2001), 78–96.
11. Throughout the essay I use the term 'English' as well as 'British'. 'English' refers to the time before the Union Act of 1707 which joined England with Scotland to form Great Britain. 'British' refers to the time after this.
12. R. B. Sheridan, Sugar and Slavery: An Economic History of the British West Indies, 1632–1775 (Kingston, 1994), 236; D. B. Gaspar, 'With a Rod of Iron: Barbados Slave Laws as a Model for Jamaica, South Carolina and Antigua', in D. C. Hine and J. McLeod (eds.), Crossing Boundaries: Comparative History of

Black People in Diaspora (Bloomington and Indianapolis, IN, 2001), 343–66, at 343 and 344–5.

13. London, The National Archives (henceforth, TNA), CO 30/2, The Barbadian Comprehensive Slave Code, 1661 (henceforth, Barbados Slave Code, 1661).
14. Ibid., Preamble.
15. Ibid.
16. An Act for good governing of Servants and Ordeyneing the rights between Master and Servants; An Act for settling the Militia within this Island.
17. B. J. Nicholson, 'Legal Borrowing and the Origins of Slave Laws in the British Colonies', The American Journal of Legal History, 38(1) (1994), 38–54, at 41, 49 and 50. Barbados was indeed the 'seed crystal', as Christopher Tomlins put it, in inspiring the slave codes of other Caribbean slave holding colonies as well as North American colonies like South Carolina and Georgia; Tomlins, 'Transplants and Timing', 397.
18. Police law was what is now known as criminal law, which can be defined as offences against the person, such as murder, rape or assault, or offences against property, such as theft or fraud; J. Holder, Principles of Criminal Law (Oxford, 2016), 1.
19. J. S. Handler, 'Custom and Law: The Status of Enslaved Africans in Seventeenth-Century Barbados', Slavery and Abolition, 37 (2016), 233–55, at 235. The English were accordingly conditioned with notions of race ideology and treatment from colonial enslavement progenitors, the Spanish and Portuguese.
20. T. D. Morris, Southern Slavery and the Law, 1619–1860 (Chapel Hill, NC, 1996), 42.
21. Nicholson, 'Legal Borrowing' and Morris, *Southern Slavery*.
22. R. B. Campbell, The Laws of Slavery in Texas (Austin, TX, 2010), 2–4.
23. Preamble, Barbados Slave Code, 1661.
24. E. A. Martin and J. Law, Oxford Dictionary of Law, 6th ed. (Oxford, 2006), 31.
25. Ibid., 745.
26. E. V. Goveia, The West Indian Slave Laws of the 18th Century (London, 2010), 20–21.
27. L. Rostill, 'Relative Title and Deemed Ownership in English Personal Property Law', Oxford Journal of Legal Studies, 35(1) (2015), 31–52.
28. Barbados Slave Code, 1661, clause 1.

29. An Act declaring the Negro Slaves of this Island to be Real Estate in Acts of Assembly Passed in the Island of Barbados (London, 1721), 62–63, as summarised in Goveia, *The West Indian Slave Laws*, 21–22.
30. Ibid., 61.
31. Ibid., 62.
32. E. Long, The History of Jamaica (London, 1774), 493–4.
33. Ibid., 495.
34. See below at 314–17.
35. M. Bailey, 'Villeinage in England: A Regional Case Study c. 1250–c. 1349', Economic History Review, 62(2) (2009), 430–57, at 430.
36. H. Cary, A Commentary on the Tenures of Littleton (London, 1828), 295.
37. For *Pearne* v. *Lisle*, see *Reports of Cases in the High Court of Chancery*, ed. C. Ambler (London, 1795), 77.
38. A. Watson, Slave Law in the Americas (Athens, GA, 1989), 63–65.
39. Co. Litt. 52. A; 9 Co. Rep. 76.
40. Ibid.
41. S. Peabody and K. Grinberg, Slavery, Freedom, and the Law in the Atlantic World (New York, 2007); P. Hyams, Kings, Lords and Peasants in Medieval England: The Common Law of Villeinage in the Twelfth and Thirteenth Centuries (Oxford, 1980), 234–6.
42. Peabody and Grinberg, *Slavery, Freedom, and the Law*, chapter 2.2.
43. Barbados Slave Code, 1661, clause 18.
44. Blackstone, *Commentaries of the Laws of England, Book II*, 92–93.
45. W. M. Wiecek, 'Somerset: Lord Mansfield and the Legitimacy of Slavery in the Anglo-American World', University of Chicago Law Review, 42(86) (1974), 86–146, at 89 n. 10, quoting J. Chitty Pleadings.
46. 5 Mod. 182 (K.B. 1697).
47. Wiecek, 'Somerset', 91.
48. Ibid., 91–92.
49. *Butts* v. *Penny* 2 Lev. 201, 83 Eng. Rep. 518 (K.B. 1677).
50. Wiecek, 'Somerset', 90–91.
51. Ibid.
52. For *Pearne* v. *Lisle*, see Ambler, ed., *Reports of Cases*, 77.

53. D. Rabin, '"In a Country of Liberty?": Slavery, Villeinage and the Making of Whiteness in the Somerset Case (1772)', History Workshop Journal, 72 (2011), 5–29, at 17.
54. 2 Salk. R, 666.
55. Rabin, 'In a Country of Liberty?', 11.
56. *Pearne* v. *Lisle*, in Ambler, ed., *Reports of Cases*, 75.
57. New York Historical Society, Sharp Papers, MS Transcript (1772), 107–8.
58. Ibid.
59. W. R. Cotter, 'The Somerset Case and the Abolition of Slavery in England', The Historical Association, 79(255) (1994), 31–56, at 34.
60. New York Historical Society, Sharp Papers, MS Transcript (1772), 43.
61. Ibid.
62. Ibid., 82, 92.
63. Rabin, 'In a Country of Liberty?', 5.
64. Watson, *Slave Law*, 66.
65. Nicholson, 'Legal Borrowing', 42.
66. Ibid.
67. Ibid.
68. The 1547 Vagrancy Act as quoted in C. S. L. Davies, 'Slavery and the Protector Somerset: The Vagrancy Act of 1547', Economic History Review, 2nd ser., 19 (1966), 533–49, at 534.
69. Morris, *Southern Slavery*, 42.
70. Gaspar, 'Rigid and Inclement', 87–88.
71. Barbados Slave Code, 1661, clause 2.
72. 1 Edw. Vic.3 (1547).
73. Barbados Slave Code, 1661, clause 1.
74. F. Aydellote, Elizabethan Rogues and Vagabonds (Oxford, 1913), 62, 64, 66.
75. A. V. Dicey, Introduction to the Study of the Law of the Constitution, 8th edn (New York, 1924), 283–4.
76. J. M. Collins, Martial Law and English Laws, c. 1500–c. 1700 (Cambridge, 2016), 44.

77. J. V. Capua, 'The Early History of Martial Law in England from the Fourteenth Century to the Petition of Right', Cambridge Law Journal, 36(1) (1977), 152–73, at 152.
78. D. Edwards, 'Beyond Reform: Martial Law and the Tudor Re-Conquest of Ireland', History Ireland, 5 (1997), 16–21; P. D. Halliday, Habeas Corpus: From England to Empire (Cambridge, MA, 2010), 68–69.
79. D. Dyzenhaus, 'The Puzzle of Martial Law', University of Toronto Journal, 59 (2009), 1–64, at 2.
80. Barbados Slave Code, 1661, clause 13. Clauses 14 and 16 also repeat how slave trials were to be carried out.
81. For Statute of Artificers, see 5 Eliz. C.4 (1562–63).
82. TNA, CO 1/15, fo. 20, as summarised in Collins, *Martial Law and English Laws*, 228–9.
83. TNA, CO 139/1, The Jamaica Militia Act, 1664, 49–51. The fugitive slaves were those left behind from Spanish colonisation of the island who eventually united with those slaves brought by the English to Jamaica to form Maroon fugitive communities.

INDEX

A

Aboriginal 254-256, 264, 269, 271, 273, 276-277

Academic 5, 164, 170-171

Account 12, 129, 168

Acquired 255, 257

Acting 124-125

Addition 65, 126, 130, 132, 301

Adjustment 276

Advocate 47, 125

Agreements 38

Allegation 221

Amendment 276

Analogy 36

Analysis 6-7, 163, 169, 211

Ancestral 144

Ancient 47-48, 53, 123, 183, 258, 272

Appeal 218-219, 221, 268, 275, 282-283, 288-289, 293-294

Arguments 35, 241

Articles 194, 239, 299

Authority 14, 30-32, 39, 42, 48, 52, 57-60, 63, 65, 67, 69, 91, 112, 117, 143-148, 150-152, 154-157, 160, 194, 268, 293

Authors 29, 37, 130, 166, 199, 212

B

Bankruptcy 183

Barbarism 171

Barrister 166, 202

Beneficial 256-257

Biography 120, 135, 137

Blackstone 13-15, 143-148, 150-162, 169, 171, 173, 176, 258-260, 272, 302

C

Calderwood 119

Canterbury 125

Catalogue 133

Catherine 261-262, 273

Chamber 88, 92-94, 103-105, 109, 115-116, 231-232

Chancellor 289

Chancery 96, 112, 131

Citation 152

Civilians 30, 130, 149

Colonies 237, 253, 259-260, 266, 270, 298, 302, 310

Commerce 230-233, 237, 240, 242-243, 245-247, 249-251

Commission 107, 201

Community 71, 85, 230, 257

Compiler 35, 52, 54-57, 59-61, 65-67, 76

Conflict 67

Context 3-4, 20, 57-59, 88, 98, 102, 131, 194, 204, 270

Contract 36-38, 199-200

Contrary 31, 220

Corpus 29, 123

Criminal 89, 109, 299, 310

Criticism 107

Crucial 174, 299

Customary 25, 28, 30, 38, 144, 152-153, 156-158, 255, 266-268, 276

D

Dictionary 85, 120, 135, 137

Director 293

Diversity 283

Doctrine 11, 254, 256-257

Domains 174, 259

Dramatic 68

E

Easements 188-191, 194, 196, 199-203, 205-207

Economic 239-240, 243, 245, 309

Editorial 54-55, 76

Education 102, 172-173, 242-243

Empire 129, 147, 149-150, 159-160, 253, 272

Epitome 32, 43

Equity 173, 184

Exercised 60-61, 254, 257

Experience 106, 158, 243, 306

F

Family 100-101, 118, 214, 288, 305

Federation 285

Formation 2, 40, 161

Fragment 221-222

Framework 235

Freedom 155, 311

G

Goodwill 262

H

Household 83, 101

Hypotheses 2

I

Imperial 128, 146, 155, 258

Insanity 284, 294

Institutes 14, 59, 123, 125-127, 129-130, 132-133, 137, 242

J

Journal 18, 78, 164-165, 215, 234, 249-250, 295, 310, 313

Judges 12, 88, 91-92, 98, 153-154, 191, 193, 195, 212-213, 218-219, 259-260, 262, 279-283, 291

Judgment 10, 87-88, 94, 102, 105-106, 212, 217-218, 220-222, 255, 280

Judicature 107, 121

Judicial 12, 87-92, 94-97, 101, 105-108, 114, 116, 124, 135, 151-153, 239, 254, 276, 281, 283-285, 287, 290, 293-294

Judiciary 12, 211-212

Jurists 15, 150, 169, 173, 177, 213, 241, 281

K

Kingship 40, 50-51, 63, 66-67, 83, 93

L

Labour 301, 306

Language 15, 62, 168, 171

Lawyers 16, 29, 39, 48, 68, 128, 131, 149

Letters 61-62, 112-113

Library 71, 73, 78, 81, 113, 132-133, 165

Literature 131-132, 134, 165-167

Liverpool 230, 232

M

Majesty 60-61

Manuscript 47, 49, 52-54, 56, 58, 70, 73-76

Medieval 18, 26-27, 41, 58, 68-69, 71-72, 74, 79-81, 84-85

Minister 289, 292

Municipal 145-148, 150

N

National 120, 137, 234-235, 241-242, 281, 293

Nature 13, 30, 38, 144-145, 211, 237, 255

Normative 28, 39, 145, 152

O

Objections 285

Obligation 212-213, 221

Offending 63

Office 99, 153

Opinion 22, 125, 128, 197, 220-221, 286

Oracles 153, 225

Ordinary 57, 293

P

Parliament 64, 107-108, 121, 155, 157, 183

Payments 220, 222

Penalty 114

Peoples 59, 253, 262, 264

Period 10, 12, 19, 25, 65-66, 128, 242, 307

Personal 89, 95, 101, 103, 106-108

Police 299, 305-306

Political 8, 30, 50-51, 60-62, 64-65, 67, 81, 84, 105, 113, 230, 232, 260, 282

Position 71, 96, 107, 156, 205

Powers 114, 147, 150, 153

Precedents 151, 223-224

Professor 169, 179, 182, 208, 214

Prologue 55, 59, 61, 80-81, 83, 85

Property 93, 201-202, 255, 260, 265, 271, 274, 298-304, 310

Protection 261, 265, 300

Public 128, 232, 239, 256, 281, 284, 288, 293, 305

Punishment 103-104, 110

R

Reasons 145, 169, 212-213, 217-218

Recognised 51, 255, 262, 269

Recovery 302-303

Reform 48, 69, 201, 232

Review 17, 69, 71, 120, 133-134, 142, 166-167, 169, 171-172, 272-273, 275, 311

S

Section 55, 145, 190, 201, 285-287

Servants 107, 299, 306, 310

Servitudes 188-190, 192-195, 198, 200, 204-205, 207

Settlers 253, 261, 265, 270

Sovereign 254, 257, 262

Speech 92, 100-102, 105, 287

Statement 31, 221, 223

Statistics 239, 243

Structure 54, 57, 168, 214, 218

Supreme 147, 149-150, 255, 266

T

Territory 256-257, 264

Theory 19, 87, 206, 215

Tractatus 35, 252

Tradition 37, 40, 52-53, 95, 106, 144, 158

U

United 126-127, 236, 260

University 1, 73, 108, 126, 165, 168, 172, 274-275, 293

www.ingramcontent.com/pod-product-compliance
Lightning Source LLC
LaVergne TN
LVHW062116200926
848484LV00007B/1679